Interpersonal Communication

second edition
Interpersonal Communication

William D. Brooks
University of Oklahoma

Philip Emmert
University of Wyoming

wcb
Wm. C. Brown Company Publishers
Dubuque, Iowa

wcb

Wm. C. Brown
Chairman of the Board

Larry W. Brown
President, WCB Group

Book Team

Thomas W. Gornick
Editor
David A. Corona
Designer
William J. Evans
Cover Designer
Edit, Inc.
Production Services
Marilyn Gartman
Photo Research

Wm. C. Brown Company Publishers College Division

Lawrence E. Cremer
President
Raymond C. Deveaux
Vice President/Product Development
David Wm. Smith
Assistant Vice President/National Sales Manager
Matt Coghlan
National Marketing Manager
David A. Corona
Director of Production Development and Design
William A. Moss
Production Editorial Manager
Marilyn A. Phelps
Manager of Design
Mary M. Heller
Visual Research Manager

Cover photo: Peter Ross

Copyright © 1976, 1980 by Wm. C. Brown Company Publishers

Library of Congress Catalog Card Number: 80-50255

ISBN 0-697-04172-7

Printed in the United States of America

Contents

2118610

Preface

The response to our first edition verified our original ideas and conceptualization of *Interpersonal Communication*. The conceptualization of the first edition rested on two premises: first, that the study of interpersonal communication ought to focus on the objective of *personal growth;* and second, that optimal personal growth in interpersonal communication occurs when cognitive, affective, and experiential learnings reinforce one another. In other words, we believed and still believe that intellectual, psychological, and experiential activities are necessary for best development in interpersonal communication.

Obviously, a textbook can more easily meet the learner's intellectual needs through the presentation of provocative, stimulating, and challenging ideas than it can meet the learner's affective or experiential needs. Interaction, insightful reflection, and evaluation are more productive vehicles for affective and behavioral growth than is a textbook. Nevertheless, the premise with which we hold is that growth in all three areas is necessary for optimum development in interpersonal communication. Even as experiential activities are necessary in interpersonal communication, so is cognitive learning necessary. We make no apology for the fact that this text focuses primarily on the cognitive. One of the unique and invaluable characteristics of human beings is that we can grow through thinking. We can use an elaborate symbol system to acquire ideas and cognitive understandings about the nature of human beings, information processing, self-concept, negotiation, conflict, and a number of other factors that are the foundation blocks of interpersonal communication. Your response in letters to us and in personal conversations, as well as in the number of adoptions and sales, has made clear that the basic foundations and philosophy of *Interpersonal Communication* should not be changed. The changes we have made in this second edition are *not* philosophical or conceptual ones. They are changes made in response to your requests for more illustrations, examples, stories, and photographs—ways of increasing clarity and interestingness. And you have asked that the intercultural material be interspersed throughout the book as each of its relative components are discussed. Finally, several of you have requested that interpersonal communication be extended beyond dyadic personal relationships and small groups to organizations. The changes we have made in this second edition are in line with those requests. More illustrative materials and clearer explanations have been given, and a new chapter, chapter 12, is devoted entirely to interpersonal communication in organizations. Our goal in this second edition, as with the first, has been to select those topics that seem to us to be so basic and important to interpersonal communication that our profession and our students dare not ignore them.

We have tried to present the ideas one needs to understand about interpersonal communication in as clear and interesting a fashion as is possible. We have attempted to illustrate these ideas so that the student may observe or identify the feelings and attitudes also involved with these ideas. It is our hope that the textbook will complement and facilitate the experiential and affective learning activities provided by the instructor as it undergirds the experiential activities with substantial knowledge and understanding.

Another goal we had with the first edition was that of avoiding a low-level "chatter" approach. We believed that it is not necessary to write at an eighth-grade level and in a "chatty" style for college students to be able to comprehend and enjoy the book. We found that assumption to be true. Students have expressed their appreciation and enjoyment of *Interpersonal Communication*. So we have attempted to maintain that objective for this second edition. We have avoided "chattiness," but we hope the text is *very personal*. We hope, also, that it is not a cold summary of experimental research findings listed as virtual laws. Although we have included discussions of the most respected scientific studies as well as the writings of humanists, psychotherapists, philosophers, and practitioners, we have attempted to make these discussions clear and interesting.

Another objective we had for the first edition, as with this second, relative to our writing was to preserve our own personalities as expressed in the writings of each of us. We have approached this book as an attempt to communicate personally with those who use it. It is our opinion that to do this effectively we must communicate as individuals, not as abstract "authors." Thus, we have not attempted to remove our personalities from our writing by having one of us rewrite the entire book or having a third person impose his or her style uniformly throughout the book. The experience for the reader should be somewhat akin to that of sitting down and chatting with both of us on various topics and recognizing that there really are two of us—two separate and distinct personalities—talking with you. There are, consequently, differences in our style of writing and in the examples we choose; yet we are alike in our conceptualization of the book, in our philosophy of interpersonal communication, and in our attitudes toward teaching and toward students. Moreover, our friendship is such that collaborating on this second edition of *Interpersonal Communication* has been an enjoyable experience for us, as it was for the first edition and the other books we have done together. We hope we can make something of each of ourselves known to you through our discussion of interpersonal communication.

This book continues to represent what we feel is a basic trend in interpersonal communication. It is an interdisciplinary book; if one views the behavioral sciences on a broad basis, then one can make a guess at the various fields we have gone to for the materials and ideas that have been incorporated into this text. Human behavior, we feel, cannot be allocated to psychology, communication, sociology, education, anthropology, or any other single field. Rather, it is our feeling that all of these areas provide legitimate bases for studying varying aspects of human behavior from different perspectives. By drawing on those different perspectives, we have developed what we hope is a complete and well-rounded view of interpersonal communication. We hope you will find interpersonal communication more understandable as a result of your reading of these materials.

As with any text, we have many persons whom we should thank—persons who read, critiqued, and made suggestions that improved the manuscript. They include James J. Bradac, University of Iowa; William E. King, St. Petersburg Junior College; Robert M. Smith, Wichita State University; Dwayne Van Rhenenen, University of Maine at Orono; Carroll Haggard, McMurry College in Texas; JoAnn Graham, Bronx Community College; and Bill Robinson, Purdue University.

William D. Brooks
Philip Emmert

Introduction

Bruce Quist

1

You and Interpersonal Communication

It is impossible for us to live our daily lives without engaging in interpersonal communication almost constantly. When we get up in the morning, we must communicate interpersonally to arrange to have access to bathroom facilities. To cooperate with the people with whom we live, we must communicate with them. Frequently, simply to get from home to school or work requires interpersonal communication to work out travel arrangements cooperatively. Once at school or at work, we find ourselves in small groups trying to solve problems and working on projects. Those of us who do not go to work or to school every day, but stay at home, find themselves interacting with children, neighbors, and friends. Those returning from school or work find themselves interacting with their family or roommates as they prepare for dinner, just as they interacted interpersonally when ordering lunch. We frequently eat meals in a small group in which we talk with one another. Often, we then spend the rest of the evening watching television, reading, or listening to the radio, but constantly interacting with other people in a small group setting.

We spend a lot of our time communicating interpersonally with other people. Communication generally takes up 70 percent of our time.[1] Most of that is interpersonal communication. That is a lot of time. Why do we spend this much time with other people communicating interpersonally?

1. David K. Berlo, *The Process of Communication* (New York: Holt, Rinehart & Winston, Inc., 1960), p. 1.

The Importance of Interpersonal Communication

Interpersonal communication is one of the most basic activities we perform—following breathing, eating, sleeping, and reproducing. It may be said that interpersonal communication is even more basic than the processes of eating and reproducing, because it may be impossible for us to engage in

Cornelius Sinclair

Interpersonal communication is the basis for friendship.

those two activities until we have mastered some aspects of interpersonal communication.

From the time we are born, it is necessary for us to communicate to satisfy our need for food. A baby cries to be fed. Mothers and fathers, through this communication, learn the necessity of feeding babies regularly, and the baby has interpersonal communication to thank for getting its daily milk. In relations between men and women, we see a complex and subtle system consisting of a collection of behaviors designed to influence the opposite sex—ultimately, for sexual reasons. Certain ways in which males and females walk, stand, gesture, and use eye contact are systematic within a culture and serve as cues to members of the opposite sex when some sort of sexual relationship is desired. We suspect that the system is so subtle that those involved in it frequently are not consciously aware of their own behavior. Nevertheless, interpersonal communication between the sexes does occur, and it appears to be necessary for the reproduction of our species. Interpersonal communication is basic to people and plays a significant role in their daily lives.

As we go to school, it is through the process of interpersonal communication that we learn how to count, add, subtract, read marks from a book, get along with our friends, and learn what behaviors we have to perform to be approved of by an authority figure called a "teacher." Even before we go to school, we learn from our parents a number of things we should and should not do to receive approval and be accepted by our friends and community. This occurs through interpersonal communication. Later, as adults, we make friends, sell cars, obtain information, pass time, are caused to laugh, and cause others to laugh through the process of interpersonal communication. Is all of this important? We think so.

Apart from its day-to-day importance, interpersonal communication assumes incredible importance within some specific situations. Males and females meet each other and establish romantic and sexual relationships by communicating. Sweethearts holding hands or a girl opening her eyes widely at a boy may be communicating incredibly complex messages.

Likewise, after the courting relationship has culminated in some form of permanent relationship (marriage more often than not, despite today's changing norms), interpersonal communication continues to play an important role. When a husband comes home from work at night, pours a beer, collapses into an easy chair, and hides himself behind a newspaper, he may be communicating a great deal. And when a wife says at bedtime that she has a headache, she has probably communicated more to her husband than the amount of pain in her head. Marriages are made and maintained through interpersonal communication. The success or failure of a marriage depends far more upon the interpersonal communication skills of the partners than on any other single variable.[2] In fact, effective interpersonal communication may be one of the most important behaviors we have.

While many of the examples just mentioned may not seem important, taken all together they assume a fairly significant importance in our lives as individuals. If we consider the role of communication throughout human history, we begin to see that it has a still greater importance to us as a species.

Speech is the form of communication that interpersonal communication usually takes. Speech is also a distinguishing feature that sets human beings apart from other animals.[3] No doubt many of you are aware of the research conducted with porpoises and chimpanzees in which scientists have attempted to communicate with these animals and teach them language systems. Although there have been some successes of a limited sort in which chimpanzees have communicated at a fairly basic level, using little plastic objects or American Sign Language instead of spoken words, neither the porpoises nor the chimpanzees have ever managed to produce spoken

2. Ben N. Ard, "Communication in Marriage," *Rational Living* 5 (1971):20–22; Harold L. Raush, William A. Barry, Richard K. Hertel, and Mary Ann Swain, *Communication, Conflict and Marriage* (San Francisco: Jossey-Bass Inc., Publishers, 1974).

3. Frank E. X. Dance, "Speech Communication: The Sign of Mankind," in *The Great Ideas Today 1975* (Chicago: Encyclopaedia Britannica, Inc., 1975), pp. 40–57.

Interpersonal communication over a cup of coffee can be most important in building the relationship between husband and wife.

Harry Smedley, Jr.

communication. This appears to be a unique characteristic of human beings. We have the physiological mechanism for producing speech and the mental capability of employing abstract language through speech. These abilities are tied to our survival and development as a species. In fact, we would suggest that the primary goal of interpersonal communication is survival—both species and individual survival.

Survival and Interpersonal Communication

Millions of years ago our ancestors became part of a mystery that would have baffled Sherlock Holmes had his primary interest been the study of communication. That mystery still intrigues us as we attempt to understand what makes human beings the unique creatures they are and why they became what they are today. Evidence gathered by anthropologists and ethologists (specialists in animal behavior) suggests that once upon a time people were not unlike close relatives of ours on the evolutionary tree—the anthropoid apes. The question that puzzles us today is: what made people different from the apes? Many think a major factor was the ability of early humans to communicate using the spoken word.[4]

That we do this is obvious. The car salesperson constantly makes use of this ability while attempting to move this year's model. In a romantic setting, women and men employ this ability in the attempt to seduce their dates. In school, teachers make use of this ability as they attempt to change and expand their pupils' understanding of the world. Even babies communicate as they attempt to make known an uncomfortable wetness to Daddy or Mommy.

Although other animals can communicate at a basic level, one of the major differences between our communicative ability and that of other animals appears to be the complexity of our communication systems. We employ language to talk about language (sometimes referred to as *metacommunication*), feelings, past and future events, ideas, and so forth.

We have become unique among all animal species in that through abstract communication we have become "time-binding" creatures.[5] Every generation does not have to relearn important facts from its own experience, because each generation learns them verbally from the preceding generations. For instance, we do not have to experience a depression to know the hardships of economic poverty, nor do we need to thrust our hands into a fire to know the searing pain of heat. These things can be learned from mothers and fathers through interpersonal communication. This ability makes it possible for us to achieve at a higher level than other animals, because each generation, instead of having to "start from scratch," can build upon the accomplishments of previous generations.

4. Harold J. Vetter, *Language Behavior and Communication* (Itasca, Ill.: F. E. Peacock Publishers, Inc., 1969), p. 16.

5. Alfred Korzybski, *Science and Sanity* (Lakeville, Conn.: Institute of General Semantics, 1958), pp. 223–24.

Communication Origins

As we were working on this book, a colleague questioned the necessity of even considering why people originally communicated. She said, "Who really cares why people communicated a hundred thousand years ago? The question is, why do we communicate today, and how can we learn to communicate more effectively?" This is a reasonable question, and the answer to it is that we feel people communicate today for essentially the same reasons they did two or three hundred thousand years ago. We do this in a different context, certainly, and within a different and more complex culture. Nevertheless, reasons very similar to those that prompted our ancestors to make their first utterances very likely motivate us today.

As detectives trying to unravel this mystery, we find that an important clue as to why human beings first communicated appears to be our relative inability to defend ourselves against other predators. We do not have the speed

6. Robert Ardrey, *The Social Contract* (New York: Atheneum Publishers, 1970), p. 355.

of an antelope or the strength of a buffalo. We do not have the claws and fangs of a tiger. And from most evidence we can conclude that our ancestors never did have these characteristics.[6]

Another clue that seems rather important is that our ancestors appear to have been meat eaters from earliest prehistoric times. There is considerable evidence to suggest that, contrary to many of our more idealistic concepts, we have always eaten meat. Furthermore, we have always killed to get this meat. There is also evidence suggesting that we could not have acquired the meat for eating through scavenging alone. Fossils indicate that humans very likely lived principally on a diet of meat provided by the killing of animals considerably larger and infinitely more dangerous than themselves.[7] We must wonder how, if we were relatively weak compared with other predators, we managed to acquire the meat that seems always to have been the principal staple of our diet.

7. Ibid., pp. 337–49.

Archeological evidence suggests that hundreds of thousands of years ago, we humans managed to evolve a society. To kill animals on the hunt and to protect ourselves from predators, we probably engaged in a great deal of cooperative social activity.[8] We did not do this because we liked other people or for any altruistic reasons, but rather because we had to. If we were to survive as a species, cooperative behavior was a necessity. Without this cooperation we could never have killed the animals for food, and we very likely could not have protected ourselves against the fierce predators of prehistoric times.

8. Ibid., pp. 359–70.

From this, we can deduce that our ancestors probably developed the ability to communicate because they had to communicate to develop the social system that was necessary for survival. *People learned to communicate in order to survive.*[9]

9. Ibid.

When we talk about survival in prehistoric times, we are referring to both our physical survival as a species and our survival as individuals. Some ethologists believe that as a species we would not have survived had we not been able to evolve a communication system. Communication can be viewed as a tool, like a set of claws or fangs, which could be used to ensure our survival. Whether we evolved the ability to speak so that we could act together and so survive, or whether the ability to speak was a biological inevitability that happened to result in our survival as a species, is a moot point.

Why We Communicate Today

Probably we still communicate interpersonally for the same reason: to survive. Of course, by survival today we are referring largely to other than immediate physical survival. Admittedly, though, the physical survival of our species still is very much dependent upon our ability to communicate (about energy supplies, population explosions, war, pollution, and the like).

Instead of using interpersonal communication to organize a hunting party for the purpose of killing game, as was done in prehistoric times, we use it to acquire symbols that represent wealth, which we then exchange for food, clothing, shelter, and so on. We are still involved in the same old physical survival race, but we communicate not only to assure immediate and long-range physical survival, but to satisfy other needs as well. Males and females communicate to satisfy the need for love, and a company foreman may communicate to satisfy the need for power. Some people communicate simply to satisfy a need for identity—to know that they are who they are. In a society as complex as ours, some barely survive and some survive very well. One point should be clear: we began to communicate interpersonally because we had to in order to survive, and we continue to because we have to in order to survive.

"Selfishness"

Although most people have little difficulty accepting our survival-oriented behavior, the implications of what we have been discussing are not so easy to absorb. Essentially, we are led to the conclusion that *all* our behavior, including communication, is to satisfy our own needs, both as a species and as individuals.

Most of us have grown up in a culture that frowns on any behavior called "selfish." Our parents, teachers, ministers, rabbis, priests, and friends have all taught us that it is bad to be "selfish." It is not surprising that most of us have accepted these admonitions as absolute truth, as we have been positively reinforced for so doing. It should be noted, however, that many people on entering their teens experience considerable frustration and anger toward their elders when they observe that many of those same elders who had admonished them during their childhood not to be selfish children behave selfishly themselves. At that point many teenagers begin to question what they have been taught, at least subconsciously. Of course, society has many rewards to withhold and punishments to administer to prevent us from expressing our doubts about hallowed truths, and most of us knuckle under, eventually even reaching the point that we accept "unselfishness" as an incontestable virtue.

If we examine each act of behavior we have ever engaged in, we can ultimately trace our motivation for each back to the satisfaction of some need of *our own*. Some philanthropists may need moral consolation to make up for the way they acquired their money, so they "atone for their sins" by being generous. Men and women working to be medical doctors may need the respect and authority of being a doctor more than they need to help people. Clergymen may need the security of the church more than they need to achieve wealth in a business. We all vary in our needs, but we act in ways to satisfy them, whatever they may be, for only through the satisfaction of these needs can we survive.

We hope it is clear that we are talking about something more than just physical survival. We are concerned with psychological survival of several different kinds. An example frequently mentioned when someone is challenging the notion that we are all self-oriented is that of the person who throws himself or herself in front of a car to save the life of a child. Inevitably we are asked if this is not an unselfish act. The answer to this question is that the act is unselfish on the surface, but if we were able to subject this "unselfish person" to psychoanalysis, we would likely discover that the sacrifice probably satisfied a number of needs. Possibly, the person needed to be a martyr, or to be respected by his or her friends, or to avoid being looked down on as a coward who would stand by and watch a child die. There are any number of needs a person might wish to satisfy that could motivate the sacrifice of his or her own life for another. We will discuss these later.

What are the needs of individuals that are satisfied by interpersonal communication? Let us look at some of them.

Social Survival

It is so necessary for human beings to be with other human beings that *Homo sapiens* has been called "the social animal." If we isolate a person in a room so that he or she has absolutely no contact with other people, after a relatively short time that person will begin to hallucinate and to lose touch with reality. We appear to acquire much of our perception of the world from the people around us. When we are isolated from people, we have a harder time accurately perceiving the world and surviving within it. Because we need people to survive physically, we seem to have developed a need simply to interact with others.

We have known a number of people who have indicated that "they don't need other people" and yet, with the exception of hermits, who are a special case, we have known very few people who managed to get along without others for very long. Even those who seem reclusive interact with other people in ways which, we are sure, they convince themselves are necessary, but nevertheless provide them contact with other human beings.

While in college, one of us had a fraternity brother as a roommate who developed a bad infection in his throat. He went to a throat specialist who, of course, provided medication, but also required that our friend not speak until this illness was gone. This went on for about five or six weeks. Although occasionally our friend whispered, by and large he simply wrote down messages and did not talk during that time. This eliminated him from a great deal of interpersonal interaction, and we recall that after some days of this kind of life he became more irritable, nervous, and edgy.

Finally, when the entire period was over and our friend's throat had healed, we discussed the experience. He told us that at times he "just wanted to scream." He needed to talk to people, even though he was something of a "loner." This was a good example of someone who really did need to engage in interpersonal communication and had that primary channel of interpersonal communication, the spoken word, denied him. It was difficult for him to survive socially and remain well adjusted without speaking. Interpersonal communication is extremely important for the social survival of all of us.

Career Survival

Effective interpersonal communication is critical to the performance of many jobs. As professors, both of us are painfully aware of the importance of talking with people in our jobs, but interpersonal communication is not only important to careers such as teaching where communication is so obvious. We know a man who works as a tool and die maker and who is highly skilled in his craft. However, for various reasons, this man never developed effective interpersonal communication skills. As a result, he sometimes has difficulty getting along with people, and is even willing to talk about his lack of concern with getting along with people on the job. Although his pay and promotions should be based upon his skill as a tool and die maker, even he will admit that he has not received the promotions and rank increases that some of his colleagues have received, simply because he did not "butter up the boss" or "get along with the right people." This is another way of saying

Richard Younker

Interpersonal communication skills affect not only a worker's career progress but also how well the worker does each particular job.

that his lack of interpersonal skills hindered his progress in his career. Many people would not think of this kind of a job as depending heavily upon interpersonal skills, but if you cannot get along with your fellow workers (even if the job that you have appears to be a purely physical process) you may not achieve at as high a level as others or receive the promotions and pay increases you might deserve. Many secretaries, contractors, bankers, lifeguards, teachers, policemen, and janitors do not progress well in their jobs and are not treated the way they feel they should be financially largely because they are ineffective at interpersonal communication. We know of no job that is totally divorced from interpersonal communication skills. Even the artist who works alone ultimately interacts with a potential customer in such a way as to get the best possible price or to receive a compliment.

Self-Concept Survival

Central to our survival is the need to think well of ourselves. Although this need will be discussed in more detail later in this chapter and in chapter 3, we would like to discuss briefly the centrality of the self-concept—our perception of ourselves—and its relationship to interpersonal communication. Have you ever wondered how you developed your self-image? How do you know who and what you are? How do you know whether you are good or bad at the things you do? How did you decide that you were a good person or not a good person? This kind of self-awareness and self-concept comes largely through the process of interpersonal communication. This process begins at a very early age. When children are born, they can be treated in a number of different ways. Parents can interpersonally communicate with them in such a way as to make them feel valued, desired, and wanted, or they can interpersonally communicate with the children in such a way as to make them feel rejected, unwanted, and worthless. This can happen as early as the first two or three years of life, although it continues throughout our lives. People tell us every day how worthwhile they consider us: by the way they look at us, by how close they stand to us, and by the way they initiate or do not initiate conversations with us. Every time we interact with other people the other person tells us how he or she regards us as an individual.

As this happens, we develop our sense of identity. If we have parents who praise us for the work we have done at school, the way we have played on the baseball team, our work in the drama club, or our accomplishments at earning a Scout merit badge, we develop a positive perception of ourselves. We begin to think we are worthwhile and a valuable part of humanity. A lot of us have had the opportunity, even when we have experienced failure, of having someone such as a friend, parent, teacher, or minister pat us on the back to say, "That's o.k. You gave it your best shot. You did your best, and we're proud of you." This kind of interpersonal comment, as insignificant as it may seem, can have quite an impact on someone as compared with the statement, "Boy, did you louse it up! You are a failure." Such a comment can make us feel worthless and reluctant to try again.

These are very simple examples, and yet we are sure you have experienced one or the other, and possibly both. The more often people interact positively with us, the more positive is the self-concept we develop. The less we experience these positive interactions, the more negatively we think of ourselves. We have known friends who were very physically attractive and intelligent but who believed they were unattractive and incompetent. This resulted from experiences throughout their lives in which their family, friends, and others communicated with them in a negative way, which ultimately contributed toward an overall negative self-concept.

Since a positive self-concept is strongly related to our survival, it is important that we be aware that the way we communicate with other people has a

A supportive parent does much to help a child develop a positive sense of identity and a feeling of worth.

Wayne Miller/Magnum Photos, Inc.

13

profound effect upon their self-concepts. A person who has a negative self-concept will not attempt new projects, initiate interactions with other people, or tackle a difficult task. Because such people are unwilling to try these things, they frequently limit their careers severely and thus do not enjoy the kind of career survival we were talking about. They frequently cut themselves off from contact with others and do not enjoy the kind of social survival that seems necessary for well-adjusted personalities.

The overall theme of this discussion has been survival. This is the primary goal or purpose of interpersonal communication—physical, social, self-concept, or career survival. A greater awareness of the interpersonal communication process will contribute in a significant manner to our survival in each of these ways. In this book we hope to consider the various component parts of interpersonal communication systems so you will better understand what is going on when people interact. With increased understanding we think you should be able to improve your own interpersonal communication competence. We now will define interpersonal communication.

Defining Interpersonal Communication

Interpersonal communication is a process in which from two to twenty persons attempt to influence one another through the use of a common symbol system, in a situation permitting equal opportunity for all persons involved in the process to influence one another. Ideally, the process causes us to be aware of others as persons rather than as objects. Persons involved in such a situation *interact,* using a language in which the symbols employed are those commonly accepted by people in the group. (The numerical limits we place on the interpersonal situation are not entirely arbitrary. With more than twenty people the opportunity for equal opportunity to influence one another is lost.)[10]

Probably as important as a definition of what interpersonal communication is would be an indication of what it is not. While the communication process is certainly present both in and out of the interpersonal context, adequate consideration of communication in all contexts would be beyond the scope of this text. The effects of context on communication are quite pronounced and have resulted in a number of subdivisions of communication studies within many disciplines.[11] Areas of study include small group communication, public speaking, persuasion, dyadic communication, mass communication, and others. These are not really *different kinds* of communication but are instead *different contexts* in which communication can occur. We feel further that several of these contexts, while validly studied separately, fall under the heading of interpersonal communication.

10. Bernard Berelson and Gary A Steiner, *Human Behavior* (New York: Harcourt, Brace and World, Inc., 1964), p. 325.

11. Daniel E. Costello, "Therapeutic Transactions: An Approach to Human Communication," in *Approaches to Human Communication,* ed. Richard W. Budd and Brent D. Ruben (New York: Spartan Books, 1972), p. 428.

Within this label we would include *dyadic communication* (between two people), communication in *small groups* (numbering from three to twenty), and much of the communication that occurs within large organizations (*organizational communication*). These phenomena fall within the purview of interpersonal communication. We will not consider either public or mass communication in this text, as we could not treat them fairly in a text focusing on the interpersonal situation.

A key criterion for determining whether or not a communication occurrence would be defined as interpersonal is related to the concept of feedback.[12] Within the communication process, do the individuals in a given situation have equal access to one another for the purpose of influencing one another? If they do, we consider the situation an interpersonal one. If they do not, the situation is not interpersonal. It is also important to stress that even though we will not be considering other contexts of communication, such as public and mass communication, the communication process in the interpersonal context is the same as that which occurs within the public or the mass communication contexts. However, we, and many other communication scholars, believe the contextual differences are significant.

Many of the communication contexts included under the heading of interpersonal communication also have been treated separately themselves. This has probably occurred because the material and research within each of these subareas is so vast as to merit intensive attention. However, even though areas such as small group and dyadic communication merit treatment and consideration in and of themselves, this does not obscure the interpersonal nature of both of these communication contexts.

12. Bruce H. Westley and Malcolm S. MacLean, Jr., "A Conceptual Model for Communications Research," *Journalism Quarterly* (Winter 1957):31–38.

Interpersonal Motivation

Important to an understanding of how to communicate effectively with other people interpersonally is an understanding of how we are motivated to do the things we do. What makes you brag? Why do you want to sit and talk with someone about a television show you saw last night? Why do you agree to get a drink of water for someone who asks you to? Why do you communicate the way you do? All of these are questions we should be able to answer if we are to communicate effectively. All of them are based on our motivational system.

The things that motivate us include our need systems, our value systems, and our environment. These three elements combine to result in our desiring things and behaving in various ways. A consideration of these three elements makes it possible for us to predict how people will respond to our messages and, furthermore, helps us to explain the messages that we receive from other people.

Need Systems

Thus far, we have made reference to a number of different kinds of needs, which scholars have postulated and classified in various ways. These needs can be grouped into four categories: physical, social, ego, and consistency needs.[13]

Physical Needs

13. W. C. Langer, *Psychology in Human Living* (New York: Appleton-Century, 1943); Leon Festinger, *A Theory of Cognitive Dissonance* (Stanford, Calif.: Stanford University Press, 1957).

14. A. H. Maslow, *Motivation and Personality* (New York: Harper & Row Publishers, Inc., 1954), pp. 80–92.

15. Ardrey, *The Social Contract*, p. 108.

By physical needs, we are referring to what Maslow[14] called physiological and safety needs and what Ardrey[15] referred to as security needs. These are probably the needs that brought about communication originally. Here we are referring to the physical needs of survival—the needs for food, for sex, for shelter, for sleep, and for physical security. People had to communicate with others cooperatively to defend their homes from outside attackers or to attack other people's homes. Men and women had to communicate effectively to have sex, which ensures the survival of the human race (although we rarely think of it in that way at the time).

Even though it may seem that we have many physical needs, actually they are rather few in number, and much of what we do today to satisfy those needs goes far beyond what is necessary. In fact, we might say that we often forget what our real physical needs are because of the encroachment of other, nonphysical needs. It is intriguing to see persons working to make money (which they think serves the purpose of taking care of their physical needs) so long and hard that they earn many times the amount of money necessary to satisfy those actual physical needs. Very few of us really need homes as nice as we have, automobiles, or all of the clothing we wear. If we compare the physical luxuries we have today with those of people who live more simply, we wonder if maybe we haven't misplaced some of our efforts—concentrating so much on getting so much more than we need. But before we condemn our materialism, we must remember that frequently we engage in behavior that brings us more material things, no longer to satisfy just physical needs, but to fulfill other needs we have—which brings us to our second need classification.

Social Needs

16. Maslow, *Motivation and Personality*, pp. 80–92.

17. William C. Schutz, *The Interpersonal Underworld* (Palo Alto, Calif.: Science & Behavior Books, Inc., 1966), pp. 18–25.

At this point we concern ourselves with social, or interpersonal, needs—the need to relate to other people. Such needs were referred to by Maslow as "love" or "belongingness" needs.[16] Another scholar, William Schutz, referred to social needs as including the needs for "inclusion," "control," and "affection." According to him, we have a need to: (1) "establish and maintain a satisfactory relationship with people with respect to interaction and association," (2) "establish and maintain a satisfactory relation with people with respect to control and power," and (3) "to establish and maintain a satisfactory relation with people with respect to love and affection."[17]

Chapter 1

In other words, all of us need to maintain some sort of interpersonal relationship with other people that is satisfactory to us. By this we mean that all of us need to love and be loved, to control others and have others control us, to relate to others and have them relate to us—with each of these behavior patterns going on in such a way that we consider both the relationships and our positions in them to be "good." That this need for interpersonal relationships is fairly basic is dramatically pointed up by studies made of orphan infants reared with and without affection. The infants who experienced affection were physically strong, healthy babies, whereas the infants who were not fondled and cuddled began to waste away physically.[18] This should indicate that we have these external needs from the time we are born and that the need for affection may even be related to our physical survival.

18. R. A. Spitz, "Hospitalism: An Inquiry Into the Genesis of Psychiatric Conditions in Early Childhood," in *The Psychoanalytic Study of the Child*, ed. O. Fenichel et al. (New York: International Universities Press, 1945), pp. 53–74; Desmond Morris, *Intimate Behavior* (New York: Random House, Inc., 1971), pp. 13–34.

Ego Needs

Ego needs of an individual can be significantly affected by one's experiences throughout life. Maslow referred to these needs as self-esteem and self-actualization.[19] Ardrey refers to the basic animal need of identity.[20] Ego needs are somewhat introspective in nature. An example would be the need to think well of oneself. The satisfaction of this need might be achieved through making a series of bull's-eyes in archery, by learning how to ski successfully, or possibly by the memorizing of a lengthy poem. In all of these cases, perception of their own accomplishments by the individuals involved would be positive, and thus the need to think well of themselves would be satisfied.

19. Maslow, *Motivation and Personality*, pp. 80–92.

20. Ardrey, *The Social Contract*, pp. 108–9.

There are probably as many approaches to ego needs as there are behavioral scientists to classify needs. One of the more prominent approaches is that of Maslow, who suggested that, among other needs, people have the need to think well of themselves—what Maslow referred to as "self-esteem needs." For instance, if Charley is a carpenter, it is a basic need of his to think he is a good carpenter. It is equally important for Phyllis to feel she is a good doctor, or for Frank to feel he is a good cook. It is necessary for us not only to accept ourselves, but also to think highly of ourselves. It is important for us to evaluate ourselves positively so we can accept ourselves as worthwhile human beings. According to many studies and scholars in counseling, psychology, and sociology, this is a very strongly felt need.[21]

21. John W. Kinch, "A Formalized Theory of the Self-Concept," *American Journal of Sociology*, LXVIII January 1973, pp. 481–83.

Maslow also suggested that we need to feel we have achieved at the highest level at which we are capable of achieving. This is what he called "self-actualization." By "self-actualization," Maslow meant that we all have abilities that we think make us able to perform at a certain maximum level. Furthermore, we have the need to *achieve* that level, thus "self-actualizing" ourselves. We suggested that individuals could enhance their self-esteem by learning how to ski. To "self-actualize," individuals would have to learn to ski as well as they thought themselves possibly capable of doing. Thus, for one person to "self-actualize" through skiing, simply managing to get down an intermediate slope might be enough. For another person to "self-actualize" through skiing, successfully engaging in cross-country skiing across the Rocky Mountains might be considered necessary. Different accomplishments are necessary for different people to "self-actualize" because they have different perceptions of their capabilities.

Some people appear to be bragging all the time. They constantly tell us how good they are or how well they do things. At first, it may seem as if they are "stuck on themselves." However, they are very probably overcompensating for feelings of inadequacy.[22] Frequently, we engage in defensive behavior when we communicate. Often this takes the form of bragging to convince ourselves that we are good so that our own ego needs may be satisfied.[23]

22. Schutz, The Interpersonal Underworld, pp. 25–32.

23. Alfred R. Lindesmith and Anselm L. Strauss, Social Psychology (New York: Holt, Rinehart & Winston, Inc., 1968), pp. 328–30.

Maslow's Hierarchy of Needs

24. Maslow, Motivation and Personality, pp. 80–92.

One characteristic of needs that probably bears mentioning at this point is Maslow's suggestion that our needs are ordered in a hierarchy.[24] The basic needs are physiological and security needs, or what we have been referring to as physical needs. Next, Maslow says, we have belongingness needs, which we are calling *social needs*. Finally come the needs of self-esteem and self-actualization, or what we have called *ego needs*. Maslow maintained that, unless people's physiological needs are met, they will not be concerned with their security needs or any other needs further up the hierarchy. Thus we would explain the old saying that "you can't preach ideology to a nation with an empty stomach" by pointing out that people who are hungry have such overriding physical needs that they cannot think in terms of ideology or be concerned with pride in nation or self, because they have not yet satisfied the more basic need levels. Maslow suggested that once a basic need, such as a physiological one, is satisfied, the person is no longer concerned with lower needs and moves on to the next higher level.

A situation has developed in America today in which labor unions, which were originally organized to satisfy the physical needs of workers, are losing members. One possible explanation for this is that union leaders are still communicating about the unions' ability to meet physical needs, even though for a number of years now (a decade or two) the majority of workers have had their physical needs fairly well met in their places of employment and by the government. They have, therefore, probably moved on to other need levels, such as social and ego needs. But the union leaders are still basing their appeal to membership on needs the workers no longer feel. The workers do not respond. So membership goes down. There are two points here: first, we cannot appeal to the next level of needs until the first level has been satisfied; and second, we cannot appeal to lower needs once the move has been made up to a higher level. These two principles are important to us in our analysis of how needs relate to the way people communicate.

There is evidence that these needs are present in people on more than a theoretical basis. In an attempt to improve production and morale in an oil refinery in the Netherlands, Willem James, who was in charge of the plant, perceived that while the workers in the refinery were organized in an efficient manner, there were a number of morale problems, so he decided to do something about them. He had been exposed to Maslow's theories and decided to put them to use in his firm.

James decided that physical needs were already being satisfied through wages and working conditions, so he attempted to meet other employee needs by giving groups of employees, as well as various individuals, problems to solve. Within the operation of the refinery there were a number of problems that needed to be solved to ensure production, so rather than tell the employees how to do their jobs, he let them go about solving the problems in their own way. Through this approach he was attempting to enhance individual self-esteem by letting the workers know he had faith in them. He gave them authority, which, of course, enhanced self-esteem and satisfied that need. He also gave them the opportunity to self-actualize by allowing them to solve problems at their highest possible level. All of these things provided an opportunity for the individuals in the plant to achieve at whatever they considered to be their maximum achievement level.

Company recognition of an employee's efforts enhances the employee's self-esteem and fosters good morale among all employees.

Dennis Brack/Black Star

Greatly increased morale and continued satisfactory production resulted from this approach. There was an interesting side effect and gratifying benefit: in addition to the satisfaction of ego needs (which we can hypothesize was the cause of the increase in positive morale), plant production actually increased, so that not only did James achieve his goal of improving morale, making for a happier family of employees, but also he managed to improve efficiency in the plant, thus increasing profits.[25] Of course, it would be easy for a rigid experimentalist to suggest that something else may have caused the increase in productivity and the improvement in morale. We would have to agree. However, the consensus among those in management is that much more than satisfaction of physical needs is necessary for the maintenance of good employee morale.

25. Ardrey, *The Social Contract*, pp. 181–86.

Examples of this are abundant. Companies such as Western Electric, IBM, General Motors, and others make every attempt to satisfy other needs in addition to the physical needs of the individual. These companies have instituted company magazines that have publicized accomplishments of various individuals on their jobs, in social activities, and the like. Births are announced, as are wins in bowling leagues, and prizes are given for suggestions that improve plant efficiency. The recognition and the activities provided by these plants help satisfy social and ego needs. It seems only reasonable that humans, being a very complex species, having once satisfied physical needs (as is true of many Americans today), would then come up with another set of needs to be satisfied. If this were not the case, we would very likely not be motivated to do anything.

Consistency Needs

26. William J. McGuire, "The Current Status of Cognitive Consistency Theories," in *Cognitive Consistency*, ed. Shel Feldman (New York: *Academic Press, Inc.*, 1966), pp. 1–46; Charles A. Kiesler, Barry E. Collins, and Norman Miller, *Attitude Change* (New York: John Wiley & Sons, Inc., 1969), pp. 155–237.

While scholars have generally classified our needs as physical, social, and ego, there is also considerable evidence that we have a strong need to be consistent.[26] The need for consistency refers to the need to have our ideas, values, perceptions, behaviors, and attitudes all consistent among themselves. If we disapprove of stealing, we can never steal anything without being inconsistent with our own value system. One of the primary ways we get children to learn honesty is by teaching them the value of honesty. We then hope their behavior will remain consistent with the value we hope they have accepted. (We also apply punishment when they are dishonest, so children avoid dishonesty to be consistent with their desire to avoid pain.)

There seem to be ways around this, though. For instance, we can rationalize our behavior—we can maintain the value that deplores stealing, and yet while working at the office take paper clips, a form of stealing. We can rationalize by saying that the corporation is so large and the paper clips are so small that "it's really not stealing at all," and besides "it won't hurt anyone." This rationalization helps us restore consistency within our own minds. If, in fact, we perceived stealing the paper clips as stealing, pure and simple, we would have an inconsistency because of our values, which would, in turn, result in pressure to restore consistency.

This need for consistency has been given a number of names. Theories proposed to explain the need for consistency include dissonance theory,[27] congruity theory,[28] and balance theory.[29] It is common, when referring to people who are experiencing inconsistency, to say that they are experiencing "dissonance." In our example, the individual uses rationalization to reduce dissonance. The implications in interpersonal communication of this need for consistency should become clear in the following example: if Charlie Smith voluntarily listens to a friend saying things that run counter to Charlie's attitudes and value system, he is confronted with inconsistency within himself. He has voluntarily chosen to expose himself to statements with which he does not agree. The inconsistency results from a behavior that is inconsistent with his own beliefs: he has listened to something that runs counter to his beliefs. How does he resolve the inconsistency? He can do this in several ways. He can rationalize by saying, "I am listening to this because if I don't I will lose my friend," a sort of "under friendly duress" reasoning. Or he can say, "I am listening because I want to hear two sides of every issue, so other friends, and I, myself, will think I am well informed, and because of this I can listen and it really isn't going to affect me." One of the ways an inconsistency such as this can be reduced, however, is by virtue of persons in this type of situation *changing their own value systems or attitudes*. In other words, they can bring their own value systems and attitudes into line with those advocated by the speaker. This restores consistency. Some communication scholars advocate the creation of dissonance deliberately through messages as a means of changing attitudes in individuals. Once having created the dissonance, the communicator relies upon the listeners to change their attitudes to restore consistency.

27. Festinger, *A Theory of Cognitive Dissonance.*

28. Charles E. Osgood and Percy H. Tannenbaum, "The Principle of Congruity in the Prediction of Attitude Change," *Psychological Review* 62 (1955): 42–55.

29. Fritz Heider, *The Psychology of Interpersonal Relations* (New York: Science Editions, John Wiley & Sons, Inc., 1958).

An Overview of Needs

One of the problems involved in a discussion of our need system is that needs are not, unfortunately, as mutually exclusive as we would like for a classification system. Certainly, many of what we have referred to here as ego needs might be classified as social needs by some people, and we ourselves would understand this. The view of our needs just presented does seem useful for our discussion of communication. It also aids us in solving the mystery we set out to solve. If we go back to the original question of why people began to communicate, we can see that they communicated to survive: to get food and to protect themselves. This need for immediate physical survival may have generated subsequent needs in humans, such as those we have been discussing. In turn these became basic needs.

Of course, it is obvious that we must minimally satisfy our physical needs so that we (and our species) survive. If we do not eat, get enough sleep, maintain the correct body temperature, and avoid things like heavy falling objects, we die. If we do not reproduce, our species will cease to exist. Both the individual and the species survive if we meet our physical needs.

The need to think well of ourselves is less directly related to survival, but is related nevertheless. People who think too badly of themselves may develop defense mechanisms that prevent them from adequately coping with their environment. These people usually end up as mental incompetents, unable to care for themselves. They are unable to assure their own survival and become a burden to other people, indirectly threatening species survival. This is why the mental well-being of others is a concern of many people. We really need all people to be "pulling their own weight" at all times. Although the relationship may not seem direct, our ego needs must be satisfied for us and our species to survive.

The sexual need of men and women for each other may also be viewed as a physical need evolving into what we would now call a social need, the need for love. Maybe at one time in our evolutionary history the social need was not a primary one, but certainly as humans evolved, the social need, the need to relate to other people, became as basic as any of our other needs.[30]

Social needs, or the need to relate to other people, appear to result in certain kinds of behaviors that are interesting to us in the field of communication. For one thing, we seem to have such strong social needs that we will engage in some very unusual kinds of behavior to satisfy them. There is evidence to suggest that this need for others may be extremely strong.[31] Peer-group pressure, or the influence of our friends and members of groups we belong to or aspire to belong to, is so great that we can be pressured to consider ourselves wrong even when we are right. We can even be caused to distort things we see because of pressure from our peers. We can be forced to change our attitudes about modes of behavior that are repugnant to us simply to assure our acceptance by a group. Studies done over the last two or three decades repeatedly indicate this overpowering need for acceptance in interpersonal relationships with others.[32] We will say things we do not believe. We will wear clothes we do not like. We will drive cars that are unsafe and buy homes that are too expensive for us to afford, to gain acceptance from groups whose approval we value. This suggests a very high degree of social needs on the part of people.

It is probable that our need for acceptance by others is related to survival. However, in this case survival does not necessarily mean survival of the individual but rather survival of the species. It may be, if we may modify Darwin's theory of evolution, that behavioral characteristics that contribute to the survival of the species have been reinforced and perpetuated genetically in individual members of the species, just as individuals who, because of desirable physical traits, contribute to the survival of the species are also retained by a society to ensure its survival. Thus, we might view a set of behaviors and codes of conduct developed by a larger group that contribute toward the survival of that group as that group's culture.

30. Richard H. Walters and Ross D. Parke, "Social Motivation, Dependency, and Susceptibility to Social Influence," in *Advances in Experimental Social Psychology*, ed. Leonard Berkowitz (New York: Academic Press, Inc., 1964), 1:231–76.

31. Ibid.

32. Serge Moscovici and Claude Faucheux, "Social Influence, Conformity Bias, and the Study of Active Minorities," in *Advances in Experimental Social Psychology*, ed. Leonard Berkowitz (New York: Academic Press, Inc., 1972), 6:157–60.

For instance, standards of conduct regarding sexual behavior toward close relatives such as sisters, brothers, daughters, sons, mothers, and fathers—incest—are very stringent. That kind of behavior is not permitted in most cultures. Some might say we have these values and codes of conduct because they are "right." However, when one considers the evidence of the biological result of the mating of fathers and daughters, brothers and sisters, first cousins, and so forth, we find that, if incest were permitted, defects would likely result that would weaken the species as a group. Therefore it seems only logical that the species would develop codes of conduct that would prevent defects and encourage mating behavior that would tend to eliminate defects and hopefully produce stronger and more "survivable" individuals. Thus, we find this need to conform to peer-group pressure, or cultural pressure, may still be survival-oriented. We are probably succumbing to species dictates so that the species may survive.

Sometimes what was once a survival behavior contributing to the survival of the group is today, owing to technological advances, no longer necessary. Because of this we see many cultural norms and values changing—and usually with considerable difficulty. A good example of this involves the changing of values regarding sexual behavior. Because of, and since, the advent of the Pill and other contraceptive methods, it no longer seems as necessary to abstain from sexual behavior with persons other than our mates as it once was. Whereas society may have needed the prohibition of promiscuous sexual behavior at one time, it may be no longer needed. Therefore, the taboo is breaking down. In addition to birth control methods, probably the advent of penicillin and its effect on venereal disease has also contributed significantly to the changes in codes of sexual conduct. It is also very possible that if the increase in venereal disease continues in spite of the presence of penicillin, we may reestablish the old sexual codes.

In addition to peer-group and cultural pressure relating to acceptance by others is the pressure of the individual's role. This is an outgrowth of a person's interaction with his or her culture and peer group in which the group, the culture, and the individual's gender, abilities, and the like create a role for the individual, just as an actor has a role in a play.[33] Our role defines what we can and cannot do, what we can and cannot say, what we are, and what we might become. When we act outside of our role, society brings pressure to bear to cause us to go back to that role and engage in the proper behaviors appropriate to it. Again, this is very likely survival-oriented. It increases the predictability of behavior of individuals, creating a more orderly society, which in turn probably contributes to survival of a society. Thus, because the individual is again in need of the group, and because the group needs to survive, the individual is very much controlled by role.

While many people refer to role as a controlling agent in and of itself, role is probably an outgrowth of pressures on the individual to behave in a manner that contributes to society's survival. Society needs roles because roles

33. Alfred Kuhn, The Study of Society (Homewood, Ill.: Richard D. Irwin, Inc., and The Dorsey Press, Inc., 1963), pp. 245–47; Erving Goffman, The Presentation of Self in Everyday Life (Garden City, N.Y.: Doubleday Anchor Books, 1959), pp. 17–76.

cause people to behave in fairly predictable ways, which makes effective interaction easier. Because we need society and because we have social needs for interpersonal relationships, we agree tacitly to play our roles properly because if we do, our needs are satisfied by society.

Our need for consistency probably relates to the requirement of prediction for survival. Although we can only guess, it seems reasonable that to survive physically in the world, we must be able to predict others' behavior and other events. If people were totally inconsistent and unpredictable, how would we ever know how to approach anyone? It would be impossible. Society could not exist without some degree of order and consistency. Just as we need others to be consistent, they also need us to be consistent for the same reasons. Hopefully, you can see that our need for consistency is related to our need and society's need to survive.

We have just discussed people's basic needs: physical, social, ego, and consistency needs, and how the satisfaction of these is related to survival. It should be evident that we need consistency in each of the other need areas. It is our feeling that much interpersonal communication behavior can be explained both in terms of our need systems themselves as well as in terms of the interaction of our needs with our values. To better understand how these relate we will now discuss values and interpersonal communication.

Value Systems

Thus far, we have discussed what many people consider the basic elements of motivation. Although the need systems discussed are of extreme importance, other motivational elements should also be kept in mind when we are trying to understand and explain behavior. Value systems are "larger" than our need systems, in the sense that they are based both on need systems and on something more. Rokeach defined a *value* as "an enduring belief that a specific mode of conduct or end-state of existence is personally or socially preferable to an opposite or converse mode of conduct or end-state of existence. A *value system* is an enduring organization of beliefs concerning preferable modes of conduct or end-states of existence along a continuum of relative importance."[34] Rokeach's view of values is that they are relative— we decide we would rather engage in one behavior compared with others or pursue one goal compared with other goals. These decisions are made relative to a continuum of relative importance we have in our minds, by means of which we decide what are preferable behaviors and goals.

34. Milton Rokeach, *The Nature of Values* (New York: Free Press, 1973), p. 5.

For purposes of understanding interpersonal communication we would like just to focus on the general concept of values and consider that all people do have value systems, or a collection of individual values concerning preferable behaviors and preferable goals. These values can include things like making money, having a big home, television sets, cars, and enough money to go to fancy restaurants. Value systems can also focus on the goal of having a close-knit family—a spouse and children, all enjoying

one another's company. In addition, there can be other goals or values. We may have the value of good workmanship as we build something out of wood and nails. We may value close friendships and good times with our friends. We may value devotion to country or commitment to God. Any of these are values that can govern our goal-seeking behavior and our day-to-day behavior.

How do we develop these values? Most of us learn our value systems as we are growing up, first from our parents, then our families, and finally people outside the family. One of the best ways to predict the belief and value systems of a person is to look very carefully at the belief and value systems of that person's parents. If you reflect for a while, you may find that you have more in common with your parents than you might ordinarily think. This becomes even more true as we get older. As we reach adulthood and our middle years, we become more like our parents than we were during our teenage years and early twenties.

It is also possible to trace our value development to the environment in which we live. People from the Midwest reared among what we might refer to as "Midwest values" apparently have a value system different from

A family that enjoys being together may have chosen this goal as a part of its value system.

people reared in New York City or Los Angeles. Likewise, a value system exists in the southeastern United States. Most of us would not notice dramatic differences among people from these different areas. If we begin to talk about a number of different subjects, however, we will begin to notice that someone from New York City values not wasting time more than someone from the South. Someone from the South may value interpersonal courtesies such as "gentlemanly" or "ladylike" behavior more than someone from New York. Likewise, someone from the Midwest may value hard work and "saving for a rainy day" more than someone from Los Angeles, whereas someone from Los Angeles may value open space, ease of transportation, and "doing your own thing" more. These are obviously a collection of stereotypes about people from different parts of the country, but we think that some elements of these values, which we have admittedly exaggerated for the sake of an example, can be found within people in these various environments. Thus, as we are growing up we not only learn our values from our parents but also from the whole environment, which includes our teachers, friends, ministers, and the like.

Every value we have results in either an avoidance or an attraction behavior on our part. If we value fine gourmet meals, we are attracted to behaviors that will ensure us the opportunity to spend enjoyable evenings in gourmet restaurants. If we negatively value pain, then we may avoid behaviors such as jogging or weight lifting. Thus values contribute toward our decision to engage in a behavior or not.

Our values relate to either end-states or modes of conduct. Rokeach referred to these as either *terminal values* or *instrumental values*. Those that are related to our modes of conduct, moral behavior, and relationships are what Rokeach calls *instrumental*.[35] These are of considerable importance to us in interpersonal communication because the way we behave interpersonally is related to our instrumental values. If we value social relationships, we will engage in behaviors and modes of conduct that are conducive to satisfactory interpersonal relationships. On the other hand, terminal values relate to end-states such as acquiring wealth, getting good grades, and "scoring" on a date. These values again can have a significant effect on the way we interact with people because they are all oriented toward some kind of terminal goal.

35. Rokeach, *The Nature of Values*, p. 5.

Importance of Self Concept

Of considerable importance to us in interpersonal communication is the notion that values can be thought of in hierarchical terms. As with Maslow's hierarchy of needs, it is possible to think of values as being ranked, with some being higher-order values and some being lower-order values. Rokeach suggested that we should think of this ranking *as it relates to our concept of self*.[36]

36. Ibid.

We value those things more highly that will reinforce and contribute to a positive self-image. Although many people express the thought that all persons should be able to have a job if they wish and earn a reasonable wage, this value is related to societal, rather than personal, need satisfaction. These same people, after discovering that they may lose some of their own opportunities when everyone has an equal opportunity for a job, may be less likely to value equal opportunities. In terms of their personal values, they may oppose such things as minimum-wage laws and affirmative action programs because the value of having a happy and comfortable life for themselves is closer to their self-concept, and thus more important than society-oriented values such as equal rights for everyone.

As we continue our discussion of interpersonal communication, this concept of the centrality of self as it relates to values will become more important. We should pay close attention to the communication behavior of others to determine what they are saying about themselves. As people speak out in favor of or against some topic, this frequently will tell us much about how the topic relates to their own self-concepts. Even though at times it may seem that people are discussing a topic "objectively," they subjectively relate the topic back to their own self-concepts. This occurs constantly in conversations and small group discussions. If we are sensitive to what people indirectly say, we can relate our messages to their self-concepts in reply so that our points reinforce their self-concepts and thus are more acceptable.

Our concern with the effect of messages on self-concept becomes more important if we consider that a simple statement by us can have a profound effect upon someone else's self-concept. A critical comment about a particular make of automobile could have a negative effect upon a friend's self-concept because of the way cars relate to that self-concept. Although the comment might seem objective to us, it may be perceived as negative by someone else. This could have a significant effect upon the outcome of any interpersonal interaction.

The Value Component in Interpersonal Communication

Although it is interesting to discuss what values are, ultimately the question most students of interpersonal communication are concerned with is what the values do for us. Values serve as standards, as motivational forces, and enable us to formulate plans and determine our self-presentation.

Because values serve as standards for us, they also determine the stands we take in our messages. For example, people who have been taught to value thrift are more likely to argue for balanced budgets in government, while someone who is taught to value fair treatment of human beings may support social programs funded by government.

Values determine the way we present ourselves to other people. In any interpersonal interaction people can be cold, warm, logical, or emotional. Much of this depends upon whether they value warmth, logic, feelings, or friendship. If we value friendship above all other things, we may throw caution to the wind regarding logic but work very hard to communicate in ways to establish and maintain friendships. Actually, none of us ever communicates entirely according to one value, so it is often necessary to relate our messages to several values if the messages are to have the desired effect.

Finally, we are concerned with values in interpersonal communication because of their motivational characteristics. Because values are an outgrowth of the needs we discussed earlier, it is not surprising that values have a significant effect on our behaviors. Different values relate to various needs, but, given our earlier discussion of self-concept, it should be obvious that many values that motivate us relate to the ego needs of self-esteem and self-actualization.

The Function of Interpersonal Communication

Consistent with our discussion of interpersonal communication in terms of survival, it is sometimes useful to think in terms of how our interpersonal communication is functioning for us in the achievement of that goal. A useful breakdown of functions is to think of either *consummatory* or *instrumental* interpersonal communication.

Consummatory interpersonal communication serves the function of *immediately satisfying* our needs, values, and goals. The interpersonal interaction itself is satisfying. There are many examples of consummatory interpersonal communication: a talk over a cup of coffee, joke-telling sessions in the dorm, and casual conversation during a date. Each of these is an example of interpersonal communication we engage in simply because it is pleasurable. It satisfies our social needs; it really does not have to lead to anything else.

Earlier we mentioned that Rokeach called values regarding our mode of conduct "instrumental values." His use of the term "instrumental" is related to the terminology we are using here. The distinction between instrumental and consummatory communication was developed by Fotheringham,[37] and we have opted to use it to suggest that some interpersonal behavior is intended to help us reach ultimate or long-term goals, rather than to achieve immediate satisfactions during interaction. Our instrumental values concerning the ways we behave with others affect the interpersonal behaviors we perform when engaged in both instrumental and consummatory interpersonal communication. When a car salesperson engages in casual conversation with someone in a car showroom, he or she is involved in instru-

37. Wallace C. Fotheringham, *Perspectives on Persuasion* (Boston: Allyn & Bacon, Inc., 1966).

mental interpersonal communication. It is instrumental in the sense that the salesperson hopes that it will accomplish the goal of selling a car. It is possible to conceive of interpersonal communication between a professor and a student as instrumental when the goal of the student is to have a grade changed rather than simply to enjoy the professor's company.

We mention these functional types of interpersonal communication to help you become more aware that we usually either try to derive immediate satisfaction from an interaction or try to satisfy long-term goals. This is true both for us and for those with whom we communicate. A better understanding of our own behaviors as well as those of other people is realized by an awareness of these instrumental and consummatory functions of interpersonal communication.

Improving Your Interpersonal Skills

This book has grown out of the belief that we can improve our interpersonal skills significantly through an improved understanding and awareness of the interpersonal communication process. We feel it would be a mistake to have skills without understanding the basis for them. A carpenter cannot simply learn how to hammer nails and saw wood. It is necessary for a carpenter to learn principles of stress as well as various design principles to know how to build in the strongest possible way. Likewise, in interpersonal communication we feel it is desirable to practice and improve interpersonal skills. There are exercises that your instructor will provide for you in class. Also, some of you may be using a workbook full of exercises intended to help with interpersonal communication skills. We hope you understand, however, that the interpersonal skills stressed in exercises are part of an understanding of the theories related to interpersonal communication. It is not enough to have the skills without the understanding. Exercises of the sort you will have the opportunity to engage in in class are extremely valuable both in helping you to practice what you are learning and in providing you with opportunities to observe the kinds of things we are discussing in this book.

Furthermore, we feel that you can better sharpen your interpersonal skills by becoming more sensitive to the processes involved. In the next chapter we will be discussing more completely the process of interpersonal communication and the various elements and contexts involved. We hope as we proceed through our discussions of self-concept, perception, the use of words, nonverbal communication, information reception, and interpersonal communication patterns that you will be more able to exercise interpersonal communication skills in various contexts such as dyads, small groups, and organizations. This increased understanding and a greater sensitivity to the elements of the interpersonal communication process should make you more adept and skilled at interpersonal communication.

2

The Process of Interpersonal Communication

Thus far we have discussed the importance of interpersonal communication and defined the interpersonal communication process. We still have not discussed in detail the various elements of interpersonal communication. In this chapter we will discuss the components of interpersonal communication systems and develop an overview of the system so that our subsequent discussion of interpersonal communication elements and contexts will be clearer. It is not enough to understand interpersonal communication generally. We must understand the components and the way they relate to one another to understand how interpersonal communication functions.

Interpersonal Communication Is a Process

For centuries scholars have discussed communication as a *linear process*. A linear process is one that moves in one direction. People have typically thought of communication as proceeding from one individual to another, as something one does to someone else. This approach to communication is analogous to warmup practice before a baseball game when the batter lofts a ball into the air and hits it to the outfield where someone else catches it. It is a one-way process in which something travels from one person to another. This, however, is not how interpersonal communication occurs. Interpersonal communication, as well as other kinds of communication, is a process in which the participants interact *with* one another.

Although Aristotle viewed communication as a process, this was not emphasized for centuries until contemporary communication scholars introduced the concept of *feedback*.[1] With the introduction of this concept, which will be discussed more completely in chapter 7, we became aware that not only did a message go from person A to person B, but also that there

1. N. Wiener, *Cybernetics* (New York: John Wiley & Sons, Inc., 1948), p. 33.

31

was a response from person B to person A. Following this line of thought, we began to refer to the communication process as *circular* rather than linear. Circular communication is communication in which messages travel from one person to another and then back. However, even the circular approach to communication understates the process nature of communication. Consider figure 2.1; the process is still unidirectional, beginning with one person, going to a second person, and returning.

Figure 2.1 The communication process.

The process view of communication suggests that communication is similar to the steady-state theory of the universe. You may have read of this theory that the universe is constantly expanding and contracting, pulsating in what is called a *steady state.* Interpersonal communication systems consist of people interacting, with all individuals involved in the interaction, influencing one another simultaneously. This view of interpersonal communication makes it almost impossible to single out at any given moment one person as the initiating communicator or the responding communicator. Both are simply communicators, who communicate verbally and nonverbally through words, gestures, and the like. Each is affecting the other, constantly and simultaneously.

A student once suggested in a description of public communication that the audience initiates the communication process. His reasoning was that, without an audience, a speaker would never begin speaking. In a way, his line of reasoning provides some insight into the communication process because he is suggesting that the mere presence or absence of one or more individuals has an effect on other people in the communication setting.

Thus, in interpersonal communication there is a constant flow of verbal and nonverbal messages back and forth between and among all the participants. There is no beginning or end to which it is possible for us to trace communication, as all individuals in interpersonal communication are mutually affecting one another all the time. While you talk with a friend, the knowledge of who that person is and what the relationship is between you, as well as your observations of how that person is sitting or looking, affects what you are saying. At the same time, what you are saying affects your friend. It would be difficult indeed to determine an initiator and a concluder in an interaction, since there are multiple, simultaneous causes and effects of events at all times in any interpersonal relationship.

This process nature makes interpersonal communication more difficult to study because we cannot really look at all aspects of an interpersonal communication system at once. In this book, we will pull out the various components and look at them separately, but we hope you will reflect on the interrelationships that may affect a specific component at any given moment. To do less and to consider one component at a time without attempting to explain interpersonal communication as a process would be to oversimplify the process and to mislead you.

Characteristics of Interpersonal Communication Systems

Although interpersonal communication shares in common a great number of characteristics with communication in other contexts, it may prove instructive to consider the basic characteristics of interpersonal communication. None of these is necessarily unique to interpersonal communication; some can be found in other communication contexts as well.

Manipulation of the Environment

We engage in interpersonal communication to affect the behavior of others in such a way as to produce mutual satisfaction of needs. This is the principle on which chapter 1 focused. As the result of our physical limitations as a species, we have been forced to develop communication as a tool to aid in our survival in the world. Interpersonal communication is a tool for survival because it permits us to manipulate the world indirectly in such a way that we can make our environment more conducive to survival. If people are distinct from other members of the animal kingdom, our major distinction is probably our manipulation of the world through communication rather than through some direct, physical means.

Furthermore, the end toward which we manipulate our environment is satisfaction of needs. We have suggested the existence of physical, social, ego, and consistency needs. Therefore, it is possible to say that all of us in interpersonal situations are attempting to speak and gesture in such a way as to cause other persons to satisfy our needs while we satisfy their needs. We are attempting not only to cause others to satisfy our needs, but also to show others how, by satisfying our needs, they will satisfy their own as well. In fact, a satisfactory, or even ideal, interpersonal relationship between people might be defined as one in which two or more people maximally satisfy one another's needs. This kind of relationship is not restricted to two people, obviously, but could involve an entire group in which all members are maximally satisfying each other's needs.

Our Past Environment

Interpersonal communication is never independent of past behavior. Because humans must learn to communicate throughout their developmental years and because the acquisition of language occurs within a specific environment, people can never be independent of those conditions under which they learn to communicate. Our attitudes have been formed as the result of a number of behavior characteristics that are rooted in our past environment.[2] Children who grow up in homes where parents constantly tell them how bad they are develop a low level of self-esteem that affects the way they communicate for the remainder of their lives. It is reasonable to suspect that the needs, fears, anxieties, desires, hopes, and dreams an individual has at any given moment in life are the product of previous influences.

2. Arthur W. Staats, "Social Behaviorism and Human Motivation; Principles of the Attitude-Reinforcer-Discriminative Systems," in *Psychological Foundations of Attitudes*, ed. Anthony G. Greenwald, Timothy C. Brock, and Thomas M. Ostrom (New York: Academic Press, Inc., 1968), pp. 33–66.

This is not to suggest that we cannot rise above our environments. Someone who is deprived in childhood can rise to great heights in the business world, in politics, or in education, for example. However, even a person who rises above a poor early environment still communicates according to behavior patterns acquired in that environment. People react in many different ways to their environment because of individual and unique circumstances at any given time. The different behaviors we manifest during developmental years condition the way in which we acquire language, the kind of nonverbal behavior we consider appropriate to a situation, the attitudes and beliefs we develop, as well as other communication habits in regard to sentence structure, message organization, and so on.[3] All of these patterns affect our interpersonal communication in some way or another. It is, of course, possible to modify past behaviors at later points in our lives, but we must consider that the desire to modify them is also a result of our previous experience.

3. Leon Rappaport, *Personality Development* (Glenview, Ill.: Scott, Foresman & Co., 1972), pp. 234–35.

Verbal and Nonverbal Systems

Interpersonal communication depends on verbal and nonverbal communication systems for maximal effectiveness. It almost seems a truism to say that we cannot communicate without spoken language. However, it is equally true that we need to communicate nonverbally.

Formal Language

A formal language system enables us to express very complex and abstract ideas, which in turn permit us to communicate about various machines, theories, formulas, and the like.[4] We are not passing judgment on the world in which we live and saying that this is the best of all possible worlds; however, the kind of world in which we live would be impossible without formal language. For us to exist without a formal symbol system would require that we regress to a very primitive form of existence. We could not live in our complex societies and have our sophisticated systems of medicine or entertainment without formal language.

If our unique characteristic is the use of communication to manipulate our environment, then one tool that makes this possible would have to be formal language. While other animals seem to possess the ability to communicate, none would appear to have this ability to the degree that people do. Certainly, we lack evidence that even the highly communicative porpoise can manipulate symbols at a level as abstract as that achieved by a human child. Whether this is a strength or a weakness we leave to you to decide. We can, however, state that the use of a commonly accepted symbol system is a necessity for human beings if they are to engage in interpersonal communication for the purpose of affecting other individuals.

2118610

A formal language system, then, is imperative for effective interpersonal communication. Of equal importance, however, is nonverbal communication, our informal language system. It is through nonverbal communication that we manage to communicate emotions and subtleties of meaning that would be lost were we restricted solely to a verbal system.[5] The emotion of love is best communicated from one person to another nonverbally rather than through words. How often we complain of inadequacy of words to express this emotion! It is not necessary to complain; we need only make use of the nonverbal skills that most of us possess to communicate love.

While research in the area of nonverbal communication is somewhat limited, it has been estimated that as much as 93 percent of our messages concerning feelings are communicated in a nonverbal manner.[6] Through nonverbal communication we manage to establish our roles, intent, and affection. It is very likely that through nonverbal communication parents communicate love and protection to a child. It is of no use to tell a child we love it, if we do not caress the child and communicate love to the child nonverbally. This is especially true of young children who have not yet mastered language skills. When we consider that for the first two or three years of our lives, we are restricted primarily to nonverbal communication for acquisition of information about the world and for manipulation of the world, we should not be surprised that researchers are becoming increasingly aware of the importance of this kind of communication.

People generally have become very sophisticated with verbal communication and are highly dependent on it to acquire the skills that are needed to

4. John B. Carroll, "Work, Meaning, and Concepts: Part I. Their Nature," Howard Educational Review 34 (1964), pp. 178–90.

5. A. Mehrabian and S. R. Ferris, "Inference of Attitudes from Nonverbal Communication in Two Channels," Journal of Consulting Psychology 31 (1967):248–52; A. Mehrabian and M. Wiener, "Decoding of Inconsistent Communications," Journal of Personality and Social Psychology 6 (1967):109–14.

6. Ibid.

Nonverbal Communication

survive in the world. However, as we become older and more skilled in the use of verbal language, we become less skilled in the use of nonverbal language. Exercises in sensitivity training are conducted for the purpose of reteaching adults to communicate nonverbally as children do. Is it possible that we lose the skill to communicate nonverbally because we become dependent on language? At present we know of no study that suggests this conclusion, but from our own observations it would seem to be the case. (More comments on nonverbal communication will be found in chapter 6.)

Context

7. J. Ruesch and G. Bateson, "Structure and Process in Social Relations," *Psychiatry* 12 (1949):105–24.

8. J. Ruesch, "Synopsis of The Theory of Human Communication," *Psychiatry* 10 (1953):215–43.

The context of the interaction determines the nature of interpersonal communication. If our past environment and past behavior patterns continue to affect the process of interpersonal communication significantly, then the context in which communication is occurring at any given moment must have at least as much effect as they.[7] We are conditioned by our role in any given situation.[8] In the office with our boss, we communicate one way. At

Interpersonal communication is affected by the role of each communicator in the interaction.

Richard Kalvar/Magnum Photos, Inc.

the bowling alley with friends, we communicate another way. If we are at a rock concert, we communicate yet another way. What we are (in terms of role) in a given situation, who we are (in terms of socioeconomic level in society), how others perceive us, and how we perceive ourselves (in terms of our work as human beings)—all condition and determine the manner in which we interact with other people.

A woman may interact with her husband in one way, but she should not interact with her co-worker at the office in the same manner. If she does (as some women do), she will very likely find it impossible to continue the same kind of interaction with her husband at home.

Contextual factors that significantly affect interpersonal communication include role, physical setting, time, urgency or nonurgency in a situation, and number and status of people present. It would be impossible to enumerate all contextual factors in an interpersonal interaction, but it is safe to suggest that these contextual factors will determine the quality and nature of any interpersonal communication to a high degree.

Mass Communication

Interpersonal communication provides the opportunity for direct communication among all parties in the communication process. This is probably the feature that distinguishes interpersonal communication from other forms of communication. Mass communication is primarily one-way, with extremely delayed feedback. It is very difficult for the receivers in mass communication to provide feedback directly to the initiating communicators. In public communication the same problem is true, although it would be possible for an audience to provide feedback to a speaker. The size of the audience in the public communication situation would generally prevent as direct a feedback as is possible in the interpersonal situation. Thus we find a distinguishing characteristic of interpersonal communication is the opportunity for communicators to affect one another mutually and immediately during the communication process.

Need Satisfaction

Ideally, interpersonal communication results in the mutual satisfaction of needs of the persons involved in the interaction. Admittedly, this statement reflects our personal value systems; however, if a positive relationship is the goal of any interaction (and we think it often is), then mutual satisfaction of needs is absolutely necessary. The result is the development of a relationship that is positive in nature. If needs are not mutually satisfied, the outcome of the interaction very likely would be a negative relationship between the people who are involved, that would leave much hatred and/or enmity between them.

Interpersonal Communication: Models and Elements

It is common for scholars to develop models of the phenomena they study. Communication models have been developed to identify the elements in the communication process. Studying these models makes it easier for us not only to recognize the components in the process, but also to check out the relationships between and among the components. Models also provide us with plans of analysis we can use to approach any communication situation in which problems have occurred. Models may suggest likely problem points in the communication process.

Harry Smedley, Jr.

Whereas two people on a teeter-totter have an action-reaction relationship, interpersonal communication is circular and is characterized by a complex interaction among people.

Scholars have identified various components of the process of communication. No one model identifies all the parts or explains all the interacting relationships. The process is far too dynamic, the elements too numerous, and the interrelationships too complex to be represented with accuracy by a few line drawings or words in any one model. Nevertheless, models do help focus our attention on those parts of the process they represent, and some parts are included in most models.

Lasswell's[9] model identifies five commonly accepted variables in the process: Who? Says what? In what channel? To whom? With what effect? All five of these variables have received considerable attention from researchers and textbook writers. Lasswell's model is a good example of a linear approach to communication.

9. Harold Lasswell, "The Structure and Function of Communication in Society," in *The Communication of Ideas*, ed. L. Bryson (New York: Harper & Brothers, 1948), p. 37.

Lasswell's Model

Schramm's Model

Wilbur Schramm's model, as pictured in figure 2.2, introduced a concept that has assumed special significance in interpersonal communication. The *source* is the brain of the person initiating a communication. It consists of ideas that the person desires to communicate. The *encoder* is a process by which the ideas are converted into symbols for transmission to another person. This is a process rather than a thing. The *signal* is the message produced and transmitted. This could consist of the words uttered by a person or any other physical stimuli produced by the initiating communicator. The *decoder* is a process by which the stimuli received (such as spoken words) are converted into ideas by the recipient of the stimuli. This is sometimes referred to as the *decoding process*. The *destination* is the mind of the person to whom the stimuli are directed. This is the person the initiating communicator wishes to influence.

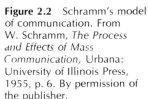

Figure 2.2 Schramm's model of communication. From W. Schramm, *The Process and Effects of Mass Communication*, Urbana: University of Illinois Press, 1955, p. 6. By permission of the publisher.

Schramm's special contribution was his suggestion that each communicator has a personal field of experience that controls both the encoding and decoding processes and determines meaning in communication. For communication to occur between people, Schramm indicated that there must be some overlap in their fields of experience, even though his is a linear model. For us to understand other persons, or for others to understand us, we should have something in common in our backgrounds that enables us to perceive the stimuli or messages similarly. In chapter 5 we will consider in greater detail the effect of our fields of experience on meaning.

Brooks-Emmert Model

In 1976 we developed a very detailed model of interpersonal communication (figure 2.3). Although the model is a circular one, it does not provide a detailed description of the communication process. The reader will note the following features not found in those models we have already considered.

1. A perception process is included to indicate that we must deal with the incoming stimuli around us. This should indicate that, while we may receive many stimuli at any one moment, there is a process we employ to organize and interpret them. (This will be covered more fully in chapter 4.)

2. Internal and external stimuli are included to point out that what we receive at any moment are not messages, but rather physical stimuli from both outside and within ourselves. There are a multitude of sensations at any moment that can include signals as well as other noncommunication stimuli. (Special attention will be given to this in chapter 4.)

Figure 2.3 Brooks-Emmert interpersonal communication model.

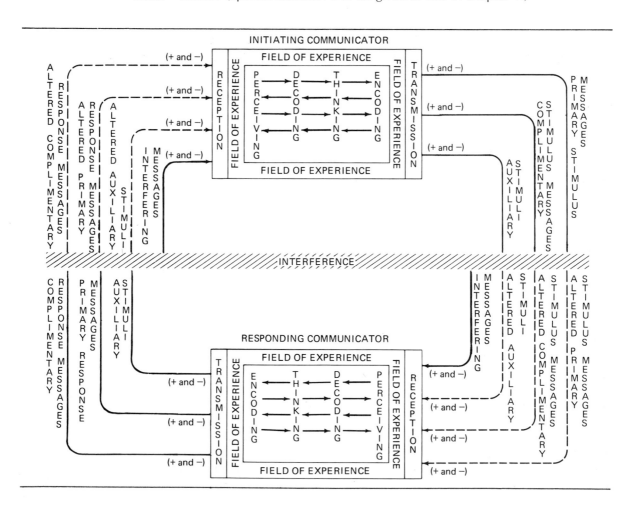

3. A thinking process is indicated. We are not really sure what occurs here, but this refers to what is frequently called *cognition*,[10] the process of developing new ideas, responding to stimuli, and so forth.

10. U. Neisser, *Cognitive Psychology* (New York: Appleton-Century-Crofts, 1967).

4. The arrows that run back and forth between the perceiving, encoding, and thinking processes in figure 2.3 indicate interaction among these processes. There is evidence that perception is affected by and affects encoding/decoding and cognition. In like manner, the reverse can be said. The interrelationships are not yet fully understood, but there appears to be considerable interplay among these processes. (See also chapter 4.)

5. The four processes just mentioned are controlled by the *individual's field of experience*. Our education, accidents, interactions with others, and even our physiological makeup significantly affect the way in which we perceive, decode, think, and encode. Obviously, this model would suggest, as did Schramm's, that fields of experience must overlap for communication to occur.

6. Our model suggests that we produce more than just one message. We produce *primary stimulus messages*—those messages produced in response to our original need to communicate and communicated by whatever means seem most effective to us. Sitting in a car at a drive-in, we would probably choose the medium of speech as the most effective and produce the sounds "I want a hot dog." This statement is our primary stimulus message because it is made in response to our hunger and transmitted by way of the medium we consider most efficient.

We also produce *complementary stimulus messages* that are our responses to the original stimuli, but are transmitted for the purpose of reinforcing the primary stimulus message. Any facial expressions, tones of voice, or gestures we might use to obtain better service at the drive-in would be complementary stimulus messages.

Finally, we emit *auxiliary stimuli* that are unrelated to the original stimulus to communicate, but that nevertheless affect other people's perceptions of our messages. If we look old, people perceive our messages one way; if we look young, they perceive our messages another way.

All of these messages and/or stimuli can influence people to satisfy our needs or not. Thus in figure 2.3 there is a plus sign to indicate that messages can be effective and a minus sign to indicate that messages can be counterproductive. (Nonverbal communication and stimuli will be considered in more detail in chapter 6.)

7. *Interference* includes any stimuli in the communication environment that can alter or distort messages. The model suggests that all messages are distorted and come through finally as altered messages. Even the spoken message changes as it causes air molecules to vibrate. No doubt you have tried to carry on a conversation when there was loud music playing. The music would be interference insofar as it made it difficult for you to hear and be heard.

8. This model also includes *interfering messages* that are present in the communication situation but are not produced by any of the persons who are communicating interpersonally. If two people are having a conversation in a room and they overhear another conversation in the hall, the hall conversation, with its semantic content, would be an interfering message.

Two points should be made about the Brooks-Emmert model of the communication process. First, the model is circular. We may consider the initiating communicator as the person who starts the interaction, but from the point when interaction begins, both communicators actually become responding communicators. That is, after we begin talking with someone, we are both responding and reacting to each other. The label *initiating communicator* is probably useful only insofar as it allows us to pinpoint the person who begins things. After that, there is no initiator, just responders. Second, the response messages each person is producing are usually called "feedback" by communications scholars. Some scholars insist that there must be feedback for there to be communication.[11] We agree with this.

11. Dean C. Barnlund, *Interpersonal Communication Survey and Studies* (Boston: Houghton Mifflin Co. 1968), pp. 24, 229–32.

Emmert-Donaghy Model

Because our earlier model is circular in nature and somewhat complicated, we now turn to a more simplified, process view of interpersonal communication in the Emmert-Donaghy model of a dyadic communication system. A dyadic communication system is an interpersonal communication system consisting of two people. This model represents what is called the *systems approach* to communication, an approach that embodies the process view of communication. Basically, the elements in a communication system, by this point of view, are limited in number. You can see in figure 2.4 that there are six basic concepts essential to an understanding of the communication process: communicators, inter- and intrafacing, relationships, feedback, environment, and interference.

Communicators

It is almost a truism to say that essential to every human communication system are communicators. Specifically, in interpersonal communication the communicators are human beings. As important characteristic of communicators is that they are composed of subsystems. Each communicator has input, output, and processing subsystems. *Input subsystems* are analogous to what we called *reception* in the Brooks-Emmert model. Input subsystems include the eyes, ears, nose, and nerves in our skin. These input subsystems allow us to receive messages and stimuli from outside and inside ourselves.

As part of our input subsystem it would also be possible to include the process called *perception*. This will be discussed in greater detail in chapter 4. In addition to physically receiving stimuli from the outside world, we must interpret them and make sense out of them. This interpreting process is

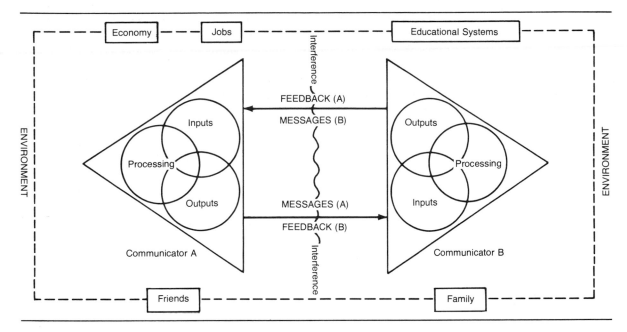

Interference

FEEDBACK (A)

MESSAGES (B)

Inputs

Outputs

Processing

Processing

Outputs

Inputs

MESSAGES (A)

FEEDBACK (B)

Interference

Communicator A

Communicator B

Friends — — — — — — — — Family

Figure 2.4 Emmert-Donaghy model of a dyadic communication system.

called *perception*. Whether this is actually an input subsystem or a processing subsystem is somewhat questionable. It is probably a part of both subsystems.

The Processing Subsystems. Processing in interpersonal communicators includes all of our thought processes. Reasoning, motivation, perception, and needs interact in ways that permit us to develop messages in response to stimuli we have received. Our processing subsystems, or thought processes, are affected by all past experiences, illnesses, emotions, and the like, that we have ever experienced in our lives. Thus, the way we decode or encode messages, as was discussed in our earlier model, is determined to a great part by what our prior experiences have been. We will be discussing the processing systems in detail in chapters 3, 4, 7, and 8, as we discuss self-concept, perception, personal needs, and information reception.

The *output subsystem* of every interpersonal communicator includes all of the messages and behaviors produced at any given time. The output subsystem includes the production of speech, the use of gestures, eye contact, and facial expressions. These outputs of ours obviously serve as inputs for other persons involved in interpersonal communication with us. We will discuss these output subsystems in chapters 5 and 6 when we discuss language and nonverbal communication. As you can see from figure 2.4, the input, processing, and output subsystems in each interpersonal communicator are mutually affected by one another. The messages we receive have an effect upon the way we think and feel. Likewise, the way we think and feel affects the way we receive messages. All this subsequently affects the way we produce messages as outputs. The interaction of these subsystems, as well as the way we interact within an interpersonal communication system, is referred to as inter- and intrafacing.

Inter- and Intrafacing

In previous communication models we have discussed interpersonal communicators as separate, individual entities who produce messages that flow between them. That process in which two human systems exist alone but interact through messages is an example of what is called an *interface* like that represented in figure 2.5. An *interface* allows messages or information to flow back and forth between two independent systems, in this case human beings. This is a very common sort of relationship between systems, and it is certainly a good example of human communication systems. In this kind of a relationship the two systems exist apart from each other and are self-sustaining.

As is the case with the processing systems just discussed, it is also possible for subsystems and sometimes even systems to overlap as do systems A and B in figure 2.6. When this happens, the systems are no longer independent but rather share common elements, which results in an *intraface*.[12] This interdependent relationship is analogous to that of Siamese twins who share a common stomach or a common heart. Although it would seem as though there are two different systems, in fact the overlap between the systems makes them so interdependent that neither can exist alone. An intraface occurs among all of the processing elements, such as motivation, perception, and reasoning.

12. Emmert and Donaghy, in press.

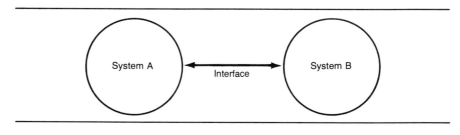

Figure 2.5 An interface relationship. From Emmert and Donagy, in press.

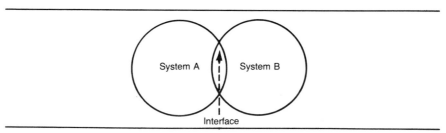

Figure 2.6 An intraface relationship. From Emmert and Donaghy, in press.

Implied in the previous discussion of interfacing and intrafacing between people is the notion of relationships. Two people who interact do more than interact with each other—they relate to each other in a specified manner. Most common are the roles we have that determine the way we relate to other people in an interaction. Two people talking in an interpersonal communication system relate to each other differently when they are parent and child than they do when they are friend and friend, or lover and lover. In each of these cases the relationships between the individuals in the system are different. Thus, whenever we talk about an interpersonal communication system, it is important that we keep in mind the nature of the relationships of the people in the system. This is why you will notice the term *role* used throughout this book. *Role* is a word that describes the relationship and the prescribed behaviors and powers that exist for an individual as he or she relates to another individual.

For you to understand the interpersonal relationship better, we would suggest a very simple model. Figure 2.7 attempts to portray interpersonal communication as a *relationship,* with no individual designated as sender or receiver. Using the example of two individuals, we would expect the goal of every interpersonal interaction to be a satisfactory *relationship.* As in figure 2.7, person A, in attempting to satisfy the needs of person B, experiences the mutual satisfaction of needs. This mutual satisfaction of needs, either directly through the interaction or indirectly through the outcome of the interaction, results in the development of a *relationship* between A and B. This relationship can be thought of as unique to the persons involved. A parallel to this would be the mixing of the substances hydrogen and oxygen. Once mixed, they become a new substance, water. Likewise, once two or more people interact, they create a new relationship.

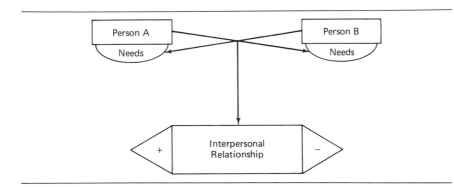

Figure 2.7 A satisfactory relationship.

In interpersonal communication we should keep in mind that often, as two people interact interpersonally, they begin to develop so many things in common that the relationship itself begins to exist as an entity. Two people can share so much that they reach a point where it is difficult for them to exist alone. This is not to say that neither one can exist alone, but rather that it is simply "unnatural" to exist alone. If they were pulled apart, each one would cease to be the same person that was formerly intrafacing with the other person. This happens to many married couples who through death or other circumstances are separated from their loved ones. At that point, the individual who remains ceases to be the same person as the one who was once intrafacing in an interpersonal relationship.

Feedback

Throughout any kind of interaction, *feedback* exists. This is a case of person A providing a message, which person B then responds to. Person B's response is called "feedback." However, it must be clear from the Emmert-Donaghy model that it is difficult to determine which is feedback and which is the message. When two people are interacting, feedback for one person is a message for another. One useful way to determine what is feedback in a communication interaction is that *feedback serves a regulatory function*. All systems, be they communication systems or not, must be regulated to survive. Without order in the system, eventually complete chaos would result, and the system could not continue to exist. In interpersonal communication systems this regulation is accomplished through response messages or feedback. Thus, we can see the importance of providing feedback for someone who is talking with us. Feedback is not simply something that is "nice" to provide. It is *necessary* for us to provide feedback in order for our interpersonal communication system to survive. If we do not provide feedback to our sweethearts, they cannot know how we feel. If they do not know how we feel, then they are unregulated relative to our own responses to their behaviors. If they are unregulated, they may eventually begin behaving in ways that are destructive to the relationship. Thus, as will be discussed in greater detail in chapter 7, feedback in any interpersonal communication system is not simply desirable, it is essential to the survival of any interpersonal communication relationship.

Environment

Emmert and Donaghy's model suggests that communication occurs within an environment. The environment is everything external to the components of the communication system. Thus, if two people are talking, everything outside those two people is the environment in which their interpersonal communication is occurring. This could include things as diverse as the economy in which they live, culture, family, and schools. The environment is important to keep in mind because not only does it exist outside the interpersonal communication system—the people within the communication system interact with it to some extent. It is impossible, for instance, for a person to be part of an interpersonal communication system and ever completely lose the influence of his or her family. At all times we are affected by our prior experiences and our awareness of what is going on in our environment.

Interpersonal communication cannot exist in isolation, but rather is affected by the environment as things filter through into the individual's internal processing system. Thus, to understand how another person is behaving, we may need to take into account the factors in the environment that that person may consider important enough to have an effect on behavior.

Interference

The final concept mentioned in the Emmert-Donaghy model is that of *interference*. Whenever communication is occurring, there can be things within the environment or within the communication setting that can distort or alter inputs and outputs. This is called "interference." For instance, if two people are talking on a Wyoming mountainside with a wind blowing at 50 mph, the

People, noise, and activity can all be communication interferences.

Karen Collidge/Taurus Photos

wind itself becomes interference in the communication process because it causes difficulty in hearing. Likewise, two people who are deaf and who depend upon sign language for communication would find that darkness during a blackout would be interference because it would prevent each one from seeing the other person's messages. This kind of interference can occur at any time in a communication setting. Likewise, another kind of interference, that within the individual, can occur at any time. This could include fears, emotions, or concerns that might exist within one or the other communicators at any given time. These can affect the way inputs are interpreted and processed. Thus, both external and internal interference can distort messages at any given time and can have a significant effect upon the outcome of an interaction.

Contexts of Interpersonal Communication

There are three basic contexts of interpersonal communication that we will include in this book. They are dyadic, small group, and organizational contexts.

Dyadic communication involves the interaction of two people. We can define this context simply by the number of people involved in it. Whenever two people are interacting, we have an interpersonal dyadic communication system. Dyads result in communication characteristics that are different from other kinds of interpersonal communication settings, and thus we will focus upon this context in chapter 10. At that point we will discuss the ways relationships are formed, maintained, and terminated. Likewise, we will discuss different types of dyadic relationships.

Small group communication is what caused us to expand our definition of interpersonal communication to include up to twenty people. The small group setting results in special behaviors by individuals that are worth consideration in and of themselves. Matters such as phases of interaction, leadership, and conformity are all of concern to people who work in small group settings. The small group context will be discussed in chapter 11.

Finally, the *organizational context* will be considered in chapter 12. In no way do we believe that a large organization such as General Motors is an interpersonal communication context. However, we can consider interpersonal communication contexts such as dyads and small groups as they occur within the larger organizational framework. The dyadic interview, methods of giving orders, and the occurrence of rumor within organizations are all very much related to the way people communicate interpersonally. It will be the function of this chapter, then, to focus upon interpersonal communication as it occurs in a larger context—that of the large organization.

As you can note from the table of contents, part 2 of this text covers the basic elements in interpersonal communication. Chapters 3 and 4 focus on the people involved in interpersonal communication. The influence of self-concept, self-esteem, the role of self-fulfilling prophecy, and person perception are discussed. Chapter 5 focuses on the use of words, or a formal language system. How can messages be understood more clearly? What are the important characteristics of word systems that can help and hinder communication? Chapter 6 considers nonverbal communication, an informal language system. What are the communicative effects of facial expressions, gestures, and vocal quality? Can we learn to communicate more effectively nonverbally? Chapter 7 deals with listening and feedback—the part of the process that brings initiating communicator and responding communicator together. In chapter 8 we consider the handling of personal needs and interpersonal communication behavior patterns. Finally, in chapter 9 we examine specifically conflict confrontation and negotiation in interpersonal communication. This chapter brings together the elements previously discussed in the total process. While these elements of interpersonal communication are not the only components in the process, they are some of the most important and the most commonly identified basic elements.

Part 3 of the text is narrower in scope, focusing upon those contexts in which interpersonal communication occurs. In that part of the book we attempt to apply interpersonal communication principles in the dyadic, small group, and organizational contexts. It is our feeling that the application of the principles within these contexts will improve understanding of the entire interpersonal communication process.

SELECTED READINGS

Ardrey, Robert. *The Social Contract.* New York: Atheneum Publishers, 1970.

Berlo, David K. *The Process of Communication.* New York: Holt, Rinehart & Winston, Inc., 1960.

Kiesler, Charles A.; Collins, Barry E.; and Miller, Norman. *Attitude Change,* New York: John Wiley & Sons, Inc., 1969.

Maslow, A. H. *Motivation and Personality.* New York: Harper & Row Publishers, Inc., 1954.

Schutz, William C. *The Interpersonal Underworld.* Palo Alto, California: Science & Behavior Books, Inc., 1966.

Stewart, John. *Bridges Not Walls.* Reading, Mass.: Addison-Wesley Publishing Co., 1973.

Elements of Interpersonal Communication

3

The Self in Communication:
The Role of Self-Concept

In his *Autobiography*, Benjamin Franklin describes how as a young man he made a list of his strengths and deficits as a person. He made this list to get at the task of correcting his deficits and taking advantage of those assets he possessed. Indeed, Ben Franklin was a very wise man, and it would be equally wise for each of us to engage in the same kind of activity. This is the sort of honest self-appraisal we all need to go through every once in a while; moreover, we need to engage in genuine follow-up action, just as Benjamin Franklin did. His specific procedure is a valid one for improving a person's self-concept.

Although there are many topics with which we will be concerned in this book, and although each of these topics may be of importance to our understanding of the communication process, the area that may have the greatest influence on one's behavior in interpersonal communication is the perception of one's self, or one's self-concept. No matter how we view the world, interpersonal communication begins within the self, and effective, wholesome interpersonal communication is closely associated with a useful and realistic perception of self.

A Definition of Self-Concept

Self-concept can be defined as *the aggregate of those physical, social,* and *psychological perceptions of ourselves that we have derived from our experiences and our interactions with others.* It is the awareness we have of being and functioning—of "self" as object. Self-concept is based on a set of experiences having the same referent, namely the *I* or the *me*. It consists of those beliefs I have about myself—about my attractiveness or unattractiveness, my intellectual ability, attitudes, beliefs, values, and my expectations of how others see me and react to me.

"Who am I?"

Harry Smedley, Jr.

Self-concept has to be achieved. It is not given. We are not born with a self-concept, but rather, we build self-concept almost entirely on the outcome of our relationships with others. Nothing resembling the concept of self could ever occur to a child who existed in the absence of others. Self, therefore, can only be understood in terms of relationships with others.

We have said that the self consists of the aggregate of our experiences in life. Many of our experiences are forgotten—that is, they are placed in our "unconscious"—but they are not lost. They can and do influence us, and sometimes they emerge suddenly into our consciousness, even surprising us. Or sometimes experiences long forgotten are brought out into the open through hypnosis. Some years ago, when one of us was working for a city police department, a man was brought into the police station suffering from amnesia. He had no identification, and no police record or military service record came to light as we tried to discover who he was from fingerprints. It was only when a specialist came and placed him under hypnosis that the man was able to tell us his name and address. Our experiences are not lost. They do exist to influence our behavior, although some experiences are in our unconscious rather than in our consciousness. In this chapter, however, we are concerned only with the conscious self. It is not so much what we *are*, but what we *think* we are, that guides our acts and behavior.

If you think about it for a moment, you know that perception of self must be extremely important, because each of us spends considerable time in thinking about self, in reflecting on the happenings, events, and interactions we have had with others—in meditating on life, the meaning of it, where we are headed, and what we really want to do.

Literature is filled with examples of thinking about self or of talking to one's self. Some excellent examples can be found in Eldridge Cleaver's *Soul on Ice;* in *Cool Cos: The Story of Bill Cosby;* and in Shakespeare's *Hamlet,* when Hamlet talks to himself, saying "O, what a rogue and peasant slave am I!"

You have thought much about yourself. How do you see yourself? Who are you? Do you like yourself? How do others see you? Who do they think you are? How do these things affect your interpersonal communication? In this chapter, we hope to present information that will give you an understanding of what self-concept is, of problems that sometimes arise in relation to understanding and identifying the self, and of how these problems cause us to adopt certain strategies and behaviors in interpersonal communication. We will identify the characteristics of a healthy self-concept, and how one may go about improving the concept of self.

We hope that as you read the remainder of this chapter you will apply it to yourself, because no other element in your interpersonal communication is more important than your perception of yourself. We tend to be what we think we are; we think we are whatever we say to ourselves; and much of what we say to ourselves is what we hear others saying about us or to us.

Development of an Integrated Self-Concept: The Many Selves

Through interaction with significant others (parents, siblings, friends, and teachers) and with reference groups (family, cliques, and clubs), we develop our concepts of self. Notice that we said concepts of self. There are many selves. Each of us is not a single self. In fact, each of us plays many roles. I am father, husband, friend, professor, administrator, employee, employer, stranger, son, and so on. Similarly, you play a number of roles. The self varies for each relationship—for each role in which we find ourselves. Add to these selves those of private self, public self, physical self, emotional self, intellectual self, and spiritual self, and it is apparent that there are many selves. This multiplicity of selves can be a hindrance to effective communication, but it is also the *means* to effective communication. If we have accurate "self-awareness" (know who we are in all these relationships and situations), then we are able to express ourselves and to interact fully and effectively across a wide range of situations and persons. The person who has integrated these multiple selves can choose that self most appropriate to the unique communicative interaction. That person can be free, loving, and affectionate when that is appropriate, and in another situation, can be controlled, logical, and intellectual when that is appropriate. In other words, the person can communicate with diversity, rather than always being the Child or the Parent in all communication situations, to use Eric Berne's *Games People Play* language.[1]

1. Eric Berne, *Games People Play* (New York: Grove Press, Inc., 1964).

Now we want to take a close look at some of the important selves. Two of the most important are the *I* self and the *me* self. *I* is the nominative case, or the active agent, while *me* is the objective case, the object of action, the one acted on or reacted to by others. *I* represents one's self-image, while *me* represents one's self-esteem. A third important self is the physical self, which refers to my perception of my body. *Body image* is the essence of my physical self. *Self-image* refers to what sort of a person I think I am. *Self-esteem* is how well I like myself. Together, self-image, self-esteem, and body image exert a controlling effect on behavior.

Self-Image—The "I" Self

Self-image comes about to a great extent as a result of our interactions with others. More specifically, it comes about as a result of our being categorized by others. This process of categorizing persons, for good or bad, is one of the basic and initial occurrences in interpersonal communication encounters. Each of us does it, and everyone else does it to us—all of us place those others whith whom we interact into categories. These categories, according to Argyle,[2] are established in terms of roles (mother, wife, husband, boss,

2. Michael Argyle, *Social Interaction* (New York: Atherton Press, 1969), pp. 131–33.

male, female, playboy), positions (social class, religious affiliation, political affiliation, age), or personality traits (intelligent, neurotic, happy, superstitious, shy, humane). As I observe the reaction of others to me, and as I am aware of how others categorize me, I develop an image of myself. I learn to predict how others will react to me and to anticipate how I will be categorized by others, and this becomes a part of my self-image and self-concept. I then behave in accordance with the image I have of myself.

Research has shown that family roles are used most frequently in the categorization process (70 percent of the time); occupation is second (68 percent of the time); marital status is third (34 percent of the time); and religious affiliation, or religiosity, is fourth (30 percent of the time).[3] Sounds familiar, doesn't it? These are the questions you are asked to answer on most forms or applications you fill out, including your enrollment form for your courses this semester, probably. Other roles are also used in the process of categorizing, however. Among these are racial, sexual, recreational, and social roles. Research has indicated that women use family roles to categorize

3. Ibid., p. 133.

THE SATURDAY EVENING POST

"The truth is, Cauldwell, we never see ourselves as others see us."

persons more than do men. Men seem to use occupational and sexual roles for categorizing persons more than do women. And religious persons use religiosity and religious affiliation to a greater extent than do nonreligious persons for identifying persons with whom they interact. Age appears to be used about equally by all.

Self-Esteem—The "Me" Self

Self-esteem, the *me* is another major component of self-concept. Like self-image, it comes about as a result of our interaction with others, but it is not the being categorized or described by others that is involved in this process. Rather, it is the being rewarded (even punished at times), the being praised or demeaned, or the being accorded prestige that creates our self-esteem. When others reward us, accord us prestige or worth, or praise and like us, then we like ourselves, value ourselves, and generally regard ourselves favorably. This is self-esteem. It is a powerful, powerful force inside us that affects our interpersonal communication behavior. A dramatic illustration of the effect of others was shown by ABC Television News in the documentary, "The Eye of the Storm." According to this documentary:

> In May 1970, Jane Elliott, an elementary school teacher in Iowa, demonstrated the effects of social role on self-concept in a racial discrimination experiment with her third-grade class. She divided her class according to the color of their eyes. On the first day of the experiment, blue-eyed children were declared superior and were "privileged." They could leave the room for a drink of water without requesting permission; they could stay out late at recess; they went to lunch early; and they sat anywhere in the room they pleased, even if it meant moving another child. During the day, the brown-eyed children, who were not "privileged," began to think of themselves as "inferior," and they scored lower than usual on card-recognition reading tests.
>
> The next day the teacher reversed the roles, making the brown-eyed children privileged. That day, blue-eyed children began to view themselves as inferior, and their reading scores, which had been superior the day they were privileged, declined dramatically.

Several similar experiments have demonstrated this powerful effect of others on us. This is the source of the *me* self-concept.

Social science researchers who have studied self-esteem identify high self-esteem as consisting of those favorable attitudes we have towards ourselves. Low self-esteem is the extent to which we have unfavorable or negative attitudes toward ourselves.

A term sometimes associated with concern over self-esteem is *self-consciousness*. Self-consciousness is the extent to which a person is shy, easily embarrassed, and anxious when in the presence of or watched by others. It is related to anxiety and is, in fact, a social anxiety. Self-con-

© Abigail Heyman/Magnum Photos, Inc.

sciousness is the opposite of social confidence or poise. Most of us, of course, are somewhat anxious in new or different social situations, but some persons experience social anxiety even in situations in which they have had considerable previous experience. They experience self-consciousness. Unfavorable or negative attitudes toward self are based on the reactions of others, on their giving or withholding praise, reward, and prestige. Researchers point out that these reactions of others are, for the most part, distributed along two dimensions: (1) status and power, and (2) warmth and friendliness.

Low self-esteem and self-consciousness are the result of others' negative reactions.

The two dimensions are labeled in various ways. Terms equivalent or roughly equivalent to status and power are *dominance, authority, strength, power,* and *control.* Terms used in place of warmth and friendliness include *consideration, love, affection, concern for people, nurturance,* and *sociability.* Hippocrates identified the two dimensions as friendliness-hostility and strength-weakness. Freud labeled them love and power. They were called affection and dominance by Leary, affection and control by Shultz, concern for people and concern for production by Blake and Mouton, employee orientation and closeness of supervision by Katz, and nurturance and dominance by Lorr and McNair.[4] You will soon discover that these concepts appear in several other chapters of this text. These characteristics of the *me* self are quite important to functioning in interpersonal communication.

Body Image: The Physical Self

4. Sigmund Freud, *A General Introduction to Psychoanalysis* (New York: Simon & Schuster, Inc., 1969); Timothy Leary, *Interpersonal Diagnosis of Personality* (New York: Ronald Press Co., 1957); William C. Shutz, FIRO: *A Three-Dimensional Theory of Interpersonal Behavior* (New York: Holt, Rinehart & Winston, Inc., 1958); Robert R. Blake and Jane S. Mouton, *The Managerial Grid* (Houston: Gulf Publishing Co., 1964); D. Katz, N. Maccoby, G. Gurin, and L. G. Floor, *Productivity, Supervision and Morale Among Railroad Workers* (Ann Arbor, Mich.: Institute for Social Research, University of Michigan, 1951); and Maurice Lorr and D. N. McNair, "Expansion of the Interpersonal Behavior Circle," *Journal of Personality and Social Psychology* 2 (1965):823–30.

A third self is the physical self—the self as object. Actually, this is the first self to be formed in a child's mind, and it continues to be a significant factor even for adults. Several researchers have found size to be an important dimension of body image. Males are most satisfied with their bodies when they are large; females are most satisfied with their bodies when they are smaller than normal.[5]

Physical attractiveness is an important factor in our body image. Although the perception of and acceptance or disapproval of one's body begins in babyhood and childhood, another significant period of special concern with the physical self is adolescence. This is a time of great impact on all areas of self-concept; and because this is so, we will give this time of life special consideration in the next few sections of this chapter, focusing on the physical self, self-identity, and identity crisis.

Figure 3.1 shows the relationship of ideal self or high self-concept to self-esteem. Low self-concept—the person you do *not* want to be—is positively correlated with low self-esteem.

Figure 3.1 Self-concept and self-esteem.

5. P. A. Smith, "A Comparison of Three Sets of Rotated Factor Analytic Solutions of Self-Concept Data," *Journal of Abnormal and Social Psychology* 4 (1967):326–33; S. M. Jourard and P. F. Secord, "Body-Cathexis and Personality," *British Journal of Psychology* 46 (1960):130–138; C. R. Rogers and R. Dymond, *Psychotherapy and Personality Change* (Chicago: University of Chicago Press, 1954); and S. Fisher and S. S. Cleveland, *Body-Image and Personality* (Princeton: Van Nostrand, 1958).

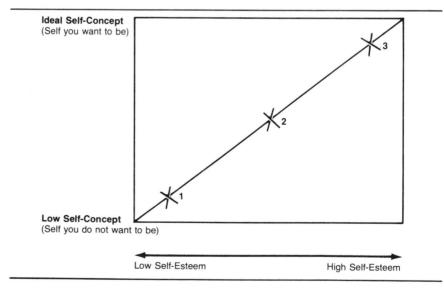

Ideal Self-Concept
(Self you want to be)

Low Self-Concept
(Self you do not want to be)

Low Self-Esteem   High Self-Esteem

Whether or not you can accept yourself and feel that you are worthwhile may depend on your beliefs about who you are. One helpful exercise is to complete the phrase "I am" with several responses that characterize yourself. After listing several phrases that complete the "I am," put each of those sentences describing yourself into one of the following categories: (1) *physical attributes*—such bodily characteristics as age, height, and weight; (2) *emotional attributes:* the feelings you possess: shy, happy, cynical, cheerful, frustrated, and so on; (3) *mental attributes*—intellectual characteristics: smart, average, or "dumb"; (4) *roles*—functions you fulfill in relation to others: class level in school, whether you are single or married, major, profession, and so on; (5) *relationships with others*—the characteristic stance you take toward others—whether you are accessible and open, closed and withdrawn, or neutral and moderate.

As the preceding exercise illustrates, we are many selves. But suppose these several selves never emerge clearly and healthily; or suppose they emerge, but they are so unintegrated as to be contradictory. In such situations, one has difficulty knowing who is the real me. When these situations occur, one has an identity problem. Usually, we first encounter this problem during our teenage years.

The Unintegrated Self: The Identity Crisis

It requires no great insight to understand that self-identity is an important factor in interpersonal communication. When one is unsure of who one is, is doubtful of one's acceptability to others, or is unable to accept oneself—in short, when one is in an identity crisis as regards one's attitudes, beliefs, values, goals, and relationships with others with respect to various roles or selves one needs to be, one's communication suffers.

It is not always easy to integrate all the selves into a consistent, coherent, unitary self-concept. When such an integration of selves occurs, we say the person has a strong self-identity. We mean that person knows who he or she is; knows how others perceive him or her; has a healthy acceptance of self; and understands his or her feelings and relationships with others.

But this is not easy. Sometimes, in fact, due to inconsistencies, deficiencies, the multiplicity of roles, and numerous other factors, we do not know who we are. Most of us, at various times throughout life, go through identity crises of varying severity. Some identity crises are small ones, and some are big ones. Most of us go through at least one period of fairly difficult identity crises, and that period is late adolescence.

With the onset of adolescence and continuing through high school and early college years, the relatively stable world of childhood becomes an unstable world of rapid change. The growth spurt and sexual development of this age create changes in identity. The physical body changes necessitate body-image changes. The new world, the adult world, that is almost upon us brings increased concern and poses serious and important questions. There is an expectancy and an urge for adolescents to establish themselves as individuals—adult individuals. Most of us experience a strong desire to break away from the dependent relationship with our parents. Add to this the fact that several important and relatively final decisions are made during these years, and one can understand how an identity crisis can exist for a few months or even a few years during this time.

We all have to sort out who we are, what we are going to believe, what things, ideas, principles, and behaviors will be valued highly and which ones will be relegated to positions of relative unimportance. Moreover, many of the decisions one makes and the goals established during this time in life are extremely important ones. What vocation should I select? Should I adopt this political attitude? What about my religious beliefs? What kind of person do I want to be as an adult? Will people like me as an adult? Whom should I marry? All these questions and virtually hundreds more are dealt with as we establish a new identity as adults. And, as previously stated, sometimes it is difficult to get all these questions answered as we interact with others and are in turn "defined" by others. Some people remain children although they get older. Sometimes the result of these years is not a clear integration of self, but a crisis in self-identity.

Children are afforded the luxury of playing at roles. As we leave childhood, however, this privilege of playing at roles begins to decrease. It is true, however, that during our high school and early college years, we do experiment with various roles and we may decide to adopt some of these roles permanently.

Although the teenage years commonly bring an identity crisis for most of us, the quest for self-identity does not stop at age twenty-one or any other age. There is continued revision of the concept of self throughout life, for life is a process and is characterized by constant changes that require adjustments. The inability to establish and retain an integrated concept of the many selves seems to be increasingly common among adults, young and old. Alvin Toffler[6] focuses attention on this phenomenon. He calls it "future shock" and says it is a product of a tremendously accelerated rate of change—changes in work, acquaintances, family, religion, sex, and almost all other aspects of our culture. One can easily become disoriented. Toffler states:

> . . . culture is itself in constant turmoil, and if—worse yet—its values are incessantly changing, the sense of disorientation will be further intensified. Given few clues as to what kind of behavior is rational under the radically new circumstances, the victim may well become a hazard to himself and others.[7]

6. Alvin Toffler, *Future Shock* (New York: Bantam Books, Inc., 1970).

7. Ibid., p. 12.

These changes in our culture create changes in the psychological climate around us. Worry, upset, uncertainty, conflict, social pressures, status shifts, life-style modifications—all of these adjustments and pressures alter our way of life and concept of who we are. Little wonder that adults in our world today can easily suffer identity crises, and, in fact, are doing so in increasing numbers. Again Toffler states:

> The striking signs of confusional breakdown we see around us—the spreading use of drugs, the rise of mysticism, the recurrent outbreaks of vandalism and undirected violence, the politics of nihilism and nostalgia, the sick apathy of millions—can all be understood better by recognizing their relationship to future shock. . . . The assertion that the world has gone crazy, the graffiti slogan that "reality is a crutch," the interest in hallucinogenic drugs, the enthusiasm for astrology and the occult, the search for truth in sensation, ecstasy, and "peak experience," the swing toward extreme subjectivism, the attacks on science, reflect the everyday experience of masses of ordinary people who find they can no longer cope rationally with change.[8]

8. Ibid., pp. 343 and 365.

Whether or not the problem is as widespread or as alarming at this time as Toffler indicates, the point that persons of any age—from teenagers to the retired—can and do experience identity crises is well taken.

In addition to the rapid changes in our physical and psychological environments that may cause identity problems and may give rise to responses such as those described by Toffler, there are other, perhaps slower-paced, causes of identity crises. For example, any of us can experience conflicting elements of motivation. We may desire one thing very much and something else directly contrary to it just as much. It is likely that most of us can recall one or more conflicting kinds of motivations we have experienced at some time, when it was necessary for us to ask ourselves what we really did want, where we really were headed, and who we really did want to be. For example, one can experience inconsistent ambitions—to be an artist or an attorney, to become an architect or to stay in the family store.

A second possible cause of an identity crisis is failure to reconcile our self-image acquired in childhood with the fact of our adulthood. Some people find it difficult to grow up. They may be adults physically and in their work role, but the concept of themselves to which they cling is that of their childhood. This situation almost guarantees the creation of an identity crisis.

A third possible cause of an identity crisis is failure to establish a central identity in terms of long-term goals and persistent striving. It becomes difficult to integrate the self if we are reacting to stimuli in the environment without focus or direction—simply responding in all directions rather than toward some integrative objective that gives meaning and permits "becoming."

A fourth possible cause is unrealistic goals—establishment of goals that fail to relate to our abilities, wealth, or opportunities.

Whatever the causes—whether Toffler's theory of rapid change in physical and psychological worlds, intrapersonal causes, or other factors—an identity crisis can be a powerfully inhibiting factor in interpersonal communication. An identity crisis in its most extreme degree is schizophrenia. There are other, lesser degrees, of course. One such type, according to Marcia,[9] is exemplified by the behaviors of those persons constituting the "playboy culture"; and there are other identifiable groups characterized by some frenetic behavior that is a response to the identity crises of their members.

9. J. E. Marcia, "Development and Validation of Ego-Identity Status," *Journal of Personality and Social Psychology* 3 (1966):551–58.

There are, of course, identity-crisis responses other than becoming schizophrenic, becoming a playboy, or joining some frenetic group. One of the responses used by some high-school and college-age persons to deal with the identity crisis common to their time of life is to call a moratorium. This means that they postpone making those decisions related to achieving integration of self, that is, those decisions that begin to define or identify them to themselves. Instead, they experiment with a number of roles and behaviors. This procedure seems to be an increasingly common feature of student life. One role is taken today, but another tomorrow; one set of values or attitudes may be tested this month, but another set may be accepted later to guide one's adult life.

Each spring there is a migration of college students to Florida, Arizona, and other warm resort places. In old cars, by bus, by plane, by bike, and by hitchhiking, thousands pour into Fort Lauderdale and other places during the spring break. They come with sleeping bags, blankets, bikinis, and guitars, to swim, sleep, guzzle beer, sprawl, and brawl. Typical of several analyses of this phenomenon is the following explanation:

> What attracts the young people is more than an irrepressible passion for sunshine. Nor is it mere sex, a commodity available in other places as well. Rather, it is a sense of freedom from responsibility. In the words of a nineteen-year-old New York coed who made her way to the festivities recently: "You're not worried about what you do or say here because, frankly, you'll never see these people again." What the Fort Lauderdale rite supplies is a transient agglomeration of people that makes possible a great diversity of temporary interpersonal relationships.[10]

10. Toffler, *Future Shock,* pp. 95–96.

Such "spring flings" are opportunities for experimentation with sundry behaviors involving little commitment, responsibility, or danger of subsequent reprisal. Society leniently affords this age group greater opportunity for using the moratorium strategy as a means of coping with ego diffusion, of attempting to discover those values, goals, and behaviors that group members will select to define themselves and to create their self-identity. The streaking fad could be viewed as quite consistent with this phenomenon. A popular news magazine stated: "Clearly, the streakers were direct decendants of the telephone-booth stuffers and goldfish swallowers of yes-

Jean-Claude Lejeune

teryear."[11] A Yalie's statement about streaking revealed the students' perception of college days as consistent with the moratorium concept. He said, "We're college students and college students are supposed to have fun!"[12]

Adults, too, use the moratorium technique, although more as individuals than as in groups. Adults may take a day off, or a weekend—even a year, when that is possible—simply to go away somewhere and "think things over." They "call time out" to integrate themselves; or, in keeping with today's more common expression, they say they are going away to "get myself together" or to "get my head together." But the moratorium technique is not a permanent solution. One cannot "go away" permanently nor can one go through life wearing a mask to hide one's identity—or wear nothing to hide it, as did the streakers. These are not satisfactory substitutes for self-integration. There are, of course, persons in our world who try to hide permanently behind false identity masks—persons who attempt to live as impostors, or who have contradictory identities like Dr. Jekyll and Mr. Hyde. There are persons who cling to unrealistic identities, who form very tenuous and precarious identities. The objective toward which we ought to be moving, however, is a healthy concept of self—an integration of the many selves—the *I* and *me*, the physical, social, spiritual, and vocational being and family member.

A moratorium can be a useful temporary response to an identity crisis, but it cannot become a permanent solution. Self-integration must still be accomplished.

11. "Streaking: One Way to Get a B.A.," *Newsweek,* March 18, 1974, p. 41.
12. Ibid., p. 42.

Relationship of Self-Concept
to Communication

Self-concept affects communication in several ways: (1) it is the basis of self-fulfilling prophecy; (2) it determines the selection and use of messages, and (3) it affects one's attitude toward communicating, i.e., communication security versus communication apprehension.

Self-Concept the Basis of Self-Fulfilling Prophecy

Each person behaves in a manner consistent with self-concept. We act like the kind of person we perceive ourselves to be. The student who has said, "I am a failure," can find plenty of excuses to avoid studying, reading, or participating in class discussion. Of course, at the end of the term that student usually receives the expected low grade. Similarly, the student who has said, "Nobody likes me," will usually find that he or she is not liked. Such persons usually do not understand that it is their behaving in a manner consistent with a deprecated self-concept (sour expression, hostility, refusal to be friendly or to participate) that invites rejection by others. It is quite important, therefore, to have a positive rather than a negative self-concept, since we tend to fulfill our own prophecies, that is, to become whatever we see ourselves as being.

Negative self-concept is developed as the result of negative experiences over a period of time. Some of the characteristics of a negative self-concept are: (1) undue sensitivity to criticism, (2) overresponsiveness to praise, (3) hypercritical attitudes, (4) a feeling of "nobody likes me," and (5) a pessimistic attitude toward competition.

You may be able to think of someone you know who has these characteristics—a person who is supersensitive to criticism, and who, you have learned, must be "handled with kid gloves" because he or she may explode, pout, or cry easily. Or perhaps you know someone who has only negative orientations. Such a person seldom has a happy word, a good word, a word of praise, or an expression of appreciation for anything or anyone. Rather, that person gripes, complains, criticizes, and debases. These are possible characteristics of persons with negative self-concepts.

On the other hand, people who have positive self-concepts may be characterized as: (1) being confident of their ability to deal with problems; (2) feeling equal to other persons; (3) accepting praise without embarrassment; (4) admitting that they have a wide range of feelings, desires, and behaviors, some of which are socially approved and some of which are not; and (5) being able to improve themselves as, for example, discovering an unlikable aspect of the self, then setting out to change it.

Richard Younker

A positive self-concept influences what we become because we tend to fulfill our prophecies about ourselves.

What you believe about self has a tremendous influence on who you become. If you label yourself as "no good in music" or a "poor public speaker," you may prove this to be so. As Condon has stated: "Responding to such labels gives us direction, even if the direction is backwards; responding to such labels helps us decide what to do and what not to do, even if the choices are not the wisest."[13] For example, if you label yourself as unfriendly, you will probably behave in a manner that is unfriendly. You will avoid opportunities to talk; you will refrain from smiling; and you will seek seclusion rather than the company of others.

13. John C. Condon, Jr., *Semantics and Communication* (New York: Macmillan Co., 1966), p. 60.

Others also play a role in this labeling of the self and the subsequent self-fulfilling prophecy. Person A's expectation of person B may become a self-fulfilling prophecy for B. Even when there is no verbal communication of that expectation, the expectation may be communicated indirectly through nonverbal communication. Rosenthal has discussed an interesting experiment in which elementary teachers were told that one group of children (the experimental group that was selected randomly from the classroom) had scored exceptionally high on a test for "intellectual blooming." In reality, the children in the experimental group were no different from the control group in regard to their real scores on the test, but the teachers believed they were different.[14] The teachers then labeled the experimental students as having high potential to bloom intellectually, and apparently the students attached the label to themselves because, indeed, the experimental group fulfilled the prophecy. Other similar experiments, reviewed by Rosenthal, have the same findings.[15] Labels are indeed lived up to.

14. Robert Rosenthal, "Self-Fulfilling Prophecy," in *Readings in Psychology Today* (Del Mar, Calif.: CRM Books, 1967), pp. 466–71.

15. Ibid.

Self-Concept Influences Selection and Use of Messages

A second relationship of self-concept and communication is that we tend to select messages to be sent that are consistent with our self-concept. Studies employing content analysis techniques have disclosed that certain types of persons utter certain types of statements. The kinds of messages we create and the treatment given them are influenced by "who the sender is." Similarly, "who one is" operates to create selective attention, so that only certain messages are selected to be received. Persons who watch only soap operas probably have self-images different from those of persons who watch only documentaries on television. One communication scholar has stated that subscribers to *Harper's* have self-images different from those of subscribers to *Reader's Digest*, and that Republicans have different expectations about their behavior (self-concepts) from Democrats.[16] As sources and receivers, we use our self-concepts to direct our behavior relative to encoding, decoding, and responding to messages. A message that is inconsistent with our view of self and of the world is often distorted or misinterpreted in decoding or is ignored entirely. Similarly, the process of encoding is influenced by

16. David K. Berlo, "Interaction: The Goal of Interpersonal Communication," in *Dimensions in Communication*, ed. James H. Campbell and Hal W. Hepler (Belmont, Calif.: Wadsworth Publishing Co., 1965), pp. 36–55.

self-concept, since we are limited in encoding to our own experiences in life. It is not surprising, then, that the messages we send identify our perception of the world and our self-concept. Have you ever avoided small talk because you were afraid of the other person? Have you ever not taken sides in a controversy because you are uncomfortable in disagreeing with others? Or have you spoken up in an argument because you had knowledge or information on the subject? Our messages are affected by who we think we are—our self-concept.

Self-Concept Affects Attitude toward Communicating: Communication Security versus Communication Apprehension

One of the most serious communication problems is *communication apprehension*. This may involve fear of public speaking, which most of us have experienced to some degree; it may also involve fear of informal and conversational speaking. The student who experiences high communication apprehension probably fears all communication situations and seeks to avoid all communication situations because his or her self-concept as a

Communication apprehension causes many people to withdraw from interaction with others and to retreat into a life of loneliness.

© Jean-Claude Lejeune

communicator is low or negative. For some, this apprehension is so strong that it is virtually disabling. This fear is the number one fear reported by Americans, who rate it even higher than fear of death.

From 10 to 20 percent of all college students and adults suffer from extreme communication apprehension.[17] The percentages are even higher for secondary and elementary school students. According to several studies, a teacher can expect that one out of every four or five students has communication apprehension severe enough to be debilitating. This fear disrupts almost every aspect of a person's life, from elementary school through adulthood. It is a communication problem making the person afflicted with it ineffective in his or her interactions with others.

The concept such persons have of themselves as communicators makes them unable to start conversations, to make small talk, to initiate friendships, and to answer questions in a classroom or in a job interview. Twenty-four percent of the students in one junior high school reported such problems.[18] The main response of these students is withdrawal from interaction with others. The low and timid voice, the avoidance of competitive play, the refusal to communicate in class, submissiveness, tenseness, and lack of popularity with classmates—these are results of low self-concept as a communicator.

Self-concept is related also to other interaction patterns and behaviors such as are discussed in chapter 8.

17. H. Thomas Hurt, Michael D. Scott, and James C. McCroskey, *Communication in the Classroom* (Reading, Mass: Addison-Wesley Publishing Co., 1978), p. 148; G. W. Friedrich, "An Empirical Explanation of a Concept of Self-Reported Speech Anxiety," *Speech Monographs*, 37:67–76, 1970; Kim Griffin, *Recent Research on Speech Anxiety, Research Monograph* P-26, Communication Research Center, University of Kansas, Lawrence, Kansas, 1967; and C. M. Phillips, "Reticence: Pathology of the Normal Speaker," *Speech Monographs* 40:220–230, 1973.

18. Gerald M. Phillips, "Rhetoritherapy Versus the Medical Model: Dealing with Reticence," unpublished paper, Pennsylvania State University, 1975, pp. 5–6.

Improving Your Self-Concept

The fully functioning self—the healthy, integrated self—possesses at least four characteristics: (1) an awareness of self; (2) an acceptance of self; (3) an actualizing of self; and (4) self-disclosure.

Self-Awareness

Before you can accept yourself or improve yourself, it is necessary to be aware of yourself. This is a necessary first step. Who are you? Of course, you are not the identical person you were four years ago, nor am I the same person I was four years ago. Also, I recognize that I will be a different person four years from now. I hope I will be a better person—better in terms of having achieved more toward some objectives I have for myself. The point is that each of us has an *historical self*. It is a part of us and is related to whatever we are at this time. Also, each of us has a *present self*, and each of us has a *future self*—a self we would like to become. Self-awareness consists of knowing the historical self, present self, and future self. As you investigate those areas, you can better answer the question "Who am I?" It may be helpful to take inventories of these three selves.

Historical Self-Inventory

1. What is my family tree?
2. Where have I lived? What were those places like?
3. Who were my first playmates? First friends? Make a list.
4. What games did I play as a child?
5. What chores did I do?
6. What trips did I take?
7. What were the best things that happened to me?
8. What were some of my sad times?
9. What were my goals?
10. What were my fears?

You can add other categories to help you become aware of your historical self.

Present Self-Inventory

1. What kinds of manual tasks am I best at? Am I good at typing? Tuning a car? Furniture repair? Gardening? Window washing? Lawn care?
2. What is my strongest special skill? Sculpting? Sewing? Macrame? Interior design? Cooking? Electronics? Auto mechanics? Woodwork? Knitting? Piano playing? Photography? Drama?
3. What sports or games do I perform best? Skiing? Bridge? Backpacking? Volleyball? Bowling? Hiking? Chess? Swimming? Motorcycling? Football? Driving? Softball? Soccer? Handball? Track? Basketball? Billiards? Wrestling? Hockey? Badminton?
4. Which school subjects are easiest for me? History? Physical education? Drama? Mathematics? Speech? Geology? Chemistry? Home economics? French? Philosophy? English? Business? Biology?
5. What do I do especially well as a communicator? Listen? Organize thoughts? Use effective language? Treat others as humans rather than as objects? Make others comfortable? Be myself? Understand others' ideas?
6. What are my strongest personal characteristics? Loyalty? Enthusiasm? Understanding? Leadership ability? Thoughtfulness? Cheerfulness? Tact? Even temper? Flexibility?
7. Whose love have I been able to return? Children? Parents? Sister(s)? Brother(s)? Boss? Steady date? Best friend? Spouse? Teacher? Grandparents? Other relatives?

This list of strengths does not completely represent your present self. You can continue it, adding other categories.

Future Self-Inventory
1. What do I want to do vocationally?
2. What are three of my most important future goals?
3. What new experiences do I want to have?
4. Where do I want to live?
5. What do I want to change about myself?

Self-Acceptance

Another factor in improving self-concept is self-acceptance. When we begin to accept ourselves and to like ourselves, our total concept of self begins to improve. It is not enough for you to be aware of yourself—your strengths and weaknesses, your positive attitudes and your negative attitudes, your confidences and your fears. You must also accept yourself. This does not mean that you come to like the negative things about yourself, but it means that you do not allow those things to disable you. You are aware of them, but you accept the fact that everyone has weaknesses, and that, therefore, not to be perfect is all right and quite normal. Self-acceptance does not mean that you cease trying to improve. You will continue to improve yourself. But it does mean that you will make the most of your strengths. You are you, with strengths as well as weaknesses, and you accept yourself that way. As you identify your strengths and develop new strengths, it is easier to accept yourself. If you develop a negative concept of self, if you cannot accept yourself much of the time, if your are unsure as to how acceptable you are to others, then the negative spiral of unacceptableness of self, low self-concept, and ineffective interpersonal communication is set in motion. But if you accept your feelings, beliefs, and relationships as "all right"—if you accept yourself and approve of yourself—you free yourself to a positive spiral of growth.

19. Thomas A. Harris, *I'm OK—You're OK* (New York: Harper & Row, Inc., Publishers, 1967).

Harris has identified four possible positions we can take relative to liking and accepting both ourselves and others.[19] The first such position is that of not accepting oneself or any other person. This is the "I'm not OK and you're not OK" position. This position is characterized by severe withdrawal from others and from self. Such a person is highly self-critical, anxious, insecure, depressed, cynical, and defensive.

A second possible position is "I'm not OK, but you're OK." A person with this attitude is fearful of his or her ability to live in the world, fearful of being inadequate for the challenges and problems of life. Such a person adopts strategies to hide and conceal the self, holds others in awe and is consequently at the mercy of others, is self-demeaning, and feels inferior to others.

A third orientation is "I'm OK, but you're not OK." This creates a superiority attitude. Such a person rejects support and help from others, avoids getting involved with others, and is ultra-independent.

Finally, there is a fourth position, that of liking oneself and others. It is the "I'm OK and you're OK" orientation. This person accepts himself or herself and others, is free, can establish meaningful relationships with others, and is reinforcing and supportive in relations with others.

Hamachek has characterized this person—the person who likes and accepts himself or herself—even more specifically and extensively than has Harris.[20] Hamachek identifies eleven characteristics of the person who likes and accepts the self. Such a person:

20. D. E. Hamachek, *Encounters with the Self* (New York: Holt, Rinehart & Winston, Inc., 1971).

1. Believes strongly in certain values and principles and is willing to defend them even in the face of strong group opinion; feels personally secure enough, however, to modify them if new experience and evidence suggest they are incorrect.

2. Is capable of acting on his or her best judgment without feeling excessively guilty or regretting these actions if others disapprove of them.

3. Does not spend undue time worrying about what is coming tomorrow, what has happened in the past, or what is taking place in the present.

4. Has confidence in his or her ability to deal with problems, even in the face of failure or setbacks.

5. Feels equal to others as a person, not superior or inferior, regardless of differences in specific abilities, family backgrounds, or attitudes of others toward him or her.

6. Is able to take for granted that he or she is a person of interest and value to others, at least to those chosen as associates.

7. Can accept praise without the pretense of false modesty and compliments without feeling guilty.

8. Is inclined to resist the efforts of others to dominate him or her.

9. Is able to admit to others that he or she is capable of feeling a wide range of impulses and desires, ranging from being angry to being loving, from being sad to being happy, from feeling deep resentment to feeling deep acceptance.

10. Is able to genuinely enjoy a wide variety of activities, involving work, play, creative self-expression, companionship, or just loafing.

11. Is sensitive to the needs of others, to accepted social customs, and particularly to the idea that one cannot enjoy oneself at the expense of others. The fully functioning self is identified by these attitudes or behaviors of liking and accepting oneself.

Self-Actualization

The third major characteristic of a fully functioning self, and an important element in communication, is the ability to see oneself as capable of meeting the challenges and fulfilling the requirements of being successful, i.e., the ability to see oneself as actualized. Such a person is confident in his or her abilities—intellectual, social, and physical—and is constantly developing and acquiring new strengths.

UPI

Self-actualization means making the "ideal self" real or *actual*. To actualize something is to bring it into being—to make it real. Self-actualization is a very important idea in self-concept and, consequently, in communication. Maslow, for example, considers self-actualization to be the highest need and highest fulfillment of a person. Self-actualization is "becoming who you want to be," and that is the greatest thing that can happen to you. It involves growth. It comes about only from your own motivation and your own willingness to work to improve yourself. As you come to know yourself, you are aware of the things about yourself you like and the things you do not like very well. If you want to change your interpersonal relationships, you are going to have to take steps to make it happen. The self-actualizing person is moving toward realizing his or her "ideal"—toward reducing the difference between the real and the ideal.

It is the self-actualized person that can most easily acquire effective interpersonal communication skills, for self-actualization is at the heart of intrapersonal and, thus, of interpersonal communication. Conversely, the person with ego-diffusion—the person torn by inconsistencies and doubts as to who he or she is, the person filled with self-hate and self-rejection, the person who dislikes and rejects others, the person who has no awareness of process and change, the person who has no awareness of becoming and of growing—this person faces a number of problems and has a number of handicaps in regard to interpersonal communication.

Each of the various interpersonal factors discussed in subsequent chapters in this text is affected by negative self-concept. The reception of information is hindered because perception is affected by negative self-concept. Language usage (both encoding and decoding) is affected. Not only are verbal messages affected, but the reception and processing of nonverbal messages are affected as well. Feedback, feelings, response patterns—all the components of interpersonal communication discussed in subsequent chapters—have their roots in the self-concept of communicators. For this reason, self-concept is discussed early in this text.

Self-Disclosure

Self-awareness, self-acceptance, and self-actualization are means to healthier self-concepts, but there is yet a fourth way to improve self-concept. It is through self-disclosure. It is strange that in this day of "busy-ness" and high interaction we can be isolated and unknown, but it is true. Although we may be surrounded by people at school, at work, and at play, we can be alone. Of course, people cannot see into our minds. They do not hear our thoughts, experience our hurts, or sense the happy feelings that surge through us. How can they know these things if we do not tell them through our verbal or nonverbal communication? If we close ourselves off to others, we isolate ourselves, and that is what is happening to many people in our world. The opposite of closing oneself to others is opening oneself. We call this *self-disclosure*. It is sharing, disclosing, and revealing something about oneself to another person.

How to Be More Self-Disclosing

Rather than being afraid to reveal ourselves to others, we have to develop a trust in others and in ourselves. John Powell, in his book *Why Am I Afraid to Tell You Who I Am?*, says that one reason we are hesitant to make disclosures is that we fear rejection.[21] When I reveal something new about myself to you, that is a significant part of me, and I am fearful that you may not accept it. I am afraid that you may laugh or in other ways reject me. Or sometimes what I want to reveal is a negative feeling I have toward you, and yet I do not want to hurt you or to have you react negatively against me. For any of these

21. John Powell, *Why Am I Afraid to Tell You Who I Am?* (Niles, Ill.: Argus Communications, 1969).

reasons, and others, it is often easier to cover up and to mask our true feelings and true selves. This motivation to "put our best selves forward so as to be liked" can lead to hiding behind a lot of false masks. Self-disclosure means that we drop the false masks and let our honest selves be revealed. This is our first suggestion for learning to be more open and for putting into practice self-disclosure:

1. *Drop the false masks.*

Too often we will not reveal ourselves, but try instead to appear to be something else. Ours is a success-oriented society, and so we are taught to appear successful. We come to believe that we simply *must* appear intelligent, healthy, clean, and attractive to other persons. Thus, we spend most of the time that we interact with others in trying to create the appearance of being *super persons*. Too many times, what we offer is a sham rather than our real selves. We are fearful that other persons may not like us, so we spend our time and energy attempting to maintain that false front. We are afraid to risk exposing who we really are. The result is that a good many relationships are based on contract between two imitation selves. We attempt to show how smart, knowledgeable, and wonderful we are, while we hide our true feelings lest we expose our ignorance or unattractiveness. This behavior is illustrated by one of the incidents in the *Peanuts* comic strip.

This is characteristic of what many of us do. We hide the fact that all we see is a ducky because we think we ought to be brilliant—that we ought to be seeing a famous painting or a sophisticated design. Yet people tend to identify with other people more readily on the basis of weak points than on the basis of strong points. The fact is that in human relationships, vulnerability is a precondition of effective communication. We should increase our willingness to be vulnerable—to reveal ourselves. All this is *not* to suggest that there is just one "real" self, or that we are always to reveal ourselves totally and immediately in every interpersonal communication situation. In fact, to try to be the same person in every situation and every encounter would be as harmful and counterproductive to effective interpersonal communication as to try to hide behind a known false image (and just as false, we might add). Each of us is made up of various selves. The relationships and roles we each play with our mothers, friends, bosses, and so on vary from person to person with whom we interact. We are not a single, absolute set of attitudes, behaviors, and relationships to all persons. The relationship we have with each is unique. The self we reveal in each of these encounters, however, needs to be an honest one—one that is congruent with our feelings, meanings, and desired behaviors in that specific encounter, and not one that is knowingly false and sham. We must risk our real selves!

When we pretend to be what we are not, three things can happen. First of all, we waste energy and concentration. Our attention is on our own performance rather than on the other person; thus we miss the messages and clues as to how others are perceiving us.

Second, pretending to be who we are not is dangerous because we may not be good enough at acting to carry it off. In fact, the truth seems to be that such acts are almost impossible to carry off. The falsity in us sooner or later slips out. This "being caught in a false face" is damaging to us as communicators in many ways, but even aside from long-range damage, who wants to be laughed at because of a silly performance in real life? We hardly want those with whom we have interacted to go away saying, "What a stupid, tragic clown! What a phony!"

A third negative outcome of pretending to be who we are not is that when the other person discovers our falsity, that person cannot further depend on anything we have to say. Rather than creating confidence and trust, we engender doubt and suspicion. That price is too high! We must learn to risk our real selves.

2. *Avoid silence and ritual responses.*

This is our second suggestion for learning to be more open and more self-disclosing, i.e., not to regress into silence and ritual responses to others.

These are two response behaviors that we ought to try to rid ourselves of because they are self-defeating. It is true that both silence and ritual communication can serve constructively in interpersonal communication if used appropriately. What we are discussing here, however, is the *inappropriate use of silence* and the *inadequacy of ritualized communication*. It is the misuse of silence as an escape or hiding mechanism that is the problem. Such use of silence is seen by others as communicating indifference and/or an unwillingness to relate. For many people such silence may not really mean that they are indifferent or unwilling to relate. They may, in fact, desire companionship, but their fear of exposing themselves is so great that they sit mute. In any event, the other person interprets that kind of silence as unwillingness to relate and reacts by rejecting the silent person. Thus, this silence behavior is counterproductive and self-defeating.

Similarly, one may use ritualized communication to avoid communication. One can hide in ritual. It is an easy way to avoid being *you*. Surely you have participated in ritualized conversations. They are extremely shallow conversations, carried on according to a kind of formula that avoids, almost entirely, honest communication. Ridding ourselves of such self-defeating response behaviors can help us improve our self-concept.

3. *Seek out trustworthy and caring persons.*

Our third suggestion for developing self-disclosure is to seek out trustworthy and caring persons. Self-concept is often improved through interaction with other persons who are trustworthy and facilitative. We observed earlier in this chapter that self-concept develops through interaction with others. To an extent, then, self-concept is related to the quality of the people with whom you interact. But primary responsibility for self-disclosure is yours.

There are yet two ideas we need to consider relative to self-disclosure. They are: (1) how much you should disclose and (2) what kinds of self-disclosure you should use.

22. Reprinted from Joseph Luft, *Group Processes: An Introduction to Group Dynamics* (Palo Alto, Calif.: Mayfield Publishing Co., 1970). *Of Human Interaction* by Joseph Luft, published in 1969, also contains the Johari window.

How Much to Disclose: The Johari Window

Joseph Luft and Harry Ingham created a disclosure model, which they named for themselves. They call it the Johari window.[22] The Johari window has four panes, representing what you know about yourself and what the other person knows of you. It is illustrated in figure 3.2.

Figure 3.2 The Johari window. From J. Luft, *Group Processes: An Introduction to Group Dynamics*, Palo Alto, Calif.: Mayfield Publishing Co., 1970.

	Known to Self	Not Known to Self
Known to Others	I Free Area	II Blind Area
Not Known to Others	III Hidden Area	IV Unknown Area

For purposes of self-disclosure, the free area represents what you willingly reveal about yourself to the other person. The hidden area represents what you could reveal but choose to keep hidden. The blind area represents what the other person knows about you that you do not know about yourself. You are blind to it; it is not in your self-awareness. Similarly, area IV is not known to you or to the other person. The process of self-disclosure enlarges area I and decreases area III. Willingness to receive information from another about yourself can enlarge area I while decreasing area II.

You might draw Johari windows that picture your relationship with other persons—one that illustrates the relationship you have with your mother, another for your best friend, and yet a third for the new person you met last week. These Johari windows would show how much you have shared and received from the other person in these dyadic relationships. As a person discloses more to the other person, the free area grows larger, while the blind area and hidden area decreases in size. Of course, the better you get to know someone and the greater the trust that develops in the relationship, the more self-disclosing and open you become in sharing feelings, opinions, and thoughts.

There are norms and rules for self-disclosure in most cultures. We do not tell a stranger our deepest, most intimate thoughts, nor do we disclose our perceived weaknesses to the waitress who serves us coffee in the restaurant, but there are important people in our lives with whom we ought to have a caring and trusting relationship and with whom we ought to share our thoughts and feelings. Research indicates that persons who do this achieve more fulfilling relationships in their lives and facilitate the growth of a healthy self-concept.

Kinds
of Self-Disclosure

The final topic we should consider relative to self-disclosure is *kinds* of self-disclosure. Identifying some of the different kinds may help one to know what kind of disclosure is appropriate in a given situation. The type and depth of disclosure ought to be determined by the kind of relationship you have with the other person.

Impersonal Information. One kind of sharing is the sharing of impersonal information. The safest or lowest level is probably that exchanged with strangers during the acquaintance process. We exchange information about the people we might both know, places we have visited, events, and similar impersonal things. This sharing indicates a willingness to be open and friendly.

Personal Information. Another level of disclosure is the sharing of personal information. We give our names, where we live, what we do, what we think,

Disclosure of deep feelings is seldom a part of the acquaintance process.

and perhaps our opinion. Only last week, I was having an interesting and pleasant conversation with a clerk in a large department store. We were exchanging personal information while she was carrying out my business transaction, and she said in the midst of our joking. "You're a Virgo, aren't you?" I admitted that I was, and she said, "I knew it! You're friendly and have a great time!" Taking a shot in the dark, I replied, "And I'll bet you're a Virgo, too!" She was, and she then proceeded to give her philosophy of work and fun. We had rapidly moved from "weather talk" to exchanges of personal information. That exchange, however, was not at the level of disclosing deep feelings or revealing frustrations, concerns, or fears, as one might in a more intimate relationship.

Disclosing Feelings.   Another kind of sharing is the sharing of feelings. Of course, we can share our general feelings in conversations with acquaintances, classmates, persons with whom we work, and so on, but these feelings are often "polite," toned down, and even disguised and distorted.

There are some common problems most of us have relative to sharing feelings. First, very often we simply do not tell others how we feel. We are afraid; we think it is inappropriate; or we assume they should "just be able to know how I feel." In fact, very often, people do not know how we feel unless we tell them. Tell the other person that "I'm happy for you," "I'm sad for you," "I like what you did," or "What you did bothered me."

Another common problem is that we express our feelings incorrectly. We hurt or anger the other person by accusing, by labeling, by being sarcastic, or by shouting commands. The other person has to guess from our behavior what feeling is underneath it. Sometimes it is fairly apparent that we are angry, but at other times, our negative behavior is so sophisticated and concealing that the other person has trouble knowing our true feeling.

What we need to do is to learn how to express our feelings in positive ways. Learning to express feelings constructively helps us in two ways: (1) finding the right words to express a feeling aids us in identifying and understanding our feelings. We handle them better inside our heart. (2) Constructive disclosure of feelings can enable the other person to help, and it can lead to a better relationship with the other person.

Self-disclosure is a necessary part of the relationship between two people.

Richard Younker

Some constructive ways of expressing feelings are: (1) name the feeling ("I'm proud of you!" or "I'm angry!"); (2) use comparisons ("I feel like I've been squished under with a steam roller!" or "I'm on Cloud Nine!"); and (3) report what action your feelings motivate ("I could give you a big hug for that!" or "I could punch you out!").

In addition to learning to express feelings constructively, and learning to disclose personal information at levels appropriate to the relationship, there are five additional guidelines we recommend. They are: (1) make a commitment to grow; (2) be willing to risk; (3) avoid manipulating others; (4) watch the timing of your disclosure; and (5) use feedback to clarify your exchanges.

First comes commitment. If you have no desire to improve your relationships with other persons, then self-disclosure will not be a concern of yours; but if you do care about your relationship with others, then you ought to make a commitment to improve, to grow, and to actualize your potential. When we feel a commitment to a relationship, we will want to share, to disclose, and engage in mutual growth with that person.

Second, we need to be willing to chance disclosure. It is worth risking being honest so that a relationship can grow. To do less results in the wearing of false masks.

Third, avoid manipulating the other person. We should not be engaged in making the other person change. It is not productive to place blame on the other person. Whether the other person wants to change or not is his or her choice and not ours. We can report our feelings and information we have that we believe will make the relationship more fulfilling for both of us, but we have no right to *tell* the other person to change.

Fourth, it is important to disclose feelings at the time we have those feelings rather than waiting until tomorrow. When feelings are expressed at the time they are felt, both parties are more likely to identify the antecedents (the events or behaviors) of the feeling. It is not helpful to store up feelings for a couple of weeks or longer and then drop them on the other person in one gigantic dose. Little growth results from that particular technique of self-disclosing.

We are not saying that you must express every feeling immediately upon feeling it. There are times when immediate expression of feelings is inappropriate. Often these are times when a third party is included in the situation.

Finally, we suggest that you use feedback to check on the meaning and feelings being exchanged. If you are not sure you understand what the other person means, ask him or her to clarify, or restate the other person's comment in other words. Paraphrasing the other person before replying is a good way to check on intended meanings. In the same way, you can check on the other person's understanding of your comments and state your meanings in alternate words when feedback from the other person indicates he or she did not understand your comments as you meant them.

In self-disclosure situations, one must be careful to avoid personal judgments, accusations, name-calling, or sarcasm. Self-disclosure of negative feelings ought to be objective and descriptive of what the other person did that elicited the negative feeling in you. The expression of negative feelings, when done carefully and with sensitivity, can be helpful to the persons concerned.

SUMMARY

Success in interpersonal communication is related directly to how you feel about yourself. Self-concept is the product of intrapersonal and interpersonal communication, but it also affects the development of effective skills in intrapersonal and interpersonal communication. It is a cause and a result, and as such, it is an important factor in growth, development, and success in our social world.

4

Perceiving and Understanding Others

As you read this book, what do you experience? That may seem a strange question, since you may prefer to be with friends engaging in some sort of recreation, rather than reading. But let us get back to the question and consider it for a moment. As you read this book, the things we hope most of you experience are the words and illustrations on the pages and, of course, the meanings we associate with these symbols. However, it must be obvious that at any given time, such as right now, you are experiencing a great deal more. For instance, depending upon the time of day, you may be experiencing any number of different kinds of feelings, such as that in your stomach. You may have a feeling of hunger because it has been a long time since you ate, or you could have a feeling of satiation if you just finished a meal.

Ordinarily, we are not acutely conscious of these feelings when engaged in activities such as reading or talking with people. And yet we are experiencing them. Likewise, we are experiencing other sensations, such as the heat or cold pervading the room we are in. If we are not in a room, we experience the presence of wind upon our skin and in our hair. No matter where we are, we also detect lightness or darkness, depending upon how our room is lighted or what the condition of the sky is. In addition to such sensations, we experience the sounds that come from heating systems, street traffic, fluorescent light fixtures, animals, and possibly conversations and/or radios or television sets outside or in our room. It is rare, indeed, to sit down and read a book and experience nothing but the book.

Perception Creates Our World

If we stop to consider all the sensations we are experiencing at any given moment, it seems remarkable that we are not driven totally out of our minds by the chaotic bombardment of stimuli we receive. Yet, for most of us, this

1. Charles M. Butter, *Neuropsychology: The Study of Brain and Behavior* (Belmont, Calif.: Brooks/Cole Publishing Co., 1968), p. 39.

2. Ibid.

Even as adults, it is difficult to sort among the stimuli that confront us every day. What you notice in this picture will be the result of your own perceptual process, which is dependent on your background.

poses no problem because of the process known as *perception*. Very simply stated, *perception is a mental process in which we select, organize, and interpret the many stimuli that impinge on us at any given moment.*[1] It is very easy to overlook the hundreds of different sensations we experience every moment of our lives. It is not possible to list them all, but if you consider the senses of sight, hearing, smelling, touch, and taste, it must be obvious that we are receivers of a multitude of sensations.

We should now indicate a major difference between *sensing* stimuli and *perceiving* them. Experiencing sensation involves the physical reception of the stimuli.[2] If the temperature of the room in which you are reading this chapter is approximately sixty or sixty-five degrees, you experience a physical sensation in your feet, especially if you have no shoes or socks on. Without prior experience, it would be impossible to translate that particular physical sensation into a meaningful concept. The concept that has meaning for us is "cold," but to say that you experience "cold" is incorrect. You actually experience a certain arrangement and action of molecules, and then, given

all the other sensations affecting you while reading this chapter, you select particular sets of physical sensations and interpret them as "cold."

In a room temperature of sixty to sixty-five degrees, you select from among the many stimuli available at the moment those that are important to you and exclude those that are not. We hope you are selecting among stimuli and organizing them so that sensations involving certain visual stimuli (books and notes) receive greater attention than the sensation you interpret as "cold."

The stimuli you select and organize for your attention are important to you because of your past experiences and needs. This would suggest, then, that as a result of our experiences with things, events, and people *we learn to perceive.*[3]

If we could bring to mind the moment of our birth, we would say it must have been a very confusing and frightening time. A baby is born into a world in which there is an unceasing presence of sensations with little or no organization or meaning. This must be very disturbing indeed. It is no wonder babies sometimes cry when they are alone. The process of perception is not one we are necessarily equipped with at birth (at least not in the same way we have it throughout our lives). Certainly, at the moment of birth, we begin trying to select from and interpret the chaotic stimuli we receive. At some early point in our lives (whether it is prenatal or postnatal, we don't know), we learn to perceive through the experiences we have.

We are concerned with the process of perception in interpersonal communication because communication involves both hearing and seeing. Since it involves visual and aural stimuli, it is necessary for us to select, organize, and interpret these stimuli whenever we are in an interpersonal situation. We perceive what we think other people are communicating to us, and likewise we have perceptions of the communicators themselves.[4] Of course, we also perceive ourselves (as was discussed in chapter 3).

To understand the role of perception in interpersonal communication, it is necessary for us to consider some of the basic principles of perception. It is obvious that we will not, in the amount of space we have in a book on interpersonal communication, be able to cover the process of perception in depth. However, it is possible for us to cover those principles of perception that are especially relevant to an understanding of the basic process and of how that process relates to interpersonal communication. That will be the objective of the first section of this chapter. In the second section, we will attempt to apply these principles of perception to the way we see other people, while in the third section, we will discuss perception as it affects interpersonal communication. We hope you will be able to ignore all stimuli unrelated to the topics of interpersonal communication and perception so you can focus your attention upon the text and your response to the text; in this way you may better understand perception and the role it plays in interpersonal communication.

3. John W. McDavid and Herbert Harari, *Social Psychology: Individuals, Groups, Societies* (New York: Harper & Row Publishers, Inc., 1968), pp. 140–44.

4. Fritz Heider, "Consciousness, The Perceptual World, Inc., and Communication With Others," in *Person Perception and Interpersonal Behavior,* ed. Renato Tagiuri and Luigi Petrullo (Stanford, Calif.: Stanford University Press, 1958), pp. 27–32.

Continuous Reception

5. Albert H. Hastorf, David J. Schneider, and Judith Polefka, *Person Perception* (Reading, Mass.: Addison-Wesley Publishing Co., 1970), pp. 7–10.

6. Ibid., p. 3.

7. Butter, Neuropsychology, p.38.

One basic principle of importance, to which we have already alluded, is that we constantly receive stimuli.[5] *The human being is an open and constant receptor.* Any individual has many receptors (related to the five senses of taste, smell, touch, hearing, and sight. The receptors are open at all times (assuming there is no physical impairment), so that we constantly receive all physical stimuli present in our environment. This means that the world around us has a kind of immediacy.[6] Everything about us is received and translated into nerve impulses and transmitted through the nervous system.[7]

It is especially important for us to realize this in interpersonal communication, because it is apparent that at any given moment, not only are we receiving stimuli from those with whom we are interacting but we are also receiving other stimuli, any of which can affect our perception of the interpersonal situation.[8] At a party we may be talking with our date, and yet we are also experiencing the sights and sounds (possibly the odors and touches) of other males and females in the room. Depending upon how we perceive these other stimuli, we may or may not interact in a manner satisfactory to our date. Sometimes this results in a couple splitting up and going home with persons other than the ones they came to the party with. This example is also an indication of just how continuously we receive stimuli and how interpersonal communication is affected by perception.

8. Bruce H. Westley and Malcolm S. MacLean, Jr., "A Conceptual Model for Communications Research," *Journalism Quarterly* 35 (1957):31–38.

How Perception Works

How we receive and process the many different stimuli about us has been a source of concern in the social and behavioral sciences for many years. Several approaches have been taken, and some rather basic assumptions have been made by different groups, depending on their approach to the perception process. Two rather basic approaches with differing assumptions have been evident over time. These are the structuralist approach and the Gestalt approach.

Structuralist Approach

9. Julian E. Hochberg, *Perception* (Englewood Cliffs, N.J.: Prentice-Hall, Inc., 1964), p. 12.

10. Ibid.

Essentially, structuralists have held that perception can be viewed as the process of combining all the sensations we receive through our different receptors into a single perception.[9] The structuralist approach assumes that there are specific receptors programmed to receive specific stimuli.[10] The approach further assumes that once the appropriate stimuli falls on the appropriate sensory receptors, the sensations received by all of them together can be added up to produce a perception. This is an additive approach. If we have a friend who is six feet tall, male, dresses in blue jeans and sweat shirts, likes symphonic music, drinks French wines, and is soft-spoken (we could

Chapter 4

add many other characteristics), it would be possible to say that our perception of that friend is the sum total of all the properties that our appropriate receptors received. This approach to perception is less in favor today, as many suggest that the perception we have of an individual (or of any physical event) consists of a great deal more than the sum of the individual parts.[11]

11. Ibid.

Gestalt Approach

While Gestalt psychologists developed their approach to psychology quite independently, many of their views of the perceptual process are something of a reaction to the structuralists.[12] Essentially, the Gestalt approach suggests that our perceptions are not the sum of many independent sensations; rather we perceive perceptual wholes.[13]

12. Hochberg, *Perception*, pp. 31–34.

13. McDavid and Harari, *Social Psychology*, p. 30.

While we may have many receptors constantly doing their job of receiving the many different stimuli present in our environment, our perception of physical events consists of more than the sum of its parts.[14] Very likely you have experienced this kind of feeling yourself regarding a friend, relative, or parent. It is not unusual for someone to ask: "Why do you love your mother?" You can list all the things she has done for you and said to you, yet this listing of events that have occurred between you and her falls short of explaining your perception of her. This is not only true in the case of mothers. It is true of any loved one. It is almost impossible to explain our feelings for another person in terms of a cataloging of his or her qualities or behaviors toward us. The whole is more than the sum of the individual components. The Gestalt approach suggests that when we perceive something, we perceive it as a whole, rather than perceiving individual parts and then putting them together.

14. S. Howard Bartley, *Principles of Perception* (New York: Harper & Row Publishers, Inc., 1958), p. 85.

This approach has resulted in some laws of perception that are accepted by many behavioral scientists today. We would like you to consider three of the Gestalt principles of perception because of their special relevance to interpersonal communication, and more specifically to the way in which they relate to our perception of other people in interpersonal situations.

Proximity

The first Gestalt principle of perception concerns what has been called the *principle of proximity* or *resemblance*.[15] It has also been referred to as the phenomenon of "grouping" by communication scholars.[16] Things located and/or grouped together in close proximity with one another are perceived as a whole. From a purely visual point of view, two people who are standing next to each other in a room filled with many people will appear to be "together." They are perceived as being a couple, or as part of an interaction unit. Similarly, two people who look somewhat alike are paired together or assumed to be relatives. Implications of this kind crop up frequently with brothers and sisters who bear family resemblances. If we see them together and we notice these resemblances, we perceive them as a "pair."

15. William N. Dember, *The Psychology of Perception* (New York: Holt, Rinehart & Winston, Inc., 1966), p. 162.

16. Ronald L. Applbaum et al., *Fundamental Concepts in Human Communication* (San Francisco: Canfield Press, 1973), p. 21.

Figure 4.1

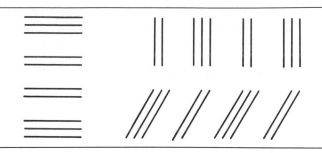

In figure 4.1, you can see examples of lines and figures that can be perceived as units of a larger whole. We tend to perceive the lines together in groups of two or three because of their physical closeness to one another. We also tend to perceive groupings of different-shaped figures when the shapes of the figures begin to resemble one another. In like manner, even though this is impossible to represent on the printed page, we group sounds according to time. For instance, Morse code symbols are perceived in units because the symbols for individual letters come close together in time.

One of the effects of the principle of proximity or grouping is observable when communicators associate themselves, as they frequently do, with persons of high prestige in the expectation that with the resultant grouping, benefits of that high prestige will rub off on them. A kind of *"gilt"* by association occurs.[17] By the same token, some communicators suffer by being on the same panel discussion with someone of low status or low repute; then "guilt" by association occurs.

17. James C. McCroskey and Robert E. Dunham, "Ethos: A Confounding Element in Communication Research," *Speech Monographs* 32 (1966):456–63.

Good Form

18. James Deese, *General Psychology* (Boston: Allyn & Bacon, Inc., 1967), pp. 277–311.

Another principle of perception suggested by Gestaltists concerns what has been referred to as the principle of good form.[18] Good form, as it occurs within our environment, is a naturally perceived whole. Take a look at figure 4.2. The dots in figure 4.2(a) can be perceived as straight lines that continue. If they are perceived in that way, they form a plus sign for us. Likewise, in

Figure 4.2

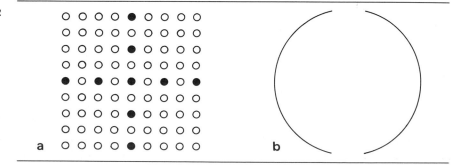

figure 4.2(*b*), you will notice what appears to be two semicircles facing each other. Whenever it is possible for *symmetry* to occur and to be perceived as symmetry, this is an example of good form. In this case, when symmetry occurs, the two semicircles are perceived as a complete circle.

The third way one can determine what is or is not good form involves what is termed *closure* or *common fate*. Closure occurs when we have an incomplete figure we can complete. In figure 4.3 you can see the letters of the alphabet. All of them are incomplete, yet you probably perceive them as whole letters and know what the letters are, simply because you engage in an act of closure, or perceiving a whole. Likewise, if we go back to figure 4.2(*a*), in which the dots form a plus sign, what is meant by common fate should become clear: the parts appear in some respect to have the same directionality, to be going to the same place.

Figure 4.3

In public speaking and composition classes, the principle of good form has been employed frequently. For instance, the necessity for balance, or symmetry, is emphasized in speeches and essays. Likewise, closure is frequently used in speaking. Whenever we say, "But you can guess the rest," we are relying on the listener to fill in what is missing. By causing our listeners to "fill in the blanks," we may well be more effective in our impact on them, since they are expending energy in helping us complete our point.

Search for Order

The third basic Gestalt principle of perception (and a very important concept for us in interpersonal communication) is what is called the *search for order*.[19] We have previously discussed the chaotic world of sensations, in which we are constantly being bombarded by stimuli of many different sorts. The Gestaltists suggest that we have the need to determine some kind of consistency or order in all this chaos. It is as though the chaos itself represents a threat to our existence. If we can extend this notion a bit further and apply to it some of the material in chapter 1, it makes sense. People are actually trying to carve out some sort of niche for themselves in the world of random events about them.

19. Deese, *General Psychology*, pp. 277–311.

One of the things necessary for us to do in meeting our needs, then, is to discern an orderliness in the world. Predictability is necessary because it enables us to manipulate the world.[20] Consider for a moment: if the world were random and had no order, it would be impossible to predict what would happen as a result of any of our behaviors. To manipulate the world

20. Hastorf, Schneider, and Polefka, *Person Perception*, pp. 1–10.

(in order to control our environment), it is necessary for us to know various kinds of cause-and-effect relationships in the world, so we try to perceive whatever order we can. This appears to affect the way we perceive things.

Bombarded by stimuli, we attempt to perceive order or organization among them. Thus, in figure 4.2(a), in which there are many dots, it is almost a natural inclination on our part to hunt for some kind of ordered perception among the available stimuli. We find a plus sign here, for all of the reasons suggested by the Gestalt perceptual principles. This search for order may account for our concern for organization in speeches, essays, and books. It could be a good reason always (even in informal situations) to put our thoughts in order before we attempt to communicate.

Basic Principles of Perception

21. Ibid.

We now turn to the thoughts suggested by Hastorf, Schneider, and Polefka to see how their views of the perception process are related to the Gestalt principle of our need for order.[21] According to these authors, there are three major predictions we can make about human reactions to the chaotic world of stimuli we have been discussing. (As we discuss these, please keep in mind both the Gestalt principle of the need for order and our earlier discussion of our need to manipulate the world around us in order to survive. We believe these are interrelated.)

Categorization Process

22. Ibid.

23. J. S. Bruner, "The Course of Cognitive Growth," *American Psychologist* 19 (1964):1–15; A. R. Lucia, "The Directive Function of Speech in Development and Dissolution: Part 1. Development of the Directive Function of Speech in Early Childhood," *Word* 15 (1959):341–52.

We structure the world of sensations about us.[22] We are not satisfied with a random set of occurrences. We order things, assign priorities, categorize, take all the various incoming stimuli, and build a structure for ourselves. We do this through a categorization process that is greatly affected by our language and by our past history. We use language in this process.[23] We can categorize different kinds of organisms such as dogs, cats, and horses, and by so doing we establish an order among living creatures. By this process we create a system with which we can deal. (We will discuss language and its relationship to the physical world in greater detail in chapter 5.)

We go even further than the simple naming of things in our categorization system; we talk about cattle as food; we talk about dogs as man's best friend. We also categorize people, and this can have a significant impact on our interpersonal relationships. For instance, we categorize one group of people as very intelligent, another group as very crafty, and yet another group as dangerous. The problem is that from there on, our structure of the world (which we have developed to aid us in coping with the world) becomes the filter through which we view it.[24]

24. Charles C. Spiker, "Verbal Factors in the Discrimination Learning of Children," *Monograph of the Society for Research in Child Development* 28 (1963):53–69.

We have some friends who are very anti-Semitic. Among their categorizations of the world is their classification of Jewish people as wealthy, clannish, and very different from "our" kind of people. Some years ago, we were invited by some Jewish friends to spend Thanksgiving with them. We did so and experienced the usual traditional Thanksgiving of the sort that Norman Rockwell used to picture in the *Saturday Evening Post.* Upon hearing of this visit, these friends reacted with "I didn't know Jews celebrated Thanksgiving." This was a very revealing statement because the categorizations, or the labels, that had been developed by our anti-Semitic friends for the purpose of structuring the world were operating to ensure that any future perceptions were in accord with their categorization system. This system would almost prevent these friends from perceiving Jewish people as ever being anything but very different from "normal people."

An interesting question is: Where do our category systems come from? They are an outgrowth of our past history. It has been observed that children who grow up in poor families actually perceive coins to be bigger than do children who have grown up in wealthy families.[25] No doubt our past history very much affects the way in which we develop a categorization process of our own. In fact, we are involved in a circular procedure in which our language and our past history conditions the way we categorize the physical world,[26] and in turn reinforces our categorization system.

25. J. S. Bruner and C. C. Goodman, "Value and Need as Organizing Factors in Perception," *Journal of Abnormal and Social Psychology* 42 (1947):33–44.

26. Benjamin Lee Whorf, "Language Mind, and Reality," *Etc., a Review of General Semantics* 9 (1952):167–88.

Stabilizing Perceptions

27. Hastorf, Schneider, and Polefka, *Person Perception.*

The second prediction of Hastorf, Schneider, and Polefka[27] is that, in addition to structuring the world of sensations in which we live, we also *attempt to impose consistency on our perceptions.* We want our perceptions to be stable. As we stand in an airport and watch a plane landing, the actual size of the plane that is being projected onto our retinal wall changes: when the plane is very distant and high, the image projected onto our retinal wall is small; as the plane nears the landing strip (and subsequently the terminal), the image actually projected on the retinal wall increases in size.

We all know perfectly well that the plane is not increasing in size. Consequently, through the process of perception (which is an interpretive process), we perceive the plane as remaining the same size but interpret the growth of the image on our retinal wall grow to mean that the plane is coming nearer us. When the plane is distant, it is smaller; when it is nearer, it is larger. At no time do we actually begin to interpret the physical world outside as being one in which objects literally grow in size as they come closer to us. In our perceptions, we impose consistency on the world and the objects about us, even though the physical stimuli we are receiving may be constantly varying in terms of size, shape, sound, and color. We do this to preserve the order we have established in our initial world-view structure. This, of course, relates to the Gestalt principle of our search for order. By imposing consistency on our perceptions, we help preserve that order.

Attaching Meanings to Sensations

28. Ibid.

29. David K. Berlo, *The Process of Communication* (New York: Holt, Rinehart & Winston, Inc., 1960), p. 31.

30. Hastorf, Schneider, and Polefka, *Person Perception*, pp. 1–18.

Finally, Hastorf, Schneider, and Polefka[28] indicate that *we attach meaning to all the sensations we have.* In some communication texts this has been termed *decoding* (we receive physical stimuli and translate them into some sort of meaning for ourselves).[29] Actually, it is important, from the perspective of interpersonal communication, to realize that the imposition of meaning on physical sensations involves a great deal more than simply associating a given meaning with a given stimulus. In fact, this is little more than what we were speaking of earlier when discussing the individual's need to structure the world.

If the structuring of the world is a process in which we are concerned with *micromeanings* (individual categorization of stimuli), then what we are talking about now should be considered *macromeaning.* We are concerned about relationships among different categories, different stimuli, and different structures.[30] This is a larger structure of the world that goes quite beyond the naming and categorization of things. It is as if we cannot stop at the creation of a simple structure. We also have to determine the relationships among the component parts of that structure. We cannot simply name dark clouds "rain clouds" and water that falls out of the sky "rain." Rather, to have an adequate predictive sense of the way things are in the world, we must establish the relationship between dark clouds and water that falls out of the sky and hits us on the face. The relationship becomes of paramount importance, just as the relationship between whistling and saying, "Here, Spot," results in a little furry four-legged creature running to our feet. These relationships are part of our total perception of order in the world, and it is the perception of relationships that enables us to make predictions in the world. Being able to make predictions, in turn, makes it possible for us to manipulate the world in ways that satisfy our needs. Thus, when we perceive a physical stimulus we do not simply interpret a given object; we also interpret that object's relationship to other objects about it.

To understand the approach just presented, picture a being from another planet happening onto one of our large athletic stadiums on a Saturday afternoon in the fall. That being would discover a tremendous number of people sitting on two sides of a rectangular field with white lines drawn all over it. (It is impossible to describe this situation without making use of some of the categories we have in our past history; but for the moment consider the plight of the extraterrestrial perceiving this and trying to understand it.)

First, it is necessary for our interplanetary visitor to structure the perceptions on a microlevel in which he, she, or it can classify people, the colors of uniforms, groups that appear to be near one another, and maybe even the existence of two different teams (because of the symmetry involved when the two are facing each other). Although our visitor may be standing at one end of the field, with the teams running close and then far away, it is certainly possible for this observer to maintain observational consistency. Then, of course, to understand what is going on, it is necessary for the visitor to attach meaning to sensations received in terms of the relationships observed among the stimuli. As a matter of fact, we can think of no other way to explain what is going on in a football game than by considering the relationships among all the participants.

Perceiving the World: A Brief Summation

Our view of perception is derived from the Gestalt approach. In interpersonal communication we are concerned with perceptual wholes. Likewise, we are engaged in a search for order in our perceptions. As a result, we attempt to structure our perceptions of the world in a consistent manner so that our sensations are not left at random and unordered. Finally, we impose upon our perceptions our own meanings and perceived relationships. All this enables us to perceive a more ordered, highly structured world; and that, in turn, enables us to predict more easily, which enables us to manipulate the world according to our needs because we are able to predict effects from causes.

How We Perceive People

Up to this point we have been considering the way in which people perceive stimuli generally. The research that has provided support for the statements we have been making up to this point was concerned with object perception or the perception of things, even though our applications have most often concerned people. It is, we hope, obvious that the concern in interpersonal communication is not with the perception of objects, but rather with the perception of people.

Try to remember the last time you met a new person. You were introduced to that person. You may have shaken hands and said a number of "nice things." That person probably did the same with you. As all this was going on, you were developing a total perception, or impression, of that person. What caused you to decide what you did decide about that person? What caused you to like or not like the person? What caused you to decide that you trusted or did not trust the person? What caused you to decide the person was intelligent or unintelligent, emotional or unemotional, warm or cold?

These are the kinds of questions that have concerned behavioral scientists in an area of study usually referred to as *person perception*. The answers to these questions about how we come to see other people are very much related to the discussion we have just completed of the process of perception

The attractiveness of movie stars significantly affects our judgment about them as human beings, even though most of us lack the information necessary for that kind of judgment.

American Stock Photos/Tom Stack & Associates

in general. Our perception of people parallels our perception of objects. We need to establish some sort of order in our perception of people, just as we do with objects. Likewise, it is important for us to develop some kind of meaning for people in terms of relationships.

Others' Intentions

31. Fritz Heider, *The Psychology of Interpersonal Relations* (New York: Science Editions, John Wiley & Sons, Inc., 1958), pp. 100–101.

One of the basic assumptions we apparently make about other people when we are developing our impressions of them is that they *intentionally* engage in whatever behaviors they perform.[31] In a way, that notion appears so obvious that it almost seems ludicrous to discuss it, yet it has far-reaching implications. We assume that someone who eats ice cream, wants to eat it. That is

Chapter 4

a very simple example, yet we make inferences far more complex than this in the same manner. If someone smiles at us, we assume the person must like us and is being friendly toward us. Likewise, if someone does not speak to us, it is not unusual to decide the person does not like us.

Inferences such as these are very typical of all of us every day of our lives. We are constantly making our own decisions about people's motivations and intentions as a result of observations of some of their behaviors. Sometimes we are correct. Sometimes we are very wrong. We nevertheless do make these inferences because, as with objects, we are attempting to structure the sensations we have of other people, develop the consistency we need, and attach meaning to our sensations. With people, however, it is a little more difficult, because people are constantly changing. Therefore, we look for common ingredients among all the different behaviors we can observe.[32] In fact, it is always interesting to consider what causes us to make the judgments we do about other people. Have you ever decided that a person you have met is a prejudiced person? How did you arrive at that conclusion?

In all likelihood, something like the following occurred: the person you ultimately labeled as "prejudiced" made a statement or two about some group that would appear to be negative. For example, suppose someone makes the statement that property values in a neighborhood tend to decline after a black family moves into the neighborhood. That statement in and of itself may not necessarily be enough cause for you to perceive the person as prejudiced against blacks, but it might start you thinking that way. Actually, the person could make a statement of that sort on the basis of information from real estate agencies. We really do not know whether or not the person is prejudiced against blacks—yet.

Suppose we are now with this person at a banquet, and there is an empty chair very close to us that this person can sit in, and another empty chair a good distance away. However, a black person is sitting in a chair next to the one nearest us, and the person whom we are observing chooses to walk the long distance to a chair between whites. At this point, we have a couple of samples of behavior, and we may begin to infer that there were certain intentions and motivations underlying these behaviors.

If we can see a consistency among these different behaviors, we begin to use that to perceive, or explain, the person. In this case we might very likely infer that the individual is prejudiced against blacks. If we are very careful in forming our opinions and our impressions and developing our inferences, we might demand more samples of behavior than that, but this is typical of the process we go through.

32. Leon Festinger, *A Theory of Cognitive Dissonance* (Stanford, Calif.: Stanford University Press, 1957).

Accuracy in Perceiving Others

A question that has been examined and investigated by a number of social and behavioral scientists for years is that of how accurate we are in judging

33. Hastorf, Schneider, and Polefka, *Person Perception*, p. 19.

34. Nico H. Frijda, "Recognition of Emotion," in *Advance in Experimental Social Psychology*, vol. 4, ed. Leonard Berkowitz (New York: Academic Press, Inc., 1969), pp. 167–223.

35. Ibid.

36. Hastorf, Schneider, and Polefka, *Person Perception*, pp. 20–25.

37. H. D. Goldberg, "The Role of 'Cutting' in the Perception of Motion Pictures," *Journal of Applied Psychology* 35 (1951): 70–71; Nico H. Frijda, "Facial Expression and Situational Cues," *Journal of Abnormal and Social Psychology* 57 (1958):149–54.

38. Michael Argyle, *Social Interaction* (Chicago: Aldine-Atherton, Inc., 1969), pp. 158–64.

39. Ibid.

40. Ibid., pp. 149–53.

41. Ibid.

other people's emotions and personalities. Our approach to the "prejudiced" person in the preceding section is one that would probably be taken by someone employing the structuralist view of perception. It is also possible to approach this question from a Gestaltist point of view, which is the way we will try to consider it.[33]

Regarding the question of how accurately we perceive emotions in other people, most of the research that has been conducted to this point would appear to be somewhat inconclusive.[34] While it is true that some fairly reasonable accuracy percentages have been obtained (anywhere from 52 to 57 percent), the emotions that have been identified by judges have been fairly general and not very specific or useful in an interpersonal communication text.[35] It seems possible to be fairly accurate in judging emotions such as surprise, happiness, fear, anger, disgust and contempt.[36]

Of course, one of the reasons why the research has been somewhat inconclusive in terms of identification of emotions is that it is very difficult to be sure which emotions are being portrayed and therefore which emotions need to be recognized. Apparently, rather than there being any definite behavioral cues for us to recognize, we are very dependent on the *context* in which people behave for us to determine what emotions are being expressed.[37] The research is somewhat incomplete on this point.

Evidence suggesting that people differ considerably in their ability to judge personality characteristics does exist, however. This is true whether the judgment is one of intelligence or personality.[38] Many of our judgments of other people, however, would appear to be the result of our projecting our own characteristics onto someone else or assuming that others are similar to ourselves.[39] It may well be that one of the reasons we are sometimes accurate in assessing another person's personality is that the individual concerned happens (fortunately) to be similar to us.

While we were discussing the perception of objects, one of the points we stressed was that background, past history, and language system significantly affect our perception of objects. This appears to be the case in terms of our perception of people, too. There are any number of factors that seem to affect the way in which we evaluate other people.

First, our own interpersonal attitudes appear to affect our judgment of other people's personalities significantly, because we are constantly looking for consistency within the world.[40] If we dislike another person, our judgment of that person's personality is very likely to be negative. If we meet person A and decide that we do not like that person, we may evaluate him or her as rude, hostile, cold, unfriendly, ignorant, and possessed of any other negative characteristics. That would be consistent with our negative interpersonal reaction.

Another factor that seems to affect our judgment of other people significantly is our role relations.[41] If there are two persons, John and Fred, the role of each relative to the other will significantly affect their perceptions of each other. If John is dependent upon Fred for pay increases and promotions, it's very difficult for Fred to evaluate John's personality. Fred will never know whether John is being friendly because he really likes him or whether he is being friendly to get pay increases and promotions.

It is also possible that a given set can affect our judgments of another person.[42] The kinds of information we have about an individual, whether true or not, will significantly affect the way we react to that person. This prior information can cause us to notice things we would not notice otherwise. It can cause us to interpret what we see differently from the way we would if we did not have the previous information. Of course, if the information tends toward the positive or the negative, it can cause us to try to bring everything else we think about the person into line with that tendency, simply to restore consistency in our perception.[43]

Our own moods and motivation at any given moment will also affect our perception of others.[44] If, for example, a young man who has not been on a date for months because he has been stationed in Antarctica meets a young lady of rather average looks and average to substandard personality, we may discover that he perceives her as being an incredibly attractive young woman and possessed of a sparkling personality. At that particular point his needs and motivations may have caused him to perceive her in a manner much different from the way he would under more normal circumstances.

Forming Impressions

Because our past history has a significant effect in determining the accuracy with which we perceive other people, one of the questions that has been raised is that of how we go about forming impressions of other people. Two approaches appear to be predominant among social and behavioral scientists interested in person perception: the *trait theory* approach and the implicit personality theory approach.

Trait Theory

The trait theory can be viewed either from a structuralist or a Gestalt point of view. The structuralist trait theory approach would consist, first, of our making separate judgments of different traits in an individual. Second, our impression of that individual would be the sum total of all the traits we have perceived. A Gestalt trait theory approach would be that our responses to each trait affect our responses to all other traits and, thus, the whole impression of an individual is equal to something greater than the sum of the individual traits. There is evidence in support of both of those approaches.

The classic research by Asch[45] supports both approaches. In his research he gave one group of subjects a set of adjectives, which included the word "warm," describing a person. Another set of subjects heard the same description, but instead of "warm" the word "cold" was substituted. Other than those two words, the lists were identical. The responses of the subjects

42. Ibid.

43. Ibid.

44. Ibid.

45. S. E. Asch, "Forming Impressions of Personality," *Journal of Abnormal and Social Psychology* 41 (1946):258–90.

indicated that their perceptions of this person were very different, depending on whether they were exposed to the word "warm" or the word "cold."

Some of Asch's further research suggested to him that "warm" and "cold" were what could be termed *central traits*. A central trait can be thought of as a characteristic that others perceive as a controlling and primary personality characteristic of the individual. Such adjectives had a greater effect upon responses than many others might have had.[46] It is possible that one of the kinds of responses we have to people is in terms of traits we sum together into a total perception.

46. Ibid.

Implicit Personality Theory

A second approach to the formation of impressions, however, is called *implicit personality theory* and seems more Gestaltist in its orientation. This approach is probably more useful in terms of interpersonal communication, and there is research that supports it. Implicit personality theory predicts that when we meet someone, we generate a set of inferences about that person on the basis of whatever stimuli we are receiving.[47] In much the manner already discussed, we look for consistencies in behaviors, we infer motivations, and from that we develop some kind of implicit personality explanation for that individual. From that point on we make use of previously held personality expectations we have generated within ourselves over time.

47. P. F. Secord, "Stereotyping and Favorableness in the Perception of Negro Faces," *Journal of Abnormal and Social Psychology* 59 (1959):309–15; J. Wishner, "Reanalysis of 'Impressions of Personality,' " *Psychological Review* 67 (1960):16–112.

For instance, if you meet someone you are able to classify as a gregarious personality, you then reach into your "storehouse" of implicit personality theories and find the things you tend to expect from people with gregarious personalities. If you associate someone who talks and laughs a lot with a gregarious personality, then you expect to see that kind of behavior from this individual. And you act accordingly.

It is important to note that our implicit personality theories are the result of a lifetime of hearing about different kinds of personalities from our friends and experiencing different kinds of people with various personalities.[48] Sometimes the predictions we make and the implicit theories we carry around inside our heads are accurate. Sometimes they are not so accurate. We are not suggesting the formation of implicit personality theories as a goal. We are only presenting what many behavioral scientists believe to be a valid explanation of interpersonal perception.

48. D. M. Gilbert, "Stereotype Persistence and Change Among College Students," *Journal of Abnormal and Social Psychology* 46 (1951):245–54.

Actually, it might be more simple to think of implicit personality theories as theories of stereotyped behaviors. We have certain stereotyped kinds of expectations for certain personalities. When we talk about implicit personality theories that people carry inside their heads, we are really talking about the stereotyped behaviors they expect from people who have specific personalities. If we expect a person with a gregarious personality to exhibit loud speaking behavior, expansive gestures, and great quantities of laughter, we have a stereotype in our heads of a gregarious person.

Richard Kalvar/Magnum Photos, Inc.

The implicit personality theory influences our actions when we meet someone we can classify as a certain type of personality.

Interpersonal Attraction

How attractive we are perceived as being and how attractive we perceive others to be plays a significant role in any interpersonal interaction. The degree to which we are willing to accept what another person says to us, as well as their willingness to accept our statements, is strongly related to the perceived attraction we feel for each other. Notice that we have used the phrase "perceived attraction" instead of referring to *attractiveness* as a quality that resides in a person. Unfortunately, in our society, we have come to speak of "attractive people," "attractive features," "attractive ideas," and the like, as though these things were attractive in and of themselves. However, this is not the case. Attractiveness is a quality that must be perceived in order to exist. The old cliché, "Beauty is in the eyes of the beholder," is more on target than many people realize.

How often have you heard someone make the following statement (or made it yourself): "I don't know what she (he) sees in him (her)"? We have all heard or made such a statement many times. The reason we frequently do not understand why someone finds a person to be attractive is because we are looking for an absolute quality of attractiveness in the person in question. Instead, we should be looking into ourselves and the person who sees the attractiveness, because attractiveness can only be perceived from the perspective of one's own background. Standards of attractiveness vary from culture to culture, from generation to generation, and from person to person. In spite of these differences in standards, we all appear to construct our perceptions of attractiveness with the same building blocks. There are three components of perceived attractiveness: a *social-liking component*, a *task-respect component*, and a *physical appearance component*.[49] We will discuss each of these components to make more clear the role of perceived attractiveness in interpersonal communication.

49. J. C. McCroskey and T. A. McCain, "The Measurement of Interpersonal Attraction," *Speech Monographs* 41 (1974):261–266.

Social-Liking Component

Whenever we make a statement such as "I like Becky," or "Mike is a great guy," we are expressing the *social-liking component* of perceived attractiveness. This component includes the degree to which we would like to have this person as a friend, how well we think we know the person, and how much we would like to meet the person. If you will think back to our discussion of social needs in chapter 1, you should recognize a parallel between this component and that set of needs. The social-liking component is, to a great degree, our response to our own social needs. As a person satisfies our social needs, we respond positively in terms of this component.

Task-Respect Component

This component involves a judgment about the expertise of an individual, most often relative to a given task. How qualified is the person to do a job? Do I want to work with this person? Can I depend on this person in a working relationship? These are the questions that are combined into a *task-respect response* to a person, and which, together, form one component of perceived attractiveness. Again, thinking back to our discussion of needs in chapter 1, you can see the parallel between this component and the ego needs discussed there. To respect another person, we evaluate that person in the light of our own self-perception, as was mentioned in chapter 3. Thus, the higher our own self-esteem, the more likely we are to perceive people positively on the task-respect component of perceived attractiveness.

Physical Appearance Component

When people talk of attractiveness, this is the component usually thought of. A person's physical characteristics are obvious to any observer and are the first stimuli we usually respond to when meeting a person for the first time. As will be discussed in greater detail in chapter 6, interpersonal communication is greatly affected by physical appearance. This is so, in great part, because the perceived attractiveness of a person is partially based upon a

Similarity of appearance often
determines how attractive we
find others.

Perceiving and Understanding Others

judgment of physical appearance. This points up the importance of paying attention to appearance, not because it is the sole determiner of our success as a communicator, but because it is one of the building blocks of attractiveness.

One of the major determiners of the extent to which people perceive us (or we perceive others) as attractive or unattractive is the extent to which we are similar or dissimilar to them. As we are more similar to a person, "homophily" is said to exist in an interpersonal relationship. As we are less similar to a person, "heterophily" is said to exist. The greater the homophily in a relationship, the greater the likelihood of the parties perceiving each other as attractive. The greater the heterophily in a relationship, the lower the likelihood of the parties perceiving each other as attractive.

50. J. C. McCroskey, V. P. Richmond, and J. A. Daly, "The Measurement of Perceived Homophily in Interpersonal Communication," *Human Communication Research* 1 (1975):323–332.

We base our judgment of similarity/dissimilarity upon the relative similarities in attitudes, family and socioeconomic background, physical attractiveness, and the like.[50] Contrary to popular opinion, opposites do not always attract. In fact, when opposites do attract, that attraction is likely to be short-lived because the necessary degree of homophily is not present in the relationship. This is why it is so important for us to establish common ground between ourselves and others in interpersonal relationships and to continue to develop common interests over time. If we do not strive for this, it is possible, and even likely, that over time, as each of us develops different interests and attitudes, the initial attraction that brought us together may diminish, resulting in a termination of the relationship.

How Does Perception Affect Interpersonal Communication?

Effect of Stability

One of the primary characteristics of our perceptions of people is that those perceptions are essentially very stable. Of course, this fits in with our need for a consistent, well-ordered world. The reason we develop our ordered and structured perceptions in the first place is to have order and consistency within a random, chaotic world of stimuli. It is not very likely that we will lose sight of our perceptions. Consequently, we tend to avoid information that will upset or contradict those perceptions.[51] We tend to distort what we see to support out perceptions, or at least to avoid contradicting them.

51. Judson Mills, "Interest in Supporting and Discrepant Information," in *Theories of Cognitive Consistency: A Sourcebook,* ed. Robert P. Ableson, Elliot Aronson, William J. McGuire, Theodore M. Newcomb, Milton J. Rosenberg, and Percy H. Tannenbaum (Chicago: Rand McNally & Co., 1968), pp. 771–76.

If Professor Smith has developed the perception of one of his colleagues as a kind, well-mannered, thoughtful person, it is not very likely that he will easily cope with information suggesting that his colleague cheats on his wife, drinks to excess, and is sometimes irresponsible. Rather, he will try to rationalize or distort the information so that he can make it consistent with his previous perception. In fact, he will even avoid information that contradicts his previous perception of this person, if possible. Our perceptions are stable and remain relatively constant, and we do whatever we can to make them so.

Our perception of things is affected by our culture in a number of ways. Erickson suggested that there are at least three reasons our culture may cause us to perceive one object instead of another.[52] First, an object may have greater meaning because of cultural associations. Second, of two objects, the one that occurs more frequently is likely to be perceived more easily than the other. Finally, because of cultural association and/or previous associations, there may be a more pleasant association related to one object than to another.

A study by Hudson suggests that we actually see photographs differently according to the culture we grow up in.[53] Hudson administered photographs to white and black subjects; the former group attended school, and the latter did not. He discovered that the subjects who attended school could see the pictures three-dimensionally, whereas the subjects not attending school did not. Evidently, the people who did not attend school were culturally isolated from photographs and thus had not learned to perceive photographs three-dimensionally. Thus, even the way in which we perceive a physical object can be affected by the kind of cultural experiences we have had.

Also of interest to us in interpersonal communication is the effect of culture on our perception of emotions in other people. People from rural cultures perceive different emotions than do persons from urban cultures when looking at the same picture.[54] For example, when looking at pictures with intense anger in arguments rural people tend to perceive less tension in the photographs than do urban dwellers. Differences of this sort could significantly affect interaction between people, as our sensitivity to different emotions can vary according to our backgrounds.

One of the reasons our perceptions are stable is of importance in interpersonal communication. As discussed in chapter 3, it is possible to develop a self-image that in its turn creates a self-fulfilling prophecy. We engage in behaviors that ensure that we will be what we perceive ourselves to be. Likewise, we can have self-fulfilling prophecies about the people with whom we communicate interpersonally.[55] Because of the self-fulfilling nature of our perceptions of other people, it appears that the following kind of relationship can frequently occur in interpersonal communication: Peggy develops a perception of Michelle in which Michelle is perceived as warm and friendly. Peggy's set of predictions for Michelle was suggested by her

Culture and Perception

52. C. W. Erickson, *Concepts of Personality* (Chicago: Aldine Press, 1963), pp. 30–60.

53. W. Hudson, "Pictorial Depth Perception in Sub-Cultural Groups in Africa," *Journal of Social Psychology* 52 (1960):183–208.

54. Leigh M. Triandis and William W. Lambert, "Source of Frustration and Targets of Aggression: A Cross Culture Study," *Journal of Abnormal and Social Psychology* 62, no. 3 (1961):640–48.

Self-Fulfilling Prophecy

55. John W. Kinch, "A Formalized Theory of the Self-Concept," *American Journal of Sociology*, January 1973.

implicit personality theories. Therefore, Peggy communicates in a warm and friendly way with Michelle because she perceives Michelle as warm and friendly. As a result of Peggy's warm and friendly communication behavior, Michelle responds similarly, thus fulfilling Peggy's expectations.

This kind of self-fulfilling cycle can occur with other perceived communication behavior, such as hostility or stupidity, as well as with warm and friendly behavior. It is not unusual for a teacher to perceive a student in a class as intelligent. From that point on, the student can do no wrong in class; the teacher knows that the student is intelligent, thus the interactions with that student will be at such a level that the teacher will cause the student to engage in behaviors the teacher perceives as intelligent because of the self-fulfilling cycle. Horribly enough, the reverse can happen. That is to say, the teacher can have prior expectations of stupidity and slowness for a student and communicate in ways that will cause the student to confirm the teacher's expectations of ignorance or slowness.[56]

56. Ibid.

Openness in Communication

57. R. Wayne Pace and Robert R. Boren, *The Human Transaction* (Glenview, Ill.; Scott, Foresman & Co., 1973); John R. Wenberg and William W. Wilmot, *The Personal Communication Process* (New York: John Wiley & Sons, Inc., 1973).

58. Kinch, "Formalized Theory."

In chapter 3 we, as do many writers of interpersonal communication textbooks,[57] suggested the value of open, trusting, and self-revealing communication. Sometimes this is simply called for as an absolute good. We would like to suggest that open, honest, and revealing communication can be either effective or ineffective, depending upon the context of the interaction. It can, for example, be very effective in eliciting trust from the people with whom we are communicating, as we indicated in chapter 3.

For the reason we have just discussed in terms of self-fulfilling cycles, by engaging in open, trusting, and self-revealing communication, we can cause others to perceive us as trustworthy, honest, and open.[58] This, in turn, is more likely to cause the others to communicate similarly. But this will not always work. Some communication contexts are competitive in nature, and in some such contexts there necessarily has to be a winner and a loser. In those situations it may not be possible to have completely open, honest communication between parties. However, for those situations in which we are trying to establish friendships and/or to continue them, the frank, open approach can certainly be effective communication behavior.

It is important to understand that a perception of trust between people is also based on predictability, which, in our estimation, is in keeping with and relates to a primary need discussed in chapter 1 and again in this chapter. That is our need for consistency in the world about us. We need to be able to predict behavior if we are to satisfy our needs. As we can predict behavior in other people, we trust them more because we are more able to satisfy our needs. Likewise, as they can predict our behavior, they trust us more for the same reason. Although predictability will not necessarily guarantee trust, it appears that trust is impossible without it. Thus, we can view predictability as a necessary ingredient for trust, even though it alone may not bring about trust.

It is entirely possible, then, that by constructing open, honest, and revealing messages about ourselves, we enable people to know us better. This in turn gives them a kind of hold over us to the extent of ensuring the kind of behavior we will engage in, and it certainly enables them to predict our behavior better. Thus, they should be able to trust us more. By having a trusting perception of us, they may respond to us in a more open manner.

While we will discuss trust in communication more fully in chapter 8, a brief comment is in order at this time. It would appear that we could use open and revelatory messages to disclose more about ourselves to those with whom we are interacting. By doing this, we allow them to know us better, predict our behavior more accurately and, hopefully, trust us more. We are not suggesting that you should constantly talk about yourself to everyone. However, it is possible to let others know "where your head is" by engaging in open, nondefensive communication with them. We do this through both verbal and nonverbal messages. We simply let others know how we really feel about ourselves, them, and the things we discuss. Thus, it is possible that open, honest, revelatory messages can in some contexts (which do not involve competition) result in an honest, trusting response from others.

SUMMARY

At this point we hope you can see that the process of perception plays an incredibly important role in interpersonal communication. It is through perception that others form their impression of us. These impressions subsequently condition the way in which we behave toward one another, and the ways in which we have toward one another reinforce our perceptions. Our perceptions are the result of our need to be able to predict and our need for consistency in the world. We will perceive whatever we need to perceive to ensure the consistency we need. Likewise, we hope it is now clear that a part of this consistency includes the necessity for explaining relationships and attaching meaning to those relationships. All this is a part of the perceptual process.

The entire process of perception and the discussion of it in this chapter should also dramatize the point that we do not ever "tell it like it is." We only "tell it the way we perceive it." And we perceive according to our past histories, language systems, and categorization systems, with all our built-in biases and expectations. These condition the way we see, hear, feel, smell, and taste the world. Likewise, everything from our past conditions the way we communicate interpersonally, because it conditions the way we perceive everything interpersonally.

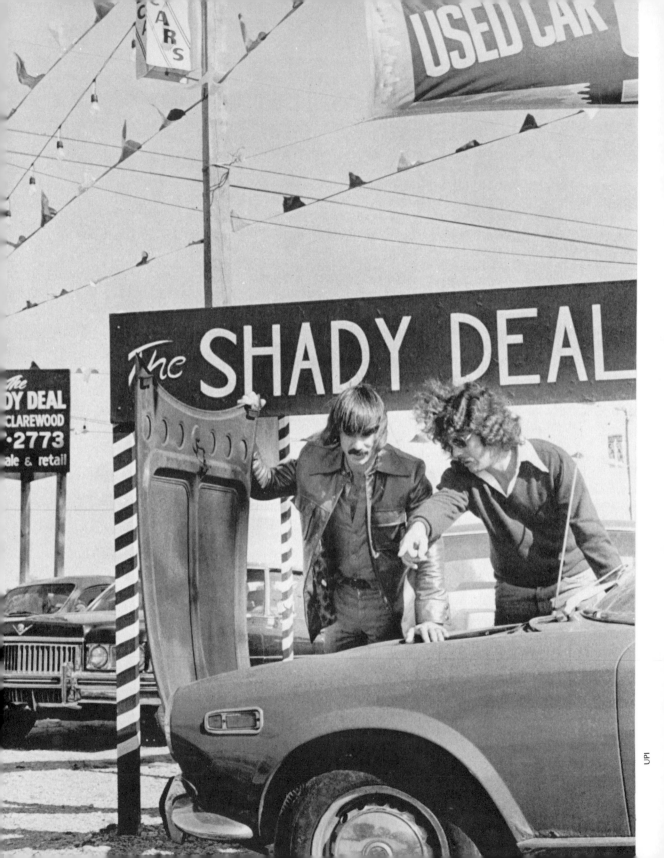

5

Words and Meaning

Probably the most important ability of human beings is the production of spoken language. From virtually the day we are born, we are confronted by other human beings making noises at us in an attempt to influence us. No doubt one of the things about us that would most impress a visitor from another planet would be our speech behavior. The use of words in the communication process is so significant that Americans spend approximately twelve years in school (not including college) formally studying language usage.

One of the big events in every parent's life is that moment when a child utters the first word. Simply being able to speak a word is an important event in the lives of human beings. It should be, too, because words play an important role in our lives. It is very likely that the first spoken words were used to position other people behind trees, indicate the location of water, and warn others of danger. Words were one of mankind's most useful survival tools, and this remains true. Today we still employ words to obtain food and housing and to defend ourselves against other people. Although our use of words has probably made the defense of ourselves and the acquisition of food and housing more indirect processes than they used to be, words are, if anything, more useful in survival behavior than in earlier times.

We make use of words in some very interesting ways. During the latter part of the winter of 1974, President Nixon, in a press conference, demonstrated this. At the time he was the target of considerable criticism from many different groups, as, later, was President Carter, because of fuel shortages. People were upset because of the shortage of gasoline and heating fuel. During his press conference, Nixon made the following statement: "The crisis is over, but we still have a problem." Essentially, Nixon was trying to change reality by changing the word used to describe it. The lines in front of gasoline stations, the shortage of heating fuel, and the higher cost of fuel continued, as they had all winter. However, the President was attempting to say that this situation no longer existed because he had called it by a different name. Frequently this strategy will work, and many politicians use it effectively. Many people, because of their lack of awareness of how words can affect us, will accept that conditions have changed because the words relating to them have been changed.

How do words enable us to change someone's perception of reality? What is it about the words *love, democracy,* or *Communism* that permits us to build beautiful relationships, destroy a life, start a war, or work for peace? Why are words so powerful? These are not academic questions, any more than the question of how we live and breathe is academic. We are talking about a basic factor in our existence: the way in which we use a tool developed hundreds of thousands, and possibly millions, of years ago to manipulate our environment and ensure our survival. To answer these and other questions, we will consider the nature of words and how we use and are affected by them in interpersonal communication.

Before we discuss the nature of words in interpersonal communication, we should consider the larger system of which words are a part—language. Although many people commonly refer to "*language* and *words* as if they were synonymous, linguists and psycholinguists suggest that they are not. Rather, *language* is a processing system in which there are two subsystems interacting to produce meaning. The first is *syntax,* which consists of the rules that enable us to determine word order and relationships among units such as verbs, nouns, and adverbs, and permits us to interpret sentences in which words have been combined. This subsystem is sometimes called "grammar."[1] Second, there is our *vocabulary,* or meaningful units or words we have learned.[2] This can be thought of as a storehouse of message units that need to be combined so that messages can be produced. Language, then, is a system for producing and interpreting messages. This is accomplished by using words and grammar together, because neither alone is sufficient for communication.

The system of grammar studied by linguists and psycholinguists is at this time somewhat removed from the pragmatic contexts of interpersonal communication. On the other hand, the study of how words come to acquire meaning and how they can affect us in interpersonal communication can be quite useful. Although there is not complete agreement among all scholars about how words acquire meaning and how they affect us,[3] we will focus here upon some of the explanations of meaning we feel are of value in interpersonal communication.

1. Dan I. Slobin, *Psycholinguistics* (Glenview, Ill.: Scott, Foresman & Co., 1971), pp. 15–20.

2. Ibid.

3. Harold J. Vetter, *Language Behavior and Communication* (Itasca, Ill.: F. E. Peacock Publishers, Inc., 1969), p. 66.

The Nature of Words

For the sake of simplicity, words can be thought of as *minimal units of meaning.* In addition, words are symbol behaviors people produce that are arbitrary in nature, can relate to some physical reality outside the person, and are used to change other people. Such symbols as words, Morse code, music notation, and even gestures refer to, or stand for, something else,[4]—something beyond themselves. They suggest some reality relevant to the people using them. The "something else" may be events outside or inside the individual. *Words are symbols that indirectly make one thing stand for another.* We will be considering words as symbols used to refer to events, concepts. or feelings to influence people in the interpersonal communication process.

Consider the word *book*—a symbol used to stand for the object you are looking at right now. Whenever we hear the word, we tend to think of objects that have many leaves of paper, writing in them, consecutive numbering, and (sometimes) covers that are harder than the inside pages. Whether or not you think of the things just listed when you hear the word *book,* notice that the word is used to represent or refer to something else that does not have to be present for you to think of it when the word is used. This is essentially what words are all about. They are a means of being able to refer to something without actually having to have the something present.

We are talking about, far more than just a reference process, however, because when we use the word *book,* what comes to mind will vary from person to person. One person may think of the Bible, another may think of a

4. Herbert Landar, *Language and Culture* (New York: Oxford University Press, Inc., 1966), p. 35.

Associations with a given word vary from person to person.

textbook, another may think of an erotic novel, and still another may think of betting on horses. It is this aspect of words that poses a problem for language theorists and language users alike. It is a rather simple matter to explain the process of reference—the process of how we make a symbol stand for something. It is another matter entirely to explain the notion of meaning, or how words cause responses in people.

The phenomenon of generating a variety of meanings in different people through the use of the same word is probably the most perplexing and intriguing aspect of language. What this really means for us is that we cannot simply use a word and always get the same response to it from different people, or even from the same person at different times. In addition to thinking of a word in terms of a symbol that symbolizes something, we should also think of a word or a symbol in any language as a stimulus we use and direct toward another person to produce a response.

In chapter 1 we defined communication as a process in which we were employing a commonly accepted symbol system to influence other people's behavior. That is the key to understanding words. If we want a glass of water, most of us say to someone who is near a faucet, "Would you please get me a drink of water?" The reason we utter those words is because we are under the impression that by doing so we stir up responses and associations in the other person that cause them to comply with our request.

Most languages are the result of a long history and, having developed over time, are identified closely with specific culture groups. People within a culture develop their own grammar and word meanings. It is interesting to note that we so identify people and their language that we use the same word to designate both the people and their language. For example, the English speak English, and the French speak French. Because language systems have developed over time, they become almost sacred in the minds of the people who speak and write them—so much so that people are inclined to be highly critical of those who deviate from common practices in their use of language.

We should also note the great number of different languages there are. The more obvious ones include the languages associated specifically with countries, such as French, German, Spanish, English, Russian, and Italian, to say nothing of the vast number of tribal and group languages emanating from smaller groups in various countries throughout the world. There also are languages of subcultures within the United States, such as those of blacks, Chicanos, and American Indians. We will discuss the relationship of language and culture later. In addition to those languages, however, there are other kinds of languages that function in much the manner we have been discussing—Morse code, which we alluded to earlier, consisting of symbols that are not spoken words but rather dots and dashes; semaphore codes consisting of flags held at different angles to each other to symbolize letters; and road signs, symbolic in form, to mention but a few.

The Nature of Meaning in Words

Meaning Is Arbitrary

5. Lewis Carroll, *Alice's Adventures in Wonderland, Through the Looking Glass, and The Hunting of the Snark* (New York: Modern Library, Inc., 1925), pp. 246–47.

6. Charles E. Osgood, "The Nature and Measurement of Meaning," *Psychological Bulletin* 49 (May 1952):197–206.

7. Alfred Korzybski, *Science and Sanity* (Lakeville, Conn.: International Non-Aristotelian Library, 1947).

8. S. I. Hayakawa, *Language in Thought and Action*, 2d ed. (New York: Harcourt, Brace and World, 1964).

9. C. K. Ogden and I. A. Richards, *The Meaning of Meaning* (New York: Harcourt, Brace and Co., 1946), p. 11.

Lewis Carroll[5] caused Humpty Dumpty to define meaning and words when he wrote, " 'When I use a word,' Humpty Dumpty said in a very scornful tone, 'it means just what I choose it to mean—neither more nor less.' 'The question is,' said Alice, 'whether you can make words mean so many different things.' 'The question is,' said Humpty Dumpty, 'who is to be master, that's all.' " Carroll suggested that the meaning of a word is arbitrary.

This view of language is one in which words by themselves have no meaning. Whatever meaning a word has is the meaning we give to it.[6] When we indicated earlier that words were symbols and suggested that a symbol was something that stood for something else, we were anticipating this idea. A symbol stands for something else—it has no meaning itself. It only *refers* to some other thing. Likewise, it should be clear that the person who makes it stand for something else is the person who uses it. Starting with Korzybski[7] through present-day general semanticists, we repeatedly find the statements, "The word is not the thing," and "The map is not the territory."[8] Essentially, language scholars make the point that the meaning of words is in us, and that the word itself does not have any meaning. The general semanticists frequently go considerably beyond this and suggest a philosophy that can be based upon their approach to language, but their admonition holds. Our language merely refers to other things.[9] It is a map that represents some reality apart from itself.

If words actually contained meanings, it would be possible for any of us in one culture to communicate with someone in another culture without difficulty. Someone who speaks English would be able to communicate effectively with someone who speaks German because the words themselves would have meaning. This, of course, is not the case. If we wish to converse with someone from Germany about a table (unless that person has acquired a knowledge of our English language), we need to use the word *Tisch* rather than the word *table*. Also, it is not very likely that we will understand what the person from Germany is talking about when he or she says *Baum*. Of course, the German speaker will be frustrated because we do not recognize the reference to an object that is composed of wood, grows with roots in the ground, has leaves, and grows tall. This example should show that words of themselves do not contain meaning; it is, rather, we ourselves who are vessels of meaning.

It should be obvious that the meanings we have for words are totally arbitrary. We could just as easily use the word *giraffe* as the word *bicycle* to represent a two-wheeled object with pedals and handlebars that one sits up on and rides. As long as everyone agreed that the word would apply to the same object, there would be no difficulty in using a word other than *bicycle* to represent the object. Many children develop their own language in which they substitute different words for those normally used. This is something of a game and they get a great kick out of it, and, of course, make fun of adults in so doing. They are also acting out the principle of arbitrary meaning.

Of course, Carroll also had another interesting point, and that was the question of who is to be the master. Will we control our words, or will our words control us? Later we will consider the effect of words upon users as compared with our present discussion of how people use the words.

Meaning Is Learned

Our position thus far has been that people acquire meanings for words. At this time, it is very difficult to say with certainty how we acquire meaning.[10] To answer this question with absolute assurance, we would need some way to open a person's brain and peer into it while he or she are acquiring meaning and actually look at the process (assuming there is a physical process to look at). This is not possible, so we cannot say for sure how meaning is acquired, although there are many theories about meaning from which to select.

There is fairly persuasive evidence, which we accept as best, explaining how word meaning develops. This approach to meaning is based upon learning theory and relies upon the stimulus-response paradigm in which we associate meanings (responses) with words (stimuli).[11]

10. Slobin, *Psycholinguistics*, p. 68.

11. Charles E. Osgood, *Method and Theory in Experimental Psychology*, (New York: Oxford University Press, Inc., 1953), p. 396.

Figure 5.1

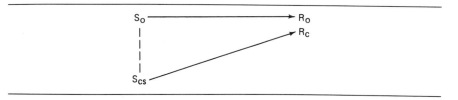

This process is depicted in figure 5.1. The original stimulus (S_0), which produced an original response (R_0), is paired, or associated with, a conditioned symbol stimulus (S_{cs}). As a result of this association, the conditioned symbol stimulus (S_{cs}) will elicit a conditioned response (R_c), which is similar to the original response (R_0).[12]

12. Osgood, "Nature and Measurement of Meaning," p. 205.

A piece of meat that has been carved from a steer, placed on a charcoal-heated grill, and done to a sizzle produces a desire to eat and perhaps even salivation. By pairing the word *steak* (S_{cs}) with the above-mentioned object (S_0) over time, the mouth-watering response that originally resulted from the original stimulus (R_0) can, through association, be elicited by the use of the word *steak*.

The simple process of association by itself will not completely explain all meaning; nor will it explain how we learn grammar.[13] However, it goes a long way toward explaining how we learn meaning, especially if we can

13. Noam Chomsky, *Aspects of the Theory of Syntax* (Cambridge, Mass: M.I.T. Press, 1965), p. 59.

Bruce Quist

The word *mother* may not be perceived positively if our past associations include too many disagreeable experiences with our female parent.

think in terms of complex groups of associations for each word. Imagine a *series of associations over time* as explaining our responses to words.

The word *mother* is one for which, when we hear it, we can have any number of kinds of responses. For many people the word *mother* produces a response that is warm and refers to a female parent. It includes any number of associations: the female parent as a source of comfort when comforting was needed; as a provider of wholesome meals; as the one who has been present at our special events; and so much more. All of these associations with the word *mother* have over time been acquired by many of us. To grasp fully what this means, it is necessary for us to try to imagine a very complex combination of all of these associations into one single response, or collection of responses, to the symbol *mother*.

This complex response is analogous to a cake. A cake is composed of many ingredients that are added at various times during preparation. The ultimate product of all of these ingredients bears little or no resemblance to the individual ingredients themselves. Our response to words is very similar to that. The individual associations and responses we have relative to a word are like the ingredients of the baked cake, merged into a response-as-a-whole, which in turn bears little, if any, resemblance to the original ingredients—the associations and responses.

14. W. D. Mink, "Semantic Generalization as Related to Word Association," *Psychological Reports* 12 (1963):59–67.

15. Carolyn K. Staats and Arthur W. Staats, "Meaning Established by Classical Conditioning," *Journal of Experimental Psychology* 54 (1957):74–80.

16. Ogden and Richards, *The Meaning of Meaning*, p. 11.

This is a very complex process and one that is very difficult to pin down empirically, and yet some studies suggest that, by providing new associations with a word, we can alter or change the response to the word.[14] Different associations and different experiences associated with words can change our responses to the words.[15] How this happens within our minds, we are not sure. We accept that it does happen, nevertheless.

One of the earlier attempts to diagram the process of meaning was that by Ogden and Richards.[16] They suggested that there is a *reference process* that occurs between a symbol and the thing symbolized. To represent this process, they created a *triangle of meaning* similar to that pictured in figure 5.2. The triangle of meaning includes the *referent* (the object referred to by the symbol), the *reference process* (the thought process by which we form associations), and the *symbol*. The reference process is a mental process in which we connect the thing symbolized with the symbol itself. The dotted line between the symbol and the referent indicates that if there is a connection between the object and the symbol, it is the person who does the connecting. *There is no direct connection between the object and its symbol.* This is the point of our discussion of the arbitrary nature of word meaning. If there is a connection between the thing and the symbol, it is through a referential process that occurs within the mind of the individual acquiring the meaning; and this is probably the result of an association process.

Figure 5.2

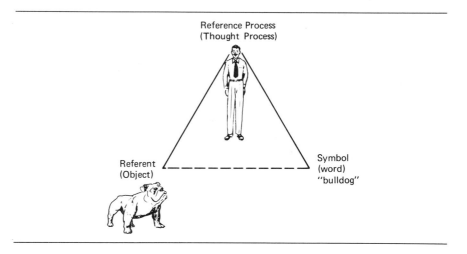

This process results in each of us having a very different meaning for every word we learn. This is evident with the word *broadcaster*. The word *broadcaster* elicits a response having something to do with radio and television from most people. In our communication classes we have asked students what the word *broadcaster* means to them. The responses have usually concerned radio and television. Students think of disc jockeys, announcers, and newscasters. In most classes, we also have usually had one or two people who tentatively raised their hands and suggested that there might be another meaning for the word. They suggested that a broadcaster is a piece of machinery used to sow seed in gardens or on farms.

Both responses are correct. A broadcaster may well be a disc jockey. Some people respond to *broadcaster* this way because they have a series of associations concerning a person who works in radio or television. The association principle is also true, of course, with a person who considers the word *broadcaster* to represent the machinery for sowing seed. Since meanings are learned through association, they are dependent upon our individual fields of experience.[17] If we have a field of experience that includes farming and farm practices, we will probably have associations for the word *broadcaster* that have to do with sowing seed.

If we return to a consideration of the word *mother*, it must be obvious that not everyone has had warm experiences with their female parents. Some have experienced a female parent who is cold, unloving, and possibly even brutal. A person who has had this kind of childhood will have a response toward the word *mother* very different from that of someone who has known a warm, sensitive, loving female parent.

17. Wilbur Schramm, "How Communication Works," in *The Process and Effects of Mass Communication*, ed. Wilbur Schramm (Urbana, Ill.: University of Illinois Press, 1955), p. 6.

Connotative Meaning

These emotional associations that affect responses to words result in what are called *connotative meanings* by many language scholars. The connotation of a word has typically been assumed to represent subjective responses to words. These include the emotional associations one person has with a word that no other person has.[18] These are the responses that are peculiar to each of us because of our own unique experiences and associations.

18. Joseph DeVito, *The Psychology of Speech and Language* (New York: Random House, Inc., 1970), pp. 12–13.

Denotative Meaning

Typically, language scholars have also indicated that there is another kind of meaning for a word. This is called *denotative meaning*. *Denotation* refers to what is commonly called the "dictionary meaning" of words. "Dictionary meanings" are simply a record of the ways most people use words. The first definition given in a dictionary reflects the most common usage of a word (and the most common associations), the second definition the next most common, and so on. Some people have even referred to this as "objective meaning," a meaning that includes properties of concepts but no emotional responses.[19]

If we are to communicate effectively with another person, the primary concern regarding language should be one to choose words for which the recipients of our message have connotations similar to ours. However, we should not assume that the way in which we have learned a word is necessarily the way other people have learned the word. Consequently, their responses to words will not necessarily be similar to our responses.

19. John B. Carroll, *Language and Thought* (Englewood Cliffs, N.J.: Prentice-Hall, Inc., 1964), pp. 26–28.

We can use a dictionary to gain an understanding of some of the associations people have for words so that we might more effectively employ words to which people will respond the way we expect them to. However, while we may learn something about the way words are used from a dictionary, we also must keep in mind that when the dictionary is published, it is already out of date. Individual words are constantly changing in respect to the way people use them. Although dictionaries can be a guide to meaning, they should always be regarded with some degree of caution.

Dimensions of Meaning

20. Donald K. Darnell, "Semantic Differentiation," in *Methods of Research in Communication,* ed. Philip Emmert and William D. Brooks (Boston: Houghton Mifflin Co., 1970), p. 181.

21. Charles E. Osgood, George J. Suci, and Percy H. Tannenbaum, *The Measurement of Meaning* (Urbana, Ill.: University of Illinois Press, 1957).

It is difficult to discuss meaning adequately without considering what has become one of the classic approaches to meaning, developed by Charles Osgood and his associates. This approach was based upon the associational view of meaning and has resulted in considerable amounts of empirical research.[20] Osgood, Suci, and Tannenbaum[21] presented evidence that indicated the existence of dimensions of meaning for words. Another way of thinking about these dimensions is to consider them the components, or building blocks, that make up meaning. An exposition of the way these components were discovered should make them more understandable.

Osgood and his associates reasoned that if we try to ask someone what a word means, the person will usually try to define it by using many different words and associations he or she has for that given word. Many of the words used to define other words are adjectives. For instance, if we asked you to define *ice cream,* you might use adjectives like cold, soft, and *good.* Osgood, Suci, and Tannenbaum took that procedure of defining through the use of adjectives a little further and made it more formal. They presented the subjects in their studies with words the meaning of which they wanted to measure, accompanied by long lists of adjectives.

These adjectives were presented to the subjects as bipolar scales (as in figure 5.3), which meant that every adjective had an opposite. If *cold* were used, its bipolar opposite was *hot.* If *soft* were used, so was *hard.* Subjects were asked to indicate on a seven-point scale the extent to which they thought the adjectives applied to the concept or word being rated. As a result of this kind of research, Osgood, Suci, and Tannenbaum discovered the existence of what they called three dimensions of meaning.

The dimensions, or elements, of meaning include an *evaluative component,* a *potency component,* and an *activity component.* The *evaluative* component in words involves a good-bad/valuable-worthless response to words. An element of meaning for every word we respond to is our positive-negative response to it. The *potency* component relates to strength and power. Part of our response to words has to do with how strong or weak we perceive the referents to be. *Activity,* the third component, involves the dynamism, or activity level, perceived in the referent of the word. This third part of our response to words is a perception of activeness/passiveness.

Mother	1	2	3	4	5	6	7	
Good	X	—	—	—	—	—	—	Bad
Fast	—	X	—	—	—	—	—	Slow
Valuable	X	—	—	—	—	—	—	Worthless
Hard	—	X	—	—	—	—	—	Soft
Passive	—	—	—	—	—	X	—	Active
Powerful	—	X	—	—	—	—	—	Weak

Good and *valuable* tap the evaluative component,
fast and *passive* the activity component, and
hard and *powerful* the potency component.

The meaning of any given word to us is a composite of these components, of course, and each of these components is affected by our previous experiences. As earlier indicated, our experiences provide us with associations for every word. Let us return to our example of the word *mother*. If our female parent were a person who did things for us when we were children, comforted us when we were hurt, dressed us warmly when it was cold, took us to movies, and had birthday parties for us (and other things desired by children), she was a person who satisfied our needs to a great extent. Thus, the evaluative component of our response to the word "mother" would probably be very positive (as marked in figure 5.3). Likewise, if our female parent has been somewhat dominant in our home, planned family activities, and has generally "taken charge," we would develop a perception of strength as opposed to weakness within the potency component. Finally, if our female parent belonged to many organizations, rushed from meeting to meeting, and chauffeured us from place to place, we would probably have a perception of her as an active rather than a passive person. Thus, the activity component of our response to the word *mother* would tend toward the active rather than the passive end of the active-passive continuum. Thus, our total response to the word *mother* would be positive, strong, and active.

Using this framework of three components of meaning, it is possible for us to compare our meanings with others' meanings. Is our meaning more positive? Is it less active? Is it stronger? These components can become guidelines for us to follow in choosing words in interpersonal communication. Whenever we are experiencing difficulty communicating, we may find

Understanding a listener's connotative meanings of words enables the effective communicator to choose words that have positive associations for the listener.

Susan Meiselas/Magnum Photos, Inc.

we have used words that are too strong and active for the person we are trying to influence. While awareness of these components will not automatically provide answers to our problems, it can provide us with insight into probable responses to our words by others.

The findings of Osgood, Suci, and Tannenbaum have further practical implications. Their research made it possible to determine which of the components of meaning is the predominant one. Apparently, the *evaluative component* accounts for more of our response to words than the other two components combined.[22] This is important to us in interpersonal communication because it suggests that the meanings of words are, to a great extent, evaluative responses, and also that whenever we are using words in interpersonal communication, the people who are listening to us are having primarily positive-negative responses to our words. It is important for us, therefore, to understand the connotative meanings of words as they relate to those we wish to influence, in terms of what are positive and what are negative words for them. It does not make much sense to use language to which we know people are going to respond negatively because of their negative associations within the evaluative component of those words. Rather, if we are trying to be effective, it seems more reasonable to use words that have positive associations for our listeners so that their responses to our whole message will be positive.

22. Darnell, "Semantic Differentiation," p. 183.

Chapter 5

There are, of course, situations for which we might choose words that people respond to negatively. That kind of situation would occur when we are trying to keep someone from doing something, or when we are trying to cause people to perceive some concept as negative. When that is the situation, we choose words that fall somewhere on the negative end of the evaluative continuum and try to associate those words with the concept we want our listeners to reject. However, when we are trying to have people accept us and the concepts we are proposing, we want to associate words that are positively evaluated with ourselves and the concepts we support.[23]

23. Staats and Staats, "Meaning Established."

This frequently occurs in politics. A politician finds out (either through polling or through very sensitive listening to constituents) that voters perceive the word *busing* very negatively and the word *prosperity* very positively. Once an astute politician has discovered this, that person will take care, in all public speeches and personal interactions, to be verbally associated with prosperity, with its positive associations. Politicians assume that if they can associate themselves with prosperity, voters are more likely to accept them. Likewise, they will try to disassociate themselves verbally from the word *busing*, in hopes that they will become more acceptable to their constituents by rejecting a word that produces a negative response.

Another important finding of Osgood and his associates has to do with the dimensionality of language across cultures.[24] Although much research concerning the multiple dimensions of meaning has been conducted in the United States with American subjects, not all such research has been. Interestingly enough, it has been determined that the dimensions of meaning found to apply to English words in the United States apply similarly to the equivalents of those words as used in other languages and other cultures. It is very rare in the behavioral sciences to have universal findings across cultures, but the research on meaning using Osgood, Suci, and Tannenbaum's technique comes close to providing us with universal results. Whereas we ordinarily must amend or qualify our statements about interpersonal communication according to culture, it is probably fair to suggest that the kinds of responses we have been talking about in terms of meaning for words are as appropriate in Japanese as they are in American English. In every culture we can expect some very similar kinds of responses in terms of the components people use to respond to words.

24. Osgood, Suci, and Tannenbaum, *Measurement of Meaning*.

Brief Summary of Meaning

To arrive at the nature of meaning, we have considered four main points: (1) words are arbitrary regarding meaning; (2) words do not have meaning of themselves—their meaning resides in people; (3) this meaning develops through a process of association that is complex and built up over years of being conditioned to words; and (4) the associated meanings we have for words can be talked of in terms of three components: evaluation, potency, and activity. Our responses along these components are the result of the different experiences and associations we have had with words and are combined into a total response to words that we call meaning. A fifth feature of importance is that the principal component of words is the evaluative component, suggesting that people respond to words along a positive-negative continuum.

We Perceive through Words:
The Sapir-Whorf Hypothesis

An important question concerning the effect of language upon us is related to what has been termed the *Sapir-Whorf hypothesis*. The Sapir-Whorf hypothesis was developed by Benjamin Lee Whorf, with considerable input by Edward Sapir, a linguist. Whorf himself was not a scholar in the formal sense. Yet, in addition to his regular career as an insurance engineer, he developed a theory of language that still causes great stimulation among scholars.[25] The hypothesis developed by Sapir-Whorf has been neither totally proved nor totally disproved,[26] thirty-five years after its formal statement.

25. Benjamin Lee Whorf, "The Relation of Habitual Thought and Behavior to Language," in *Language, Thought and Reality*, ed. John B. Carroll (Cambridge, Mass.: M.I.T. Press, 1956), pp. 134–59.

26. Slobin, *Psycholinguistics*, pp. 120–33.

27. Benjamin Lee Whorf, "Science and Linguistics," in *Language, Thought and Reality*, pp. 207–19.

The notion proposed in this theory is that our perception of reality and the world around us is determined by the thought processes we use and that these thought processes are determined by the language system we have learned. This means that we perceive according to the words and language system we have learned.[27] Examples given are numerous. For instance, Eskimos have many different words for snow, whereas people who live in a southern climate in the United States may simply use one: the word *snow*. According to the Sapir-Whorf hypothesis, a person from the south who has only one word for snow will only see one kind of physical reality when confronted with samples of frozen moisture falling out of the sky. However, an Eskimo with a language that enables him or her to differentiate among many different kinds of snow with many different words will be able to see many different forms of snow. Skiers are able to distinguish and have words for somewhere up to about half-a-dozen different kinds of snow. For someone who grows up in the Midwest and is not a skier, however, *snow* usually refers to one of two types: wet snow and dry snow. A corollary of the theory that the words we learn determine the reality we perceive is that the environment in which our culture developed has shaped the language system our society later teaches us. Thus, we find ourselves faced with a circular process in which the reality that faced our ancestors shaped the language, and in turn, the language subsequently shapes the reality any of us are able to perceive because we developed within and learned a language system.

This theory is consistent with the discussion in chapter 4. As you recall, in that chapter we discussed the process of perception, and it was indicated that, according to some scholars, to perceive it is necessary for us to categorize. We use a language system to categorize the physical stimuli. This is what the Sapir-Whorf approach suggests. As we are confronted with numerous stimuli, we select among, categorize, and attach meaning to what we see, hear, and feel. We do this according to our language system.

A number of our students have complained that the first course in almost every discipline, whether it be in communication, psychology, chemistry, or history, consists of nothing but a lot of new words (and often these are new words referring to many familiar things). We would have to agree that this is probably the case. Beginning or introductory courses in most areas of study spend a great deal of time defining the jargon of the discipline. Every field appears to have its own words for use in talking about the phenomena studied in that particular field. Each of you has probably experienced and/or are experiencing the practice right now of learning new words to describe phenomena around you, and you are undoubtedly finding that this may be a necessary process. It is our feeling that basic courses focus upon providing to students beginning a discipline a new vocabulary because *it is necessary to have the language to discuss the concepts of that field effectively.* More specifically, it is not only necessary to have the language to *discuss* the concepts; it may be necessary to have the language if we are to *perceive* instances of the concepts to which the words refer.

The term *feedback* has become a popular word in recent years. It is, of course, a term people in communication are happy to see become popular because it is so much a part of our discipline. We wonder if people have not (in addition to learning and adopting the word *feedback*) in recent years also changed their perceptions of the way people relate to one another and interact with one another because of the use of the term. We cannot *prove* that the use of the term *feedback* in recent years has caused a change in the way people interact, but we suspect that this new word, and other definitions and concepts associated with it, may have affected the way people perceive communication.

Probably the most acceptable interpretation of the Sapir-Whorf hypothesis is the modified version of Whorf's original statement. Rather than suggesting that our thoughts are totally determined by our language, this version offers a facilitation approach that suggests that our language system makes it easier to think about some things than about other things.[28] This version of the Sapir-Whorf hypothesis does not say it is impossible for us to think certain thoughts or to perceive certain realities, but rather that our language system makes it easier for us to perceive some realities and think certain thoughts. The words we learn, and the meanings associated with them, do have an effect on the way we perceive things. Likewise, the structure of the language we learn affects the way we think about things.

It has always intrigued us that in the German language verbs usually come at the end of a sentence. To listen to and to understand German

28. Slobin, *Psycholinguistics,* p. 125.

speech requires that we use a kind of thought process different from that required for comprehending English, in which verbs typically follow the subject in a sentence. When listening to German, we must retain much more in our heads before we know what verb is being used. Is it possible that this wide difference in grammar causes differences in thought? We do not really know, but the modified approach to the Sapir-Whorf hypothesis seems reasonable to us. The structure of our language could affect the order in which we think about things and thus, the way in which we perceive the world.

The meanings of the words we have acquired through the years would seem to have similar effects. It is possible that the combined effects of language structure and word meanings could facilitate our thinking about some things more easily than others. It has been said that you cannot translate a poem from one language to another. Simply translating the words does not translate the essence of the poem. Possibly, poets have meant that thoughts in one language may not be expressible in the word equivalents of another language. This does not necessarily mean that thoughts in one language are impossible to express in another language, but rather that the same thought would have to be expressed very differently.

What does this theory mean to us in interpersonal communication? Simply this: we have all grown up within a specific language system, and each person in any interpersonal situation may have grown up in more than one language system. (We all come from our own subcultures, in which we have learned our languages under different circumstances. Consequently, our language systems condition us to think differently about things, or at least facilitate our thinking about different things.) We should always be concerned with the nature of the language system of the persons with whom we communicate. Does their language system hinder thinking some thoughts? Do they lack certain words, which prevents them from perceiving some things we perceive? These same questions should be applied to ourselves. Do the persons with whom we talk use words and language structure that are unfamiliar to us? If so, could this be the reason we do not see things the way they do? If we begin to suspect this may be the case, it may be desirable to try to learn their language system, or at least try to understand it better. This may enable us to understand and resolve differences more easily.

How Words Affect Interpersonal Communication

At this point you should better understand the nature of words and how words come to have meaning for us through symbolization and association processes. We will now consider the effect of the symbolization process on us in interpersonal communication.

Excellent examples of the modified Sapir-Whorf hypothesis abound in America. We have cultural groups such as blacks, WASPs, males, females, Spanish-Americans, Japanese-Americans, and American Indians. The culture of a person, be it a majority or minority culture, has a significant effect upon language usage. Arabs have six thousand words for *camel*. Our category systems are very much bound up in our vocabularies.

Andrea Rich suggests that our symbol system can be viewed as an extension of culture.[29] We feel that words permit us to express those things that are of importance in our culture. Because, as discussed earlier, the weather is an important factor in the Eskimo culture, they have developed a vocabulary that reflects this and have a number of terms for ice and snow, whereas a person growing up in the Midwest may only be able to distinguish two kinds of snow. The difference is the result of the differing importance of snow in the cultures. Rich concludes that "language, then, our conventionally agreed-on system of symbols, codes our experience; enables us to communicate that experience to others; structures our thoughts, perceptions, and actions; and serves both as an expression of and an influence on our culture."[30]

The kind of problems resulting from cultural differences in word meaning is made more clear by the experimental finding that Italians react to the words *thieves* and *criminals* as having a more successful and less foolish connotation than is the case for most Americans.[31] This may suggest a more generally positive perception of criminals in Italy than in the United States. Perhaps Italians and Americans, when communicating about criminal activities, have difficulty achieving understanding if they are unaware of this difference in the perception of these words.

A similar problem exists between WASPs and ethnic minorities in our country. Blacks, for instance, appear to have learned words in a different manner from whites. It has been suggested that many adult blacks function linguistically within the context of two different language systems: black language and a white language.[32] Depending on the socioeconomic level of an individual black person in America, he or she may function in the context of at least three language systems—a language system referred to as standard American English, another language system common to blacks living in ghettos in America, and still another language system of middle- and upper-class blacks. It is possible, however, that the language system of middle- and upper-class blacks is more comparable to standard American English than to anything else.

It is necessary for members of different cultural groups to take into consideration the existence of different responses to the same words when communicating interpersonally with members of another cultural group. Lewit and Abner suggested that cooperation is possible when words mean the same to both whites and blacks.[33] Cooperation and trust may fail to be

29. Andrea Rich, *Interracial Communication* (New York: Harper & Row Publishers, Inc., 1974), p. 129.

30. Ibid., p. 131.

31. Ephraim Rosen, "A Cross-Cultural Study of Semantic Profiles and Attitude Differences: (Italy)," *Journal of Social Psychology* 49 (1959):137–44.

32. David Lewit and Edward Abner, "Black-White Semantic Differences and Interracial Communication," *Journal of Applied Psychology* 1, no. 3 (1971):276.

33. Ibid.

© Leonard Freed/Magnum Photos, Inc.

Interpersonal communication between cultures is hampered by the differing perceptions of words.

produced, however, in spontaneous, natural situations if the interacting person hears familiar words but infers meanings different from those of the speaker. This problem is not simply one arising between whites and blacks. This problem is present whenever members of two or more cultures attempt to communicate with one another. Whenever individuals from any subculture attempt to communicate within an interpersonal context, there are significant problems when words are used for which the subcultures have different meanings (especially if the communicators are unaware of these differences).

Of recent vintage, though possessing roots that go down throughout history, the feminist movement has focused upon the unequal treatment of women in our country. Women have been paid less for doing the same jobs and have been denied jobs because of their sex. While that is what the feminist movement has focused on, we would like to point out that in reality we have two very separate cultures: a male culture and a female culture living side by side in America.[34]

The various factors that constitute culture can be applied to the making of a differentiation between the male and female worlds in this country. Ex-

34. Barbara W. Eakins and R. Gene Eakins, *Sex Differences in Human Communication* (Boston: Houghton Mifflin Company, 1978), pp. 1–21.

periences of males and females differ to a marked extent in this country. The beliefs, values, and attitudes are very different. The meanings attached to a given word also differ greatly for males and females. Today there is a controversy over abortion. Could a male and a female possibly perceive the meaning for the word "abortion" in the same way? Of course not; their experiences with it are different. It is something that happens to a woman. It does not happen to a man, who can be only indirectly involved in an abortion. Obviously, personal involvement does not exist for males.

Likewise, if a male and a female have had sex together and some time later the girl, upon discovering she is pregnant, says to the male, "I am pregnant," could we for a moment suggest that the word *pregnant* has the same meaning for the male as for the female? Again, it is not something that happens to a male. It seems to us that many males forget that the female experience is one that differs from the male experience. Frequently, males try to make decisions for females on matters that they cannot approach in the same way as females because they do not have the same point of view—they do not perceive the same meaning. Of course, the same thing holds true for the other side of the coin. As long as wars are fought by men, can *war* ever mean the same to males and females? We doubt it.

There are many other words and concepts we could focus on to point out cultural communication differences. We would like to suggest, however, that you consider all the different things different groups interact about and how different cultures could cause people to approach words differently.

Abstraction Process

A concept discussed by general semanticists for years, and which is of interest to us in interpersonal communication, is the abstraction process. In our previous discussion of perception, in chapter 4, we stressed the chaotic nature of the world and the different stimuli impinging on us. We went on to say that the perception process was our only defense against this, and that it consisted of arranging the world into some kind of pattern so that we could impose an order on the world.

In chapter 4 we also suggested that we employ categories for the purpose of classifying the stimuli we perceive. There are numerous furry, four-legged animals with tails and barks running around our neighborhoods. It is easier to deal with these animals if we can classify them and have some set of predictions for that classification. The classification we use is that of *dog*. There are any number of predictions we can make regarding what these animals might do on our lawns, what kinds of noises they might make under different circumstances, and whether they might or might not be friendly and thus either do us bodily damage or make us feel good under certain circumstances. This is the process of abstraction. To conceive of the category *dog* it is necessary for us to abstract from each of these furry creatures those characteristics they all have in common. By noting those characteristics, we are

35. Alfred Korzybski, "The Role of Language in the Perceptual Processes," in *Perception: An Approach to Personality*, ed. Robert R. Blake and Glenn V. Ramsey (New York: Ronald Press, Co., 1951).

able to depict a class of animal life. This class is an abstraction. The abstraction process not only includes noting similarities but also overlooking differences. [35]

It should be obvious that we overlook some very significant differences. One of us has an English bulldog that is short, squat, very broad-shouldered, has teeth that stick out, is bowlegged, and almost waddles when he walks. A neighbor has another dog that is about twice as tall as the bulldog, has long silky black hair, and has a very long tail, as opposed to the bulldog's short curly tail. The dog is also incredibly graceful and able to jump great heights, as opposed to the bulldog's inability to do so. The neighbor's dog is called a black Labrador.

Were we to go by color, or by size, even by the way the animals move, one might be inclined to question their even being classified in the same category. And yet the two animals do have a number of characteristics in common. Although their movement abilities may differ, many of their behavior patterns are quite similar, as are many of their apparent interests. Both are interested in chasing birds, barking at a stranger intruding upon their property at night, and playing with balls and sticks. We could also classify them in terms of their genetic similarities. They seem to have some common ancestry, perhaps discoverable if one checks back far enough. Thus, we classify them as *dog,* a creature that inevitably walks on four legs, has a tail, barks, and appears to be friendly more often than not toward people.

The abstraction or categorization process that we employ to handle incoming stimuli in our day-to-day world, could also be termed a *stereotyping process*. We stereotype dogs according to the characteristics they appear to have in common. Abstraction and stereotyping can be very useful, as was pointed out in the chapter on perception. It is impossible to handle every incoming stimulus individually and separately. Rather, it is necessary to have a system that permits predictions. If it were necessary for us to approach each dog as a totally different creature, without any basis for prediction (which we would have to do if we had no category or stereotype to guide our responses), we would probably go mad. Rather than do that, we employ abstractions and stereotypes, which provide us with some predictive ability.

If you had no ideas about a group of people called *doctors,* and what they can and cannot do, you would probably never go to one. If you did go to one, you would not know how to act in the presence of that person. However, given the abstraction/stereotype most people have of medical doctors, you are able to choose to go to one when you consider yourself sufficiently ill to require this individual's services. You also have a basis for responding to the advice this person gives.

Although the abstraction process is useful, there are some real problems it can create in interpersonal communication. For example, we may assume that because we have an abstraction/stereotype of a given category, the

The word *dog* refers to both of these very different animals! *Dog* is an abstraction we may or may not agree about.

characteristics of that category will necessarily hold true for every member. Using the category of *doctor,* it is quite possible for us to assume that if our abstraction concerning doctors includes people who have a certain amount of training and a certain amount of expertise regarding knowledge of the human body, then we may be inclined blindly to accept the advice given by any doctor, when, in fact, there are a number of doctors who, for one reason or another, may be inadequate for our needs.

General semanticists have suggested that the abstraction process causes us to overlook the differences in people and things, simply because they are all in the same category.[36] (They suggested the same thing about stereotyping, because abstraction and stereotyping are similar processes.) Their implied warning is a valid one as applied to interpersonal communication, for if we respond to stereotypes and abstractions rather than to the person with whom we are trying to communicate, we can become very ineffective. Likewise, if the language employed by the other person is such that we respond to our stereotypes rather than giving consideration to the fact that the other person may have some kind of idiosyncratic difference in their meaning, we may respond to the wrong concept. We would be responding to our abstraction, not to the concept the other person intended.

General semanticists have suggested the devices of "indexing," "dating," and the use of quotation marks to aid us in avoiding this kind of error.[37] We can index dogs by considering them "dog_1," "dog_2," "dog_3," whenever we see a dog. This should remind us that all dogs are not necessarily friendly, and that we must test this assumption with each dog.

Likewise, we need to remember that the abstraction of *mother* is one we may have developed some years back. We also need to remember that *mother* has probably changed in the intervening years, as we live in a process world in which everything changes continually.[38] By employing dating procedures, we can remember that people and things change. Mother $_{1985}$ may not be the same as mother $_{1965}$. Consequently, we need to respond to her differently. Terms change over time. Words and their meaning change over time. Inflation $_{1980}$ is not the same as inflation $_{1970}$. Thus when discussing inflation and ways to combat it, we may have to think in very different terms in 1980 from the way we did in 1970.

Finally, the use of mental quotation marks may remind us that the meaning we have for a word is an abstraction and can be very different from the meaning someone else has. For instance, when we are discussing the term *democracy,* it would be of use to keep in the backs of our minds imaginary quotation marks around that word because "democracy" for us may represent something very different from "democracy" for another person. If such is the case, we may at any time during a conversation simply stop the conversation and say: "Wait a minute. Tell me what you mean by 'democracy' and I'll explain what I mean by 'democracy.' " By going through that process, it may be possible to restore understanding.

36. Roger Brown, "How Shall a Thing Be Called?", *Psychological Review* 65, no. 1 (1958):14–21.

37. Korzybski, *Science and Sanity,* pp. 1–18.

38. Korzybski, "Role of Language."

We are not trying to say that the abstraction process in and of itself is necessarily bad. On the contrary, it should be obvious from the earlier discussion of perception that abstraction, categorization, and stereotyping are necessary for us to cope with a multitude of stimuli in the world. We are, however, cautioning that the abstraction process can cause us to use words in a way that leaves out characteristics. Thus, to communicate with one another and have common meanings and common responses to words, it is necessary for us to remember that the abstraction process occurs also with the person with whom we are communicating, and always to try to check with them to make sure that our responses to words are compatible with theirs.

Hidden Antagonizers

In *Language in Thought and Action,* S. I. Hayakawa[39] referred to the existence of "snarl words" and "purr words." He suggested that we use words that are in some respect similar to sounds issuing from animals, and more particularly the cat family. An example of snarl words would be, "You're a male chauvinist pig." A statement such as that is an indication of a feeling of hostility. The words do not necessarily indicate anything about the person to whom the comment is directed. What is being said is: "I feel the following way about you, and it's a very hostile way, and so consequently, I will snarl at you." Hence the expression "snarl words."

39. Hayakawa, *Language in Thought and Action,* 2d ed.

Likewise, the comment, "You're beautiful tonight," is not really as much about the person to whom the comment is directed as it is about feelings of the communicator toward the person who is receiving this utterance. In essence, what the communicator is saying is, "I love you and I feel good about you, and so consequently, I am going to indicate my happiness to you." The person does this by using what Hayakawa referred to as "purr words."

It is our feeling that we can go beyond Hayakawa's original comments about snarl words and purr words. It is rather obvious when we are saying hostile things like, "you're a louse," or "I don't like you," that these are snarl words. But it seems to us that there is an entirely different kind of word that merits attention and requires caution when communicating. We call these *hidden antagonizers*—words perceived negatively by the recipient of our message because of the associations and connotations for that person. They are "hidden" antagonizers because the user is unaware that the words are snarl words to some people.

In recent years a problem which has confronted many whites in this country is the question of what word should be used to refer to people of African ancestry with dark skin.[40] The terms *Negro* and *colored* have been rejected by many of these people. Other terms now in use include *black, Afro-American,* and *African.* The use of words such as *colored* or *negro* in speaking to some of these persons, produces a response very similar to that which would result from the use of snarl words—an intense response, which is

40. Lerone Bennett, Jr., "What's in a Name?", *ETC., A Review of General Semantics* 26, no. 4 (1969):399–412.

extremely hostile, and which is very difficult ever to atone for. The same kind of thing appears to be true for adherents of the women's liberation or feminist movement.

Some words, that whites commonly use have intensely negative connotations for members of certain minority groups—not only blacks but also Chicanos, American Indians, and so on. Frequently unaware of these negative connotations, whites proceed to use these hidden antagonizers with alarming regularity when interacting with members of other cultures. The responses obviously are negative, and cooperation and trust are no longer possible. On the contrary, they are destroyed if they ever existed in the first place. Certainly cooperation and trust are not created when words are employed this way.

It is also evident that whites are not the only cultural group that uses these hidden antagonizers. One study revealed that blacks frequently employ words that are far more threatening to whites than blacks realize. Words such as *honky* seem to be far more threatening to whites than blacks intend them to be. On the contrary, when whites employ derogatory terms toward blacks such as *nigger,* the response of blacks to those terms is very close to the response expected.[41]

41. Daniel J. Roadhouse, "Analysis of Interracial Differences toward Derogatory Terms." Paper, University of Wyoming, A, 4, 1974.

Why this is so, we can only speculate, but we would imagine that blacks have been subjected to so much abuse by whites for so many years that it is not an unusual thing for them to be at the receiving end of derogatory messages. Thus, they do not react as intensely as whites under the same or similar circumstances. White society in America today finds itself in the position of being on the receiving end of insults, which is something of a new experience, and because it is, we suspect that whites react more intensely to a derogatory term than minority groups, such as blacks, would predict. Our past experience is what determines the meanings the words hold for us, and the way in which we respond to those words. It should be obvious that the past experiences of people in different cultural groups are considerably different.

While conducting a communication workshop, we used the term *women's lib* during discussion. After we uttered the term, we found ourselves being attacked verbally by a woman for having used it. Evidently the term *women's lib* was a snarl word for this person, but we had not known it was going to be. Finally, after some interaction, we and the woman managed to reach an understanding, and the ultimate outcome was that we refrained from using that term for the balance of the conference and began using the term *feminist movement*. It took this encounter for us to become aware of some very negative connotations associated with the term *women's lib* that are not associated with the term *feminist movement* for some women.

Many of our words can become snarl words for someone else without our ever intending them to be so. While Hayakawa referred to the use of snarl words as a manifestation of hostility on the part of the communicator, it

Awareness of past experiences of the listener might have helped Vice-President Agnew avoid the use of hidden antagonizers.

seems legitimate to suggest that, by the same token, the listener's role in converting seemingly innocent words into snarl words (even though the talker did not intend them that way) is a manifestation of that person's hostility. In recent years hidden antagonizers have become talked about more and referred to more often. Words that label various ethnic groups, such as *Polack* and *Jap,* have received publicity, thanks in no small measure to former Vice-President Agnew's use of them. The use of male pronouns to refer to both sexes in textbooks has been attacked by members of the feminist movement for the effect it has upon young girls. Blacks, Chicanos, and Indians have pointed out many terms that are offensive to them.

Some terms have been hidden antagonizers for years. The recent focus upon them is probably the result of an increased willingness to talk about ethnic problems and interracial interaction in the United States. The problem is very real, and one that is deceptive. It is possible for a communicator to think, "Well, I didn't mean anything derogatory or hostile when I used that term." This is really quite beside the point. Former Vice-President Agnew, during one of his press conferences, used the term *Polack.* There was a controversy immediately following that, and many troubled letters were addressed to the former vice-president. Mr. Agnew's response, it was interesting to note, was that he had not intended any slight when he used the term. Our point here is that it did not matter whether he intended the slight or not. The response of the listener to the words we use is all that really matters, because that response is the one with which we have to deal. If we have used hidden antagonizers in our communication (even though they were hidden from us) and they antagonize someone listening to our message, our ability to continue the relationship with the person to whom we are speaking may be completely destroyed. There may be no way we can go back and pick up the relationship, regardless of the meanings we intended.

What do we do with regard to hidden antagonizers? Because they are hidden from our awareness, we obviously do not know we are about to use them when we do. The only advice we can give is based upon common sense. Listen to people around you, and read about different ethnic, religious, and special-interest groups. Find out what is offensive, unacceptable, and would antagonize people with whom you may interact. Remember, the hidden antagonizers are not ones that are necessarily obvious, nor are they words everyone will be aware of as being hidden antagonizers. Try to get to know better the people with whom you communicate, so you will know what thoughts and words they are sensitive to.

Remember, the meanings of the words you use in your messages in interpersonal communication will be determined by the fields of experience of people who are listening to you talk. You will have your own meaning, but this will almost be irrelevant, because your concern in interpersonal communication is with the effect you have on the other person. Thus, your first concern must be the field of experience of the other person, and the possible responses that person may have to words you use.

Of course, when we mention hidden antagonizers, what we are really referring to is the way people respond to words in terms of the evaluative component of meaning. Recall, we said that the primary response of people to words is determined by the evaluative component of the words we use. Consequently, our concern here is with words that are going to provoke a negative response. These we determine not in terms of our own fields of experience, but in terms of the fields of experience of our listeners.

Reaching Agreement

Since words can provoke hostile responses, words can keep us from ever reaching agreement with people to whom we are speaking. Likewise, words can facilitate agreement. It is impossible for us to reach agreement on any matter so long as we are reacting to words differently from the way the people to whom we are talking are reacting. If we are discussing freedom of speech, it is imperative that we and the person with whom we are talking both have similar referents for the abstraction *freedom of speech*. If one of us means by this the freedom to express any political philosophy in a public forum and the other person means the showing of pornographic films, it may be very difficult for us to come to an understanding. One of us may be supporting freedom of speech and the other may be opposing it, but we are neither in agreement nor disagreement because we are talking about two different things. We cannot reach agreement because, though we use the same words, our points of reference are different. For us to reach agreement in any discussion, it would appear to be necessary for us to reach agreement on the meaning of the language we are using in the discussion. How can we do this?

Let us return to Lewis Carroll and the discussion between Alice and Humpty Dumpty. We really cheated when we presented the discussion earlier, because we left out the first part. " 'I don't know what you mean by glory,' Alice said. Humpty Dumpty smiled contemptuously. 'Of course you don't—till I tell you.' "[42]

42. Lewis Carroll, *Through the Looking Glass.*

The interesting thing about this interaction is the way in which Alice approached Humpty Dumpty. He had obviously used a word, *glory*, in a way that did not make sense to her, so she asked him what he meant. He then proceeded to define it for her ("a nice knock-down argument" was his definition). While this may seem very simplistic, it is not a bad idea for us in interpersonal communication. That is to say, why not simply ask, "What do you mean by *freedom of speech?*" Rather than continuing an argument on whether or not we should permit freedom of speech, it would make sense to find out whether or not the thing we are arguing about is the same for both of us.

It is entirely possible that a simple definition of the term *freedom of speech* will not be adequate. In fact, recalling our earlier comments on the abstraction process, remember that *freedom of speech* is a very abstract phrase and can refer to many different concrete events. Likewise, it is necessary for us to keep in mind that any verbal definition we offer for *freedom of speech* may also be somewhat abstract. It may be far removed from the concrete events we are using it to represent.

It may be necessary for you to say to the person with whom you are talking something like this: "Well, I think I understand your verbal definition. Let me see if the following example is what you mean." And then it would be possible for you to give a concrete example, such as, "Do you mean freedom of speech to include the right to shout 'Fire!' in a public place when there is no fire?" At this point the other person can say, "Well, no, I don't intend freedom of speech to include that." Then it is possible for you to say, "Then *freedom of speech* doesn't really mean *absolute* freedom of speech and it does not include all examples of speech." It would be possible to go through some kind of exchange of this sort, using examples and verbal definitions to pinpoint more accurately the way in which each of you is using words. If we can determine what the concrete reality is that the other

© Mike L. Wannemacher/Taurus Photos

person is using his or her words to represent, it is then possible for us to reach some sort of agreement on (1) the words we are using and what we intend them to mean, and (2) what the point of discussion is.

It is important to note also that one of the ways in which we can help someone else understand what we mean by a word is by attempting to describe our own field of experience so the other person can come to understand how we learned the word and, thus, our meaning for it. Conversely, it would help us understand another person's meaning for a word if we could determine what associations the other person has for his or her words and how they were acquired (through what field of experience). Having this background, we might better understand why such persons are sensitive to a word we are not sensitive to.

One of us has a sixteen-year-old daughter who, when she was between two and three years old, experienced a very severe infection in her throat, cheek, and mouth. During this period her cheek, jaw, and throat were very swollen and incredibly sensitive to pain. She was taken to a number of doctors and dentists who attempted to determine the cause of the infection. In the course of so doing, these doctors and dentists touched the infected area and were required to probe and take samples for analysis. All of this was extremely painful to a little girl at an age when it could not be adequately explained. Although this experience was not her first in a doctor's office, it was one of the most dramatic of her life to that point, and appears to have become associated in her mind with the phrase *doctor's office*. To this day, at age sixteen, she is tense in a doctor's office and, more specifically, if she is told that it is necessary for someone to look into her mouth or take a throat culture, tension turns to fear. The associations she has are extreme, but they are a good example of how understanding a person's fields of experience can help us better understand why they are responding the way they are to words and phrases we may use in interaction with them. Thus, in addition to asking what the other person means when they use words, we may want to ask how they came to have the associations they have.

Of course, the maximum agreement we can reach will be when we can find similar experiences to which we can relate the words we are using. It is probably a good idea whenever there is word disagreement between us and another person to search for common elements in our fields of experience.[43]

43. Schramm, "How Communication Works," pp. 3–26.

SUMMARY

In this chapter we discussed meaning in words and the fact that it is arbitrary in nature. We suggested that meaning is very likely acquired through a complex association process, which results from our field of experience. This process causes meaning in words that is best understood in terms of three components: evaluation, potency, and activity. Moreover, we indicated that the primary component of meaning is evaluative. We are constantly responding to words in positive or negative ways. We also discussed the Sapir-Whorf hypothesis: that language either determines the way we think and perceive the world or (at least) makes easier certain ways of thinking and perceiving the world. This is, in turn, tightly bound to the cultural group from which we have learned our language.

Finally, we discussed the abstraction process and the sometimes remote contact some words have with the concrete referents to which they apply. We also pointed out the existence of "hidden antagonizers" and suggested the importance of being aware of how other people respond to our words, not just to our responses. Much of what we know about language is very tentative at this point, and much more needs to be tested. The concepts we have covered in this chapter, however, have some basis in research and are also consistent with the personal experiences of both of us. Also, the concepts are accepted by many scholars and have considerable practical significance for interpersonal communication. It is our feeling that keeping in mind these characteristics of language while communicating should improve interpersonal effectiveness.

6

Nonverbal Communication: Influence without Words

You have, no doubt, had the experience of meeting someone for the first time whom you found you liked immediately. Sometimes, too, you have experienced just the reverse—knowing nothing about a person on first encounter and immediately disliking that individual. When meetings like this occur, whatever it is that causes us to respond with either like or dislike probably represents a combination of many things, such as the way the person's hair is worn, the clothes, the bodily movements, facial expressions, how close the person stands to us (or how far away from us), and his or her relative physical attractiveness (or lack of it). All of these combine to give us our impression of an individual (although our impression can subsequently be modified through the interactions that follow). These factors, which can influence us, are termed *nonverbal communication*.

1. Randall P. Harrison, "Nonverbal Communication," in *Handbook of Communication,* ed. Ithiel de Sola Pool et al. (Chicago: Rand McNally & Co., 1973), p. 93.

2. Ibid.

Importance of Nonverbal Communication

Today, *nonverbal communication* is used to refer to everything from hand gestures[1] to smiles[2] to alpha waves on a biofeedback machine.[3] Depending upon whom we wish to listen to, *nonverbal communication* can refer to anything we can see, hear, feel, or smell, with which we can associate meaning.[4] On the other hand, some scholars suggest that for something to be nonverbal communication there must be communicative intent present.[5]

Regardless of which approach you adopt, it must be obvious that we live and communicate in a world filled with nonverbal stimuli that can significantly affect interpersonal communication. The number of nonverbal behaviors that can influence others is so vast that our discussion can become confusing. We use gestures, facial expressions, smiles, and even eye contact (or lack of it) to communicate that we like or do not like someone. The

3. Larry L. Barker and Loretta A. Malandro, "Research Problems and Directions." Paper presented at University of Wyoming Conference on Communication and Growth—Promoting Behavior, Laramie, Wyoming, June 1974.

4. Jurgen Ruesch and Weldon Kees, *Nonverbal Communication* (Berkeley, Calif.: University of California Press, 1956), p. 189.

5. P. Ekman and W. V. Friesen, "The Repertoire of Nonverbal Behavior: Categories, Origins, Usage, and Coding," *Semiotica* 1 (1969):49–98.

clothes we wear can influence others. The way in which we wear our hair—even the kind of eyeglasses we select—can influence other people. These and many more behaviors can be deliberately manipulated and employed as symbols to influence another person, just as we employ words to influence.

While some people may not be aware of the importance of nonverbal communication, Mehrabian suggests that the amount of liking we have for another person is primarily communicated by us in this way.[6] Mehrabian's formula indicates that of the total affection or liking that we communicate to another person, only 7 percent is communicated by words. Thirty-eight percent is communicated by how we use our voices (rate, pitch, and volume of speech). Fifty-five percent is the result of facial expressions (smiles, eye contact, and frowns).

More recent research calls into question some of Mehrabian's figures, with words accounting for a greater relative percentage of meaning than is the case with Mehrabian's formula.[7] Even in this contrary research, however, nonverbal communication still accounts for more meaning than do words. Whether we accept Mehrabian's earlier figures or the most recent research, at least we know that nonverbal communication is very important in communicating liking for a person.

Mehrabian's formula (with the same relative importance for words, vocal quality, and facial characteristics) would apply to the communication of any emotion or feeling. Whenever we indicate our liking or disliking of something—our acceptance or rejection of something—we are communicating feelings. Probably most of our communication at home is feeling-oriented—expressing our feelings—and hence nonverbal communication is playing a major role in what we communicate.

Most of us actually speak words for only 10 to 11 minutes a day.[8] While that may seem like a low estimate, words uttered in the average sentence last for about two and a half seconds. Although we may be involved in conversations that last for hours, the actual time we spend uttering words is nevertheless only about 10 or 11 minutes a day. Thus, if you can think of your average day and the amount of time you spend in conversation (which is probably much more than 10 or 11 minutes a day), it becomes obvious that while you are involved in conversation, a lot must be going on in addition to the speaking of words. Quite logically, if you are involved in conversation for three hours during the day and if, out of that three hours, only 10 or 11 minutes is involved speaking words, then you are left with 169 to 170 minutes of conversation to account for that does not involve words. This is the time you spend communicating nonverbally.

It does not take a scholar, however, to recognize the importance of nonverbal communication. Males and females have recognized the importance of nonverbal cues from the beginning of man's history. The way a woman walks, the way a man moves, and the ways in which they look at each other

6. A. Mehrabian and S. R. Ferris, "Inference of Attitudes from Nonverbal Communication in Two Channels," *Journal of Consulting Psychology* 31 (1967):248–52; A. Mehrabian and M. Wiener, "Decoding of Inconsistent Communications," *Journal of Personality and Social Psychology* 6 (1967):109–14.

7. T. G. Hegstrom, "Message Impact: What Percentage is Nonverbal?" *Western Journal of Speech Communication* 43 (1979), pp. 134–142.

8. Mark L. Knapp, *Nonverbal Communication in Human Interacting*, 2d ed. (New York: Holt, Rinehart & Winston, Inc., 1978).

can determine how they will spend an evening, either in loneliness or in romantic companionship. Parents and children have recognized the importance of nonverbal communication for years. The way a parent raises or lowers his or her voice and the way a child manages to develop a tear in one eye can have far more to do with the outcome of an interaction than the words that are spoken between them.

While we are focusing upon interpersonal relations, we should note that politicians have long recognized the importance of nonverbal communication. As an example, politicians have always been concerned with their appearance—how they look to others. This concern with nonverbal communication was very high in Richard Nixon's 1968 Presidential campaign. The staging of his TV appearances, the clothes he wore, and the absence of the lectern behind which he would speak were all the result of a concern for the image created by nonverbal factors.[9] Mr. Nixon's campaign was so intensely directed toward creating an image through the use of nonverbal cues that he hired a team of' media specialists who could put together the image

9. Joe McGinnis, *The Selling of the President, 1968* (New York: Trident Press, 1969), pp. 62–76.

Nonverbal communication has become an effective part of our presidential campaigns.

Stern—M. S./Black Star

10. Ibid., p. 178.

he wished conveyed, through nonverbal' means, to the people of the United States. Many of the commercials on television designed to cause people to vote for Richard Nixon contained very little of Mr. Nixon himself.[10] They contained a sound track of him speaking (so the words of Nixon were present), but there was an attempt, through photography, to present a series of nonverbal images on the screens of America's television sets that would not only arrest the attention of the viewer but would also distract the viewer's attention from the words spoken by Nixon. The results of the election would suggest that this attempt was successful and that nonverbal communication may have at least as great an impact in politics as words.

During the 1976 campaign similar attention was paid to Mr. Carter's nonverbal behaviors. There was a studied attempt to present Mr. Carter informally. He was often pictured in jeans, walking in peanut fields, and even draining a pond on his property. This "down-home" approach was intended to enable the average voter to identify with the candidate. Finally, his smile was emphasized, on the assumption that this would make him more attractive to voters. These strategies apparently worked, although barely.

Although we speak only ten to eleven minutes a day (and write even less than that), we spend at least twelve years of our lives receiving formal instruction in the use of words. But today, at elementary, secondary, and also university levels, the attention paid to nonverbal communication is scant. There are few courses in nonverbal communication comparable to our standard English courses. More and more colleges and universities are beginning to develop such courses, but it is apparent that we learn most of our nonverbal communication during the early years of our lives, and we need formal instruction in this subject far earlier than it is currently being offered. Is it any wonder that many of us fail so miserably in our attempts to influence other people if we consider the lack of training we all have in nonverbal communication? We have been placed in a situation in which much of our total communicative effort depends upon a skill for which few of us have received formal training. It is not surprising that we err in our communication efforts. It is more surprising when we succeed. Fortunately, we manage to learn some skills of nonverbal communication on our own in our haphazard "pick-it-up-on-the-streets" manner.

It is our intent to provide in this chapter a more complete understanding of nonverbal communication and, hopefully, to whet your appetite for further study. Though it is obvious that we cannot completely cover the entire area in one chapter, we believe that an introduction to the subject is better than no information at all. We feel that, if you are at least aware of the elements that are of importance in nonverbal communication, you will be able to exercise greater control over your own nonverbal behavior and improve your nonverbal skills. The activities and exercises your instructor will provide for you should enable you to apply much of the information we will present in this chapter.

Two Points of View

Consider the following situation: two men are sitting in chairs set very close to each other in a room, talking. Mr. A says to Mr. B, "I have a cold today. You probably shouldn't sit very close to me." At that point Mr. B moves to a chair farther away from Mr. A. There would be no argument among communication scholars that communication occurred between Mr. A and Mr. B. Mr. A employed a symbol system that was common to both men and used it in such a way as to influence Mr. B.

Consider another situation still involving Mr. A and Mr. B, sitting as they were in the first situation, in chairs close to each other. Mr. A involuntarily sneezes, pulls out a handkerchief, and wipes his nose. At this point Mr. B rises from his chair and moves to another chair in the room, farther away from Mr. A. The effect of Mr. A's communication in the first situation is no different from the effect of Mr. A's sneeze in the second situation; however, there may be a difference in terms of communication.

Some scholars suggest that all behavior in an interactional situation is communication.[11] We will refer to this viewpoint as the *unintentional approach* to nonverbal communication. Other scholars contend the term "communication" should be reserved for those behaviors done with intent to influence another person.[12] We will refer to this viewpoint as the *intentional approach* to nonverbal communication. Ekman and Friesen, who subscribe to the intentional approach, have distinguished three levels of nonverbal cues: informative, interactive, and communicative behavior.[13]

11. P. Watzlawick, J. H. Beavin, and D. C. Jackson, *Pragmatics of Human Communication* (New York: W. W. Norton & Co., Inc., 1967).

12. Ekman and Friesen, "Repertoire of Nonverbal Behavior."

13. Ibid.

Informative Behavior

According to Ekman and Friesen, a nonverbal cue may provide us with information about someone because we are able to interpret it. In our example, the man who sneezed did not intend to communicate that he had a cold and that Mr. B should move. However, the sneezing behavior, while it lacked any intent to influence Mr. B, was perceived and interpreted by Mr. B as information that Mr. A had a cold. This would be an example of informative behavior.

Interactive Behavior

Nonverbal behavior can also influence the interaction that occurs between people, even though it is not intended to do so. It is not an unusual thing in interpersonal communication for us to observe another person shifting his or her position in a chair. It is possible for us to observe this, assume boredom, and therefore bring our interaction to a close more rapidly. This is called interactive behavior, because it affects interaction even though it is not intended to communicate.

Although he may not intend to convey a message, information concerning the man's lack of desire to communicate can be inferred from the way he holds his newspaper.

Harry Smedley, Jr.

144   Chapter 6

Finally, Ekman and Friesen suggest that nonverbal behavior can be communicative whenever the behavior is performed for the purpose of influencing another person. A young man on a date may put his arm around the shoulder of the girl he is with for the purpose of making her realize he feels affection for her. The nonverbal behavior of putting his arm around her shoulder is done with communicative intent and thus, the nonverbal behavior can be considered nonverbal communication.

Whether we choose the intentional or unintentional viewpoint, it must be obvious that all nonverbal behavior has communicative implications. However, it is necessary for us to refrain from inferring a communicative intent every time someone engages in a nonverbal behavior that has meaning for us. This has led to some real problems, as it did, for example, during World War II when American servicemen in England made the mistake of assuming that all nonverbal behaviors of British girls were intended as messages. In America, when a male and a female are on a date, it is the female who has the responsibility for determining how intimate the behavior may become. It is the female in America who says "stop." This is frequently communicated nonverbally. In England, on the other hand, that was not the custom. Women did not act as regulators, but instead the male was expected to determine how far they would go in their romantic behavior. It was the male who was supposed to say "stop." When American servicemen and English girls were out on dates, therefore, the American servicemen could observe English girls engaging in behavior that contained no communication to "stop." In fact, the English girls were nonverbally quite responsive to the American servicemen. Therefore, assuming that the English girls' behavior was a message saying "go," the Americans engaged in behavior that resulted in very negative perceptions of American servicemen. It also resulted in a perception by American servicemen that English girls were less than "nice."

The reason for this misperception was the assumption that all behavior is communication simply because it can be interpreted meaningfully. To be sure, behavior can be interpreted. We are engaged in a deductive process in which we are trying to deduce or infer from observed stimuli something beyond those stimuli. Thus, all behavior can be interpreted meaningfully and affect communication, even though the intent to communicate may be absent. This means that all we can ever do is make inferences about the nonverbal stimuli we observe. Nonverbal stimuli have no inherent meaning, but must be interpreted.

Unfortunately, it is not unusual for us to observe nonverbal behavior in the course of interpersonal communication and assume that the person engaging in that behavior must be intending a message for us. Sometimes that is the case, sometimes it is not. It is important for us to remember when we are observing nonverbal behavior that the person may or may not intend a message. The observer is never in a position to know whether communicative intent is present or not. Therefore, it is really not possible for a receiver to determine whether or not the behavior being observed is an intended message. It is certainly possible for a receiver of stimuli to make inferences and to interpret stimuli; however, it is necessary for us at all times to remember that we are making inferences.

A best-selling book called *Body Language* by Julius Fast[14] has taken the approach that all behavior has communicative intent. In this book he suggests that a woman who sits with her legs apart, touches her breast with her own hand, strokes her thighs as she talks, walks with a languorous roll to her hips, engages in very direct eye contact, touches a male when asking for a light for her cigarette, adjusts her skirt as she sits close to a man, and thrusts forward her breasts is intentionally communicating messages that she wishes to go to bed with the man. There seems to be very little doubt, according to Fast, that all of these things are intended messages indicating a woman's desire for sex with a male. Unfortunately, we do not really know that. It is important for us to realize that, to know that all of the behaviors just mentioned indicate sexual availability, we would have to know the intent of the woman. This is not possible. What is possible, though, is for us to observe these behaviors and then make an inference that the woman is (or is not) available for sexual activity. We should never forget that we are making an inference, however, and that our inference can be right or wrong. If a male observes these behaviors and assumes that sexual desire is the intended message, he may make a serious error.

One of us had an interesting experience while discussing nonverbal communication with some students in a class. It was revealed that several of the female students considered it to be nonsexual behavior, when they were sitting with a date watching a football game, movie, play, or concert, to rub their date's thighs. This was very surprising because, for our generation, for a female to rub her date's thigh was the kind of thing that was an invitation to sexual activity. Evidently, to some younger females today it is perfectly permissible to take one hand and place it on a date's thigh and stroke and caress the thigh while sitting side by side watching some sort of entertainment. If a male were to perceive this as an intended message of invitation and act accordingly, disaster could result. If the young man responds with sexual play, he may have his face slapped, the date may terminate, and he may never see the young lady again.

This discussion has been based on a semantic quarrel among scholars, with one group of scholars wishing to define nonverbal communication as requiring intent and another group of scholars trying to define nonverbal communication as not requiring intent. Obviously, neither definition is correct or incorrect. We discussed it to call your attention to the fact that

14. Julius Fast, *Body Language* (New York: Pocket Books, Inc., 1971).

whether or not you interpret all behavior as intended messages is important because of the possible effect your interpretation may have upon your response to what you receive as stimuli. If you perceive all behavior as intended messages, it is possible for you to commit errors of the type just discussed. It is our feeling that it is safer to assume all nonverbal communication, as well as the words we receive, to be stimuli that we can receive and interpret, but which do not have inherent meaning. We should not necessarily assume them to be messages resulting from intent by the person producing them. Rather, we should pay close attention to all available nonverbal stimuli and try to make inferences about them. But still it is important to remember that we are making inferences and should be prepared to readjust them at any moment. As long as we remember that the meanings we assign to nonverbal behaviors are inferences and nothing more, it matters little whether we subscribe to the intentional or unintentional point of view.

In organizing this chapter, we will be modifying Ekman and Friesen's categories of nonverbal cues. We will consider nonverbal cues as *communicative, informative,* and *attributive* cues. Communicative cues are used as intended messages to influence others. Informative cues provide information to the observer, even though the observed does not intend them to. Attributive cues have no direct relationship to message intent, yet affect message interpretation. It is impossible to have mutually exclusive categories. There are obviously some nonverbal cues that could be considered communicative, attributive, or informative, depending on the situation. Nevertheless, we shall attempt to proceed in this manner so that we may adequately consider nonverbal events that affect interpersonal communication.

Nonverbal Behavior in Interpersonal Communication

Communicative Behaviors

Many factors affect our perception of other people—not only what they say and do; there are many nonverbal behaviors that affect the way we receive messages and the way we perceive them. Communicative behaviors of importance include such things as people's appearance, movements, face, voice qualities, their use of space and time, and their use of touch.

Appearance

Often a person's general appearance is communicative behavior. We most often have our hair cut and styled in ways we think will favorably influence other people. We wear clothing we consider appropriate for an occasion because if we are wearing appropriate clothing, we feel we have greater influence on those with whom we are interacting. Women use makeup to influence people. Likewise, in recent years, facial hair on males has played a significant role in interpersonal relations. Even pipes and cigarettes can be used by us to tell others about ourselves.

We can deliberately manipulate all of these things and use them in a symbolic manner for the purpose of influencing other individuals. Thus, these can be considered communicative behaviors. The length of our hair and the way we have it combed and styled affects other people's perception of us.[15] At one time wearing long hair was a symbol of a particular life-style and political philosophy. For a while the long hair worn by hippies and liberals was adopted by many other people, and it became difficult to stereotype someone with long hair. This phase of behavior has, incidentally, become more ambiguous (and thus less useful for communication) as we have observed of late that there has been a trend back to shorter hair for both males and females.

15. Ruesch and Kees, *Nonverbal Communication*, p. 41.

Even with the current changes, hairstyles are used with communicative intent. This is nothing new. In the first letters from Paul to the Corinthians, Paul discussed the desirability of women wearing their hair long. He also was concerned that men should *not* wear their hair long.[16] Today our concern with hair is every bit as strong as it was at that time, and we continue to worry about how hair is arranged and/or covered.

16. Roy B. Chamberlin and Herbert Feldman, *The Dartmouth Bible* (Boston: Houghton Mifflin Co., 1961), p. 106–7.

The clothing we wear can have a significant effect upon the way people perceive us. Leonard Bickman pointed out that college students, aware of people's responses to various styles of dress, dressed "conventionally" when they were campaigning for Senator Eugene McCarthy in 1968.[17] The tactic was known as the "clean for Gene phenomenon" and has been a strategic weapon ever since. The reason students dressed "straight" at that time was because they knew they were going to be interacting with people to whom "hip" or "college" dress would be unacceptable. Even today, knowledgeable young people "dress up" for job interviews. They employ their clothes as a form of communication to be more effective in securing jobs.

17. Leonard Bickman, "Social Role and Uniforms: Clothes Make the Person," *Psychology Today* 7 (April 1974):48–51.

There are any number of norms for the clothing we wear that depend upon the communication setting. We know a student who had a summer job inventorying water supply availability in rural Missouri. When the student first conducted the survey and asked farmers to respond to questions, he wore a suit, white shirt, and tie. The first couple of days the student discovered he was not getting very much cooperation from the farmers and decided that the way he dressed might have something to do with it. He began to wear work pants, jeans, and workshirts rather than suit and tie, and discovered that the farmers were responding much more cooperatively. *What is appropriate dress depends upon the situation and the people with whom we are interacting.* It should be obvious that the clothing we wear can have a significant effect upon our general appearance and people's responses to us, and thus can be used as nonverbal communication.

Charles Harbutt/Magnum Photos, Inc.

Recently, facial hair has assumed increased importance. For several decades American males did not wear beards and mustaches to any great extent. In recent years young people began wearing beards, mustaches, and long sideburns to a much greater extent than they had been. There are very definite responses to beards and mustaches. People wearing beards are frequently perceived as more sensitive, more masculine, more intelligent, and warmer than people who do not wear them. It is also true that people who wear beards are perceived as more deviant, more likely to be radical, more independent, and less group-oriented.[18] An individual who decides to grow a beard is usually making a conscious decision, with the intent of affecting other people's perception of him.

Females employ makeup to influence other people. The cosmetics industry is one of the major industries in America today. Women color their hair, add color to their lips, highlight their cheeks, accentuate their eyes, extend their eyelashes, and do other things to change their appearance. What the effect of all of this is we are not entirely sure, although some uses of makeup

Clothing can be an effective form of nonverbal communication.

18. D. G. Freedman, "The Survival Value of the Beard," *Psychology Today* 3 (1969): 36–39; Marion E. Starling, "Nonverbal Communication: A Study of the Effects of Men's Hairstyles" (paper, Purdue University, May 1972).

may be related to research findings on nonverbal communication. For instance, the use of eye makeup by women may be an attempt to make the eyes look larger. Research indicates that when the pupils of the eye are dilated, a woman is perceived as more sexually attractive to males than when the pupils are not dilated.[19] It may be that for centuries women have recognized that if they could make their eyes appear larger, this might be perceived as more sexually attractive.[20] Of course, women have never really talked about it in these terms; they simply talk about being more or less attractive, depending upon how makeup has been applied.

Pipes, cigarettes, and cigars can be aspects of appearance that some people deliberately manipulate to affect others. One phenomenon associated with college life many of us have observed is that of the young male attempting to learn how to smoke a pipe. Not atypically, the pipe is used to create the image of someone who is solid, calm, and thoughtful. It is not surprising that many undergraduate males wish to convey that impression. Likewise, first-year graduate students frequently begin smoking pipes—very likely for the same reasons.

The cigarette is a nonverbal appearance behavior that begins to interest us when we are in high school, and sometimes earlier. In America, people smoking cigarettes have been portrayed in films and on television as being sophisticated and worldly. Of course, many of us, while growing up, wish to achieve that maturity and sophistication and thus smoke cigarettes in the hope that this will make us more like the jet-setters we wish to emulate.

Cigarettes, cigars, and pipes are perceived differently when smoked by males and females. Some things appear to be more acceptable for males than for females in our society. For instance, cigars and pipes are not yet accepted as appropriate for females and thus cause a female who smokes a pipe or a cigar to be perceived as more radical or more "different."

As was mentioned in chapter 4, when we first meet people, we develop an implicit personality theory, which we use to predict their behavior and to govern our own communication behavior. The aspects of appearance just discussed, and others, determine, to a large extent, what that implicit personality theory will be. The way we are perceived and our subsequent effectiveness (or lack of it) as communicators is significantly affected by our appearance. Although it may seem like "selling out" to some people when we dress for an occasion, or for people with whom we will be interacting, it is actually good communication sense.

Movement

19. J. W. Stass and F. N. Willis, Jr., "Eye Contact, Pupil Dilation, and Personal Preference," *Psychonomic Science* 7 (1967):375–76.

20. Richard G. Goss, "Reflections on the Evil Eye," *Human Behavior* 3, no. 10 (October 1974):16–22.

21. Albert E. Scheflen, *Body Language and the Social Order* (Englewood Cliffs, N.J.: Prentice-Hall, Inc., 1972), pp. 57–132.

In addition to appearance factors that we use to influence other people, the way we move significantly affects others also. One of the ways we use movement is to regulate interaction with others.[21] We employ gestures, eye contact, head nods, and changes in body position or posture to indicate when we are finished with a thought. By so doing, we indicate that the person we are talking with should talk. Sometimes we do this to show that we are bored or that we wish to leave. There are many different interaction regulators.[22]

During a conversation, when we are listening to someone else, we employ head nods to indicate agreement or disagreement and to indicate continued interest in what the other person is saying. Likewise, the person who is speaking uses head nods and changes in eye contact to indicate when he or she has finished speaking and is waiting for us to talk. Typically, when we have finished our thought, we raise our heads and look expectantly at the other person.[23] This is our signal to the other person to begin responding. We can use the head nod to regulate what is said and when it is said. When we are listening we nod our heads in what would ordinarily be an affirmative manner simply to indicate that we understand what is being said and that the other person can continue talking.[24]

We frequently use body position or posture to indicate that a conversation should continue or not continue. For instance, if we are trying to conclude a conversation with another person and we are standing, we may begin to angle ourselves toward an exit from the room. We may even begin to move in the direction of a door. Each of these behaviors conveys to the other person our desire to terminate the interaction.[25] If we are sitting during a conversation, it is not an uncommon thing for us to lean expectantly forward to indicate interest in the conversation and to indicate that we wish to continue with it.[26] Likewise, if we have been sitting back in a chair listening to someone else talk and we begin to move up toward the front of the chair, we may be indicating that we are ready to conclude the conversation.[27]

The use of the hands and arms to reinforce words is one of the first things many people associate with the term *nonverbal communication*. The gesture, which is what we usually call this use of the hands and arms, can be a very useful form of communicative behavior. We use hands and arms to reinforce our words. Simply the way in which our palms point (whether up or down) appears to have significant effect upon how other people interpret the words we are uttering.[28] If our palms are down, people see us and our message as much more assured, certain, and aggressive. When our palms are up, we appear to be more uncertain, to be qualifying what we are saying, and sometimes even asking for someone to help us out.

The hands can be used to communicate far more, though, than merely additional meaning for words—hands and fingers can be used as symbols themselves.[29] The A-OK gesture which became associated with the space program in the 1960s is now an accepted part of the nonverbal repertoire of most people. This symbol, which is as good as saying the words, "A-OK," communicates much all by itself. Likewise, the middle finger extended upwards in our society is a negative, obscene communication. In addition, the black power movement has used the upraised, clenched fist as the sign of unity and brotherhood (and some would add aggressiveness toward whites).

22. Ekman and Friesen, "Repertoire of Nonverbal Behavior."

23. Allen T. Dittmann and Lynn G. Llewellyn, "Relationship between Vocalization and Head Nods as Listener Responses," *Journal of Personality and Social Psychology* 9 (1968):79–84.

24. Ibid.

25. Randall P. Harrison, *Beyond Words* (Englewood Cliffs, N.J.: Prentice-Hall, Inc., 1974), pp. 49–51.

26. Albert Mehrabian, "Relationship of Attitude to Seated Posture, Orientation and Distance," *Journal of Personality and Social Psychology* 10 (1968):26–30.

27. Abner M. Eisenberg and Ralph R. Smith, Jr., *Nonverbal Communication* (Indianapolis: Bobbs-Merrill Co., Inc., 1971), p. 26.

28. Harrison, *Beyond Words*, p. 134.

29. Ekman and Friesen, "Repertoire of Nonverbal Behavior."

30. A. E. Scheflen, "Quasi-Courtship Behavior in Psychotherapy," *Psychiatry* (1965):245–57.

The way we cross our legs seems to affect the way others perceive our messages.[30] It is possible to appear relaxed in the legs-crossed position. Likewise, it is possible to cross our legs in a masculine or feminine manner. There appears to be one way of crossing legs for males in which the angle of one leg is resting upon the knee of the other. With females, however, it is more common to have the back of one knee resting over the other knee. This is not to suggest that people who cross their legs with one ankle over a knee are masculine, or that people who cross their legs with the back of one knee over the other knee are feminine, but this is a stereotype that exists in our society and as such certainly affects communication.

Facial Expression

31. Knapp, *Nonverbal Communication*, p. 263.

32. Ruesch and Kees, *Nonverbal Communication*, p. 18.

The face is probably the most expressive part of our bodies.[31] Because we have so many muscles and organs within the face, it is possible for us to express complex emotions. It is interesting to note that infants respond to faces more readily than they respond to other objects.[32] Likewise, when a "face shot" occurs on television, the attention level goes up considerably. We pay close attention to faces because we learn a great deal from looking at other faces. We can see the eyes, the mouth, and the area around the eyes and mouth with the various muscular positions that can be assumed.

33. P. Ekman and W. V. Friesen, "Nonverbal Leakage and Clues to Deception," *Psychiatry* 32 (1969): 88–106.

34. Knapp, *Nonverbal Communication*, p. 268.

Not only does the face communicate a great deal, it also appears to be the kind of nonverbal behavior that we seem best able to control.[33] It is with the face that we lie the best. While lack of eye contact causes some people to interpret a person's message as insincere, practiced liars find that they can make extremely good use of direct eye contact, appearing sincere while lying to conceal their insincerity. It is very difficult for people to determine accurately whether a communicator is sincere and when not sincere.[34] People learn to make faces very early in childhood—even learning to smile when they are unhappy. Thus, it is not surprising that we become very adept at concealing our emotions in our faces.

35. Ekman and Friesen, "Nonverbal Leakage."

While our attention may be drawn to faces, it is also true that we can gain information about another individual through other parts of his or her body just because of the facial control most of us have.[35] It is possible for us to see subconscious communication occurring through the hands, feet, or body posture.

Paralanguage

36. G. L. Trager, "Paralanguage: A First Approximation," *Studies in Linguistics* 13 (1958): 1–12.

37. Ibid.

The word *paralanguage* refers to those nonverbal characteristics associated with the production of words through speech.[36] These characteristics include pitch, voice quality, and rate and rhythm of speech. While some people do not think of vocal characteristics as nonverbal (probably because of their association with words), this is a very important aspect of nonverbal communication.[37] We employ variations in all these paralinguistic factors to convey emotion. Those who have had the opportunity to listen to radio

Not only pictures but facial
expressions may be worth a
thousand words.

drama or readings by accomplished actors on recordings will recognize at once the incredible flexibility of the voice and the capacity of the voice to alter the meaning of words. The words in a book or a transcript of a speech are not just the spoken words written down. In fact, we do not generally write down many of the vocal characteristics of an utterance. Typically we write the words alone, and this is by no means all of the message.

Pitch alone conveys much. A high-pitched voice can convey excitement or fear. A low-pitched voice can convey seriousness, sadness, and sometimes affection.[38] One of the criticisms drawn by many students in speech courses is that they lack vocal variety. Usually instructors who offer this criticism mean that there is not enough pitch variation, or that the pitch is too monotonous—too constant. We even use the word "monotone" to describe the voice of a person who does not vary pitch sufficiently. Obviously, there is no absolute standard regarding pitch, and we do not really mean that people should have their pitch going up and down without reason, but rather that pitch can be used to reinforce and strengthen the impact of words used in a message.

We use the pitch of our voices to say something about ourselves and to influence other people. Females, upon reaching womanhood, typically experience a lowering of the voice similar to that of males, although not to the same extent. However, some women do not allow themselves to lower their voices, maintaining instead a high-pitched voice which, according to some authorities, is associated with their childhood. In other words, women who do not wish to become women but wish to remain little girls may continue to speak in a high-pitched "little-girl voice," which they hope will influence others to continue perceiving them as little girls rather than as women. This then removes the threat of their having to perform as women and to assume responsibilities as women.[39] No doubt this sometimes occurs with males, although in our society the value of masculinity and of becoming a deep-speaking male seems to urge young boys in the opposite direction to that of young girls in terms of pitch.

Even when males and females have been matched by height and weight with the same anatomical structures, including even larynxes of the same size, male-female voice quality differences are still there.[40] Researchers conducting this type of research suggest that boys and girls form words differently, with girls smiling more when they speak. Since smiling has the effect of shortening the vocal cords, this could also explain the higher pitch of female voices. The smiling behavior, of course, is a culturally learned nonverbal behavior.

While some people think voice quality is a totally biological phenomenon, it can be altered by the individual and is used by all of us to influence others. A harsh, cutting nasal voice has one effect on people, whereas a soft, well-modulated voice has a completely different effect on them.[41] Most of us learn to produce sounds with different vocal qualities because of the envi-

38. Knapp, *Nonverbal Communication,* pp. 340–349.

39. D. W. Addington, "The Relationship of Selected Vocal Characteristics to Personality Perception," *Speech Monographs* 35 (1968):492–503.

40. J. Sachs, P. Lieberman, and D. Erickson, "Anatomical and Cultural Determinants of Male and Female Speech," in *Language and Attitudes: Current Trends and Prospects,* ed. R. W. Shuy and R. W. Fasold (Washington, D.C.: Georgetown University Press, 1973).

41. Ibid.

ronment in which we are reared. In the southwestern United States we find a voice quality that is very different from that of people living in the southeastern United States. We can discern still another voice quality for people living in the northeastern United States. In fact, we can find pockets within individual cities in which the voice quality differs markedly from that of most people in the region in which the city is located.

These regional differences are acquired during childhood. We do not all consciously control our voice quality, but we probably subconsciously develop a voice that enables us to project a desired image. Obviously there are some limits to the extent to which we can change our voice quality, but singing teachers, voice coaches, and speech teachers throughout the country have experienced considerable success in showing people how to change the quality of their voices.

Just as we have stereotypes for people with hair of different lengths, we have stereotypes that are applied for relating people with different kinds of voices.[42] A deep voice tends to come from a larger man, whereas a high-pitched voice tends to come from a smaller, thinner man. An interesting piece of research, certainly, would be to determine the effect of totally incompatible voices and bodies in terms of the differing stereotypes that people have.

We use volume to complement the meaning of words.[43] As we become more excited or angry, or when we simply want to make a point more emphatic, we tend to increase the volume with which we speak. As we wish to become more affectionate, considerate, and understanding in our speech, we tend to reduce our volume. Couples making love never shout at each other. Romantic feeling appears to be most effectively communicated to another person through the use of soft, breathy voices speaking barely above a whisper. Volume is an effective paralinguistic factor in communication.

Finally, the rate at which we speak, and the rhythm, have a significant effect upon interpersonal communication.[44] As we increase our rate of speech, we change the listener's perception of the importance of what we are saying. Someone who is speaking rapidly tends to convey an impression of excitement and importance, whereas someone who speaks slowly conveys a relaxed atmosphere with no need for hurry or excitement. The rhythm with which we speak can vary. Some people speak in short spurts, while some tend to speak in a rather consistent fluent manner (although total fluency does not appear to exist with anyone). Severe nonfluencies, which are sometimes called "stuttering," decrease other people's perception of our credibility.[45] They tend to perceive us as less dynamic and as less qualified; the perception of trust, however, remains unaltered.

There is an organization called Toastmasters International that is, among other things, very concerned with nonfluencies in speech. This organization so firmly believes that nonfluencies are detrimental to effective communication that during some of their chapter meetings a person who is called the

42. Ibid.

43. Hall, *Silent Language,* pp. 163–64.

44. W. B. Pearce and F. Conklin, "Nonverbal Vocalistic Communication and Perceptions of a Speaker," *Speech Monographs* 38 (1971):235–41.

45. K. K. Sereno and G. J. Hawkins, "Effect of Variation in Speaker's Non-fluency upon Audience Ratings of Attitudes Toward the Speech Topic and Speaker's Credibility," *Speech Monographs* 34 (1967):58–64.

" 'ah' counter" drops a marble in a coffee can to produce a sharp sound every time a speaker utters a verbalized pause or an "ah." The Toastmasters' feeling is that this kind of nonfluency interferes with effective communication, and thus they try to reinforce it negatively.

There is evidence to indicate that speech that is too fluent may be perceived negatively also.[46] If we speak too fluently or too glibly, we may be perceived as "slick" and possibly untrustworthy. We have for some time felt that one of Richard Nixon's primary problems was that his speaking was somewhat too fluent. Mr. Nixon had been a college debater and had been in public life for many years, and therefore he acquired an extremely fluent speech pattern and rhythm. His speaking voice and rate were measured and constant, and there were very few nonfluencies and hesitations in his speech. As a result, he seemed practiced and nonspontaneous at all times. This may have contributed to a perception of untrustworthiness and sometimes a lack of warmth by the public. We cannot single out any one factor to explain public opinion polls, but even when Mr. Nixon's popularity was high prior to some of the scandals of 1972, 1973, and 1974, it was very difficult to find people who felt warmly toward the man. Many people respected him and acknowledged his expertness, but did not respond to him as a warm human being. It is our feeling that this may have been caused in part by the overly fluent manner of his speech.

46. John E. Dietrich, "The Relative Effectiveness of Two Modes of Radio Delivery in Influencing Attitudes," *Speech Monographs* 13 (1946):58–65.

Time

47. Hall, *Silent Language,* pp. 15–30; 146–64.

In Hall's *The Silent Language* one of the factors discussed extensively was the importance of people's use of time and space in communication.[47] According to Hall, we can use time to influence other people just as we can use words. For instance, if we place a phone call to someone at midnight, the time we have chosen will cause the receiver of the call to perceive that our call is more important than he or she would perceive it as being if we placed it at 3:00 in the afternoon. We do not normally place a telephone call in the middle of the night unless there is an emergency. Thus, when we choose to place a call at night, the call acquires added importance and emphasis.

Likewise, we can use time to communicate by our way of timing our arrival for an appointment. It is possible for us to arrive early for an appointment to communicate interest in the meeting we are attending, or it is possible for us to arrive late for an appointment to communicate lack of interest or indifference toward the meeting. People use time as communication for complimenting others by being on time; and sometimes we use lateness to "put people down" by suggesting to them that they really do not count enough for us to make an attempt to arrive on time.

It is also possible for us to use time to cause people to make decisions differently. Abraham Lincoln's practice of scheduling controversial topics for discussion at his cabinet sessions at the end of the meeting, late in the afternoon, is one now-famous case in point. President Lincoln was employing time to force quick decisions—decisions that might have taken much longer had the topic been raised at an earlier hour. By introducing topics late in the afternoon, we force members of decision-making groups to make their decision more quickly (to avoid running into the approaching dinner hour). On the other hand, if we introduce a controversial issue at the beginning of a meeting, early in the afternoon, we might discover ourselves faced with a very long discussion because people perceive no reason to hurry. Thus we have a prime example of how time can be used effectively to influence others.

Space

Space also can be used as communication. It is possible to communicate a positive evaluation of another person simply by standing close to him or her.[48] We stand closer to people we like and farther from people we dislike. It is as though we will permit people we value to invade our own personal territory, but not those we do not like. Robert Ardrey has suggested the existence of what he has termed "the territorial imperative" in animals.[49] According to him, all animals, including humans, have well-defined territories around themselves, which they will defend rather than permit them to be invaded. This is probably the basis for our use of space in communication. If so, it is possible that the use of space to communicate liking is, in part at least, genetically acquired as well as culturally learned.

Our use of space varies from culture to culture, however, as the norms regarding distance between people during interpersonal communication are considerably different for various groups. Hall indicated the existence of at least four different kinds of distance that middle-class Americans in the northeast employ in communication.[50] They are "intimate," "personal," "social," and "public" distance. If you will look at table 6.1, you can see the different interpersonal communication behaviors appropriate to each of these four distances and the close and far phases of each of the four distances.

Intimate distance can range anywhere from no space between persons to 18 inches. The close phase of intimate distance ranges from no space to 6 inches, and the far phase ranges from 6 to 18 inches. We use intimate distance with persons we like extremely well. Intimate distance—admitting people to our personal territory—is used to express positive evaluation of them. It also involves considerable physical contact with other persons. Of course, the smells and feel of the other person are available to each, thus bringing into play other senses than sight and sound in the communicative process.

Personal distance is a noncontact distance which in the close phase includes distances from one and one-half to two and one-half feet and in the far phase from two and one-half to four feet. Within the personal distance we have interactions with our friends and our family. Hall mentions that a wife

48. A. Mehrabian, "Some Referent and Measures of Nonverbal Behavior," *Behavior Research Methods and Instrumentation* 1 (1969):203–7.

49. Robert Ardrey, *The Territorial Imperative* (New York: Dell Publishing Co., Inc., 1966).

50. Edward T. Hall, *The Hidden Dimension* (New York: Anchor Books, Doubleday & Co., Inc., 1966), pp. 111–29.

Use of space in an office can
speak loudly.

UPI

Table 6.1

Distance		Measurement	Examples
Intimate			Lovers embracing, soft whispering occurs (if anything at all is spoken)
	Close phase	0–6″	
	Far phase	6″–18″	Mother–child looking at book together; close friends discussing secret; audible whispering
Personal			Husband and wife planning a party; parent–child in friendly conversation; soft voice when indoors; full voice outdoors
	Close phase	18″–30″	
	Far phase	30″–4′	Discussion of subjects of personal interest and involvement; social exchange over cup of coffee
Social			Impersonal business discussions; discussions with fellow workers on the job; conversations during casual social gatherings
	Close phase	4′–7′	
	Far phase	7′–12′	More formal business discussions; distance at which we engage in activities where we wish to be alone, such as reading; when talking at this distance the voice is noticeably louder than for the close phase
Public			Voice is loud but not full volume; one person addressing a small group
	Close phase	12′–25′	
	Far phase	25′ or more	Public speeches before very large groups; interpersonal communication probably not possible; this is the minimum distance kept between the public and public figures (such as politicians and movie stars) most of the time

is permitted within the close phase of personal distance, but for another woman to step that close presents a very different situation in which a norm has been violated.

Social distance prevails in such social interaction as parties. The voice is kept at a normal level. The close phase, ranging from four to seven feet, is the one in which impersonal business often occurs. We tend to work and have social relationships in the close-phase, social-distance situation. The far phase of social distance ranges from seven to twelve feet. Business and social discourse sometimes occur in this phase; however, the discourse is usually of a more formal character than that occurring at the close phase of social distance. In the far phase the voice level is, of course, noticeably louder than for the close phase, since the distance can range to upward of twelve feet. People can continue to work in the presence of another person without appearing rude, as is observed frequently in many offices in which a number of people work together. Interpersonal communication can occur at this distance, but with increased difficulty.

Public distance can range in the close phase from twelve to twenty-five feet and in the far phase from twenty-five feet on up. Although it is possible for interpersonal communication to occur at this distance, it is rare, especially in the far phase. At this distance the principles of public communication become operative. Public-speaking texts focus on public-distance situations.

We are not usually concerned with public distance in interpersonal communication. There are interpersonal situations involving all three of the other distances. Probably the most important thing to keep in mind is not merely what these distances are but the fact that the distances mentioned are appropriate to certain kinds of communication behaviors in specific relationships and situations. We obviously do not use intimate distance when we are engaging in a business discussion with a real estate agent. Likewise, the use of the far phase of social distance with a member of the opposite sex when we are on a date would seem very strained and formal indeed. It is important for us to keep in mind that we must use the appropriate distance for the situation, or we may find that the space we are keeping between us and the people with whom we are communicating will interfere with our communication effectiveness.

Tactile Communication

We all begin our lives as infants with the use of touch to communicate. This is the only kind of communication a father or mother has available with which to influence the child. Desmond Morris, in *Intimate Behavior*, suggests that we never get over the infant satisfaction with touching.[51] He believes we learn to associate comfort with both touching and the rhythmic beating of a heart. Thus, whenever we share moments with someone we love, we begin to perform very childlike behaviors with each other. We

51. Desmond Morris, *Intimate Behavior* (New York: Random House, Inc., 1971), pp. 13–34.

begin to treat the person we love as one would treat a child, and we allow ourselves to be treated as a child by the person we love. This enables us to enjoy some of the caressing and touching we have associated with some very satisfying and warm moments in our life: those of infancy and childhood.

Another point regarding tactile communication that should be considered is habits of touching. People touch one another more in some cultures than in others.[52] In some cultures to touch a member of the opposite sex is taboo. Likewise, within a culture such as that of the United States, there are many different subcultures and consequent mores, which are of considerable importance regarding touching behavior. We can probably increase our interpersonal effectiveness by using touching behavior that is consistent with the backgrounds of the people with whom we interact. Tactile communication can play an important role in dyadic communication because we usually stand more closely together in this communication context.

52. Sidney M. Jourard, "An Exploratory Study of Body-Accessibility," *British Journal of Social and Clinical Psychology* 5 (1966):221–31.

Cultural Differences

Just as words are perceived differently from culture to culture, so also do different cultures communicate nonverbally in very different ways.[53] These differences, combined with a tendency to forget that we *infer from* and *interpret* nonverbal behavior, can be problematic, as already mentioned, and are significant enough to deserve discussion.

53. Edward T. Hall, *The Silent Language* (Greenwich, Conn.: Fawcett Publications, Inc., 1959).

Edward Hall compared middle-class white Americans with people of other cultures in their use of distance during interactions. He discovered significant differences from culture to culture. The interaction distance preferred by Latin Americans in interpersonal communication is considerably less than it is in the United States.[54] The distance comfortable for a Latin American is so close that it tends to evoke either hostile or sexual feelings in North Americans. One can easily picture a conversation between a North American and Latin American in which the Latin American is continually advancing toward the North American and the North American is constantly retreating. The result is that the Latin Americans perceive us as cold, withdrawn, and unfriendly, and North Americans perceive Latin Americans as breathing down their necks, crowding them, and spraying their faces.

54. Hall, *Silent Language*, p. 16.

Sometimes the differences in nonverbal communication between cultures can be quite subtle, and it is this very subtlety that can cause problems, because the differences are present and yet they are not immediately obvious to us. For instance, while Japanese, Chinese, and Occidentals interpret facial expressions similarly, they apparently differ in the degree of emotion being perceived. People from Japanese, Chinese, and Occidental cultures perceive that a person they are all observing is happy or that another person they are observing is sad in a fairly similar manner. However, the *amount* of happiness or sadness perceived by the groups will differ considerably from culture to culture.[55] The problem, then, is not one in which the *cultures*

55. W. Edgar Vinacke, "The Judgements of Facial Expressions by National-Racial Groups," *Journal of Personality* 17 (1949):407–29.

Nonverbal communication differences between cultures vary from extremely subtle to quite obvious.

Jill Freedman/Magnum Photo's Inc.

cause individual members to perceive emotions in a totally different manner; rather, the perceived *intensity* of the emotion will differ.

In addition to the visual kinds of nonverbal communication behavior, which are affected by the culture in which we are reared, there are also differences from culture to culture in terms of paralanguage. One of the more interesting variations between cultures would have to be that of accent or dialect in speech. This is of such importance that Andrea Rich considers the accent or dialect to be the most relevant element in paralanguage in terms of communication from culture to culture.[56] It is true that accents and dialects tend to accompany cultures. There is an accent that accompanies black ghetto residents, another accent in the speech of some Jewish-Americans, still another accent in the speech of most Chicanos, and many others. Even regions within a country have their own distinctive accents.

What is the effect of different accents upon interpersonal communication? According to Haines, an individual's accent can significantly affect perception of his or her credibility.[57] Without going into which accents have how much credibility, it is enough to suggest that accents help identify a person's culture, and as a result of that, a perception of credibility by the

56. Andrea Rich, *Interracial Communication* (New York: Harper & Row Publishers, Inc., 1974), pp. 189–190.

57. L. S. Haines, "Listener Judgements of Status Quos in Speech," *Quarterly Journal of Speech* 47 (1961):164–68.

listener is developed. Messages produced by a person with an accent are accepted by recipients to either a greater or lesser degree simply because of the accent. Announcers in broadcasting generally strive for what has been termed *General American Speech*. People in the fields of speech and speech pathology are able to identify General American Speech, a fairly accent-free speech form. It is the kind of speech we hear from someone like Walter Cronkite, John Chancellor, or Harry Reasoner on news broadcasts. We would suggest that deviations from General American Speech cause changes in the perception of credibility. Extreme deviation probably results in some kind of a decrease in perceived credibility in most cases.

Sometimes cultures will develop their own specific nonverbal messages, which are peculiar to that particular culture, for expressing some kind of an emotion or thought. For instance, in America, blacks exhibit a behavior called "rolling the eyes." It is a distinct eye behavior that is used to express impudence and disapproval of a person who has authority over them or who is dominant. The primary message communicated with rolling the eyes is that of hostility. Blacks, especially females, roll their eyes while being lectured to as a result of their having broken a rule. Also, the practice of rolling the eyes is used sometimes to express disapproval of another person.[58] One of the nonverbal behaviors of blacks which is probably most misunderstood by whites is that of turning one's back to the person with whom one is communicating interpersonally. For many whites, to have another person turn their back to them while communicating in a dyad or even in a small group is very insulting. However, within the black culture, turning one's back to another person during a conversation is an indication of friendship and trust. One of the most friendly greetings that can be given from one black to another is that of walking up to the person, saying something warm and friendly, then turning around, with back toward the person just greeted, and walking away a few steps. The reason this is the friendliest greeting one black can give another is that essentially the nonverbal message is something to the effect: "Look, I trust you so much that in greeting you I unhesitatingly place myself in a vulnerable position."[59]

It is apparent from this discussion that we could go into any number of nonverbal behaviors. We could consider handshakes, eye contact, head nods, sitting positions, standing positions, walking, patting on the back, touching behaviors, rate of speaking, volume, and many other nonverbal behaviors that we employ to communicate with others. All of these will vary from culture to culture. Some cultures will share some nonverbal messages; however, whenever we are communicating with someone from another culture, it is imperative for us to be aware of the probability that some of the things we are doing nonverbally, which may be normal and natural within the culture in which we have been reared, may offend or threaten a person in another culture. Likewise, if we find ourselves being put off, thinking that others are insulting us because of the way they are behaving nonverbally, we

58. Kenneth R. Johnson, "Black Kinesics: Some Nonverbal Communication Patterns in the Black Culture," in *Intercultural Communication*, L. A. Samovar and R. E. Porter, ed. Wadsworth Publishing Co., Inc. (Belmont, Calif.: 1972), pp. 181–89.

59. Ibid.

must be open to the possibility that what we are responding to is not directed toward us personally but rather is a nonverbal behavior characteristic of the cultural background of the person with whom we are communicating.

Appearance, movement, facial features, voice qualities, space, time, and touching behavior can all be intended messages. They play a part in the interpersonal communication process that is as important as that of any other factor. Increased sensitivity to nonverbal communication should result in improved interpersonal communication.

Informative Behaviors

In addition to the nonverbal behaviors we perform as intended messages, we have behaviors that can be interpreted by those who observe them even though they are unintentional. Because we can infer considerable amounts of information from them, Ekman and Friesen called these *informative nonverbal cues*.[60]

60. Ekman and Friesen, "Repertoire of Nonverbal Behavior."

If you were involved in a discussion with Mr. X, and during the course of this discussion you and Mr. X began to disagree over some point and this disagreement developed into an argument, in the midst of which you could observe Mr. X's face becoming a bright shade of red, you might deduce an internal state of anger. Of course, Mr. X would not intend to communicate his anger if he wanted to continue the relationship with you and to have a conversation that is "civilized." However, because of the presence of adrenaline in his bloodstream (which results from his excitement over the disagreement), his blood vessels would dilate, his heart would pump blood rapidly, and a flushed face that you could observe would result. From this you could infer a heightened state of excitement and/or anger. Thus the nonverbal behavior—reddening of the face—would be informative for you. Even though he intended no message of anger, it would be possible for you to observe Mr. X and deduce a state of mind he might never wish to reveal.

There are many behaviors such as this. Jade dealers in the Far East are reputed to be able to determine when someone is interested in a particular piece of jade by noting the dilation of the pupils of the customer's eyes. It has been observed that dilation of the pupils of the eyes is correlated with increased interest or attention to something.[61] The jade dealer infers from his observation that the customer likes a particular piece of jade; thus, the behavior has been informative and the dealer can then act upon that knowledge to effect a satisfactory transaction.

61. Stass and Willis, "Eye Contact, Pupil Dilation."

Why are these behaviors informative? Behaviors such as blushing and pupil dilation are simply stimuli that an individual emits in response to feelings. These nonverbal behaviors are such that, given appropriate past experiences, we can infer many things about a person. Thus informative behaviors are stimuli from which we can infer information. Our inferences may or may not be correct, but most of us act on them nevertheless. This makes sense, just so long as we remember that we are acting on inferences.

Nonverbal attributes include a number of physical characteristics that are unrelated to any specific message intent and yet can have a significant effect on our effectiveness in interpersonal communication. These attributes include a person's height, gender, skin color, size of nose, eye color, and other physical characteristics. These are factors that we know affect the outcome of interpersonal communication. We know, for instance, that a premium is placed on male height. Males who are tall are perceived as more credible than males who are not tall.[62] During the twentieth century, we could have predicted with astounding success the winner of national presidential elections simply by the height of the candidates.

Studies indicate that higher salaries are paid to taller employees, even when their qualifications are equal to those of shorter employees.[63] Job applications that are identical except for a difference in height result in tall applicants being hired more often and receiving better salaries. Likewise, women pay considerable attention to the height of the males they date. Women prefer tall men. Height affects our interpersonal effectiveness.

Skin color also appears to have a significant effect upon communicative effectiveness. Many studies conducted in the fifties investigated the effect of skin color on communicator credibility. The findings consistently indicated that Caucasians were more likely to be perceived as more credible (thus to be more effective in persuasion attempts) than persons with black skin.[64] Of course, skin color is not related to message intent, but it nevertheless affects the outcome of an interpersonal interaction. The same thing has been true of gender. Even females perceive males as more credible.[65] Whether or not we are born as male or female, black or white, will have a significant effect upon the outcome of our communication attempts. Of course, the studies that have produced these results have been conducted within the context of the university community. This is primarily an upper-class, WASP community in America, and thus these results are culturally biased.

One of the nonverbal attributes that people in America do not generally like to discuss is the influence of physical attractiveness. In this country we like to think that we judge people on their merits. We do not like to think or believe that one person has an inherent advantage over another person merely because of the facial or body structure with which he or she was born. However, some research would suggest that while physical attractiveness is a somewhat ambiguous quality, people who are more physically attractive are liked more and are considered to be more intelligent, personable, sensitive, warm, responsive, kind, interesting, modest, sociable, and outgoing than people who are not physically attractive.[66] Men and women who are not physically attractive are perceived to have a deficiency of those qualities we have just attributed to attractive people. Some people do have more going for them simply because of the luck of birth, and these people have a head start in interpersonal communication effectiveness. Certainly

62. C. D. Ward, "Own Height, Sex, and Liking in the Judgement of the Heights of Others," *Journal of Personality* 35 (1967):381–401; P. R. Wilson, "Perceptual Distortion of Height as a Function of Ascribed Academic Status," *Journal of Social Psychology* 74 (1968): 97–102.

63. S. D. Feldman, "The Presentations of Shortness in Everyday Life—Height and Heightism in American Society: Toward a Sociology of Stature," reported in "Physical Attractiveness," Ellen Berscheid and Elaine Walster, in *Advances in Experimental Social Psychology*, vol. 7, ed. Leonard Berkowitz (New York: Academic Press, Inc., 1974), pp. 178–79.

64. E. Aronson and B. W. Golden, "The Effects of Relevant and Irrelevant Aspects of Communicator Credibility on Opinion Change," *Journal of Personality* 30 (1962):135–46.

65. Franklon Haiman, "An Experimental Study of the Effects of Ethos in Public Speaking" (Ph.D. dissertation, Northwestern University, 1948); "The Case Against Chauvinism: A 20-Year Bill of Particulars," staff report in *Human Behavior* 1, no. 3 (May/June 1972):46–49.

66. K. K. Dion, E. Berscheid, and E. Walster, "What Is Beautiful Is Good," *Journal of Personality and Social Psychology* 24 (1972):285–90.

their credibility is much higher to begin with, hence, for example, the use of movie stars in testimonial-type advertising.

It is also evident that even after we have interacted a great deal with someone, we respond significantly to the way the person looks. It seems that the physical attractiveness itself continues to have its effect even though we may already have become aware of attitudinal differences and personality deficiencies.[67] We still continue to perceive someone more positively if they look nice. These findings have any number of implications, and one of the most important for us to recognize in interpersonal communication is that, since physical attractiveness plays a significant role in interpersonal communication, it is to our advantage to make ourselves as physically attractive as possible, given the limitations with which we have been born and the opportunities available to us (thanks to hairdressers, cosmeticians, plastic surgeons, and clothiers). It is not just a matter of vanity to make ourselves more attractive, it is sound interpersonal communication. The more attractive we are, the more success we are likely to experience in our interactions with other people, other factors being equal. This is probably true in social situations, learning situations, and job situations. While these situations may not directly relate to attractiveness, we are frequently judged on the basis of our attractiveness anyway, and this judgment has a significant effect upon the way people receive our messages. Thus, it is to our advantage to determine what is perceived as attractive by those with whom we interact and to strive toward that ideal, not because we are trying to conform or because we are vain, but because we wish to become the most effective interpersonal communicators possible.

At this time we should restate that there are no universal standards of attractiveness, as was discussed in chapter 4. What is attractive in one cultural context may be repulsive in another. Whereas height may be an important attractiveness ingredient to white Anglo-Saxon Protestants in America, it may be of little importance in some other cultures. While size of a woman's feet may have been of considerable importance to the Chinese at one time, it has never been as important to American men as bust size. Thus, in trying to be attractive, we must make our attempt in terms of the culture of the person we wish to have perceive us as attractive.

It is impossible for us to consider every nonverbal attribute that can possibly affect the outcome of interpersonal communication. However, many physical characteristics over which we have little or no control can nevertheless be interpreted and affect communication. We would suggest that, for the most part, these factors cannot be changed (it is difficult to make oneself taller once growing has stopped—elevator shoes to the contrary notwithstanding; it is difficult to change one's skin color; and it is difficult to change one's gender). It appears to us that the most reasonable approach to nonverbal attributes is for us to be aware that these factors influence communication. With this awareness we can be prepared at all times to perform

67. Berscheid and Walster, "Physical Attractiveness," pp. 205–6.

Physical attractiveness is an influential part of effective interpersonal communication.

whatever communicative behaviors are necessary to make up for any adverse effects of nonverbal attributes. Likewise, we should be prepared to take advantage of any positive nonverbal attributes that might work for us.

Environmental Influences

68. Knapp, "Nonverbal Communication," pp. 83–113.

69. A. G. White, "The Patient Sits Down: A Clinical Note," *Psychosomatic Medicine* 15 (1953):256–57.

70. L. B. Wexner, "The Degree to Which Colors (Hues) Are Associated with Mood-Tones," *Journal of Applied Psychology* 38 (1954):432–35.

71. W. Griffitt, "Environmental Effects of Interpersonal Affective Behavior: Ambient Effective Temperature and Attraction," *Journal of Personality and Social Psychology* 15 (1970):240–44.

In addition to the behaviors we have that affect communication, we are all subject to environmental influences in any interpersonal communication situation.[68] The color of the room we are in, the temperature, the day on which we are communicating, the size of the room, the shape of the room we are in, the furniture we are sitting in, and the arrangement of the furniture can significantly affect the way in which we interact with another person.[69]

Color is another environmental factor that influences communication. There is no question but that the color of our surroundings will affect us.[70] Warm colors such as yellow and red appear to make us more responsive and excitable; cool colors such as blues and greens appear to be more restful and make us quieter and more unresponsive.

The temperature of a room can also have a significant effect upon us, if for no other reason than to cause us to become more or less attentive to the interaction in which we are involved.[71] Suffice it to say that there are many environmental influences, even down to the hardness or softness of the chair in which we are sitting, that will affect the way in which we interact with others. The comfort or the lack of comfort we experience will have a significant influence upon us. These and other nonverbal environmental influences do have a significant effect upon the interpersonal communication process.

In this chapter we have tried to consider the existence of nonverbal communication in the interpersonal setting. The idea of influencing others without words through a nonverbal symbol system is not a new one but has recently come under more extensive investigation by behavioral scientists. We have considered the different approaches to nonverbal communication—the intentional versus the unintentional approach. A major consideration of this chapter has been the use of inference in observing nonverbal behavior. We have tried to suggest that we are constantly interpreting and inferring from nonverbal stimuli. We never really know when another person is attempting to communicate with us nonverbally. Thus, we run the risk of responding as though some behaviors involved intended messages by others when such is not the case. This can lead us into some significant problems.

The different communicative behaviors over which we have control and which we use for the purpose of influencing others include appearance, the way we move, the use of the face, paralanguage, the use of space and time, and even tactile communication. Likewise, we have considered informative behaviors, or those behaviors that we can observe in other people and that may provide us information about them. We have also considered nonverbal attributes, largely physical characteristics unrelated to specific message intent, which affect our effectiveness in interpersonal communication. The effect of environmental factors is also considered. We have included in several of the sections a discussion of the effect of culture on our use of nonverbal communication. We hope this chapter will cause you to be more sensitive to nonverbal communication in interpersonal situations.

SELECTED READINGS

Fast, Julius. *Body Language*. New York: Pocket Books, Inc., 1971.

Hall, Edward T. *The Silent Language*. New York: Fawcett Publications, Inc., 1959.

Harrison, Randall P. *Beyond Words*. Englewood Cliffs, N.J.: Prentice-Hall, Inc., 1974.

Knapp, Mark L. *Nonverbal Communication in Human Interaction*. 2d ed. New York: Holt, Rinehart & Winston, Inc., 1978.

Mehrabian, Albert. *Silent Messages*. Belmont, Calif.: Wadsworth Publishing Co., Inc., 1971.

Ruesch, Jurgen, and Kees, Weldon. *Nonverbal Communication*. Berkeley, Calif.: University of California Press, 1956.

Scheflen, Albert E. *Body Language and the Social Order*. Englewood Cliffs, N.J.: Prentice-Hall, Inc., 1972.

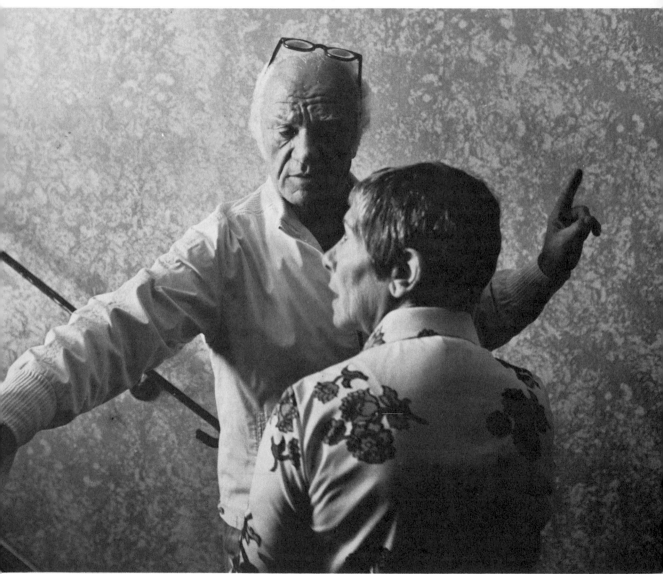

7

Listening and Feedback

This chapter focuses on two important phenomena in communication—listening and feedback. One type of information received via listening is the way others are responding to us (feedback information). Not all feedback information is received by listening, of course. Feedback information may come to one by any of the senses and, therefore, the feedback section of this chapter includes more than listening. Since much feedback is received via listening, however, the two processes are naturally related and are treated together in this chapter.

We will discuss the listening process, the various purposes of listening, the most common problems of listening, ways to improve listening, and how to take notes effectively. Feedback will be defined, the sources and types of feedback will be identified, the effects of feedback on listening and on the communication process will be discussed, and suggestions for using feedback effectively will be given. The chapter concludes with a section on feelings. Feelings often play a dominant role in communication, and they are known for the most part via feedback. Why it is important to express feelings, why inhibiting feelings and feedback can be harmful to communication, and the consequences of giving ambiguous feedback are topics considered in the final section of the chapter.

Listening

The Importance of Listening

It has been said that as much as 98 percent of classroom time in communication classes emphasizes sending skills, while less than 2 percent focuses on receiving skills. Yet what the listener brings to the communication situation is of prime importance to effective communication. The listener needs to be aware of what is at stake in the communication situation, and the sender needs to understand both the listening process and the listener to achieve the response that is desired. Unfortunately, listening behavior is often over-looked or ignored.

Various studies have shown that adults spend about 70 percent of their waking hours engaged in communication activities, with about 10 percent of this communication time spent in writing, 15 percent in reading, 30 percent in talking, and 45 percent in listening. Hence, 75 percent—later studies show up to 90 percent—of all human communication is carried on by speaking and listening. The extensive use of the telephone, movies, radio, television, and public address systems have amplified the importance of listening. Our democratic form of government is based on a well-informed public; modern entertainment depends on a variety of good listening habits; many jobs and positions depend heavily on effective listening; and learning in school relies on listening ability. In the classroom and in everyday life, effective listening helps one to get along and to learn.

The evidence is overwhelming that without specific training we do not develop listening skills that are adequate to meet the needs of modern life. The data indicate that most of us are poor listeners. We can accurately recall only 50 percent of the information we hear immediately after hearing it. Confusion, misinformation, and misunderstanding are common products of our communication experiences. Effective listening can make the difference between knowledge and ignorance, information and misinformation, involvement and apathy, and enjoyment and boredom.

The Listening Process

At the outset it seems desirable to define *listening*. In a sense, listening is a combination of what we hear, what we understand, and what we remember. Hearing, the first element, is the detection or perception of sound. It is the response of the nervous system of the human body to the stimulation of a sound wave. A listener does not receive a word or message instantly, but rather accumulates sounds, receiving a word after a brief but measurable interval of time. The listener accumulates sounds bit by bit, identifies short sound sequences as words, and then translates these words and groups of words into meaning. It may be helpful to think of the act of listening as comprising three stages: hearing, identifying and recognizing, and auding. The diagram in figure 7.1 illustrates these three states.

The first stage, *hearing*, is the process by which speech sounds in the form of sound waves are received by the ear. The second stage, *identifying and recognizing*, is one in which patterns and familiar relationships are recognized and assimilated. Through auditory analysis, mental reorganization, and association, the sounds and sound sequences are recognized as words. The third stage, *auding*, is the translation of the flow of words into meaning. Auding involves one or more avenues of thought—indexing, comparing, noting sequence, forming sensory impressions, and appreciating.

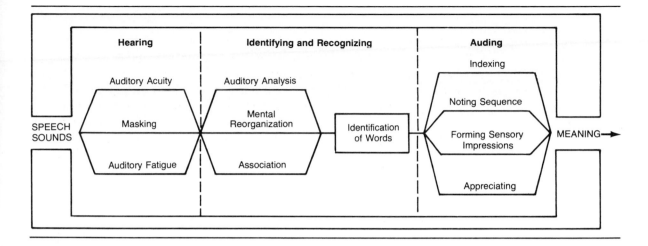

As identified in figure 7.1, one of the first factors to affect the hearing of sound is auditory acuity—the ability of the ear to respond to various frequencies (tones) at various intensities (levels of loudness). Human speech frequencies range from 125 to 8,000 cycles per second, although most words fall between 1,000 and 2,500 cycles per second—the critical range of auditory acuity.

The loudness of sound is measured in decibels and ranges for speech from fifty-five decibels (soft talking) to eighty-five decibels (loud conversation). A person is said to have a hearing loss when he or she requires more than the normal amount of intensity (volume) to hear sounds of certain frequencies. A requirement of fifteen to twenty decibels over normal would be considered a significant hearing loss. Any loss of this amount in the critical range of 1,000 to 2,500 frequencies is especially serious, since it affects the intelligibility of speech.

Another factor influencing hearing is *masking*. When background noise, especially competing conversation, enters the ear in the same frequency range as the speech one is intending to receive, the extraneous noise is said to *mask* the intended oral message. When the extraneous sound is composed of all frequencies, it is called *white noise*. White noise is sometimes produced when a large number of persons (a roomful) talk in loud voices—all at the same time.

Auditory fatigue is yet another factor that can affect hearing. Continuous exposure to sounds of certain frequencies can have the effect of causing a temporary hearing loss. A monotonous tone or a droning voice can have the effect of creating auditory fatigue. Studies today are showing that hearing losses, some of an enduring nature, are resulting from prolonged exposure to noise in urban communities. Some researchers suggest that music played at high volume for prolonged periods can cause a hearing loss.

Figure 7.1

Prolonged exposure to loud noises and music may cause permanent hearing loss.

The second stage in listening—recognition and assimilation of patterns and relationships—can be affected by the quality of auditory analysis, mental reorganization, and association. *Auditory analysis* refers to the process of comparing the incoming sounds with sounds that are familiar to the individual. Sounds are recognized in terms of their likenesses and differences.

The second part of the process of this stage is mental reorganization. In mental organization the listener applies some system that will aid retention and will structure the incoming sounds. We may syllabify a word, for example, as we pronounce it to ourselves. If we hear a series of numbers, we may place them in groups of three, or we may repeat the series to ourselves several times. Whether we group, recode, or rehearse, we are engaged in mental reorganization.

Finally, sounds are associated with prior experiences with sounds. Words used in speech may be entirely strange to the listener—for example, a foreign language—or they may have become associated with subjective meanings quite different from those the sender had in mind. In any event, there is a process for identifying words in which the listener's experience, background, and memory are used to create associations in regard to the incoming sounds.

The third major stage of listening is auding, the process of assimilating the continuous flow of words and responding to them with understanding or feeling. Again, the listener's experiential background is brought into play along with various skills in thinking to make sense of the stream of words that is being received. The listener may index, make comparisons, note sequence, or react by forming sensory impressions or appreciating what is heard.

The term *indexing,* as it is used in auding, refers to the outlining or ranking of information according to importance. It is the searching for main ideas and supporting or secondary ideas; it is the separating of the relevant from the irrelevant; and it is the structuring of bits and pieces into more meaningful wholes. Some persons who are exceptionally skilled in indexing apparently have an ability to visualize an outline of incoming information.

Another aid to the assignment of meaning is arranging the material according to time, space, position, or some other relationship; that is, by noting sequence. All these functions aid the listener in creating a layer or framework into which information can be placed and related. Material is easier to remember if the order of events and placement of parts are noted.

Sometimes the listener reacts with the senses to incoming information. Probably the sensory response most frequently used in association with incoming information is sight—the ability to add a visual dimension to the information. Some persons are apparently highly skilled in forming sensory impressions so that they taste words describing tastes, smell descriptions of smells, and generally translate words into sensory images, thus adding to the meaningfulness of the verbal message.

A final function that may be engaged in during the auding stage is appreciating, that is, responding to the aesthetic nature of the message. Appreciation can play an important role in listening to public speeches that are ceremonial in nature and in the reception of messages that are intended to activate the feelings and emotions of the listener.

All these elements and more are used in dynamic relationships to carry out the process of listening—the process by which information is assimilated, ideas are received and reacted to, and interpretations, judgments, and applications are made to derive meaning from the messages received.

**Purposes
of Listening**

The development of good listening ability involves recognizing that there are specific purposes in listening, each with defined requirements and skills. The three most important purposes are (1) listening for enjoyment, (2) listening for information, and (3) listening to evaluate critically. We may listen, of course, with all three purposes in mind. We may also enjoy while we learn, but the most effective listening appears to occur when we know what we are listening for and listen with that specific purpose in mind.

Listening for Enjoyment

Appreciative listening can increase our enjoyment of life, enlarge our experience, expand the range of what we enjoy, and decrease the tension of daily life. Much of the daily conversation in which each of us engages serves a social purpose—the enjoyable function of sharing feelings and responses to build and maintain positive, supporting relationships. In addition, we engage in listening to satisfy our desire for appreciating and experiencing art and beauty. In the adult world, listening for enjoyment is composed of listening to music, listening to stories or drama on television, engaging in social conversation, and, for some persons, listening to live drama, oral interpretation, or literature read aloud.

Learning to listen effectively is an integral part of listening for enjoyment, for information, and to make critical evaluations.

Jean-Claude Lejeune

Many people cheat themselves out of pleasant and beneficial listening experiences because they have a limited, narrow experience in appreciative listening. When we deny ourselves the pleasure of aesthetic listening, we are always the losers. Persons who believe they have to get practical information from all the material they listen to condemn themselves to a poverty of cultural experience. Similarly, persons who do not attempt to expand their experiences in appreciative listening shortchange themselves. To limit ourselves to a diet of soap-opera listening is to miss the opportunity to live more richly, deeply, and pleasantly through expanded aesthetic appreciations.

Listening
for Information

Another purpose of listening is to receive information—to acquire an answer to a definite problem or question, to listen for direction, to listen to the news of current interest, and to acquire the opinions and views of others. We have noted previously in this chapter the important contribution that listening makes to learning in general and the important relationship between listening ability and the acquisition of a viable picture of the world and ourselves. Further, as a student in college, you are keenly aware of the central role listening plays in the acquisition of information and understanding.

Listening to Make
Critical Evaluations

The word *critical* can be a source of confusion. We use the term here to refer to careful evaluation rather than to negativism, to aggressive attack, or to the constant challenging of statements. The antagonistic, challenging aspect of being critical can be the antithesis of effective listening, as we shall note later when we discuss special problems in listening. Even critical listening in the positive sense of the term (to evaluate carefully) can have dire consequences if the listening objective of receiving information accurately is interfered with by inappropriate timing of the evaluative process. If we attempt to examine carefully each sentence and idea during a speech meant to transmit information, the efficiency of our listening for information will be seriously decreased. And if an antagonistic, criticizing process is engaged in as we listen to the speech meant to inform, the results are disastrous: faulty analysis, snap judgments, distortion, and impeded learning. Once again, it should be stressed that the purpose for which we listen must be considered if we are to listen effectively. We need to have evaluative assimilation in informational listening, but the careful evaluative assimilation should be withheld until we have fully comprehended the entire message. We are usually well repaid for postponing evaluation.

On the other hand, if the purpose of our listening is to make a decision—a judgment—then we profit by adopting an evaluative attitude more immediately. We profit by evaluating the strength of each main point advanced and by a careful testing of the reasoning used and the quality of the evidence used in supporting the point. Such weighing and evaluating is most effectively done point by point rather than by waiting until the end of the speech. Critical listening makes us aware of prejudices in ourselves and in others. It forces us to judge on the basis of facts and information rather than on emotions and falsehoods. It calls for patience, objectivity, and the testing of thinking and reasoning.

The important point to keep in mind at this time is that we may have various purposes in mind when listening, but the specific purpose for which we listen ought to determine the skills called into play. The major concern of any listener is to discover the purpose and nature of the performance of the message involved and to make an adjustment to it.

Misconceptions about Listening

Poor listening can occur as the result of false assumptions about listening, poor listening habits, and ignorance about good listening techniques. We will consider, first, four unfounded but widely held assumptions about listening. These misconceptions, and recent evidence suggesting how badly we have been misled by them, are deserving of our attention.

Listening Is Easy

A serious assumption that interferes with improving listening is the assumption that listening is easy, that listening is passive—a process in which we relax and receive information. This misconception suggests that the listening process is one in which the listener is not actively involved. Nothing could be further from the truth. Listening—especially critical and informational listening—is difficult and fatiguing because it requires continuous, active mental effort. It is true that in some communication situations listening is voluntary; yet if we listen only when we want to or are tempted to, we hear only what we want to hear and only what captures our fleeting attention. We are afflicted with nonlistening habits. Effective listening requires skills and behaviors characteristic of emotional and mental maturity. Productive listening is work. It requires effort and purposeful activity.

Listening Ability Is Largely a Matter of Intelligence

The relationship between listening ability and intelligence is not nearly as close as many have assumed. Intelligence has something to do with listening, of course, just as it has something to do with many behaviors—especially with all intellectual activities—but we listen with more than intelligence. We listen also with our experience and with our emotional and psychological capacities. Many reports have tended to disprove a close relationship between listening and intelligence.

Daily Use of Listening Eliminates the Need for Special Training

Another naive assumption is that training in listening is unnecessary because, like learning to walk, we just learn to listen as a part of the process of growing up. The truth is that no amount of practice and use of listening will ensure improvement in listening if the practice is not accompanied by intelligent monitoring and guidance. Evidence tends to show that the kind of practice most people get in the process of growing up develops and reinforces listening faults as much as it does listening skills.

Improving Reading Ability Also Improves Listening Ability

Educational research has shown this assumption to be false. The best way to improve listening skill is to receive direct training in that skill. Improvement in reading does not transfer to listening ability.

Problems in Listening

Another cause of poor listening is the development of bad habits in listening. Eight of the most common problems in listening follow.

Premature Dismissal of a Subject as Uninteresting

One rationalization for not listening is that the subject is uninteresting. When we decide that a subject is uninteresting, listening is greatly impaired; in fact, it may be entirely turned off. But uninteresting subjects are not necessarily without value. To equate interestingness with valuableness is a mistake. It reveals an underlying attitude that says, "Interest me and entertain me! If you succeed, then this information is valuable to me." This attitude is a denial of the role the listener plays in the communication situation. Knowing that communication is transactional, we can easily predict the effect on the speaker that is produced by the nonverbal communication of such an attitude by the listener. Further, some messages lacking in interest may contain highly important and relevant information, but if we have prematurely decided not to listen, we will not receive that information. Undoubtedly, some students do not learn because they do not listen. When the responsibility is placed entirely on the speaker, little communication can occur. To stop listening prematurely because you think a subject is uninteresting is a bad habit that can be broken by listening to all kinds of subjects.

A second bad listening habit is that of avoiding difficult material. Too many of us listen only as long as it is easy, comfortable, and entertaining. If the material becomes difficult, we just decide not to listen. That habit, of course, deprives us of many opportunities to learn and to acquire new insights and understandings. Many students who fail in college do so because they have acquired the habit of not listening to anything difficult. Throughout life they have seldom been subjected to any oral discourse that was difficult to understand. In college they find themselves listening to lectures in which new and sometimes complex concepts are presented. When students lack experience in listening to things that require mental exertion, or when they have developed the habit of avoiding or ignoring the difficult, they will find themselves handicapped. If you are afflicted with this bad listening habit, the only solution is to make a planned effort to listen to difficult material. Try to include news commentaries, discussions, and lectures in your listening.

Criticizing Delivery and
Physical Appearance

A third common problem in listening is that of focusing on the external aspects of the speaker and listening only if the speaker's appearance and delivery are attractive. If the appearance is not to their liking, or if the delivery is either vocally or physically distracting, some persons become so busily engaged in mentally criticizing the delivery or appearance that they fail to listen to the message.

A junior in college—a prospective student teacher—was recently interviewed by me and another person. It was apparent from observation of the other person during the interview that he was not hearing what the student was saying because the student's general appearance had distracted the interviewer into being critical. This was even more apparent in our private discussion following the interview, when he confessed that he had heard almost nothing the student had said because the student's appearance was so distracting. This listener used a "different" appearance to rationalize poor listening. Many of us have fallen into this habit. If the speaker has an annoying mannerism, we focus on that and decide that we cannot listen. We spend the time mentally criticizing either the physical appearance or speech delivery at the cost of not receiving accurately or beneficially the information sent to us.

Faking Attention

It is not unusual to observe someone faking attention in church. Faking attention can also be observed in classrooms, and it occurs frequently even in dyadic communication situations. The faker probably assumes that "if I look as though I were listening, the speaker will be pleased." The speaker may indeed sometimes be deceived, but in most instances the only person deceived is the one faking the listening. Listening requires energy, effort, and the use of specific skills. When our energy is used to fake attention, we cannot listen. On occasion, faking attention can be exposed by a carefully inserted question. Besides suffering the embarrassment of being caught looking like a smiling statue or of failing to respond in the right way at the right time, the faker is cheated of an opportunity to learn from what is said.

Listening Only for Facts

Another problem in listening is that of listening only for facts. Focusing on "getting the facts" can develop into a bad habit in listening. We can become so busily engaged in listening for and trying to remember facts that the ideas are missed entirely. Memorizing facts is not a way to listen. Facts are useful in constructing and understanding ideas; as such they should be considered secondary to the idea. When people talk, they want you to understand their *ideas,* and grasping ideas is the skill that is basic to effective listening.

Letting Emotion-Laden Words Arouse Personal Antagonism

Another habit detrimental to listening is that of allowing the emotions to take control of behavior. When that which we are hearing is something we do not want to hear—something that angers or frightens us—we may develop the habit of blocking it out. On the other hand, if the words are "purr words" for us, we are apt to react with positive emotions, accepting everything that is said—truths, half-truths, or pure sham. Our emotions act as filters to what we hear. When we hear something that is opposite to our beliefs, values, attitudes, prejudices, or convictions, we react quickly and emotionally. We become fearful and may begin to argue mentally with the speaker. We plan rebuttals to what has been said, and in the meantime have not heard anything else; we think of questions we can ask to "put down" the speaker; or we may just turn to thoughts that support our own feelings on the topic. Any of these behaviors may become so habitual that as soon as we hear words, ideas, or arguments that strike our emotions, we react by not listening. Our antagonistic and negative behavior becomes as automatic as if an "antilistening" button were pushed. This may be our response *unless* we have learned to master this behavior and to become good listeners.

Wasting Advantage of Thought Speed over Speech Speed

A final poor habit of listening has to do with how we use the extra time available as a listener. There is a great difference between *speech speed* and *thought speed;* we speak and think at different speeds. The average rate of speaking is about 125 words per minute, but the brain can handle words at a much faster rate. It is not uncommon, for example, to find people who can read at rates of 1,200 words per minute and easily understand what they have read. Some individuals have read as rapidly as 10,000 words per minute and then scored over 80 percent on factual tests of the material. Numerous experiments in compressed speech (speech that is speeded up mechanically) have shown that people can listen effectively at speeds four or five times faster than normal speech. The brain *handles* words at a lightning pace, but when we listen, the brain *receives* words at a snail's pace. Hence, there is a gap between processing what we hear and receiving the words because of the rate at which they are spoken. We cannot think more slowly; we continue to think at high speed while the spoken words arrive at slow speed. What this means is that there is a lot of time available for our brains to sidetrack us. Our brains can and do work with hundreds of thoughts other than those spoken to us. We use the extra thinking time when we listen, but how do we use it? We often fall into the habit of wasting it, and sometimes this takes us into daydreams, fantasies, or other activities unrelated to the message we came to hear. Even if we catch ourselves and come back to what the speaker is saying, it will be more difficult to understand. We have missed something in the speaker's line of thought, and it is now more difficult to grasp the ideas expressed. What is being said seems less interesting, and our old daydreams beckon us to return. Most of us have had such experiences as students in a classroom, but we must break the habit of wasting thinking time if we are to realize our full potential as listeners. The proper use of this spare time will be discussed in the section that follows.

How to Improve Listening Behavior

The objectives you should pursue to improve listening behavior include the elimination of poor listening habits already acquired and the development of basic skills and attitudes essential to good listening. If you desire to improve your listening, you may find the following eight suggestions worthwhile and helpful towards achieving this objective.

Listen to Difficult Material

The poorest listeners are inexperienced listeners, listeners, who are unacquainted with lectures, documentaries on radio or television, panel discussions or interviews on television, or public speeches given in lecture halls. Good listeners develop an appetite for a variety of spoken messages. They have even learned to enjoy the challenge of difficult subjects. They like intellectual stimulation and growth. If you want to become a better listener but feel handicapped by the bad habit of avoiding difficult presentations, then you should resolve to eliminate this handicap by participating as a listener in a wide variety of communication situations.

*Determine Purpose
Behind Communication
Situation and Your
Subsequent Role
in Listening*

If the communication is persuasive in purpose, you know that you will be engaged in critical listening. The material in this section of the chapter will identify specific skills involved in critical listening in addition to those involved in achieving your objective of developing basic skills and attitudes essential to good listening. If the communication is to inform or instruct, you will be concerned with receiving the ideas and concepts as clearly, accurately, and fully as possible. One objective for improving listening behavior is to acquire the habit of determining *why* you are listening.

*Create an Interest
in the Subject*

The key to being interested in a subject is its relevancy or usefulness to you. Senders do not always point out clearly how the information can be useful to you. Sometimes it becomes necessary for you purposefully to seek out ways in which this information can be beneficial. Sometimes, as a listener, you need to ask yourself, "What's the speaker saying that I can use? What worthwhile ideas has the speaker?" Research studies are unanimous in their discovery of the tremendous significance of the interest factor in listening proficiency. Good listeners seem to be interested in whatever they are listening to. Good listeners seldom find topics "dry."

We know that as interest goes up, concentration and learning efficiency increase also. The real problem is to determine what you can do when you are not interested to provide a stimulus for interest. For one thing, subjects tend to be interesting when they have immediate application. Hence, look for immediate reward. If necessary, however, discover for yourself how the information will be useful at a later time and place. Introspection to questions such as "Why am I here? What initial motive brought me to hear this speaker?" and "What selfish uses can I find for this material?" usually will help you to discover genuine interest in the topic.

Effective listening is closely related to personal growth, and for selfish and personal reasons it is necessary for us to try to become genuinely interested in receiving ideas. This objective relates to one of the common problems in listening discussed in the previous section—the problem of allowing distracting appearance or delivery to dominate one's attention and thinking. Our goal must be to listen to the message and not be distracted by the delivery or the appearance of the person. Our aim is to find out what the speaker is saying, to find out what knowledge and information the speaker has that we need.

Every speaker has peculiarities, and if you allow yourself to be bothered by a droning voice, a shrill pitch, a persistent cough, socially inappropriate dress, and so forth, you will more often than not be led away from concentrating fully on the message. Unfortunately, speakers often have some eccentricity. It may be poor eye contact, an accent, or some distracting bodily activity. It is possible, however, for you, the listener, to make the decision to adjust to those situations—to tell yourself that it is the message you want and that the idiosyncrasy of the speaker is unimportant. People can be rational. They can learn to control their behavior. Listeners can learn to adjust to speakers, and when they make that adjustment a natural part of their behavior, they will become more effective listeners.

Keep Your Emotions in Check

An important objective for improved listening is to learn to hold your fire, to learn not to get too excited about a speaker's point until you are certain you thoroughly understand it. The aim is always to withhold evaluation until comprehension is complete. Effective listeners keep open minds. They try to identify the words or phrases that are most upsetting emotionally and purposely to "cool" their reactions to them; otherwise emotions are aroused and deaf spots are created that impair listeners' ability to perceive accurately and to understand. Deaf spots are always areas of great sensitivity—areas of our strongest values, convictions, and prejudices. A single emotion-laden word or an argument may trigger our emotional blockage, and when this occurs, our listening efficiency drops toward the zero point.

There are some steps you can take to strengthen your behavior control. When you hear something that really upsets you, first, you can extract those words or phrases that are most upsetting to you emotionally and make a list of them. Second, you can analyze why each word influences you as it does. Ask yourself what the original basis for your reaction to that word is. Third, it may be helpful to discuss each of these words with a friend or classmate. You may discover that these words carry unique and purely personal connotations for you that are without foundation. In any event, getting these words out into the open and identifying them will be of great help in enabling you to cool your reactions to them.

Listen Primarily for Ideas and Patterns of Reasoning

The seventh objective for effective listening is to attain the ability to recognize main points and central ideas. Good listeners focus on ideas. They have acquired the ability to discriminate between fact and principle, idea and example, and evidence and argument. Poor listeners tend to be unable to make these distinctions. They fall into the poor listening habit identified earlier in this chapter—the habit of listening for facts. Good listeners know that it is important to get the main idea as quickly as possible and to comprehend the underlying structure of the message or the particular argument being given.

Use Spare Time Wisely

The final objective suggested for a self-improvement program in listening is to make the wisest possible use of the spare time created by the difference between speaking rate and thinking rate. The good listener acquires the ability to capitalize on thought speed. Most of us can think easily at about four times the average rate of speaking. That is, we have about four hundred words' worth of thinking time to spare during every minute a person talks to us. This major handicap to effective listening can be converted into our greatest single asset.

The answer lies in using the spare time purposefully to enhance our understanding of the message we are receiving. Listening authorities suggest that the following mental activities be used to fill this spare time: (1) anticipate what will be said; (2) note the adequacy with which each point is supported; (3) mentally review; and (4) listen "between the lines" for additional meaning. These are the ingredients of concentration in listening. The listener has time to engage in these "extra thoughts" while at the same time listening to the other person.

Listening between the lines is listening for hidden or unstated meanings, new meanings—that is, meanings other than those assigned by us initially—listening for what is not said as well as what is said.

Note Taking

Note taking is not an unusual activity for serious-minded students in educational institutions as well as participants in industrial and organizational training programs. Note taking can be highly beneficial to learning, although for some who have not learned to listen and to take notes efficiently, it can be a waste of time if not a hindrance to learning. So common is the inability to take notes efficiently that many colleges and universities, which realize the importance of this practice to learning, include instruction and training in note taking in their orientation programs for freshmen. Note taking in the classroom setting is a direct application of "listening for information" skills.

I can remember well an undergraduate history course I took in which note taking was a necessary part of learning the material covered. The evaluation of how much one learned in the course was derived solely from two examinations, both based entirely on classroom lecture material. Nothing in the text or assigned readings was tested. I was away from class one week on a choir tour and, before leaving, I arranged with a friend to use her notes when I returned. When I returned and saw her notes, I understood why she had not done well on the first test in the course. She tried to take down in narrative style every word the professor said. The result was that most of what the professor said did not get on the paper. She attempted to do in longhand what would have taxed a person skilled in shorthand to do.

Suggestions for Taking Better Notes

1. Decide whether or not you need to take notes. Probably one should not take notes indiscriminately. I believe I have known a person or two who got into such a habit of taking notes on everything that I suspect that when someone greeted them in the hall, they must have written it in their notebook. Notes are sometimes unnecessary and may get in the way of learning. There are no general rules applicable to everyone concerning when to and when not to take notes. It is an individual matter depending upon such things as your own concentration and retention abilities, whether the information will be used immediately or at some later date, and the purpose of the listening.

2. Decide what type of notes you should take—key-word or outline, partial outline, or complete outline. The key-word type of note taking provides the least cues of the three types, but it also permits you to pay maximum attention to the speaker—the nuances in the verbal or nonverbal secondary messages. If the key words are indeed *keys for you,* that is, if they are positively associated with meanings so as to be keys that open and recall whole areas of thought for you, then the key-word type of note taking can be highly efficient.

If, however, there are important ideas that cannot be represented by a word or phrase, then you will want to use either the partial outline or the complete outline. The difference is that, in a partial outline, you take notes on only areas of the presentation with which you are unfamiliar, while other topics in the presentation are not recorded in your notes, since you are already familiar with those areas. For example, if, in your communication class, various patterns for organizing materials were discussed and you knew the chronological and topical patterns but had not heard of the motivated sequence pattern, you might take notes on the motivated sequence but not on the time or topic patterns. Your partial outline notes do not represent all the messages in outline form. They represent only the new information that you may need to recall and review at a later time. The complete outline form of note taking is one that gives you a relatively complete record of what was said. The important thing is for you to determine which type is best for your needs in the particular situation.

3. Identify the organizational pattern of the message and let your note taking reflect that pattern. Some students attempt to force every lecture, re-

gardless of how it is organized, into their own favorite pattern. Sometimes the speaker may have no particular pattern. If that is the case, then you will want to adapt to that reality and not try to give the message an organizational pattern. The sooner you identify the speaker's pattern of organization—or the fact that the speaker has no clear-cut organizational pattern—the easier it will be for you to adjust your note taking to the situation.

4. Keep your notes brief so that they are notes—not narratives or verbose descriptions. The briefer your notes, the more time you have for listening and thinking and the less time you will spend writing.

5. Keep your notes clear. Do not clutter the page with words, scribbling, or doodling that becomes noise at a later time. Do not crowd words or phrases together. Give yourself enough room to keep your notes clear. Also, learn to use indentation to show visually the subordination of developmental ideas to major points.

6. Practice the principles for effective listening identified earlier in this chapter. At the heart of effective note taking is skillful listening.

Rewards of Good Listening

All of these objectives—listening to materials of various degrees of difficulty, determining the purpose of the communication, creating a personal interest in the message, adjusting to the speaker and the environment, holding the emotions in check, focusing on ideas and patterns, and using spare listening time efficiently—are quite worthwhile, especially for college students who spend an extraordinary amount of their time talking and listening.

Your successful effort to reach these objectives in your own listening behavior will be richly rewarded. You will not only improve your own listening ability and decision-making ability, but you will also gain an appreciation of speech communication. You will gain new insights into the speaking process as well, and as you become a more competent speech communication critic, you may also become a better communicator. Further, you will be better prepared to handle the steadily increasing avalanche of communication in the world, which threatens to inundate modern man. In this day of communication explosion and saturation, it is more necessary than ever that we acquire the ability to listen effectively and discriminatingly. In a world of conflicting views, half-truths, indoctrination, and propaganda, the competent person must be able to listen critically; to listen for valid information; to listen for enjoyment and renewal of spirit. The poor listener is severely handicapped today. Without the skills that permit you to be an effective receiver, you might easily be overcome by the incoming streams of messages. Having become a good listener, you will find that great personal satisfaction and reward can be derived from effective listening.

Feedback

A second concept related to the receiving of information is *feedback*. Actually, effective listening depends on feedback. Effective listening occurs only when the cues we send back to the other person allow that person to know we have received the message. It is on the basis of that feedback that the message can be adjusted to improve its understandability. This corrective function is the primary purpose of feedback.

Feedback Defined

Wiener, one of the first persons to be concerned with feedback, defines it as "the property of being able to adjust future conduct by past performance. Feedback may be as simple as that of the common reflex or it may be a higher order feedback, in which past experience is used not only to regulate specific movements, but also whole policies of behavior."[1] The essential characteristic of this definition has been accepted generally by communication scholars, i.e., that corrective function is the heart of the feedback process. Feedback, then, enables communicators to correct and adjust messages to adapt to the receiver. Without feedback there is no way to monitor the communication process, no way to seek integration and agreement. Rather, we are left with a haphazard, random, or chance system of influencing others and of cooperating with others. Without feedback there is no systematic way to adjust to change, and change, as we have noted before, is inherent in process. Barnlund, in discussing feedback, emphasizes these points strongly. He states:

> Feedback is a requirement of all self-governing, goal seeking systems whether they are mechanical devices, living organisms, or social groups. To obtain this feedback an autonomous system must be able to observe or scan its own performance, compare intended and actual operation, and use this information to guide future action.[2]

Effective communication exists between two persons when the receiver of a message gives it the interpretation intended by the sender. Effective communication results from the ongoing corrective process made possible by feedback.

One point should be made clear in our discussion of feedback, and that is that both communicators are senders and receivers simultaneously. We have discussed feedback as though it were coming from one person (the receiver) to another person (the sender) in a linear manner, that is, first the original message and then the feedback response. Actually, as we have indicated earlier, the process is complex and characterized by simultaneous interaction. Feedback is flowing both ways. It is not unidirectional! Feedback comes from both communicators and exerts a mutual influence. This is the

1. Norbert Wiener, *Cybernetics* (New York: John Wiley & Sons, Inc., 1948), p. 33.

2. Dean C. Barnlund, *Interpersonal Communication: Survey and Studies* (Boston: Houghton Mifflin Co., Inc., 1968), p. 229.

essence of interaction and the basis of transaction. According to Ashby, a leading British proponent of the concept of systematic feedback, feedback exists between two parties when each affects the other, when the relationship is characterized by a simultaneity of response.[3] Nevertheless, if feedback is ignored and not sought, communication failure can result. Sometimes people are so preoccupied with themselves and their message that they do not listen to or observe the feedback of others, or they do not seek feedback from the other person to check on the other's interpretation of the message. Communication without feedback is one-way communication. Two-way communication occurs when senders obtain feedback concerning how receivers are decoding the senders' messages. In two-way communication, through the use of feedback, messages are modified so that they communicate more accurately with receivers. Through feedback, accuracy of understanding is facilitated; and accuracy of understanding improves the development of fulfilling relationships and of working together effectively.

3. W. Ross Ashby, *Introduction to Cybernetics* (London: Chapman & Hall, 1956), p. 53.

Sources and Types of Feedback

There are a number of ways of categorizing the different types of feedback. We will look at six of those ways.

Internal or External Feedback

Feedback can be classified as either internal or external. When we monitor our own performance and think about what we are saying as we encode the message, or when we reflect about something we have just said, we are using internal feedback; but when we are listening to the verbal response of the other person, or observing that person's nonverbal responses, we are using external feedback. We may also hear what we are saying as we say it (external feedback) and rephrase it to give it added meaning (internal feedback), thus using both sources, external and internal, for self-feedback. Johnson described internal and external feedback well when he said:

> Put very simply, internal feedback is at play in the speaker who is being reflective about something he has just said, while external feedback is operating when the speaker is being sensitive to the reactions of other people to what he has said. When external feedback is at work it necessarily affects—and is affected by—the internal feedback that is going on at the same time. The two kinds are doubtless even more closely interwoven than this would indicate, however; even if no other persons are present, the reflecting that is done by a speaker or thinker on what he has just said or thought is influenced in some degree by his past experiences—and his contemplations of future experiences—with external feedback. So, when we say that there are two kinds of feedback we do so with the realization, of course, that while they might be

4. Wendell Johnson, *Your Most Enchanted Listener* (New York: Harper & Row Publishers, Inc., 1956), p. 174.

distinguished, one from the other, they cannot possibly be disentangled. As his own listener, every speaker attends as best he can as though with the ears of a multitude.[4]

Johnson's description of internal feedback identifies our private expectations and evaluations of the adequacy of our messages. You have probably had the experience of rehearsing a speech, or a conversation you were going to have. You tried out phrases to see if they sounded right. This was an example of internal self-feedback. Internal feedback is taking place all the time as we communicate with others. As we speak, we get set for certain responses. These expected responses result from internal feedback. We hope that our internal feedback matches the external response of the other person. In other words, sometimes we correct what we intend to say before we say it on the basis of our internal feedback, and sometimes the listener actually responds as we anticipate. When that happens, the internal and external feedback match quite closely. Both kinds of feedback are necessary to effective communication. Reliance on either one alone decreases the efficiency of the adjustive process.

Internal and external feedback.

© Richard Kalvar/Magnum Photos, Inc.

Another classification system for feedback is positive or negative, a category system focusing on the reinforcement aspect of feedback and one that has been used extensively in feedback research. This kind of feedback tells us whether our message is received correctly or not, and whether or not our message is accomplishing our objective. As Berlo states, "if the public buys more (positive feedback), the advertiser keeps his messages. If the public quits buying the product (negative feedback), the advertiser changes his messages."[5] A person receiving positive feedback tends to continue the behavior—to produce the same kind of message, that is, to send more messages similarly encoded and similar in their purposes; but the person receiving negative feedback tends to cease or modify the behavior—to change the

5. David K. Berlo, *The Process of Communication* (New York: Holt, Rinehart & Winston, Inc., 1960), pp. 113–14.

Not all feedback is positive.

message. Both kinds of feedback are important to the communication process, since negative or positive feedback provides the source with information as to whether the message is successful in accomplishing the source's objective—in satisfying the need that motivated the communication.

Reinforcement or Correction Feedback

A third way of looking at feedback is in terms of its serving either as a reinforcement (positive or negative as just discussed) or as a monitoring function for corrective purposes. In other words, many researchers have pointed out that not all feedback is used as reinforcement. Sometimes feedback data are used to compare what was wanted (ideal or expected goal) with what was obtained (actual result). Keltner has pointed out that feedback is much more complex than just positive or negative reinforcement.[6] Berlo makes the same point as he explains this corrective, monitoring, or cybernetic function.[7] He says this function emphasizes the interdependence of two or more elements in a system, that is, of both the sender and the receiver. Together, they constitute a system during a communication transaction, and feedback is the means by which each adjusts to the other for the purpose of integration. When this is the purpose for which feedback is put to use, reward or punishments are secondary. Rather, this function of feedback is control, balance, or integration of the elements in the total system, that is, an integration of the sender and receiver as a system in interpersonal communication. This integration or control for the purpose of maintaining a harmonious system is called *homeostasis*.

6. John W. Keltner, *Interpersonal Speech Communication: Elements and Structure* (Belmont, Calif.: Wadsworth Publishing Co., Inc., 1970), p. 90.

7. Berlo, *Process of Communication*, p. 111.

Indirect or Direct Feedback

Feedback may be classified, also, as indirect or direct, purposive or nonpurposive. In other words, some response messages are purposefully constructed by the receiver and sent directly to the sender. Other responses of the receiver may be beneath the awareness level and are not purposefully constructed, but are simply "given off." Such informative behaviors were discussed extensively in chapter 6, on nonverbal communication.

Purposive feedback is originated by the receiver and directly sent to the source for the purpose of providing information relative to the primary message. It is intentional feedback communication. Indirect feedback is not information purposively selected and sent, but is instead nonpurposive and unintentional feedback communication. Let us look at some examples.

Our local newspaper, like many other newspapers, features a "Letters to the Editor" section. Each day, among the letters appearing in the column can be found one or more "angry-reader" letters. These are written to "straighten out" the editor on some issue. Such letters are dramatic examples of purposive and direct feedback.

UPI

A common example of indirect and unintentional feedback is the situation in which a person sends one feedback message verbally, but also sends another feedback massage, a nonverbal message that clearly contradicts the verbal. The nonverbal feedback message may have been communicated by posture, tension, movement towards or away from, facial expression, breaking and refusing eye contact, tone of voice, rate of speech, or any one of numerous nonverbal ways of communicating. The person responding did not intend to send a contradictory message, but it was "given off" nonetheless, and we got the unintentional feedback. As noted in chapter 6, these unintentional nonverbal behaviors often have to do with feelings, likings, and preferences.

Immediate
or Delayed
Feedback

Feedback may be immediate or delayed. In face-to-face communication, whether formal or informal, public speaking or group discussion, we have access to immediate feedback. Such feedback gives face-to-face communication great adaptive and corrective potential; but in mass communication, feedback is of necessity delayed. Immediate feedback is not possible in mass communication, since the sender of the message is not in the physical presence of the receivers. Only delayed feedback in the form of letters, phone calls, decrease or increase in number of viewers as measured by the rating services, and decrease or increase in sales of products advertised provide feedback information.

Verbal or Nonverbal
Feedback

Finally, feedback may be classified according to the channel used, that is, as either verbal or nonverbal. Nonverbal cues such as facial expression, posture, gestures, sighs, tone of voice, and other bodily movements or physical responses may provide important feedback to the sender, as explained in the illustration in our discussion of nonpurposive or unintentional feedback above. In fact, nonverbal messages are often used as much as or more than verbal messages by police, medical doctors, psychiatrists, therapists, and others in investigative or interviewing situations.

Effects of Feedback

Experiments in which feedback was the manipulated variable have demonstrated dramatically that feedback does have a powerful effect on communication and communicators. Its effect on various dependent variables has been investigated and reported in the journals of several academic areas—communication, education, psychology, business administration, and speech sciences, for example.

One of the landmark studies of feedback effects is that of Leavitt and Mueller.[8] They tested four variations of feedback: (1) none, (2) seeing each other only (receiver was not allowed to talk), (3) yes-no by receiver (the sender could check on his messages by asking questions to which the receiver could answer yes or no), and (4) free feedback (all verbal and nonverbal messages between sender and receiver were allowed). The procedure for their experiment called upon the sender to describe verbally some patterns or geometric designs that the receiver was to draw. The sender could not draw the design; he or she could only tell the receiver how to draw it. The design drawn by the receiver was then compared to the criterion model, that is, to the design the sender had been looking at and from which the verbal description had been given. The results showed that with greater amounts of feedback, communication was slowed down. The slowest communication was the free feedback condition. As we would guess, corrective and adaptive communication takes time. If you want fast communication, then one-way communication is faster than two-way. Of course, you may be misunderstood entirely, but you will at least have fast misunderstanding. A second effect Leavitt and Mueller discovered was that accuracy of communication increased as feedback increased. With free feedback, the patterns drawn by the receivers were almost exactly like the criterion pattern. And the third effect of greater amounts of feedback was that the receivers felt more confident about the communication outcome. Conversely, as feedback decreases or, even worse, is absent, accuracy decreases, miscommunication and confusion increase, and anxiety sets in.

A second kind of feedback studies have investigated positive and negative feedback. One effect of "reinforcement feedback" (positive or negative feedback) is that the sender's encoding process changes. A series of experiments has demonstrated that communicators in public speaking situations, as well as communicators in interpersonal communication situations, have encoding problems when they experience severe negative feedback. Speakers even *make changes in the content* of their messages when they receive strong negative feedback. Negative feedback tends to disrupt the encoding process, sometimes to the extent of altering words. If the feedback is positive, however, there are fewer disruptions. Also, with positive feedback more opinion statements are used, while with negative feedback opinion statements tend to decrease.

Before concluding this section on feedback effects, we must call attention to two special topics that relate directly to feedback effects. One is self-concept, a topic discussed at length in chapter 3; the second is feedback effects in times of personal crisis.

Self-concept, as pointed out in chapter 3, is built largely on the basis of feedback received from others. As the individual receives open and honest feedback, he or she becomes aware of himself or herself in relation to others. This is possible only through interaction with others—interaction that

8. Harold J. Leavitt and Ronald A. H. Mueller, "Some Effects of Feedback on Communication," in *Interpersonal Communication: Survey and Studies*, ed. Dean Barnlund (Boston: Houghton Mifflin Co., 1968), pp. 251–59.

utilizes feedback. For as you provide feedback to others, they come to know themselves and you and, conversely, through their feedback to you, you come to discover yourself.

The second situation in which feedback effects are especially important is in times of personal crisis. Feedback can serve persons in crisis situations in an empathic and facilitative capacity. There are times in the lives of most of us when we need a person to talk to—someone who will listen to us and who will provide empathic feedback, both verbal and nonverbal. We know from experience as well as from scientific study how important it is for each of us to have someone—a close friend, husband or wife, or family member—to whom we can turn to share our deep and personal problems.

Conversely, most of us, at one time or another, have had the experience of playing the other role, that of providing an empathic ear for a close friend. If you recall such an experience, you know that the primary function was that of providing supportive feedback. That feedback, undergirded by love and caring, is of such importance in crisis situations that we would be remiss to ignore it in this discussion of the effects of feedback. And, though it may

Each of us needs someone to turn to in times of personal crisis.

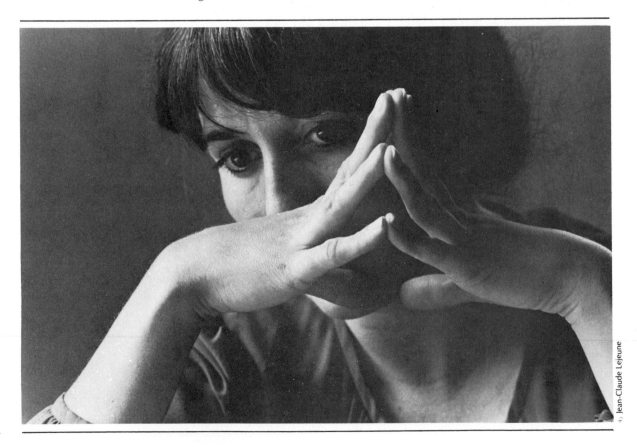

be a "special" topic as regards feedback effects, it is not an uncommon problem. Certain crisis situations are common to most of us, and generally, these situations require an empathic feedback role on the part of others for us to cope with the problem effectively. Death, divorce, retirement, and accidents are examples of common experiences that are traumatic to various degrees. In such times as these, empathic and supportive feedback are an essential part of the process of resolving the situation and adjusting to the change that has occurred. Brockopp and Hoff relate an incident that illustrates how important empathic feedback can be, at least in the initial stage of a crisis situation:

> A girl called the crisis center upon the advice of her mother as she could not stop crying one morning following a suicide attempt with her mother's pills. Intake interview revealed a very depressed, anxious and desperate girl with a history of family conflict, drug involvement and a prior suicide attempt. After separate sessions with the girl and her divorced mother, family therapy was initiated with a total of six sessions including one with an older friend who allegedly initiated the girl into the drug scene. The focus in family crisis therapy was on the meaning of the girl's suicidal and drug behavior in relation to total family problems. By the end of the sessions there was evidence of marked improvement in communication between mother and daughter, relief of depression, crying and suicidal ideation and attempts.[9]

9. G. W. Brockopp and L. Hoff, "Crisis Intervention Services and Community Mental Health Programs," Crisis Intervention 4 (1972).5.

The story illustrates the role crisis centers can play for persons who have no one to whom they can turn in times of crisis.

Two different student teachers with whom one of us has worked during the past few years have described in their teaching logs incidents in which high school students in crisis situations sought help from them—student teachers—there being no one else the students felt they could turn to. In one of these situations, a boy, quite distraught (he had raped a girl), wanted help, but did not know what kind of help he wanted. However, he could not bring himself to talk with the school counselor, an older friend, his physician, or any teacher. The student teacher was able to provide the empathic and supportive role the boy needed and was eventually successful in getting him to see a priest.

The other situation involved a boy who sought out the student teacher to talk about a crisis situation, informing the student teacher that he "was going to kill himself tonight." The next morning he was found dead in his car, where he had gassed himself. These are two examples of persons seeking an empathic relationship. In one instance the person providing an understanding ear was successful. In the second instance, tragedy resulted despite the attempt to provide empathic feedback.

Quite obviously, considering this and similar tragedies, one of the problems in crisis situations is that the person experiencing the crisis has no one to whom to turn and is not always aware that intervention assistance is available. He or she may have no knowledge of or contact with intervention services. Many communities have been concerned with this problem, have organized crisis centers and hotlines, and have undertaken wide educational and publicity campaigns to deal with the problem. If the individual facing a crisis communicates with empathic, knowledgeable others in an open and clear manner, he or she will gain information from the exchange of ideas and emotional strength from the helpfulness and supportiveness of caring people. These elements are necessary components of constructive decision making and of satisfactory crisis resolution. Through communication we adapt to our environment. The facing of a crisis and the constructive resolution of a crisis is adaptation to the environment—adaptation to change; and empathic, supportive feedback is an important component in that process.

These are not the only ways in which feedback affects communication, but they represent a sampling of the many effects that feedback has on the communication process. Since feedback is so important to communication, are there guidelines for how we might use feedback?

Effective Use of Feedback

The guidelines we suggest are commonly cited for effective interpersonal communication in various settings—instruction, transactional analysis, and problem-solving discussion, for example. They are:

1. Effective feedback, used for reinforcement, is both positive and negative.

2. Effective feedback, used to monitor the process, is descriptive rather than evaluative. By describing, the individual is left free either to use feedback or not to use it at all. And descriptive feedback does not provide as much defensive behavior.

3. Immediate feedback is more effective than delayed feedback. Generally, it is most useful if provided at the earliest opportunity.

4. Effective feedback is specific rather than general.

5. Effective feedback is directed toward behavior that the sender can do something about, rather than toward behavior or circumstances over which the person has no control.

6. Effective feedback is constructive rather than destructive. It is motivated by the desire to help the sender, and is given in that spirit. It is directed toward the objectives of increasing fidelity in the exchanges of meaning and of enhancing integration.

7. Effective feedback does not overload the communication channels by imposing all of one's interpretations on the message received. Rather, the objective is to provide only necessary feedback—enough information, but not too much.

The next step, it seems to us, is for you to check your own feedback behavior. How effective is this part of your interpersonal communication? Questions such as the following can help you assess your use of feedback.

Do I make a habit of giving feedback and of using the feedback I receive from others? Or do I ignore feedback?

Do I use replicative feedback, rather than always asking the other person to restate, or asking what was meant?

Do I encourage feedback by using it out of a positive orientation, rather than criticizing or condemning through it?

Am I specific rather than general?

Do I avoid overloading feedback with details and unrelated data?

Do I provide clear and consistent feedback rather than ambiguous or contradictory feedback?

Feedback and Feelings

Much of the feedback we receive or send is via the nonverbal channels and has to do with affective messages—with feelings. Feelings are a legitimate part of interpersonal communication and an inherent part of the feedback process. They should not be ignored in the study of feedback.

Can you imagine human communication devoid of feeling, or a relationship existing between two persons with no feelings included? Such a situation is impossible! Only in "Star Trek" do we have a being devoid of all feeling. The Vulcan, Spock, can engage in interpersonal communication and keep feelings entirely out of it, but you and I, like Captain Kirk, Scotty, and the others aboard the *Enterprise,* cannot engage in interpersonal communication without feelings being involved. We cannot afford to ignore this important element in feedback. The remainder of this chapter focuses upon feelings in the feedback process. We are concerned with four topics: (1) the importance of expressing feelings, (2) consequences of suppressing feelings, (3) ways of feeding back feelings, and (4) ambiguous feedback and feelings.

*Importance of
Expressing Feelings
via Feedback*

Feelings expressed (or repressed, for that matter) tend to elicit the same kind of behavior from the other person. Argyle states: "During social interaction it is very common for an act by A to be followed by a similar act from B. This we call response matching. . . . Similar response matching takes place with regard to emotional state, bodily contact, and other elements to social behavior."[10] Numerous studies, reviewed by Argyle in his discussion of reciprocity behavior, have verified this phenomenon. These studies, made between 1955 and 1969, found that length of utterances follows this rule, as do

10. Michael Argyle, *Social Interaction* (New York: Atherton Press, 1969), pp. 171–72.

length and frequency of pauses and interruptions. Jokes lead to jokes; giving opinions leads to the other person giving opinions; showing solidarity, disagreeing, and asking questions, all lead to similar response behavior; smiling elicits smiling; and self-disclosure leads to self-disclosure. The reciprocity phenomenon operates equally well with the feedback of feelings. This is why the feeding back of feelings is important in interpersonal communication.

Being friends, for example, is a two-way street. For two persons to be friends, they must engage in behaviors that enable a mutual liking, trusting, and knowing to develop. We tend to like those persons who like us, and to trust those persons who trust us. It is not surprising, then, that the feeding back of feelings of liking and of warmth tend to elicit from the other person expression of feelings of liking and warmth, or that the expression of dislike and coldness causes the other person to feel dislike and coldness. The feelings we express toward another tend to be reciprocated by the other. To know and understand this principle of reciprocity gives us an important insight into the process of interpersonal communication.

Another reason for the importance of feeding back feelings in interpersonal communication is that such expression is the necessary key to the establishment of a relationship. To create liking and trust, it is necessary to provide honest feedback. The expression of feeling such as caring or warmth is the vehicle by which liking is indicated; and to express liking, we must be able to feed back our feelings clearly, honestly, and constructively to the other person.

Inhibited Feelings and Suppressed Feedback: Effects on Self-Concept and on the Interpersonal Communication Process

11. David W. Johnson, *Reaching Out* (Englewood Cliffs, N.J.: Prentice-Hall, Inc., 1972), p. 90.

One of the consequences of suppressing feedback and inhibiting the expression of feelings, according to Johnson, is that the quality of problem solving goes down.[11] Some persons believe the opposite. They believe that any expression of feelings interferes with problem solving. Supposedly, when we engage in logical problem solving, feelings should be left out of the process. Actually, however, feelings are a valid part of the process, and when they are ignored and suppressed, our thinking and decisions are poor. Unresolved feelings can contribute to biased decisions. We suspect that almost all of us have, at one time or another, accepted a poor idea because we could not handle or would not express a feeling we had. We could not say to the person suggesting the idea, "I like you very much, but I don't like that particular idea." We may have just suppressed the feeling and acceded to the idea, and we may have rejected good ideas for similar reasons. Bales' research has revealed that the quality of problem solving is improved when participants freely give both positive and negative statements. When either is suppressed, communication quality is diminished.[12]

12. Robert F. Bales, "In Conference," *Howard Business Review* 32 (1954):44–50.

Another consequence of suppressing feedback of feelings is that it can affect our perception of persons, events, and information. Feelings not dealt with can create blind spots of misinterpretation and distortion. The greater the suppression of feelings, the greater the number of blind spots in our reception of information.

A third consequence of suppressing affective feedback is the creation of an unreal and nonauthentic person. People have emotions. Even as we think and observe, so are we happy or unhappy, fearful or secure, depressed or joyful. Feeling is not a once- or twice-a-day experience. Feeling is with us all the time, just as thinking is. In fact, feeling accompanies thinking, and, probably, certain kinds or ways of feeling go with certain kinds or ways of thinking. Thus, to try to suppress feeling in communication is to deny yourself, for among the things that make you uniquely you are your feelings and emotions.

The psychologically healthy person does not inhibit feelings and suppress feedback. The healthy person is attuned to feelings, accepts them, and integrates them into his or her communication, thinking, and relating to others.

If you are to know the real person, you need to know the feelings that are associated with that person's ideas and decisions. If a person will not share these feelings with you but suppresses that feedback, or if you will not allow that person to express these feelings, then it is not the real and authentic person with whom you are communicating. Gut-level communication, as well as head communication, is an important aspect of the total person. The dishonesty that results from suppressed feedback of feelings creates artificial persons and superficial relationships. Whether in marriage, organizational committees, or whatever, when persons pervert or destroy their authenticity by suppressing feedback of feelings, their relationships are set on a dangerous and self-destructive path.

In summary, suppressing feedback results in serious three-way deterioration: in the quality of problem solving, in information reception, and in creating and sustaining productive relationships.

Ways of Feeding Back Feelings

We have noted thus far that feelings are a legitimate part of interpersonal communication and that there can be negative consequences of suppressing feedback of feelings. Let us turn now to how feelings are fed back. What are the ways we use to express them?

First, before you can feed back feelings easily and constructively, you must develop an awareness of your feelings and emotions and learn to accept them. How have you been behaving toward your feelings as you communicate with others? It might be helpful if the next time you engage in an

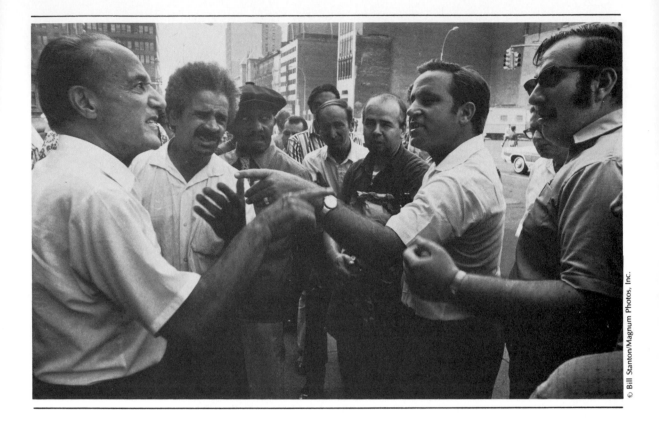

© Bill Stanton/Magnum Photos, Inc.

Emotional feedback is both verbal and nonverbal.

argument with someone, you will intentionally think about your feelings. How are you feeling? Are you afraid? Angry? Jealous? If you can admit your feelings, take a good look at them to identify them, estimate their strength or intensity, and try to discover what caused them or where they came from, then you can know yourself better. Further, if you feed back your feelings in respectful but honest ways, you can function in interpersonal communication situations as your real and whole self.

You will find that you and others tend to feed back feelings in two general ways! verbally and nonverbally.

We Feed Back Feelings Verbally

13. Johnson, *Reaching Out*, p. 91.

Johnson has suggested that a person unaware of feelings, unaccepting of feelings, or unskilled in feeding back feelings will use the following forms of verbal expression of feelings:[13] labeling others, giving commands, asking questions, making accusations, engaging in name calling, making sarcastic remarks, and expressing approval or disapproval. In contrast, the self-directed feedback of emotions and feelings by persons who are aware of their feelings and who understand their emotions usually takes one of the following forms: identification or naming of the feeling, reporting as to the form of action the feeling motivates one to take, and describing the feelings as a simile or metaphor.

One should note that the first type of feedback of feelings (those more characteristic of persons not accepting or perhaps even unaware of their feelings) is directed toward the other person. The second type of feedback is directed toward the self. It identifies and names the feeling by saying, "I am afraid," "I feel angry," or "I feel confident." It reports action you want to take by saying, "I could kiss you!" Or it may utilize a figure of speech: "I feel as though a bulldozer ran over me." All these statements refer to the self, while name calling, commands, accusations, sarcastic remarks, and sharp questions are directed toward the other person.

John Powell has discussed five principles that ought to guide you in emotions and feelings.[14] The principles are:

1. Feeling statements should not imply a judgment of the other person. Describe your own feelings and emotions rather than labeling the other person.

2. Emotions are not moral (good or bad). Do not link emotions to sinfulness. Experiencing fear or anger does not make you a bad person.

3. Emotions and feelings must be integrated with intellect and reasons. You need to understand that emotions are normal and useful and to accept the fact of their usefulness intellectually.

4. Emotions and feelings must be reported if you are to allow others to know you.

5. With rare exceptions, emotions must be reported at the time they are experienced. Reporting a feeling the following day is not the same as reporting it at the time it is experienced. Emotions are transient and difficult to recapture.

We express emotions and feelings verbally, but it is important that we learn to express them verbally in a healthy and productive way.

14. John Powell, S.J., *Why Am I Afraid to Tell You Who I Am?* (Niles, Ill.: Argus Communications, 1969), pp. 50–85.

We Feed Back Feelings Nonverbally

Some scholars believe that much of the meaning exchanged by persons in communication situations is carried by nonverbal messages—as much as 65 percent.[15] So important are the nonverbal aspects of communication that an entire chapter (6) is devoted to them in this text. In that chapter, we called attention to the fact that nonverbal communication is especially important to the expression of feelings, that it plays a *primary* role in the communication of feelings and emotions. We noted that facial and vocal cues appear to be the most important nonverbal cues for communicating feelings and emotions, although it is the totality of the person's behavior—an amalgam of all of the nonverbal cues—that give us the best idea of the feeling or emotion

15. J. D. McCroskey, C. E. Larson, and M. L. Knapp, *Introduction to Interpersonal Communication* (Englewood Cliffs, N.J.: Prentice-Hall, Inc., 1971).

communicated. We discussed touch as a form of nonverbal communication and pointed out that it is an extremely important way to communicate feelings in intimate communication. One noted psychiatrist has stated: "Many of the difficulties most of us have in communicating even with those persons closely related to us could be overcome if we would simply employ the language of physical contact more."[16] Touch seems to be quite important to all human beings and to animals as well. Mothers touch their children to comfort them and hold them to give them reassurance. Unfortunately, there is a reluctance to touch among adults in our culture. The result is that as adults we are denied much of the language of physical contact. We are "uptight" about communicating our feelings and emotions by touch. Our culture bias against touching is emphasized well by Flip Wilson's "Don't touch me! You don't know me that well!" admonitions to his TV guests.

Many psychologists are stressing the importance of nonverbal communication as a means of helping persons to relate to one another. Julius Fast, in his book *Body Language*, describes a party where the guests were forbidden to speak.[17] They could communicate only through touch and other nonverbal means. They discovered that they could communicate feelings and emotions, and that they did, in fact, build unique and unforgettable relationships without words. We do communicate our feelings and emotions nonverbally. The way we walk, sit, and stand; the way we turn our heads, arch our eyebrows, smile, or frown; the tension, affection, or calmness in one's touch—all these cues help reveal one's feelings.

As children, each of us probably used our entire bodies to communicate our feelings. We shouted, stomped, jumped, yelled, smiled, frowned, and cried as we openly expressed our true feelings. Somewhere between childhood and maturity too many of us learned to suppress our feelings, to reject our feelings, and to be coldly rational. We learned to say things we did not mean, to act intelligent when we did not understand at all, to thank people and compliment them when there was no appreciation in us. We hid our feelings behind verbal screens rather than expressing them clearly and constructively through our nonverbal communication. In short, we did not learn to provide open, constructive feedback. We need to rediscover something of the honesty of childhood and find our way to healthy relationships through honest and constructive feedback.

16. Smiley Blanton, "The Magic of Being in Touch," *Reader's Digest,* August 1965.

17. Julius Fast, *Body Language* (New York: Pocket Books, Inc., 1971).

Death of Feelings: A Societal Disease

Today, according to the writings of some of our best observers of the condition of man, one of the growing, serious illnesses of thousands of persons in highly developed and industrialized societies is the death of feelings or the absence of significant emotional involvement. People are coming to live ever more shallowly and transiently. Relationships (emotional involvement and feelings) have become superficial. Ralph Greenson has described this superficiality—this death of emotional involvement.[18] He has observed various types of persons who deny themselves authentic relationships. They have lost or suppressed ability to have authentic feelings and to become emotionally involved to build significant and lasting relationships.

18. Ralph Greenson, "Emotional Involvement," in *The Exciting Ear,* ed. Eleanor McKinnery (New York: Pantheon Books, 1966).

One such group are those persons who have no relationships with people—only with things. Life, for them, is lived at the superficial level of things. They work for things, talk about things, and are primarily concerned with things. They strive for wealth and accumulate possessions. They move from larger to larger homes, from one expensive car to more expensive cars, from one investment to even larger and greater investments. But these people live in emotional poverty. In their hunger for authentic involvement, they seek things. They become involved with inanimate objects.

A second group of persons, who limit themselves to superficial relationships, Greenson describes as people whose lives are overrun with frenzied activity, as chronically intense, entranced, and enthusiastic. They are party givers and party goers. They are instant first-namers and strive for instant warmth and affection. Greenson states:

> . . . to make sure it's instant warmth, they give you some alcohol and stir you around in the group, and now everybody is dissolved in this kind of amorphous glow that looks like a relationship—except that you can't remember who these people are. . . .how are these people really involved? Not in the sense I mean. This is again a pseudo-involvement; a search for involvement, a frantic wish to become involved, but they can't really do it because it is indiscriminate; it is almost impersonal. . . . These are people who have a terrible need to be popular. [They are unable] to discriminate between friends, acquaintances, strangers, and enemies. If you're there—you're my friend, in fact you're my dearest friend and I call you "honey" and "darling." And this is a typical sign that they call anybody and everybody darling and honey.[19]

19. Ibid., p. 42.

A third group who lives in superficial rather than authentic and emotionally valid relationships are the pseudosexual people. Greenson describes this group as follows:

> . . . now you find a very interesting group of people who apparently are very prone to have sexual relations, but they have sex without passion and also without guilt . . . if you listen to their sexual adventures —which they are quite willing to tell you—you find they are so boring—which is remarkable; it used to be that sexual stories or adventures were exciting; not with this particular group of people. They, again, are boring because they're indiscriminate; this is not a person falling in love with another person . . . no, it is only another conquest in a series of conquests or another step in some kind of a ladder that leads nowhere. These people are collectors, building a collection that they add certain trophies or people to . . . it's a degradation of the whole meaning of sexuality and of passion; as I said, these people are not passionate;

Superficial relationships and lack of significant emotional involvements are becoming more widespread in our highly developed industrialized society.

they don't love, they don't become infatuated. They just feel some bodily needs and try to find some kind of a person to satisfy them with—and this is how they live.[20]

20. Ibid., p. 44.

Greenson has observed in his work as a psychoanalyst these types of persons who have developed communication and life-styles characterized by superficial relationships rather than by authentic relationships based on true feelings and honest involvement. For these persons, and they do include virtually thousands in our society, feelings are dead. We believe that as people lose their capacity to experience feelings, to care about the feelings of others, and to express feelings in feedback to others, the quality and effectiveness of interpersonal communication suffers.

Ambiguous Feedback

It is sometimes difficult to know with any degree of precision the feelings of another person because in many instances those feelings are ambiguous and embedded in contradictory messages. The ambiguity or contradiction may be in the nonverbal area alone, or it may be between the nonverbal and verbal messages. Sometimes a person may say one thing and do another. Perhaps right now you can think of someone whom you believe likes you, but you just are not sure because the person has never said so. Or maybe someone keeps telling you how much he or she likes you, but the person's nonverbal behavior does not seem to be what you would expect it to be if he or she did like you. There are contradictions and ambiguity in the feedback. Why?

Feedback may be ambiguous because of contradictions in nonverbal messages or contradictions between verbal and nonverbal messages. There is, almost always, some ambiguity in nonverbal feedback. This is true in part because the same feeling can be expressed nonverbally in dozens of ways, Think of all the ways you might use to express anger—ways from furious bodily activity (stomping feet, waving arms, and so on) to stiff rigidity. Moreover, any single nonverbal cue can be used to express any number of emotions or feelings. A blush, for example, can indicate anger, embarrassment, pleasure, or hostility. Moreover, there are wide differences among cultures, subcultures, and even social groups as to the meaning of many nonverbal feedback cues. There is, consequently, plenty of room for error in our interpretation of nonverbal feedback. The fact is that the language of nonverbal communication is subject to the same kinds of ambiguity of meaning as is verbal language.

The second source of confusion in interpreting feedback of feelings stems from the contradiction of verbal messages by nonverbal behavior. For example, on a certain morning one of us was in conference with an administrator at the university and, as the time neared noon, he began shifting in his chair and glancing at the clock. Noticing his own behavior and the effect it produced, he said, "Oh, don't rush. I have plenty of time," But his physical behavior as well as the tonal qualities of his voice said clearly that he was worried about the time. The verbal and nonverbal behaviors were contradictory.

What happens when verbal and nonverbal behavior is contradictory? We tend to believe the behavior that we think is more difficult to fake. Generally, we assume that nonverbal feedback is more difficult to fake than verbal. We are more likely to believe nonverbal feedback than verbal feedback when the two are in contradiction. Sometimes, however, we are left in a state of not really understanding the person. Or we may pay no attention to the nonverbal feedback and accept the verbal feedback of feelings as true when, in fact, we recognize the feelings to be untrue. When there is ambiguity or contradiction in feedback, and when we cannot resolve the confusion, states of anxiety, suspicion, and guardedness arise in us.

21. Paul Watzlawick, Janet H. Beavin, and Don D. Jackson, *Pragmatics of Human Communication,* (New York: W. W. Norton & Co., Inc., 1967), pp. 211–18.

This phenomenon has been called the *double bind*.[21] In a double-bind situation, the receiver is caught between contradictory messages. It is essentially a "damned if we do and damned if we don't" situation. An example is the fellow who received two new shirts, one blue and one yellow, from his grandmother. The next day, to please his grandmother, he wore the yellow shirt, to which she reacted by saying, "What? You don't like the blue one?" Another example of a double bind that children sometimes experience, which has destructive and debilitating consequences, is the situation in which a child observes anger and hostility in a parent, while the parent

22. Ibid.

denies the anger and insists that the child deny it, too.[22] The child is then faced with the dilemma of whether to believe the parent or to believe his or her own senses. If the child believes the parent, a needed relationship is maintained while the child denies reality; or the child can disbelieve what the parent says, maintain a firm grasp on reality, and damage a vital relationship. Double binds of this kind that are long-lasting can contribute to

23. Ibid.

pathological behavior.[23]

The objectives toward which we should be striving are to feedback our feelings clearly, accurately, and constructively. We need to learn to make our verbal and nonverbal feedback congruent. And we need to learn to become aware of ambiguity and contradiction in the feedback of others.

SUMMARY

In the first part of this chapter we have emphasized the importance of listening—discussed the process of listening, identified its purposes, and explained some common misconceptions and problems. Also, specific suggestions were made as to how one might improve listening, including suggestions for taking notes.

The second concern of the chapter was feedback as a special kind of information reception. We emphasized the importance of feedback as the means for generating adaptive and corrective behavior necessary to transactions. We identified six types of feedback. The effects of feedback on communicators and on the process of communication was reviewed. Finally, eight guidelines for effective feedback were identified. The chapter concluded with a section on feeding back feelings, an especially important kind of feedback, since feelings have such a powerful impact on relationships and the process of interpersonal communication generally.

We have observed that feedback of feelings is a legitimate part of human communication. We took a look at how feedback of feelings affects communication—how feedback can elicit reciprocal behavior, how it enables relationships to be established, and how it permits the authentic person to emerge. Further, we considered the consequences of suppressing feedback. Problem-solving proficiency is decreased when feedback is suppressed. Perception and receptivity to information are impaired when feelings are kept bottled up rather than constructively fed back. Finally, we identified some ways for feeding back feelings constructively.

SELECTED READINGS

Barbara, Dominick A. The Act of Listening (Springfield, Ill.: Charles C Thomas, 1958).

Barker, Larry L. Listening Behavior Publisher, (Englewood Cliffs, N.J.: Prentice-Hall, Inc., 1971).

Fast, Julius. Body Language (New York: Pocket Books, Inc., 1971).

Johnson, Wendell. Your Most Enchanted Listener (New York: Harper & Row Publishers, Inc., 1956).

Kelly, Charles M. "Empathic Listening." In Small Group Communication: A Reader, ed. by Robert S. Cathcart and Larry A. Samovar. 2d ed. (Dubuque, Iowa: William C. Brown Co., Publishers, 1974).

Nichols, Ralph G., and Stevens, Leonard A. Are You Listening? (New York: McGraw-Hill Book Co., 1957).

O'Banion, Terry, and O'Connell, April. The Shared Journey: An Introduction to Encounter (Englewood Cliffs, N.J.: Prentice-Hall, Inc., 1970).

8

Interpersonal Communication
Patterns and Orientations

Which shoe do you put on first? The right or the left? Do you sleep in the same position or pattern of positions each night? We are creatures of habit. We develop patterns of behavior as we adapt to our environment. This is true of our communication behavior, too. We develop habitual responding behaviors and habitual patterns or orientations as we interact with others. This chapter is concerned with habitual orientations that seem to be especially important in interpersonal communication. They are: (1) trust and supportiveness versus suspicion and defensiveness; (2) open-mindedness and flexibility versus closed-mindedness and dogmatism; and (3) attraction and affection versus alienation and hostility. These orientations dictate to a great extent the typical response behavior of persons as they interact. The effect of these patterns of behavior on interpersonal communication is quite pronounced; and if we are to understand fully the process of interpersonal communication and to improve our interpersonal communication skills, then we need to understand how these psychological orientations affect communication, how such orientations come about, and how we can modify them or influence their effect on our communication behavior.

You have noticed that these psychological orientations are arranged in pairs of opposites. One cannot be both open-minded and closed-minded at the same time; one cannot be both loving and hostile; one cannot be both trusting and suspicious. For that reason, we consider these orientations in pairs.

Moreover, as an orientation develops, it tends to become more and more generalized so as to apply to an ever greater number of situations and persons. And, too, these response sets tend not only to become broader in their application, but to become habitual as well. For that reason, these orientations can be either a great help in interpersonal communication, or a great hindrance and inhibitor of successful communication with others. Let us consider first interpersonal trust and supportiveness and their opposites, suspicion and defensiveness.

Trust or Defensiveness

The importance of trust in interpersonal relations has been emphasized in the teachings of philosophers and religious leaders for hundreds of years. The characteristic has received renewed attention in our lifetime from psychologists, communication scholars, and human relations experts. Among those who have placed trust as the foundation stone of satisfying interpersonal relationships or of wholesome development of the person through interaction with others are: Allport (theory of personality development),[1] Fromm (art of loving),[2] Buber (nature of good interpersonal relationships),[3] Gibb (group behavior),[4] Rogers,[5] and Deutsch.[6]

Cooperative and positive relationships demand a high degree of trust by each person. Unless a climate of trust exists in interpersonal communication, not much progress can be made. From the first meeting of persons (the acquaintanceship process) through ongoing relationships such as marriage, the basic foundation is the ability of the communicators to trust each other. The establishment of such a climate is the first and most important task they face. Once such a climate has been created, fears of rejection, betrayal, and harm disappear and feelings of supportiveness, acceptance, openness, and safety emerge. Of all the factors in interpersonal communication, this factor—a trusting and supportive climate—is of paramount importance. The absence of a trusting and supportive climate ultimately fosters a climate of suspicion and defensiveness that is dangerously destructive in interpersonal relationships.

1. G. W. Allport, *Personality and Social Encounter* (Boston: Beacon Press, Inc., 1960).

2. Erich Fromm, *The Art of Loving* (New York: Harper & Row Publishers, Inc., 1974).

3. Buber, Martin, *I and Thou* (New York: Charles Scribner's Sons, 1970).

4. Jack Gibb, "Climate for Trust Formation," in *T-Group Theory and Laboratory Method: Innovation in Re-education*, ed. L. P. Bradford, J. Gibb, and K. D. Benne (New York: John Wiley & Sons, Inc., 1964), pp. 279–309.

5. Carl Rogers, *Client-Centered Therapy* (Boston: Houghton Mifflin Co., 1951).

6. M. A. Deutsch, "Trust and Suspicion," *Journal of Conflict Resolution* 2 (1958):265–79.

Trust Defined

What are the essential characteristics of trust? What does trusting behavior look like? How do you recognize it? Many scholars have written about trust, and there is a generally accepted definition of what it is and what its characteristics are.

Trust has been defined as "reliance upon the behavior of a person in order to achieve a desired objective, the achievement of which is uncertain in a risky situation."[7] That definition means there are at least four elements in trusting behavior. They are: (1) a trusting person is willing to take a risk. You are in a situation in which the behavior of the other person can help you or hurt you in terms of your needs and goals. We all run that risk when we trust another. Conversely, if there is no risk involved, trust is unnecessary. You would not be trusting that a specified outcome would occur, but would know that it would occur and be able to predict the outcome with 100 percent confidence. The phenomenon of trust operates only when there is an element of risk. If you operate on the principle of "play it safe" and never run a risk, then you never experience trust. (2) A trusting person realizes that it is the future behavior of the other person that will determine whether he or

7. K. Giffin, "Interpersonal Trust in Small Group Communication," *Quarterly Journal of Speech* 53 (1967):224–34.

she, the trusting person, will be harmed or helped. (3) A trusting person recognizes that any loss incurred as a result of misplaced trust will outweigh any gain that can come as the result of a trust fulfilled. In other words, the person stands to lose something of significance. (4) A trusting person is confident that the other person will behave in such a way that beneficial consequences will result.

Factors Related to Trust and Supportiveness

Why does one trust? The reasons for trusting seem to lie in two areas—within the person and within the situation.

According to Deutsch and others, at least two basic intrapersonal factors are related strongly to trusting or not trusting.[8] Those factors are self-esteem and authoritarianism. Self-esteem in relation to its role in self-concept was discussed extensively in chapter 3. Now we see that it is closely related, also, to interpersonal trust. A second factor within the person that is related to trust is authoritarianism, which is related to closed-mindedness or dogmatism. That factor is discussed later in this chapter. Suffice it to say here that these two factors appear to be closely related to trust. They are related in opposite ways, that is, authoritarianism is related negatively to trusting (authoritarian persons tend to be more suspicious and defensive than nonauthoritarians), while self-esteem is related positively to trusting. (Persons of high self-esteem tend to be more trusting and supportive than persons of low self-esteem.)

8. Deutsch, "Trust and Suspicion," p. 270.

In addition to these intrapersonal factors, there are at least four situational factors, as identified by Deutsch, that appear to be related to trust.[9] They are: (1) characteristics and intentions of the other person, (2) power relationships, (3) the nature and quality of the communication between the two persons, and (4) the presence or influence of a third person. These situational factors probably interact with the intrapersonal factors (esteem and authoritarianism) to determine the degree of trust and supportiveness or suspicion and defensiveness existing in the relationship. The intrapersonal factors probably give each person an inclination to respond defensively or supportively, or to trust or not trust, but the specific situation itself triggers the response and influences the intensity of the response. A person who is usually not defensive can become defensive in certain situations. You may have found yourself defensive in some specific incident. Something about the situation elicited defensiveness. A graduate student who was studying defensiveness and supportiveness in selected dyadic communication situations described the "prospectus meeting" each graduate student goes through as a situation that automatically triggers defensiveness. (The prospectus meeting at this university is a meeting open to the entire faculty.) The graduate student presents the proposal as to what he or she wants to study for this thesis or dissertation. If

9. Ibid.

you want to put the situation into your own frame of reference as an undergraduate student, imagine yourself appearing before the faculty of the department to explain and justify the topic you had selected for a term paper. This particular student's prospectus, which was distributed to the faculty of the department, described the situation from the student's point of view as follows:

> Tentative title: ON DEFENSIVE AND SUPPORTIVE CLIMATES IN DYADS: EFFECTS ON PERSUASIVE STRATEGY AND CHANGES IN INTERPERSONAL PERCEPTION
>
> (The scene is a classroom in a large, well-known university. A prospectus meeting is in progress. Joe Student, the candidate, is seated in the front of the room, sweating blood. Professor James C. Hot Shot opens the questioning.)
>
> HOT SHOT: Well, Joe, I see you're a little nervous.
>
> JOE S.: I guess I am, Professor.
>
> H.S.: Well, you needn't be. None of us here is going to hurt you, are we, gentlemen? (Entire faculty shake heads in unison, smiling.) Now, why don't we get started? Joe, I see your proposal deals with attitude change in dyads.
>
> J.S.: Yes, sir, it does.
>
> H.S.: Well, I haven't had a chance to read through your prospectus completely, but in looking at the reference page (of which there's only one), I notice that you failed to include the important research of Fisher and Cutbait (1961). Can you explain why you did not include this material, Joe?
>
> J.S.: I did read Fisher and Cutbait, sir, but it seemed to have little relevance to what I'm doing. After all, Fisher and Cutbait's research deals with *effects* of persuasive messages while my study is going to focus on the messages themselves, and—
>
> H.S.: (interrupting) The messages themselves! Good God, boy, this is a department of psychology! Leave the study of messages to the speech people; after all, it's not very important anyway. I see no point in continuing this. Come back when you've designed an attitude change study.
>
> J.S.: But Professor, I . . ., I . . .

Albeit somewhat exaggerated, the above scene serves to illustrate an important point: in any communication situation, the amount and type of interaction is controlled by the participants, creating a "climate" which influences subsequent interaction. All of us have experienced this phenomenon of "climate," and we realize that communication climates can range from that of enemies locked in mortal combat to free, open, and loving exchanges.

In describing the climate established in the exchange between Joe Student and Professor Hot Shot, we might readily apply Jack Gibb's (1961) term, "defensive"[10] (as opposed to "supportive"); furthermore, we could apply Gibb's schema to describe what it was about the interchange that created the "defensive" responses. More difficult to

10. Jack R. Gibb, "Defensive Communication," *Journal of Communication* 11 (1961):141–48.

pinpoint, however, would be *why* the climate became "defensive" in the first place. Were Joe and/or Professor Hot Shot having a "bad day"? Were they caught in an habitual behavior pattern? Was there something about the prospectus meeting that made them prone to defensiveness?[11]

11. Used by permission of William F. Eadie.

There are situations that possess characteristics conducive to defensiveness, and there are situations that facilitate trust. *One factor in such situations is the other person*—characteristics, reputation, and intentions.

Characteristics and Intentions of the Other Person

The other person's expertness, for example, is one of the characteristics we can use as a measure of the trust that can be placed in the person. If that person is an expert on the problem being discussed by virtue of ability, skill, or experience, then we will have more confidence and be encouraged to trust the person more than if the person were not an expert. Or the person may possess important information on the topic or be known for sound judgment and wise decision making. Any of these characteristics could have an effect on trustworthiness.

A second factor relative to the other person is reliability. By reliability we mean dependability, predictability, honesty, or consistency. When the other person's reputation for honesty is perceived as high, then we are encouraged to be more trusting.

The intentions of the other person also have an effect on trust. Each person engaged in communication has his or her own goals. The intentions of the other person are perceived, generally, in terms of favorable or unfavorable, congruent with one's own intentions or contradictory to one's own intentions. As congruent intentions or goals are evidenced, trust is engendered. Sometimes the goals of the two persons are congruent. Such a goal situation fosters cooperative behavior and trust. Sometimes the goals are not congruent. Such a goal situation fosters competitive behavior.

Brooks conducted a study in which forty-five pairs of persons were asked to solve problems by communicating under different goal relationships.[12] Each member of a pair had three sets of cards. One set possessed true information, another possessed false information, and the third set possessed true but irrelevant information. The sender knew which cards possessed what kind of information and could exchange any card from any of the three sets for a card possessed by the other member of the pair. One of the three goal relationships established for each pair was competitive in that one person could win only if the other person lost; the second goal relationship was congruent in that the two persons could win only if both cooperated and aided one another; and the third goal relationship was one of independent goals; that is, either individual could win or lose regardless of the cooperativeness or participation of the other. The results indicated that when the

12. William D. Brooks, "An Investigation of Three Goal Relationships upon Communication Efficiency, Amount of Communication, and Honesty in Communication." Unpublished manuscript, University of Kansas, 1967.

goals were congruent, cooperative behavior did follow. The efficiency of problem solving was higher in the congruent-goal situation than in the competitive-goal situation or in the independent-goal situation. The amount of communication was highest in the congruent-goal situation, and honesty of communication was highest in the cooperative- or congruent-goal situation. In the cooperative situation, virtually no false information was sent (2 percent of the messages), but in the competitive-goal situation, 68 percent of the messages sent were either false or irrelevant. The study indicates that goal relationships are related to honesty, amount of communication, and efficiency in communication. Although the experiment was a contrived game situation, the findings are in agreement with other studies and do confirm that the goal relationship is an important factor in the creation of trust.

One example of a competitive goal situation is the "prisoner's dilemma," which the following situation illustrates:

> Two suspects are taken into custody and separated. The district attorney is certain that they are guilty of a specific crime but he does not have adequate evidence to convict them. His strategy, then, is to point out to each prisoner the alternatives open to him, i.e., to confess to the crime or not to confess. The district attorney points out that if he confesses and the other prisoner does not, then the confessor will receive lenient treatment for turning state's evidence, whereas the latter will get "the book" slapped at him. Shall he confess and guarantee his getting minor punishment, or shall he run the risk of full punishment because his partner confesses? If neither would confess, perhaps neither could be found guilty.

In 1960 a dramatic, real-life application of the prisoner's dilemma—the competitive-goal situation—was used to gain confessions from Hickock and Smith in the Clutter family murder case, a multiple murder made infamous by Truman Capote's book *In Cold Blood,* and, subsequently, by the movie of the same name. Alvin Dewey, Kansas Bureau of Investigation agent and former FBI agent, and three other FBI agents used the competitive-goal situation in the interrogation of Richard Hickock and Perry Smith. Capote relates in his book, which is based on interviews with Hickock and Smith by Capote over several months while he lived in Garden City, Kansas, how the fear of each of the prisoners that his partner would confess and escape the blame grew. They were kept separated from each other from the outset, of course. Perry Smith, according to Capote, wanted to "talk to Dick, was fearful that Dick's guts were unreliable, that he panicked too easily . . . he'd give an arm, a leg to talk to Dick for just five minutes."[13] And Dick was equally eager to converse with Perry. "Perry, if he lost his nerve and let fly! . . . I should have silenced Perry on a mountain road in Mexico!"[14] In the end, after hours of interrogation and after alibis were repeated and repeated, it was Richard Hickock who admitted that they had carried out the whole thing, but that Perry was guilty of all four murders. It was only after hours of talk with Perry

13. Truman Capote, *In Cold Blood* (New York: Random House, Inc., 1965), pp. 226–27.
14. Ibid., p. 228.

Chapter 8

UPI

Actors Robert Blake and Scott Wilson pose beside photos of killers Perry Smith and Dick Hickcock in the film *In Cold Blood.*

Smith in which parts of Hickock's hour-long tape-recorded confession were repeated that Smith was convinced that his partner had turned on him. It was then that Smith unloaded all the gory details of the multiple murders. The competitive-goal situation, the prisoner's dilemma, had worked for the investigators. This competitive-goal situation destroyed Smith and Hickock's climate of trust.

It is clear from numerous research studies and from real-life incidents we have observed that goal relationships are related to cooperative and competitive strategies; and it is also quite clear that cooperation versus competition is a powerful element in fostering trust or in destroying trust. Any of these factors in the other person—goals or intentions, reputation or reliability, expertise—are factors in the situation that relate directly to the creation of a climate of trust or of suspicion.

Power Relationship

15. Deutsch, "Trust and Suspicion," p. 265–79.

A second situational factor related to trust is the power relationship of the persons involved. According to the research of Deutsch and others, a power hold over the other person causes one to trust that other person more.[15] It is not unusual for gangs, for example, to require a new member to commit some heinous crime that is observed by members of the gang. By having witnessed the new member commit such an act, the gang has gained power over the new member. The gang can "trust" the new member, because they "have the goods on" him or her and can "blow the whistle" on him or her at any time. One of the explanations suggested for Patricia Hearst's alleged part in the robbery of the San Francisco bank is that it may have been such an initiation rite. The same concept has been propounded as an explanation for the Zebra killings in the San Francisco area.

Nature and Quality of Communications

16. J. Loomis, "Communication and the Development of Trust and Cooperative Behavior," *Human Relations* 12 (1959):305–15.

A third factor in the situation that can affect trust is the nature and quality of the communication between the persons involved in the encounter. When the communication is open, when intentions and goals are identified, and when expectations and plans for reacting to violations are stated, then trust is encouraged.[16] When those things are kept hidden, trust is more difficult to establish.

Presence of a Third Person

17. J. N. Farr, "The Effects of a Disliked Third Person upon the Development of Mutual Trust." Paper presented at the American Psychological Association's Annual Conference, New York, 1957.

Finally, a fourth situational factor related to trust is the presence of a third person, or the knowledge that the communication will be given to a third person.[17]

These four situational factors—other person, power relationships, nature and quality of the communication, and presence or influence of a third person—are related to the development of trusting behaviors or defensive and suspicious behaviors.

Factors Related to Suspicion and Defensiveness

Defensive communication is the opposite of trusting communication. For many people, defensiveness is the overriding psychological orientation they take toward interpersonal communication. The basic reason for defensive communication lies, probably, in unmet interpersonal needs. As discussed in the first part of this book, we communicate to satisfy our needs, needs that go far beyond food and shelter, some being quite sophisticated and psychological in nature. Communication is our primary vehicle for satisfying these needs. Consequently, as our communication is successful in helping us, we are reinforced and we develop confidence in our communication; we view communication positively; and we develop positive relationships with others.

However, when we are not able to meet our needs through communication with others, we lose confidence in our coping ability and become less confident of others, even to the point of becoming defensive and guarded in our communication with others. Such behavior, of course, is counterproductive—the more defensive we become, the less effective our communication becomes. Little wonder that we then become anxious about our getting along in the world, and that a general feeling of anxiety results. Unresolved anxiety then leads to more defensive tactics in interacting with others. Fear, anxiety, doubt—these feed defensive communication behavior. You have probably observed defensive communication in others. You have observed the fear in their posture, eyes, facial expressions, and body movement. You have noticed their withdrawal behavior—turning away from you, avoiding eye contact, shifting their weight backwards, stepping backwards, or hesitating verbally.

Not only is defensive communication the result of unmet interpersonal needs and the absence of factors conducive to trust, but it can be influenced by factors outside the self as well. As with trust, there are internal factors (fear, anxiety, an experiential history of being suspicious and defensive), and there are external factors. Among the most powerful external factors are the communication behaviors of the other person. In other words, a person's communication behavior can stimulate defensiveness or trust in the other person. Unless we understand that certain communication behaviors tend to elicit defensiveness, we may find ourselves in situations in which the other person becomes defensive without our understanding why. Gibb has identified communication behaviors that tend to stimulate defensiveness in the other person, as well as those behaviors that tend to create supportive climates and reduce defensiveness. There are six pairs of behaviors in Gibb's category system. Those in the left column, when perceived by a receiver, tend to arouse defensiveness, while those in the right column are interpreted as supportive and tend to reduce defensiveness.[18]

18. Gibb, "Defensive Communication."

Gibb's Defensive and Supportive Behaviors

Defensive Climates	Supportive Climates
1. Evaluation	1. Description
2. Control	2. Problem Orientation
3. Strategy	3. Spontaneity
4. Neutrality	4. Empathy
5. Superiority	5. Equality
6. Certainty	6. Provisionalism

Gibb's categories of behaviors associated with defensiveness or trust grew out of his analyses of tape-recorded discussions that revealed that defensive communication increased as those behaviors in the left column were used and decreased as those behaviors in the right column were used. Let us consider each pair of behaviors in greater detail.

Evaluation or
Description

It appears that when one person is evaluative of another, there is a tendency for the other person to become anxious and defensive. Through verbal or nonverbal codes one person can communicate evaluation of another. Each of us, of course, makes judgments about others and forms attitudes toward others; but we can attempt to reduce the number of blunt and strong evaluative messages we send others. It is true that we use communication to elicit cooperation from others so that we and they enjoy a mutual satisfaction of needs. Sometimes our communication requires us to talk about the other person to that person, but when we do, we ought to be descriptive rather than evaluative if we want to be supportive rather than defensive. When we gripe or complain about another to his or her face, we can know (providing we have learned this principle of communication) that the other person will become fearful and defensive. Knowing that, we would be foolish to gripe or complain to others about themselves—to call attention to their weaknesses, to tell them how bad they are—in short, to speak negatively of others or to put them down. It should not be surprising that children who are subjected only to evaluative communication by their parents become anxious and defensive; or that a wife or husband constantly "put down" by her or his mate acquires defensive communication strategies rather than trusting and supportive ones. Gibb has observed that as one communicates more descriptively, defensiveness decreases. If one can remove the evaluative labels, supportive climates can be fostered. You will recall that we identified this same principle earlier when we discussed self-concept, feedback, and expressing feelings as we respond to the other person.

Control or Problem
Orientation

If our intentions are to control the other person—to change the other person's mind, to get the other to do something, or in some way to influence the other—the other person will often become defensive. We resent being dominated by another person. We want to be responsible for ourselves and not to be controlled by another. When another tries to control us, we resist—we become defensive. If the other person wants to make our decisions for us, it means that that person believes we are ignorant, unwise, uninformed, or in some way inadequate to live our own lives. That's really a put-down! No wonder we resist that definition of ourselves.

On the other hand, when the other person cooperates relative to our mutual problem, works with us, respects our ability to work on the problem,

© Eric Kroll 1979/Taurus Photos

Defensive behavior reduces the effectiveness of interpersonal communication.

and has no predetermined solution or answer to shove down our throats, we respond positively. We see that behavior as supporting and helpful. That behavior, consequently, engenders trust rather than defensiveness.

Deceptive Strategy versus Spontaneity or Openness

When we perceive the other person as having a hidden plan he or she is trying to work on us, we become defensive. Hidden motives and strategies in and of themselves arouse suspicion. We are suspicious of that which is concealed, of that which is gimmicky or tricky. Gibb has found from his analyses of the tapes of sessions of training groups that persons often perceive the strategies of their colleagues,[19] and when they do, they become defensive. On the other hand, behavior that appears to be free of deception and that is spontaneous tends to reduce defensiveness. This does not mean, however, that we are to be absolutely frank and totally open in every encounter. Rather, spontaneity and openness should be tempered with consideration for the depth of our relationship with the other person—the ability of all persons involved to accept the responsibility that full frankness and total openness carries with it. The same principle applies to the extent of the

19. Gibb, "Defensive Communication," p. 145.

spontaneity and openness we should display relative to self-disclosure—a concept we discussed when we were talking about self-concept and feedback. There lurks a danger in totally disclosing ourselves to every person encountered; moreover, there can be danger in too much "telling it like it is." Nevertheless, we often err in the opposite direction—in not being as open and spontaneous with the other person as the situation warrants. And, when we are not open but are engaged in a deceptive strategy, such behavior, when discovered by the other person, destroys trust.

Neutrality and Empathy

The fourth set of behaviors related to suspicion and trust is neutrality and empathy. The problem with neutrality is that it sometimes appears to be the same as lack of interest. It may be looked upon as a lack of concern. We want people to be genuine, to be involved—involved with us—not against us. Communication with "low affect," as Gibb calls it, sometimes communicates "not caring"; and if the other does not care about us, then we tend to become more guarded rather than open and trusting. If, however, warmth and caring are communicated, trust is encouraged. Empathy is supportive and engenders a climate of trust.

Superiority and Equality

The communication of superiority in wealth, power, social position, intellectual ability, or in any other way arouses defensiveness in the receiver of such messages. The communication of equality reduces defensive behavior in the receiver. Absolute equality seldom exists, of course, but the person who values others, respects them, and likes them does not see the differences as important. Consequently, such a person does not communicate superiority, but respect and admiration. Such messages tend to elicit trust from the receiver.

Certainty and Provisionalism

The final set of behaviors identified by Gibb are certainty and provisionalism. Certainty can be equated with being dogmatic, and provisionalism can be roughly equated with being flexible and open. Since one of the psychological orientations yet to be discussed in this chapter is dogmatism as opposed to flexibility, we will not further discuss certainty and provisionalism except to emphasize their interrelatedness with trust and suspicion.

We have now identified factors conducive to trust and factors conducive to defensiveness, but what we are concerned with, primarily, is "How can I become trusting rather than defensive?" "How can I influence the development of a trusting climate?" and "How can I help another with whom I am communicating to become less defensive?"

Patterns of trust and affection begin to be established at an early age.

Bruce Quist

A part of being trusting rather than suspicious lies within the self, as we have already observed. As with self-concept, the development of a psychological orientation toward communication—trust or suspicion, for example—has been going on for a long time. Change may require some hard thinking about ourselves. Also, like self-concept, the development of trust has a reciprocal component to it—that is, as we learn to behave so as to reduce defensiveness in others and so to stimulate trust from others, we come to develop trust within ourselves for others. What can we do to influence the development of trust for us in the other? Griffin and Patton have said we can demonstrate expertness, reliability, and dynamism.[20] In other words, we can be concerned and involved (dynamism), be honest and predictable (reliable), and have something to offer another by way of helping (expertise). The use of our expertise would have to be such as not to be perceived as superiority, to be consistent with Gibb's observations. Then, according to Gibb, we could aid the development of trust for us in another by being descriptive, problem-oriented, spontaneous, empathic, equal, and flexible in our communication with the other person rather than being evaluative, controlling, planning, neutral, superior, and dogmatic.[21] Johnson points out that interpersonal trust is built between two persons during what he calls "a commitment period."[22] During this period the two persons disclose more and more of themselves and of their reactions to each other. Their behaviors and attitudes are disclosed during the commitment period, and a communication climate is created. It is then that we can best influence the development of a climate of trust. Rejection, ridicule, the put-down—these communication patterns can destroy trust and stimulate fear, anxiety, and defensiveness. The concept of reciprocal behavior is again observed as a powerful determiner of interpersonal communication behavior. If this is so, then we can influence trust through our own behavior with others. Trust, like its opposite, suspicion, is a powerful factor in interpersonal communication. The quality of our interpersonal communication is affected by the psychological orientation we develop in terms of these bipolar variables—trust and supportiveness, or suspicion and defensiveness.

20. Kim Giffin and Bobby R. Patton, *Fundamentals of Interpersonal Communication* (New York: Harper & Row Publishers, Inc., 1971), p. 164.

21. Gibb, "Defensive Communication."

22. David W. Johnson, *Reaching Out* (Englewood Cliffs, N.J.: Prentice-Hall, Inc., 1972), pp. 44–48.

Open-Mindedness versus Closed-Mindedness

A second psychological orientation that can affect personal communication is open- or closed-mindedness. (Closed-mindedness is sometimes called *dogmatism*.) This psychological orientation has to do with one's pattern for processing information. Hence, open- or closed-mindedness is closely related to the discussion of our use of language in chapter 5.

One of the names associated most closely with the scientific study of dogmatism (closed-mindedness) is Rokeach, who studied dogmatism in *The Open and Closed Mind*.[23] He defined dogmatism as "(a) a relatively closed cognitive organization of beliefs and disbeliefs about reality, (b) organized around a central set of beliefs about absolute authority which, in turn, (c) provides a framework for patterns of intolerance toward others."[24]

23. Milton Rokeach, *The Open and Closed Mind* (New York: Basic Books, Inc., 1960).

24. Rokeach, "The Nature and Meaning of Dogmatism," *Psychological Review* 61 (1954):194–204.

Table 8.1

Open-minded	Closed-minded
1. Evaluates messages objectively, using data and logical consistency	1. Evaluates messages on the basis of inner drives
2. Differentiates easily. Sees the shades of gray, etc.	2. Thinks simplistically, i.e., in black-and-white terms
3. Is content-oriented	3. Relies more on the source of a message than on its content
4. Seeks information from a wide range of sources	4. Seeks information about other beliefs from his own sources rather than from the sources of the other beliefs
5. Is more provisional and willing to modify his beliefs	5. Rigidly maintains and defends his own belief system
6. Seeks comprehension of messages inconsistent with his set of beliefs	6. Rejects, ignores, distorts, and denies messages inconsistent with his own belief system

The dogmatic person has a closed orientation to the world. This closed, rigidly set view of how the world is and of what is absolutely true and absolutely not true affects the person's information processing. It affects the person's perception of incoming stimuli, and it affects acceptance or rejection of information. A flexible or open-minded orientation, on the other hand, permits us to process information more accurately and beneficially. Let us examine in more detail the characteristics of the dogmatic or closed-minded individual and the characteristics of the open-minded individual.

1. *Evaluates messages on the basis of inner drives.* The dogmatic person evaluates incoming messages on the basis of inner drives, inner standards, and internal pressures rather than on the basis of logical consistency, observations, or scientifically produced data. It would not matter to a closed-minded person how "good" the evidence was, or how "compelling" the logic of an argument. The dogmatic person would reject the most objective, fair, and logically compelling argument if it was in disagreement with his or her beliefs. The dogmatic person is intolerant of discrepant information. Such an orientation makes adjustment to the environment and to the changes that are an inherent part of any process (and living and communicating are processes) quite difficult. The dogmatic orientation commits

25. Rokeach, *Open and Closed Mind*, p. 57.

a person rigidly to a set of internal forces. All incoming information is then quickly evaluated on the basis of its conformity to those inner black-and-white rules. Rokeach has identified those inner pressures as "habits, beliefs, perceptual cues, irrational ego motives, power needs, the need for self-aggrandizement, and the need to allay anxiety."[25] The dogmatic person maintains beliefs in the face of contradictory information and evidence.

2. *Uses simplistic thinking.* The dogmatic individual uses simplistic thinking. Everything is black or white, absolutely right or wrong, and absolutely true or false. There is little ability to discriminate—to see the partly true and partly false, the somewhat-but-not-exactly. The more open-minded individual, however, notices the differences, can discriminate, and can tolerate uncertainty of the shades of gray. The dogmatic person sees a wide discrepancy between his or her beliefs and those beliefs outside his or her system, while the open-minded person does not need to separate them so widely.

3. *Is source-oriented.* The closed-minded person seems to be more source-oriented than message-content-oriented. The source—who is sending the message?—is more important to a dogmatic person than the content of that message. Whether the message is accepted and believed depends on who the source is; the person is unable to distinguish easily between information and the source of information. The dogmatic person is "authority bound." Dogmatic persons tend to be more anxious and insecure. It may be, then, that they need authorities who are absolute so that they can feel secure. The open-minded individual is, on the other hand, content-oriented. Such a person is able to think in terms of the message, with less emphasis on the sender.

4. *Seeks information from his or her own sources.* The dogmatic individual tends to seek information about new beliefs only from his or her "sources." A person who is dogmatic about religion, for example, will get all information about other religions from people of his or her own religion. The dogmatic person would not likely accept information from a person of another religion about a religious belief. Only the dogmatic person's own sources can be trusted to "speak the truth," whereas the open-minded person shows willingness to adjust—to modify beliefs.

5. *Rigidly maintains and defends his or her belief system.* The closed-minded person rigidly defends his or her system of beliefs. It is as if the change of one small belief would cause the person's whole world of beliefs to come tumbling down. The open-minded person holds beliefs more provisionally and is able to adjust them, or even to discard a belief if the data warrant.

6. *Is unable to tolerate inconsistency.* Because the closed-minded person cannot tolerate inconsistency, dissonance, or contradiction, that person tends (consciously or unconsciously) to reject, ignore, distort, or deny messages inconsistent with his or her own belief system. A more open-minded

person seeks clarification and understanding of messages inconsistent with or contradictory to beliefs and can tolerate greater dissonance.

The preceding characteristics of dogmatic individuals may be regarded as among the most decisively limiting variables in interpersonal communication. Even though that is true, you will note that we do not attempt to set forth ways for overcoming such an orientation, as we did in the case of lack of trust. The reason we do not prescribe how not to be closed-minded is that closed-mindedness is a personality variable, and thus truly a psychological orientation; trust and affection, on the other hand, are relationship variables. Trust and affection can be built or destroyed in relationships; hence they are not "possessed" by one person as a behavior pattern, but are shared with another person in interaction. Probably the most helpful suggestion we can make relative to closed-mindedness or dogmatism is to consider how best to interact with dogmatic persons.

From what we know about the behavior characteristics of the dogmatic, closed-minded person, we can consider the effects our own behavior will have on such a person and then behave in ways that will maximize the chances of a constructive and productive encounter with that dogmatic individual. If you carefully consider the six characteristics of a dogmatic person discussed in this section in relation to the topic and the objective of the interaction, you will have an indication of the way that dogmatic person will interpret your messages and will react to you in the communicative encounter. Let us now turn to yet another behavior pattern or orientation, that of affection or alienation.

Attraction and Affection versus Hostility and Alienation

The striking thing about love and will in our day is that, whereas they were always in the past held up as the answer to life's predicaments, they have now become the problem. It is always true that love and will become more difficult in a transitional age, and ours is an era of radical transition—we cling to one another and try to persuade ourselves that what we feel is love, and we are too insecure to take the chance that it might not be. The bottom then drops out of the conjunctive emotions and processes, of which love and will are the two foremost examples.[26]

Rollo May places love at the forefront of those orientations necessary to interpersonal communication. He states:

> . . . with rising divorce rates, the increasing banalization of love in literature and art, and the fact that sex for many people became more meaningless as it was more available, love seemed tremendously elusive if not an outright illusion. The sexual form of love understandably

26. Rollo May, *Love and Will* (New York: W. W. Norton & Co., Inc., 1969). p. 13.

became our preoccupation; for sex gives at least a facsimile of love. But sex, too, has become Western man's test and burden. The books that roll off the presses on sex technique have a hollow ring, for most people seem to be aware on some scarcely articulated level that the frantic quality with which we pursue technique as our way to salvation is in direct proportion to the degree to which we have lost sight of that salvation. It is an old and ironic habit of human beings to run faster when we have lost our way, and we grasp more fiercely at research, statistics and technical aids in sex when we have lost the values and meaning of love. Whatever the merits or failings of the Kinsey studies and the Masters-Johnson research, they are symptomatic of a culture in which the personal meaning of love has been progressively lost.[27]

27. Ibid.

Rollo May is not the only person writing of love and its opposite, alienation. The importance of this variable—the affection-alienation variable—is recognized by scholars from many areas of study. Certainly, this psychological orientation cannot be ignored in a study of interpersonal communication. Therefore we turn our attention to a consideration of four topics: (1) attraction, (2) affection, (3) alienation, and (4) hostility.

Attraction

When we talk of interpersonal attraction, we are referring to the positive attitudes, the moving toward, or the liking one person has for another. Not all the determinants of our liking of another person lie within the other person; some of the causes and correlates of interpersonal attraction lie within ourselves. Although the characteristics and behavior of another play an important role in determining whether or not we find him or her attractive, researchers have found that liking often does lie in the eye of the beholder. Therefore, included in our consideration of interpersonal attraction are qualities of the attracted as well as qualities of the attractor.

Accidental Happenings

One element that operates in interpersonal attraction is accidental happenings, either good or bad. Good happenings cause us to like the recipient of the happening, but bad happenings cause us to draw away from that person. Even when the thing that happens is beyond the person's control, it can affect our attitude. There is evidence that we tend to like those who have succeeded (everybody likes a winner) and dislike those who have failed. One reason given in explanation for this phenomenon is that we want to believe that people get what they deserve; that people are responsible for their own fate; that the world is a predictable place. Walster's research reveals that persons who hear about an accident, for example, want to blame someone (preferably the victim) for the accident. Moreover, his research shows that the desire to hold the victim responsible increases proportionately with the severity of the consequences of the accident.[28]

28. E. Walster, "The Assignment of Responsibility for an Accident," *Journal of Personality and Social Psychology* 3 (1966):73–79.

29. Lerner, M. J., "Evaluation of Performance as a Function of Performer's Reward and Attractiveness," *Journal of Personality and Social Psychology* 1 (1965):355–60.

A dramatic illustration of this phenomenon is an accident that occurred a few years ago on the Wabash River at Lafayette. Five men left Logansport, Indiana, in two small boats to go downriver some thirty-five miles. One of the boats, with three men in it, ran out of gas, and when the engine stopped, the boat began to take on water. In the attempt to transfer one man to the other boat, both boats were upset, dumping all five men into the forty-six-degree flood waters. Although people were on the scene of the accident almost immediately, only two of the men were saved, and not all of the bodies of the others had yet been found some three months later. It was a terrible tragedy, but the shocking thing to many of us was the reaction of some persons with whom we talked. They not only blamed the victims for possible errors in judgment (standing in a boat, being out on a flooded river, overloading a boat, and so on), but also made statements to the effect that the victims deserved what they got. Lerner has conducted several experiments indicating that people convince themselves that chance occurrences to others are deserved.[29] So it is that persons who win, who are successful, and to whom good things happen are valued higher and admired more than persons who lose, who fail, and who have suffered unfortunate events.

Unjust Treatment

A second factor in interpersonal attraction has to do with unjust treatment of one by another and the effect produced by that unjust treatment. Regarding that effect, Tacitus stated centuries ago: "It is a principle of human nature to hate those whom you have injured." Several recent experiments have demonstrated that a person who behaves in a cruel or generous way toward another tends to change his or her attitude toward the recipient of the behavior so that it is consistent with his or her treatment of that person. A person who harms another tends to develop a dislike for the person harmed; and a person who does a favor for another tends to feel increased liking for the other.[30]

Rewards

Liking may also be produced by rewards provided by others. We like those who reward us and dislike those who punish us. Several researchers have suggested that interpersonal relationships always cost us something along with giving us something, and that liking is a function of comparing the cost to the reward (reward − cost = profit).[31] If the relationship is profitable, or if mutually satisfying rewards are obtained each from the other, interpersonal attraction is high. When people praise us, our liking for them increases. If we find interpersonal communication with a person to be socially rewarding, enjoyable, or exciting, we will experience greater attraction to that person.[32] Conversely, if we make no effort to enjoy talking with others, we should not be surprised that we are not attractive to or liked by others. Again, we see the direct relationship between being likable and interpersonal communication.

30. See K. E. Davis and E. E. Jones, "Changes in Interpersonal Perception as a Means of Reducing Cognitive Dissonance," *Journal of Abnormal and Social Psychology* 61 (1960):402–10; J. Davidson, "Cognitive Familiarity and Dissonance Reduction," in *Conflict, Decision, and Dissonance*, ed. Leon Festinger (Stanford, Calif.: Stanford University Press, 1968), pp. 45–60; D. C. Glass, "Changes in Liking as a Means of Reducing Cognitive Discrepancies Between Self-Esteem and Aggressiveness," *Journal of Personality* 32 (1964):531–49; and T. C. Brock and A. H. Buss, "Effects of Justification for Aggression in Communication with the Victim on Post-Aggressiveness Dissonance," *Journal of Abnormal and Social Psychology* 68 (1964): 403–12.

31. See G. C. Homans, *Social Behavior: Its Elementary Forms* (New York: Harcourt, Brace & World, 1961), p. 150; and J. W. Thibaut and H. H. Kelly, *The Social Psychology of Groups* (New York: John Wiley & Sons, Inc., 1959), pp. 81–82.

32. See, for example, D. Landry and E. Aronson, "Liking of an Evaluation as Function of His Discernment," *Journal of Personality and Social Psychology* 9 (1968):133–41; R. E. Brewer and M. B. Brewer, "Attraction and Accuracy of Perception in Dyads," *Journal of Personality and Social Psychology* 8 (1968):188–93, and D. Byrne and W. Griffitt, "Similarity vs Liking: A Clarification," *Psychonomical Science* 6 (1966):295–96.

By improving our skills in interpersonal communication, we can discover others and they can discover us, and a mutually satisfying situation can be created. Reinforcing each other, each of us will come to like the other.

Stress

Another factor in the realm of interpersonal attraction is stress or anxiety. There is now considerable evidence indicating that when persons are under stress they desire the presence of others.[33] The evidence suggests that persons under stress prefer to be with those who are in the same situation as they are, or with whom they have had significant interaction previously. Persons are often in a position to comfort and reassure one another. The mere presence of others appears to produce psychological and physiological responses helpful in reducing anxiety. Combat studies of bomber crews have shown that the presence of others does reduce anxiety created by severe battle stress.[34] Anxiety and stress motivate people to seek others.

Social Isolation

Social isolation is a fifth element to be considered in interpersonal attraction. There is ample evidence that isolation of itself creates a powerful desire for interpersonal contact and is a strong facilitator of interpersonal attraction. Man is a social creature, and social isolation for any prolonged period of time is a painful experience. As Schachter has pointed out, the autobiographical reports of criminals in solitary confinement in prison, of religious hermits, of prisoners of war, and of castaways clearly reveal that isolation is devastating.[35] One of the rewards another person can provide to the lonely or isolated person is sheer physical presence as a fellow human being.

Propinquity

33. See S. Schachter, The Psychology of Affiliation (Stanford, Calif.: Stanford University Press, 1959); H. B. Gerard and J. M. Rabbie, "Fear and Social Comparisons," Journal of Abnormal and Social Psychology 62 (1961):586–92; I. Sarnoff and P. G. Zimbardo, "Anxiety, Fear, and Social Affiliation, Journal of Abnormal and Social Psychology 62 (1961): 356–63; P. G. Zimbardo and R. Formica, "Emotional Comparison and Self-Esteem as Determinants of Affiliation," Journal of Personality 31 (1963):141–62; and J. M. Darley and E. Aronson, "Self-Evaluation vs. Direct Anxiety Reduction as Determinants of the Fear-Affiliation Relationship," Journal of Experimental Social Psychology Supplement 1 (1966):66–79.

Propinquity (proximity or distance between persons) has been shown to influence one's choice of friends. Simply stated, the finding is that, other things being equal, the closer two individuals are geographically to one another, the more likely it is that they will be attracted to each other. Studies supporting this finding are numerous and consistent. They have shown that proximity is directly related to friendship formation, to mate selection, and to a decrease in prejudice. It has been found that increased contact between white persons and black persons results in a reduction of prejudice, whether the contract is on the job,[36] in an integrated housing project,[37] in a university classroom,[38] or among policemen.[39]

It has been found that persons who live in apartments near stairways are better known and more popular than persons living in the other apartments in a building. In classrooms, apartment houses, college dormitories, housing projects, and other situations, the finding of numerous studies is consistent—proximity is directly related to liking. Persons in closer proximity (centrally located physically) tend to interact with others more, form social bonds more quickly, and experience greater attraction and liking. Conversely, persons on the edge or isolated from others tend to experience less interaction and less popularity. The implication of this finding for each of us ought to be clear. Liking and attraction comes more easily as we are in closer proximity to others, and it is more difficult to establish those relationships when we are not in proximity but are, instead, isolated from others. If you find it a little difficult to get acquainted with others or to talk with others, perhaps you will want to place yourself in the "middle of the action" when you can. Certainly, going into the corner or as far away as you can will only serve to intensify your problem.

Studies have indicated, also, that liking and proximity tend to adjust themselves so as to go together; that is, as liking increases, persons come into closer proximity. As an example, perhaps you or someone you know has had occasion to move from one floor to another floor in your dormitory so as to be nearer to a person you or the other person liked; or maybe you moved from one house to another for the same reason.

All these studies on proximity and liking may bring to mind the old saying "Absence makes the heart grow fonder," which we may need to qualify by adding "when no one else is around!" Well, that is not quite true, because there are variables other than proximity at work in interpersonal attraction. Proximity is not the "whole story"; and as we said at the outset of the discussion on proximity, "other things being equal, proximity determines interpersonal attraction." It is clearly true, however, that proximity is a powerful influence in bringing about liking, and liking is related directly to interpersonal communication. Liking facilitates interpersonal communication, and through more effective interpersonal communication, we increase our own likeableness and interpersonal attractiveness. It is an interactive process, and it is possible to influence the process so as to create an upward spiral—a mutual, positive, ever-improving situation.

Similarity of Personality

Another factor in liking and interpersonal attraction is similarity of personality. One hypothesis, supported by the finding of several studies, is that friends perceive each other as being more similar in personality than do nonfriends.[40] Do persons who are attracted to each other actually possess similar personality characteristics? Research findings tend to support the folk saying, "Birds of a feather flock together." Reader and English gave a battery of personality tests to friends and nonfriends and found a significantly higher positive correlation between friends' personalities than between nonfriends' personalities.[41] The finding of personality congruence should not be surprising inasmuch as it is consistent with other findings relative to the similarity of friends, to the effect that friends are similar on dimensions such as attitudes, socioeconomic class, religion, values, and beliefs. Whether friends

34. D. G. Mandlebaum, *Soldier Groups and Negro Soldiers* (Berkeley: University of California Press, 1952), pp. 45–48.

35. Schachter, *Psychology of Affiliation*, p. 6.

36. Palmore, E. B., "The Introduction of Negroes into White Departments," *Human Origins* 14 (1955):27–28.

37. M. Deutsch and M. E. Collings, "The Effect of Public Policy in Housing Projects upon Interracial Attitudes," in *Readings in Social Psychology*, 3d ed., ed. Eleanor Maccoby, T. M. Newcomb, and E. L. Hartley (New York: Holt, Rinehart & Winston, Inc., 1958), pp. 612–23.

38. J. H. Mann, "The Effect of Interracial Contact on Sociometric Choices and Perceptions," *Journal of Social Psychology* 50 (1959):143–52.

39. See, for example, L. Festinger, S. Schachter, and K. Bork, "Social Pressures in Informal Groups" (New York: Hayes and Brothers, 1950), Mark Abrahamson, *Interpersonal Accommodation* (New York: Van Nostrand Reinhold Co., 1966); and R. F. Priest and J. Lawyer, "Proximity and Peership: Bases of Balance in Interpersonal Attraction," *American Journal of Sociology* 72 (1967):633–49.

40. See E. G. Beier, A. M. Rossi, and R. L. Garfield, "Similarity plus Dissimilarity of Personality: Basis for Friendship," *Psychology Report* 8 (1961): 3–8; and J. A. Broxton, "A Test of Interpersonal Attraction Predictions Derived from Balance Theory," *Journal of Abnormal and Social Psychology* 63 (1963): 394–97.

41. N. Reader and H. B. English, "Personality Factors in Adolescent Female Friendships," *Journal of Consulting Psychology* 11 (1947):212–20.

become similar as a result of their associating together or become friends because they are similar is not clearly known. Research findings on this question are contradictory.

Similarity of Attitudes

A final element to be considered in interpersonal attraction is similarity of attitudes and beliefs. As is the situation with similarity of personality and attraction, so it is with similarity of attitudes and attraction—we do not know whether persons are attracted to each other because they have similar attitudes and beliefs or whether, as a result of their attraction and association, they come to develop similar attitudes and beliefs. Perhaps it is some of both. We do know, however, that there is a tendency to make attitudes or orientations toward objects and ideas congruent with attitudes toward the other person in interpersonal communication. One of the best explanations of this phenomenon has been given by Heider.[42] His P-O-X balance theory explains how orientations held by each person toward the other are related in a balanced way to the orientations each holds toward the object of communication. In the model picture (figure 8.1) "P" is talking to "O," the other person, about "X," an object of communication. If "+" indicates a positive attitude or evaluation toward the object of communication or a liking for the other person, and "−" indicates a negative attitude or evaluation toward the object of communication or a dislike of the other person, then "balanced situations" can be illustrated, as is shown in the figure.

42. Fritz Heider, *The Psychology of Interpersonal Relations* (New York: John Wiley & Sons, Inc., 1958).

Figure 8.1

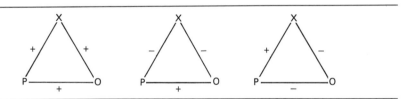

If the relationship between person (P) and the other person (O) is positive (+) and P has a positive attitude (+) toward an issue (×) (let us use euthanasia as an example), then the other person will probably have a positive attitude toward euthanasia, too (left); or, if the persons have a positive relationship and one of them has a negative attitude toward the object, then the other one will probably also have a negative attitude toward the object (center); and, if the relationship between P and O is negative and P has a positive evaluation of X, then P assumes that O has a negative evaluation of X (right). The theory suggests that there is a tendency for people who like each other to share likes and dislikes and for people who dislike each other to disagree in likes and dislikes.

Heider's balance theory not only recognizes that attitudes between people as well as their attitudes toward common objects of social reality are important factors in interpersonal communication, but that the two factors are interrelated.

However, unbalanced orientations do occur, and would include situations such as those illustrated in figure 8.2:

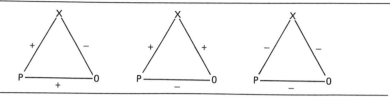

Figure 8.2

The model at left shows two persons who relate positively to each other (P and O), but P has a positive attitude toward X (euthanasia) while O believes euthanasia is murder and a moral sin. The middle illustration, as well as the one on the right, shows persons who do not like each other and yet they agree perfectly on euthanasia, one pair approving euthanasia and the other pair disapproving euthanasia. In all three examples things are not the way they are "supposed to be" as far as the people involved are concerned. Therefore, through communication, persons attracted to each other tend to bring their attitude and belief systems into balance, to preserve states of balance, or to resolve states of imbalance. For example, one couple we know, interpersonally attracted to each other to the extent that they were married, had opposite orientations toward bowling. She like to bowl, but he cared not the least for it. Interestingly enough, however, today he too enjoys bowling and participates in a bowling league. Clearly, a situation of imbalance was turned into one of balance.

We suspect that most of us have had the experience of hearing someone we liked very much say something with which we could not agree and did not like at all. Maybe your friend spoke out against the Equal Rights Amendment, while you were very much for it. You probably experienced what is called *dissonance*—a state of imbalance. What feelings were created in you, and what did you do or think to resolve the situation for yourself? You may have found it very difficult to maintain the same attitudes toward your friend and toward the Equal Rights Amendment. Research findings suggest that some alteration of our attitudes or beliefs is necessary. We cannot maintain, exactly as they were, our previous attitudes and beliefs, since they would be in a state of imbalance and we cannot maintain that inconsistency. In the example above, it would be possible for you to change your attitude toward your friend (you think less of your friend now); or you could change your attitude toward the Equal Rights Amendment ("I didn't realize it meant all that!"). Another option is to get your friend to reconsider this orientation toward ERA ("You didn't really mean our Equal Rights Amendment, did you?''). Another option that you may select is: ''forget it,'' ''repress it,'' or ''remember to avoid bringing this subject up when talking with this person.'' In some instances, we may have learned indirectly of a friend's attitude toward an object of communication; or by inference from various related cues, we may suspect that our friend has an attitude opposite to ours on some topic. In such situations we may purposely avoid the topic. This option of ''leaving the field'' psychologically is often used by persons to avoid situations of imbalance.

We have discussed briefly eight factors that affect interpersonal attraction, and we have found that interpersonal attraction exerts a powerful influence on interpersonal communication. When there are strong, positive relationships between persons, a high probability exists that communication will be successful; but when there is a strong dislike between persons, communication will be severely handicapped. To ignore this powerful influence or to fail to understand it is to fail to understand the process of interpersonal communication. And, understanding the interpersonal communication process, one can work to influence communication in positive directions.

Affection

By *affection* we mean loving, caring, and accepting. Affection is having a positive attitude toward another. It is manifesting a positive general response tendency. Most scholars write about affection in terms of caring, of being willing to become involved with another, and of sharing another's joy or sorrow, fortune or misfortune. It seems to us that one of the differences in the pictorial reporting of the war in Vietnam as compared to the pictorial reporting of World War II is that far more emphasis was given to caring for, and the sharing with, those suffering because of the war in Vietnam. The reporting of World War II seemed to be restricted to pictures of victory, to the placing of flags atop a mound, and to triumphant marches through city streets. But the photographers and reporters of the war in Vietnam, at least some of them, showed us pictures of persons caring—of marines caring for injured civilians, of wounded caring for each other, of a soldier carrying a crying child. These pictures and stories portray the caring side of man. They portray persons recognizing the pain of another human being, persons willing to share in that pain and willing to respond to the needs of others.

Affection is identified by Schutz as one of the basic interpersonal needs.[43] Like trust, it functions reciprocally—as one demonstrates affection or caring toward another, the other tends to react in like manner. Thus, interpersonal needs are fulfilled. One of the basic behaviors related to affection in interpersonal communication is self-disclosure. Jourard has stated:

> Effective loving calls for knowledge of the object. . . . How can I love a person whom I do not know? A truly personal relationship between two people involves disclosure of self one to the other in full and spontaneous honesty.[44]

43. William C. Schutz, *The Interpersonal Underworld* (Palo Alto, Calif.: Science & Behavior Books, 1966), p. 25.

44. Sydney Jourard, *The Transparent Self* (Princeton, N.J.: Van Nostrand Reinhold Co., 1964), pp. 25–38.

Bruce Quist

Without self-disclosure it is virtually impossible to form a close relationship with another person, to develop an orientation of affection and caring toward that person. A relationship develops only as two persons learn about each other. You cannot be valued by another for who you are if the other cannot know who you are. As two persons share their reactions to situations and to each other, they are pulled together, but if they stay silent and refuse to share or disclose, they remain strangers and alienation (aloneness) results. Without disclosure, how can one know the needs of another so as to respond in ways that foster the other's happiness and growth? How can one share with another in working toward some objective if they have not engaged in enough mutual disclosure of selves to anticipate each other's reactions, needs, and wants, and the parts each will play in the interaction?

There has been considerable research on self-disclosure and its effects on interpersonal communication. Research shows, for example, that self-disclosure enjoys an interactive relationship with trust.[45] The stronger the trusting climate, the greater the self-disclosure; and the more one comes to

Affection and acceptance can become patterns of behavior.

45. Jourard, *Transparent Self.*

know another, the greater the opportunity for the development of trust. The more self-disclosing you are to another, the more likely that the person will be self-disclosing to you. Self-disclosure tends to elicit liking, or to be a prerequisite for it; and you are more likely to disclose to a person you know, trust, and like than to a person you do not know, trust, or like. The interacting relationship among these factors is strong indeed. Nevertheless, many people find it difficult to share themselves openly with others so as to develop strong, positive relationships with them. Even in the closest of groups—the family—an absence of love and caring can exist. If family members do not disclose, but withdraw from one another, how can they really know one another? Jourard has said, ''For lack of mutual disclosure, children do not know their parents; fathers do not know what their children think, or what they are doing. Husbands and wives often are strangers one to the other to an incredible degree.''[46] In Ionesco's play, *The Bald Soprano,* for example, a man and woman happen to meet and begin to converse. They discover as they become acquainted and self-disclose that they ride the same train, that they live on the same street, that they both have a seven-year-old daughter, and amazingly, that they live in the same apartment. In fact, they discover they are married to each other! They are husband and wife!

46. Ibid.

Alienation

47. Giffin and Patton, *Fundamentals of Impersonal Communication,* p. 186.

48. See David J. Burrows and Frederick R. Lapides, eds., *Alienation: A Case Book* (New York: Thomas Y. Crowell Co., 1969) for illustrative cases of alienation and its withdrawal characteristics.

Alienation refers to being estranged or withdrawn from other persons. An alienated person holds negative attitudes toward other persons and has a feeling of ''aloneness.'' Alienation does not mean simple disagreement with another person.[47] Disagreeing with another is communication, but alienation is nonparticipation. It is withdrawing from purposeful interaction. It is being apart from others.[48] Alienation cannot occur between a person and someone that person has never known. Rather, it is a withdrawing from a relationship—an estrangement. It can happen between two persons or between a person and a group (family, for example). The alienation we are most interested in is that between two persons—that which results in a breakdown of a relationship or changes a positive relationship into a negative one. Often such alienation (that between two persons) is partial, that is, one person feels he or she is denied the right to communicate with the other on certain topics—not on all topics—or has been made to understand that he or she cannot communicate at certain times or under certain conditions. Of course, if one is denied the opportunity to communicate on certain topics or at certain times, then withdrawal from the relationship is a natural consequence. Alienation is the result of being denied or of being ignored. If this happens enough times and with many persons with whom we normally interact, then anomia-alienation sets in.

Anomia-alienation is a general unwillingness to communicate. We can easily understand how such alienation works against effective interpersonal

© Raimondo Borea

communication in numerous ways. Besides the obvious, the nonoccurrence of effective communication, this type of alienation is counterproductive to trust, supportiveness, self-disclosure, helpfulness to others, the enhancing of self-concept, and virtually all of the other variables related to interpersonal communication that we have discussed in this text. This aspect of alienation, anomia-alienation, has been shown to affect severely other variables directly related to interpersonal communication.[49]

Alienation is withdrawal from and nonparticipation in interactions.

But how widespread and significant is alienation, the opposite of love and involvement? According to many writers today, it is quite widespread—so widespread, in fact, that even the comic books of today have altered their heroes to fit or identify with their readers. No longer are comic book heroes the protectors of virtue and the objects of praise and adulation. Today, comic book heroes are pelted with bottles, insulted, and put down. The superhero of yesteryear is today's antihero. Howe has stated:

49. Judee K. Heston and Michael Burgoon, "Unwillingness to Communicate, Anomia-Alienation, and Communication Apprehension as Predictors of Small Group Communication." Paper presented at the Speech Communication Association Convention, New York, November 1973).

> ... the $50-million-a-year comic book industry is changing. No longer do heroes fly around zapping just any old lawbreaker. The new hero frets over social problems, like pollution, slum control and civil rights, and he often suffers from identity crises. ... Even Superman is in for a

50. Richard J. Howe, "Updating Superman: Comic Book Heroes Are Being Modernized; They Struggle with Alienation and Social Ills," *Wall Street Journal*, April 15, 1970.

51. May, *Love and Will*.

change. In future issues he will come to feel that he is a stranger in an imperfect world, his editors say. Surveying ant-like hordes of human beings from a skyscraper, he muses in one forthcoming issue, "For the first time in many years, I feel that I'm alone."[50]

Similarly, Rollo May writes about what he calls "the alienated state of mass communication" in which the average citizen knows dozens of TV personalities who come smilingly into his living room but in which he himself is never known. In this state of alienation and anonymity, painful for anyone to bear, the average citizen may well have fantasies that hover on the edge of real pathology.[51] The classified ads in figure 8.3 give evidence of the loneliness and alienation in our society. Of course, down the continuum from alienation are violence and hostility. Again Rollo May explains how hostility follows alienation:

> In New York City, it is not regarded as strange that the anonymous human beings secluded in their single rooms are so often connected with violent crime and drug addiction. Not that the anonymous individual in

Figure 8.3

CLASSIFIED ADS   UNDERGROUND PRESS

New York is alone: he sees thousands of people every day, and he knows all the famous personalities as they come, via TV, into his lonely room. He knows them all. But he himself is never known. His smile is unseen; his idiosyncrasies are unimportant; his name is unknown. He remains a foreigner pushed on and off the subway by tens of thousands of other anonymous foreigners. This is a deeply depersonalizing tragedy.

This aloneness is transformed into loneliness. The lonely man lives and breathes and walks in a subtle and insidious loneliness. It is not surprising that he trains a gun on some anonymous passer-by. And it is not surprising that the young men in the streets, only anonymous digits in society, should gang together in violent attacks.

Loneliness and its stepchild, alienation, can become forms of demon possession. Surrendering ourselves to the impersonal daimonic pushes us into an impersonal anonymity; we serve nature's gross purposes on the lowest common denominator, which often means with violence.[52]

52. May, *Love and Will.*

Hostility

Unlike alienation, in which one withdraws into aloneness, hostility is participatory. It is overt negative behavior. It may be cold and calculating, but it exists as a force *against*. Hostilities refer to aggressive behavior, and hostility in interpersonal communication refers to aggressive, negative communication behavior.

Statements indicating a wish or intention to commit a destructive act, statements attributing undesirable qualities or unfavorable characteristics to another person, and statements denying another person desirable qualities or favorable characteristics are examples of direct hostile communication. Hostility can take any number of forms. One-upmanship is one form. Squelching is another form, as is the nasty comment disguised as a joke. If you can recall any of these forms of hostile communication that you have heard in the last few days, you will note how very calculated they were.

One of the major difficulties in handling hostility in interpersonal communication lies in providing opportunities for people to release their hostility. Unless some provision is made for their release, hostile feelings tend to be perpetuated so that the ultimate result is a total breakdown in communication. The problem is that as hostility against us increases, the tendency is for us to withdraw or leave the scene; thus, the means or opportunity for reducing this hostility is lost. Withdrawal is also accomplished by a cessation of talking and listening.

If we do not withdraw from the communication situation, some adjustive techniques for reducing hostility may be available. In the days of early man, hostile and aggressive feelings led to physical attack. Contemporary man has come to disapprove of fighting as a means of handling hostility, although apparently there is still a social norm in the lower socioeconomic strata that when someone insults you, you should punch him in the nose. This norm is not as characteristic in other classes, however. For the most part, physical aggression as an adjustive technique is socially and legally rejected. There are other adjustive techniques available, however. One form is verbal aggression. When hostility occurs and the individual resorts to verbal aggression, you, as a knowledgeable communicator, can understand that the verbal aggression is an adjustive behavior—an outlet for the aggressor's hostility. Further, you also know that the verbal aggression can have a cathartic, cleaning effect; it can result in reduced hostility. Your understanding of this process can permit you to help in the solution of the problem rather than to "feed the fire."

Another adjustment technique is rationalization. The frustrated and hostile individual can speak of an unattainable goal as an undesirable one. Such a public commitment of one's thinking tends to validate the inference. By verbalizing the change of goals, frustrated people convince themselves that they are right. Thus, those statements they want to believe actually come to be believed. This is the process of rationalization—one of several processes whereby we adjust to feelings of frustration, hostility, and aggression. Most of us have used rationalization many times.

Although rationalization may allow us to reduce our tensions and to allay hostility, it carries some dangers. We can do two things that will improve our communication effectiveness in connection with rationalization: (1) if we observe another engaged in rationalization, we can be wary of accepting that person's evaluations; and (2) we can learn to identify our own rationalizations as such, which may enable us to break the habit of saying things we later regret.

Still another way we may react when experiencing hostility is to reject all or any part of proposals made to us. Such rejection is psychological aggression or attack. Some persons assume a general pattern of giving negative responses to almost all messages because that kind of response has become habitual as a result of their having reacted that way in response to felt hostility. Such a person has developed a general negative-response tendency.

SUMMARY

In this chapter we have focused on three pairs of psychological orientations or behavior patterns that have been shown to be directly related to interpersonal communication. These behavior patterns include: (1) trust or defensiveness, (2) open-mindedness or dogmatism, and (3) affection or hostility. We ought to emphasize again that most of us find ourselves at various points along the continua of these orientations. What our specific response tendency is in a given interpersonal communication situation can vary with the topic, with who the other person is, and with other factors in the situation. We have noted that psychological orientations result from factors within the person as well as from factors within the situation. Our objectives for this chapter have been three: (1) to help you to understand more fully how psychological orientations and behavior patterns affect the process of interpersonal communication, (2) to make suggestions that might help anyone who wants to modify attitudes or response tendencies in interpersonal communication, and (3) to indicate how you might influence the behavior of those with whom you communicate in a positive direction.

SELECTED READINGS

Deutsch, Morton A. "Trust and Suspicion." *Journal of Conflict Resolution* 2 (1958): 265–79.

Gibb, Jack R. "Defensive Communication." *ETC., A Review of General Semantics* 22 (June 1965).

Haney, William V. *Communication: Patterns and Incidents.* Homewood, Ill.: Richard D. Irwin, Inc., 1960.

Johnson, David W. *Reaching Out.* Englewood Cliffs, N.J.: Prentice-Hall, Inc., 1972.

Kiesler, Charles A.; Collins, Barry E.; and Miller, Norman. *Attitude Change.* New York: John Wiley & Sons, Inc., 1969.

Rokeach, Milton. *The Open and Closed Mind.* New York: Basic Books, 1960.

9

Conflict and Communication

Apparently no form of life exists without struggle and conflict. Interpersonal-communication conflicts may range from subtle disagreement to overt hostility. We experience conflict daily at various levels of intensity. However, conflict is an area scholars have tended to ignore in their study of communication. Only during the past few years have teachers and researchers in communication turned their attention to the study of conflict as an interpersonal-communication phenomenon.

Although conflict may be a necessary element of growth—a positive factor—it can also have a destructive effect on a person. Conflict is a part of all healthy relationships, but it can destroy our relationships unless we learn to handle and manage it. Whether conflict is harmful or helpful depends on how it is used and on how constructively one copes with it. That is the challenge, and therein lies the objective of this chapter—to learn about conflict and the factors at work in it. We will consider five topics in this chapter: (1) developing an attitude toward conflict, (2) types of conflicts, (3) possible conflict outcomes or resolutions, (4) interpersonal negotiation and facilitating cooperative behavior, and (5) mediation or arbitration.

In a world growing smaller via technology, becoming more crowded with people, and experiencing a rapidly increasing rate of interaction, interpersonal conflict takes on added importance. The moderation of excessive conflict and the constructive use of conflict require us to understand the interpersonal-conflict phenomenon, as well as to understand and acquire skill in communication as it relates to effective conflict resolution. The social importance of conflict management and resolution, and the central role communication plays in successful conflict resolution, make this area one of the most significant in interpersonal communication. But before we delve further into the study of conflict, let us define it.

Deutsch defines *conflict* as a situation in which "incompatible activities occur."[1] Thibaut and Kelly explain that when two persons are in conflict, each behaves in a way that will provide the greatest reward and the least cost or punishment.[2] *Conflict,* in the language of Boulding, refers to a "situation of competition in which the parties are aware of the incompatibility of

1. M. Deutsch, "Conflicts: Productive and Destructive," *Journal of Social Issues* 25 (1969):7–8.

2. John W. Thibaut and Harold H. Kelly, *The Social Psychology of Groups* (New York: John Wiley & Sons, Inc., 1959), pp. 100–125.

3. Kenneth E. Boulding, *Conflict and Defense* (New York: Harper and Brothers, 1962), p. 5.

potential future positions and in which each party wishes to occupy a position that is incompatible with the wishes of the other.''[3] Conflict situations often include messages of threat as well as messages of promise. In short, as persons in conflict situations try to get what they want—try to win from the other—they often threaten the other person with punishment or sanctions, or they make promises of rewards to the other person if he or she will behave according to the promiser's wishes. Thus, inherent elements in the definition of conflict are *threat* and *promise*. Bowers defined and explained these elements when he stated:

> Imagine two parties to conflict, Archer and Target. A threat exists when one (say, Archer) predicts that he will impose negative sanctions on the other, these sanctions to be contingent on some behavior of the other. A promise simply changes the sign of the sanction: Archer predicts that he will deliver positive sanctions to Target contingent on some behavior of Target's.[4]

4. John Waite Bowers, ''Guest Editor's Introduction: Beyond Threats and Promises,'' *Speech Monographs* 41 (March 1974).

In real life it is usually not so simple; one person seldom has all the power to reward or to punish another person. In many interpersonal situations, the interdependence of the persons involved and the complexity of interpersonal relationships ensures that both parties in conflict have some power. One may have more power than the other, but the other probably has some power, too. Again, Bowers says:

> Both parties to conflict in everyday life often control both kinds of sanctions for each other and . . . the behavior of parties in conflict is best explained by their taking account of both rewarding and punishing contingencies. But English (for one) has no word to characterize a message expressing such a double contingency [as threat and promise]. So I invented one: ''thromise.''[5]

5. Ibid.

Now that we have defined interpersonal conflict and have called attention to its two major vehicles, promises and threats, we will turn to a topic that is of great importance for any communication student who wishes to learn how to deal with conflict constructively—namely, attitudes toward conflict.

Developing a Healthy Orientation to Conflict

Challenge and conflict bring about productive change, provided the conflict is handled creatively and constructively. In fact, Simmel's thesis, expressed in both of his classic works, *Conflict* and *The Web of Group Affiliations,* is that conflict is a form of socialization—that no organization or group

Even at the international level, the constructive use of conflict is important to the peace and development of all people.

Conflict and Communication

6. George Simmel, *Conflict,* trans. Kurt H. Wolff, and *The Web of Group Affiliations,* trans. Reinhard Bendix (Glencoe, Ill.: Free Press, 1955).

7. Lewis Coser, *The Functions of Social Conflict* (Glencoe, Ill.: Free Press, 1956), p. 31.

8. David W. Johnson, *Reaching Out* (Englewood Cliffs, N.J.: Prentice-Hall, Inc., 1972), p. 203.

9. George R. Bach and Peter Wyden, *The Intimate Enemy: How to Fight Fair in Love and Marriage* (New York: Avon Books, 1968), pp. 25–26.

10. Coser, *Functions of Social Conflict,* p. 31.

11. Ibid., pp. 26–28.

could exist without conflict.[6] Another scholar has stated: "No group can be entirely harmonious, for it would then be devoid of process and structure."[7] And Johnson tells us:

> Moreover, every interpersonal relationship contains elements of conflict, disagreement, and opposed interests. Interpersonal conflict exists whenever an action by one person prevents, obstructs, or interferes with the actions of another person; there can be conflicts between goals, ways of accomplishing the same good, personal needs, and expectations concerning the behavior of the two individuals. It is inevitable that you will become involved in conflicts whenever you have a relationship with another person. A conflict-free relationship may only be a sign that you really have no relationship at all, not that you have a good relationship.[8]

The total and permanent absence of conflict, even if it were possible, apparently would not be a desirable situation. It may be that there is a real need for persons who are intimate to have some conflict—some disagreement. Bach and Wyden have indicated that closeness is characterized by disagreeing and making up—that the desire to be in harmony with the other person creates a need for conflict just to establish and maintain our notion of harmony and agreement.[9] We would guess, however, that many of us have assumed that controversy, confrontation, and conflict are automatically undesirable, that they are to be avoided at all times and at all costs. We may have held the false idea that the primary purpose of learning, or of communication, was the elimination of problems and conflict. Such is not the case. Challenge, questioning, choosing, and testing are necessary elements in growth and in life. Of course, conflict and confrontation can be destructive; as the signs say, "WAR MAY BE HAZARDOUS TO HEALTH." The point is that we need not fear conflict or try to avoid or cover up conflict. Conflict may be harmful or helpful, bad or good, destructive or facilitative—depending on how we cope with it. The attitude that appears to be warranted is that which recognizes the inevitability of conflict and its growth and thereby facilitates the beneficial potentials of conflict. Further, we can have a positive, confident attitude toward developing an understanding of conflict and of the role played by interpersonal communication in constructive conflict resolution. Coser calls for this same positive and acceptive attitude toward conflict.[10] He points out that sociologists, in their early study of conflict, looked on it as something totally undesirable, a disruptive force in society. Their objective was to find ways to eliminate conflict, an objective that was counterproductive.[11] Now, according to Coser, sociologists recognize that conflict has desirable qualities as well as negative ones. They recognize that conflict creates associations, that it provides a means for the retention of differences, disagreements, and changes—all factors of importance to the growth, adaptive ability, and subsequent preservation of the organization. Those same values of conflict apply equally well to persons. Thus, interpersonal conflict, like organizational and group conflict, is necessary. Keltner says, "The closer the relationship, the more intense the conflict; contradiction and conflict not only precede unity but are operative in it at every moment of its existence."[12]

12. John W. Keltner, *Interpersonal Speech Communication: Elements and Structures* (Belmont, Calif.: Wadsworth Publishing Co., Inc., 1970), p. 230.

Types of Interpersonal Conflict

Conflict can involve disagreement over seemingly insignificant things, just as it can involve disagreement over major things. Some topics that were identified by a group as things that have caused conflict were: fingernail biting, what one should eat, use of tobacco, use of marijuana, use of alcohol, use of drugs, what we should believe; driving habits, whether or not to get a job, lifetime goals, how to spend leisure time, how clean our living areas should be, who our friends ought to be, how to relate to other persons, how to spend our money, and how high to make the fence. Some of these topics may seem ridiculously insignificant, but to the persons with the conflict, it was *not* ridiculous. Each of these topics involves persons desiring *control* or influence over others. Each is important. It is not for any person outside the conflict to judge its importance to those involved in it.

Interpersonal conflict can be categorized in several different ways, two of which are considered here—type of goal or objective about which the conflict revolves, and level of intensity of the conflict.

Categorizing Conflict in Terms of Type of Goal or Objective

There are at least three types of goals or objectives with which interpersonal conflict may be concerned. They include: (1) goals or objectives that are nondivisible or nonsharable; (2) goals or objectives that may be divided and shared in various proportions between the parties in conflict; and (3) goals or objectives that may be fully claimed and possessed by both parties in the conflict.

Nondivisible- or Nonsharable-Goal Conflicts

Some objects of conflict are not divisible. Both contestants cannot win; if one wins, the other must lose. There can be no ties and no sharing of the desired objective. In the contest of basketball, for example, the rules of the game are such that the objective is nonsharable. One team must win and the other must lose. Similarly, if two men are competing to "win the hand" of a girl they each want to marry, both cannot win—at least not as far as marrying the girl under the existing laws of our country is concerned. The loser might win "other" objectives, but both cannot marry the girl. Marriage is a "winner-take-all" objective. In war, unconditional surrender represents a defining of the objective as nonsharable. As we shall see further along in this chapter, not all conflict resolutions result in producing a winner, either total or partial. Sometimes conflicts are resolved without either adversary having won. Both suitors may lose the girl; or they may cease to engage in the conflict. They may leave the scene of conflict, both having decided that the costs for attaining their objective were too great.

Win-all-or-nothing conflicts can be extremely difficult and dangerous conflict situations. Such conflicts, if carried out fully to the end, result in total loss for one of the adversaries. Such conflicts are then life-or-death struggles.

Partially Sharable Goal Conflicts

Sometimes conflict objectives are sharable. Although each participant may desire to win all, it is possible that he or she will win some and lose some, while the adversary also wins some and loses some. Deutsch, as well as most other scholars who have studied conflict, states that most conflicts are of this type—they have sharable objectives, or can be redefined so as to make sharing possible.[13] In such conflict situations, there can be a cooperative interest in reaching an agreement, since both parties can win some, and that may be preferable to losing all.

13. Deutsch, "Conflicts," pp. 7–8.

One of the difficulties in conflicts of this type is that they may not be perceived as conflicts in this category. Rather, they may be misperceived as win-lose conflicts, as black-or-white situations. Once a conflict is perceived or defined to be in that category, resolution becomes more difficult.

Another thing that can happen to conflict with sharable objectives is that, through inappropriate communication behavior of the parties involved, they may escalate into conflicts whose goals are nonsharable. We will return to a discussion of these problems later on in this chapter, but let us now consider the third type of conflict objective.

Fully Sharable Goal Conflicts

Fully sharable objectives are congruent goals—goals that may be possessed by both parites to the conflict. Such conflicts cease to be conflicts as soon as they are perceived correctly by the persons involved. When participants understand that they both can win fully, a natural, cooperative situation is created. Competition, controversy, and combat cease.

Categorizing Conflict in Terms of Level of Intensity

Interpersonal conflicts can be categorized according to level of intensity. Although any number of levels of intensity might be identified, we have arbitrarily selected three general levels of conflict—controversy, competition, and combat.[14]

As we use the term in this context, *controversy* refers to a difference or disagreement that is perceived by the parties to the conflict as controllable through some acceptable procedure and resolvable to at least the partial satisfaction of both. In controversies, the parties desire a solution beneficial to both. They do not want to destroy each other. This spring, as every spring, teachers' associations and boards of education are locked in conflict of this controversy type. Neither desires to destroy the other. Both are necessary for the production of services (education for children and youth) they both desire. There are specific, rational, and peaceful procedures through which they engage in the conflict; thereafter, hopefully, resolutions will be arrived at that permit both parties to fulfill their desires and to function at some reasonable level of satisfaction.

14. Keltner also uses these levels of intensity to categorize conflicts. See *Interpersonal Speech Communication*, pp. 223–24.

The term, as used here, refers not to a disagreement over values, policies, or facts, but to a course of action on the part of each party that can enable each party to win. *Competition* involves winning and losing. The parties may engage in the competition according to a defined set of procedures or rules (as in basketball, baseball, or poker), or they may compete without written or agreed-on rules to govern their behavior (as in the situation of two fellows trying to win the same girl), and the prize may be all or nothing (as in basketball) in which one wins and the other loses, or the prize may be sharable proportionately to the success of the competitors (as in track, in which one wins first, another second, and so on). In any event, in competition there is a commitment to winning the prize at the expense of the opponent, whereas in controversy each party will be happier if the source of the controversy (the disagreement, misunderstanding, or misinterpretation of facts) can be removed so that the parties may cooperate rather than compete. Although there is a strong winning motivation in competition, it stops short of destruction of the party to the conflict. Winning the goal is enough. The winner does not need to destroy the opponent. Many games exist to fulfill the functions of competition. And, undoubtedly, competition and controversy play important roles in the growth of persons, groups, or societies.

Here we have the top level of intensity—the third type of conflict. Combat may grow out of competition, just as competition may emerge from strong controversy; but, regardless of its origin, combat involves action against an opponent with the intent of harming or destroying that opponent. *Combat* refers to a fight. There is a significant difference between a fight and a game—between combat and competition. Rapoport has described that difference:

> In a fight, the opponent is mainly a nuisance. He should not be there, but somehow he is. He must be eliminated, made to disappear or cut down in size or importance. The object of the fight is to harm, destroy, subdue, or drive the opponent.
>
> Not so in a game. In a game, the opponent is essential. Indeed, for someone who plays the game with seriousness and devotion, a strong opponent is valued more than a weak one.[15]

15. Anatol Rapoport, *Fights, Games, and Debates* (Ann Arbor: University of Michigan Press, 1961), p. 9.

Games have rules and rationality, but the saying goes, "Anything's fair in love and war!" At least, there is a strong motivation to harm, injure, or destroy the other in conflicts that have escalated in intensity to the level of fight or combat.

Conflict Resolution: Possible Outcomes

Thus far we have discussed the role of conflict and types of conflicts. Now we turn to an identification of the possible resolutions of conflict. We will consider the possible resolutions to conflict in a sequence the reverse of that in which we discussed types of conflict.

There are four possible outcomes in conflict situations: (1) victory for one and destruction for the other, (2) cessation without victory or destruction, (3) partial victory and partial defeat for each party (partially-shared-goals resolution), and (4) coming to understand or creating a situation in which the goals are fully sharable and congruent.

Victory and Destruction

One possible end to conflict at the combat level is the total victory of one party and the total destruction of the other; or, in the case of games and competition-type conflicts, the conflict terminates when the winner has been determined and the prize, or proportions thereof, awarded according to the rules or agreed-upon procedures.

Cessation

Some combat situations are resolved without total victory and total defeat. Sometimes one contestant (or both contestants) perceives that there is nothing that can be done to ensure victory or to improve his or her position. There being no way to carry the combat to a victorious conclusion for either party, both decide to cease. Neither wins, and neither is destroyed. They

UPI

have fought to a draw and decide to stop. When one party (or both) decides that the cost of continuing the conflict, of seeing it through to victory, is greater than what can be won, when the cost of the conflict outweighs what can be gained in victory, contestants will often decide to cease the conflict.

Inability to resolve conflict through communication sometimes leads to violence and force as responses to conflict.

Partial Victory and Partial Defeat

A third possible outcome of a conflict is to deescalate it or redefine it so that it becomes a shared-goals situation, a situation in which one party can win without the total destruction of the other party, or where both parties can win some and lose some—a situation in which the goal can be shared in some way.

Conflicts are sometimes resolved by the parties agreeing to partial victory and partial defeat for each. Half a pie is seen as better than none at all. Some games have this type of resolution built into the rules. In the 1974 Indianapolis 500, each of the thirty-three contestants won some money, with even the thirty-third-place winner (Dick Simon of Salt Lake City) receiving over $13,000. The 1974 winner, Johnny Rutherford, received more, of course, some $245,000 plus, but each contestant in this very competitive game-conflict won part of the total pot.[16] The goal was shared. This type of resolution is probably the most used in interpersonal conflict. It involves compromise, bargaining, and negotiating.

16. *The Journal and Courier*, 28 May 1974, p. B-1.

Fully Sharable Goal: Integrative Unity

The fourth possible outcome is to come to realize that the goal is fully sharable, or to redefine the situation and develop an integrative unity so that no conflict exists. Both parties integrate their desires and cooperate fully so that both are winners. Full integration and satisfaction of both parties are the outcomes. Once data have been provided, interpretations verified, values agreed upon, or misunderstandings cleared up, the parties involved in the controversy perceive their goals or desires to be compatible and congruent. There is then no basis for conflict. In fact, there is no conflict resolution necessary—only an awareness of the *congruent* goal is needed. To reach fully integrated unity, i.e., fully sharable goals, or to reach partially shared goal situations requires interpersonal communication and negotiation, the next topic to be discussed.

Principles of Negotiation through Interpersonal Communication

Interpersonal negotiation is especially important in partially-shared-goal conflicts. Its purpose is the satisfactory resolution of conflict. This section of this chapter focuses on the process of interpersonal negotiation. We will identify and discuss principles that seem to be helpful in interpersonal negotiation.

1. *Maintain open communication lines.* Studies seem to indicate that opportunity for full, free communication and use of that opportunity are related positively to cooperative behavior and subsequent conflict resolution. Steinfatt, Seibold, and Frye state as a result of their experiments in conflict resolution: "When full communication is allowed, real reward produces more cooperation than does imaginary reward. This apparent interaction is in addition to an apparent main effect for communication across reward conditions."[17] They were studying the effects of imagined and real reward on cooperation in conflict resolution, as well as the effect of communication on cooperation. They found that communication by itself had an effect on

17. Thomas M. Steinfatt, David R. Seibold, and Jerry K. Frye, "Communication in Game Simulated Conflicts: Two Experiments," *Speech Monographs* 41 (1974):34.

cooperative resolution of the conflict, and it also interacted with reward to facilitate cooperation. They concluded, "Communication, the opportunity to exchange information concerning the possibilities of the situation, is necessary; without communication no creative solutions occur."[18] Unless the communication lines are open and used, conflicts go unresolved. It ought to be apparent, then, that pouting, "clamming up" so as not to communicate, and fleeing from the conflict are counterproductive behaviors. They make about as much sense as does the ostrich's sticking his head in the sand. Rather, one of the most important variables in conflict resolution is willingness and opportunity to engage in full communication. There is a great deal of evidence that the presence of a channel in which worded messages can be sent and exchanged, in contrast with the absence of such a channel, clearly increases the amount of cooperative behavior.[19] There is evidence, also, that the use of two channels is clearly superior to one. Johnson states: "The greater the number of channels used the more effective a message will be inducing cooperative behavior and . . . the greater the simultaneous and serial redundancy of messages aimed at inducing cooperative behavior the more effective they will be."[20]

One of the problems in marital conflict often encountered by marriage counselors is that the couple has closed all lines of communication. One of the first tasks is to get the channels of communication open, to restore the opportunity for communication, and to get the persons involved to communicate with each other. A well-known scholar in marital and family communication has pointed out that the use of all channels—verbal and nonverbal—is a characteristic of successful conflict management and resolution. Her studies show that families successful in the management of conflict exchange information through verbal and nonverbal channels much more frequently than do families that are unsuccessful in managing conflict.[21] An increase in the number of channels used and open face-to-face communication serve to increase cooperative behavior and facilitate interpersonal negotiation.

2. *Work for accuracy in communication.* Be accurate in what you say. Don't jump to conclusions or speak in "allness statements." Be careful with what you say. Just as it is common for individuals in conflict to close down communication channels instead of moving toward fuller and freer communication, so, too, it is common for individuals in conflict to communicate threats and statements that are not accurate rather than communicating objective and accurate information. When persons in conflict refuse to communicate with each other, or when they communicate inaccurate or less than honest information, there is not much hope for inducing cooperative behavior and moving toward beneficial conflict resolution. Johnson states, "Only when communication is aimed at creating an agreement fair to all parties involved is it helpful in resolving a conflict constructively."[22] The studies of Pilisuk and Skolnick show that when intentions are communicated

18. Ibid.

19. M. Deutsch, "Trust and Suspicion," *Journal of Conflict Resolution* 2 (1958):265, P. G. Swingle and A. Santi, "Communication in Non-Zero-Sum Games," *Journal of Personality and Social Psychology* 23 (1972):54–63; and G. H. Shure, R. J. Meeker, and E. A. Hansford, "The Effectiveness of Pacifist Strategies in Bargaining Games," *Journal of Conflict Resolution* 9 (1965):106–17.

20. David W. Johnson, "Communication and the Inducement of Cooperative Behavior in Conflicts: A Critical Review," *Speech Monographs* 41 (1974):73.

21. V. M. Satir, *Conjoint Family Therapy: A Guide to Theory and Technique* (Palo Alto, Calif.: Science & Behavior Books, Inc., 1964).

22. Johnson, "Communication and Inducement of Cooperative Behavior," p. 213.

23. M. Pilisuk and P. Skolnick, "Inducing Trust: A Test of the Osgood Proposal," *Journal of Personality and Social Psychology* 8 (1968):121–33.

24. Ibid.

25. Shure, Meeker, and Hansford, "Effectiveness of Pacifist Strategies," pp. 106–17.

26. Pilisuk and Skolnick, "Inducing Trust."

27. Mark L. Knapp, Roderick P. Hart, and Harry S. Dennis, "The Rhetoric of Duplicity: An Exploration of Deception as a Communication Construct." Paper presented at the convention of the Speech Communication Association, New York, November 10, 1973.

with integrity, increases in cooperative behavior follow, but when one person is deceptive, there is a decrease in trust and cooperative behavior and an increase in competitive behavior.[23] Moreover, they say, "there is often a tendency to make deceptive use of the signaling of planned behavior in conflict communication."[24] Shure, Meeker, and Hansford have found that as competition increases in conflict situations, subjects think their opponent is trying to deceive or trick them.[25] As honesty is revealed, however, cooperative behavior increases. The problem is that there is a tendency to engage in deception as competitiveness increases.[26] Knapp, Hart, and Dennis state:

> Duplicity seems to be a constituent of nearly everyone's communicative repertoire. The rudiments of lying are often learned at an early age, by observing the communicative strategies employed by parents and peers and by undergoing punishments for being truthful. From introspection alone, it seems clear that lying is an adaptive behavior first practiced in situations where it is a harbinger of success or, at least, promises to help us avoid negative sanctions.[27]

If cooperation in conflict is to be increased, then honesty and accuracy in communication seem to be necessary.

3. *Keep the content of messages substantive and orientational rather than emotional.* Keep emotion controlled. Hostility begets hostility. Overcommunication expressed through violent and hostile action, or undercommunication expressed through silence, sulking, and leaving, are examples of hostility, and they stimulate hostility from the other person. Communication is then blocked. *How* one person speaks to the other becomes more important than *what* is said. A periodical article describes it well.

> We asked readers what they are most likely to do when they are displeased with their husbands and what their husbands are most likely to say—say nothing, brood about it, hint that they're unhappy, express their feelings or start an argument. We also asked how often they and their husbands behave in these different ways when they do argue—leave the room, sulk, sit in silence, swear, shout, hit out, cry or break things.
>
> The most happily married wives are those who say that *both* they and their husbands tell each other when they are displeased and thus try to work out their displeasure together by communicating in a calm and rational way. They also say that they and their husbands rarely or never fight in any of the different ways we listed; that is, they seldom resort either to the active-aggressive fighting (swearing, shouting, hitting out, crying or breaking things) or to passive-aggressive fighting (leaving the room, sulking or staying silent).
>
> The wives who are most unhappily married are in relationships where one or both partners can't talk calmly about what's bothering them.[28]

When the content of messages is primarily substantive and orientational rather than emotional or affective, cooperative behavior is induced. Re-

28. *Redbook,* June 1976.

search by Bales indicates that threat statements, although common in conflict negotiation, are detrimental to consensus seeking, whereas high-orientation statements are helpful.[29] Similar effects of threat statements have been found by Deutsch and Krauss.[30]

Threats communicate a potential harm. High-threat verbal behavior is characterized by a large number of statements reflecting antagonism toward the person. High-orientation verbal behavior includes statements of procedural suggestions, relevant facts, and conciliation or willingness to consider other alternatives and ideas. Another way of talking about this same variable is in terms of substantive versus affective content. We should not confuse affective or threat statements with those that identify rules or sanctions. The latter type of statements may be helpful in inducing cooperative behavior if they are objective, accurate, honest, and related procedurally. Affective, threat statements are charged with negative emotionality—anger, antagonism, and hostility against the person. As the content of bargaining communication increasingly allows for the honest expression of intentions, expectations, conditions of retaliation, and conditions of reconciliation, it will be more successful in inducing cooperative behavior.[31] A host of other researchers say the same thing.[32]

Terhune found that messages specifically reducing the ambiguity of intentions and expectations significantly improved cooperative behavior.[33] Messages that emphasize reciprocity of choice, the desirability of cooperative choices, or threatened penalties for noncooperation are effective in inducing cooperative behavior.[34] When messages are orientational and substantive, when they clarify and emphasize expectations, procedures, sanctions, and promises of reward, then cooperative behavior is likely to be facilitated. When deception, antagonism, and threat against the person characterize the content of bargaining communication, competitiveness rather than cooperation tends to result, and escalation into combat rather than constructive resolution is encouraged.

4. *Use a rational, problem-solving approach.* A rational, problem-solving approach is the best procedure for handling conflicts. There is no substitute for data. They are essential to answers that stand the tests of logical correctness. Other answers—those not based on fact and data—have as much chance of being illogical and false as they do of being accurate and correct. The hope of human beings is in their ability to use their intellect rather than their hunches, emotions, instincts, or physical strength.

Using a rational, problem-solving approach means that I need to:

a. *Get accurate information.* In any communication setting, and especially in conflict situations, we communicate best when we are informed. Therefore, in conflict situations, we need to practice saying, "Whoa! First, I must get my facts straight! I must make sure I have accurate data!" If you are lucky enough to be in conflict with a person who is operating from data, too, interpersonal negotiation is considerably easier.

29. Robert F. Bales, *Personality and Interpersonal Behavior* (New York: Holt, Rinehart & Winston, Inc., 1970).

30. Morton Deutsch and Robert M. Krauss, "The Effect of Threat upon Interpersonal Bargaining," *Journal of Abnormal and Social Psychology* 61 (1960):181–89.

31. Johnson, "Communication and the Inducement of Cooperative Behavior," p. 73.

32 J. L. Loomis, "Communication, the Development of Trust and Cooperative Behavior," *Human Relations* 12 (1959):305–15; G. Evans, "Effect of Unilateral Promise and Value of Rewards upon Cooperation and Trust," *Journal of Abnormal and Social Psychology* 69 (1964):587–90; Shure et al., "Effectiveness of Pacifist Strategies"; R. Radlow and M. F. Weidner, "Unenforced Commitments in 'Cooperative' and 'Noncooperative' Non-Constant-Sum Games," *Journal of Conflict Resolution* 10 (1966):497–505; and Swingle and Santi, "Communication in Non-Zero-Sum Games," pp. 54–63.

33. K. W. Terhune, "Motives, Situation, and Interpersonal Conflict Within Prisoner's Dilemma," *Journal of Personality and Social Psychology*, Monograph Supplement 8 (1968).

34. Radlow and Weidner, "Unenforced Commitments," p. 499.

35. W. Charles Redding, *Communication within the Organization* (New York: Industrial Communication Council, 1972), p. 87.

b. *Avoid information overload.* Researchers have discovered that when a person is inundated with information, problems arise.[35] This overload can be in terms of quality or in terms of the nature of the content. Either way, the ability of the person to handle the information is inadequate. A person can handle only so much information at one time. You have experienced situations when you simply had to get away by yourself and "clear your head," not only because of the amount of cognitive data you had been taking in, but also because of the amount of affective data. Emotions get bound up in certain situations, and especially in conflict situations. So be sensitive to the amount of information—emotional and intellectual—that the other person is bombarded with and that you are "taking on."

c. *Avoid ambiguous communication.* Ambiguity leads to misunderstanding. What you want is understanding. Ambiguity results from too little information—information *under*load? It results, also, from too general information and from contradictory information. These problems have been discussed earlier. Once again we emphasize them in relation to conflict situations. The aim is for specific, objective, concrete communication.

d. *Avoid polarized communication.* Polarized communication results from oversimplifying. The conflict becomes black and white, right and wrong. Both persons think they are right; each believes the other is wrong; each thinks he or she is the one maligned; and each knows his or her "answer" is the "solution."

e. *Define the conflict.* What is its cause? What type of conflict is it? What events led up to the conflict? What event triggered it? What is the true size of this conflict? The smaller it is and the more specific it is, the greater the probability of resolving it satisfactorily. The larger it is and the more vague it is, the greater the difficulty of resolving it. Further, the conflict can be defined as to type. Conflicts are either nonsharable goals (win-lose situations), sharable goals (joint problem), or fully congruent goals (no conflict at all if the data can be flushed out, i.e., both win fully). Of course, joint-problem conflicts offer a greater possibility of satisfactory resolution than do win-lose conflicts.

f. *Generate possible solutions.* Both parties should work cooperatively in doing this. Flexibility in considering possible solutions is important. An awareness of alternatives in the situation is important to the problem-solving approach.

g. *Evaluate the possible solutions and select one implement.* Included in this discussion should be a consideration of how the plan will be checked later to see if it has solved the problem. There needs to be some way of discovering whether or not the solution is mutually satisfying.

36. Nancy A. Reiches and Harriet B. Harral, "Argument in Negotiation: A Theoretical and Empirical Approach," *Speech Monographs* 41 (1974):36–48.

5. *Know when to consider trades and compromise.* Reiches and Harral have written specifically about the role of argument.[36] They state, as we have emphasized, that argumentation does not occur in a "total-conflict situation," an all-out victory-or-defeat effort. Rather, in argumentation, they say,

"one wins relative to his own goals and value system: satisfaction with the bargaining outcome does not necessarily imply crushing one's opponent. Negotiation, then, can be compared to a variable-sum game, a game that blends conflict and cooperation, a game of *mutual dependence*."[37] Trades are made. Person A gives up one thing wanted by Person B, and Person B gives up another thing wanted by A. Each deems it advantageous to win some rather than to attempt to win all but risk losing everything. Each sees advantage in compromise.

In *compromise* each of the parties to the conflict is willing to give up goals or values to preserve or win other goals or values of higher priority. Each party settles for something less than what was wanted. Very often, if not always, parties who resolve conflict via compromise *possess a common goal of high priority*. Each gives up lesser goals so that both can have part of the important goal—the shared value. The tragedy is that often, even when the conditions for compromise exist, as when there is a basic agreement on the important goal, agreement may be destroyed or ignored because of negative interpersonal relationships —lack of trust, hostility, and closed-mindedness.

6. *Structure cooperative action.* We can facilitate cooperative behavior by creating situations or structuring actions that tend to elicit cooperation. Johnson states:

> Perhaps the surest way of resolving a conflict constructively is to involve yourself and the other person in a situation where you have to cooperate with each other to achieve mutually desired goals. Cooperative interaction means that you and the other person will engage in joint action to accomplish a goal you both desire. Two individuals who both wish to build a sandcastle and help each other to do so are in cooperative interaction. The members of a football team take cooperative action to win a game. A teacher and a student planning an assignment to maximize the students' learning are in cooperative interaction. Two individuals who wish to deepen their relationship and thus spend time on a joint activity are in cooperative interaction. Any time you and another person have the same goal and help each other accomplish it you are in cooperative interaction. Cooperative interaction has very powerful, positive effects upon the relationship between two individuals. Cooperation produces increased liking for one another, increased trust, and a willingness to listen to and be influenced by each other. Friendships are largely based upon cooperation. The development of a fulfilling friendship rests upon the ability of two individuals to define mutual goals (even if the goal is to fall in love) and then cooperate in obtaining them. In a conflict situation, the primary way to ensure a constructive resolution is to work out a cooperative solution.[38]

Numerous studies have verified the positive relationship between cooperative interaction and conflict resolution.[39] If cooperative interactions can be created or structured, conflict may be resolved constructively.

37. Ibid., p. 37.

38. Johnson, *Reaching Out,* pp. 215–16.

39. See the March 1974 issue of *Speech Monographs* (vol. 41). This issue is devoted entirely to conflict resolution, and numerous studies of this topic are reviewed.

Mediation or Arbitration

Mediation refers to the use of a third party in the conflict-resolution process. The contestants agree to allow a third party, an outside party, to assist them. The mediator has no power to make decisions. The mediator cannot make trades or compromises for the contestants, but serves as a catalyst. He or she reasons, persuades, provides data, and attempts to facilitate a resolution to the conflict.

Arbitration often follows unsuccessful attempts at conflict resolution through interpersonal negotiation and mediation, and it goes even further than mediation. Arbitration is characterized by giving the power of decision to the "outsider"—the arbitrator. The parties to the conflict give up their right to make decisions in the resolution of the conflict. The arbitrator functions as a judge and jury, hears the arguments, considers the evidence and the cases presented, and makes a decision relative to the awarding of the goal sought by the contestants. Arbitration is used, for the most part, when public interest demands that certain conflicts be resolved.

Mediation and arbitration become necessary when a conflict cannot be resolved through principles of negotiation.

Wide World

SUMMARY

We have considered three major topics in this chapter on conflict. First, we have observed that conflict is a necessary part of life, that it is not a realistic or healthy objective to avoid or flee from conflict. Persons that are exactly alike and without differences are not persons. They might be clones, but they are not persons. Each person is unique and is different from others. In every relationship there will be differences and conflicts. The healthy attitude, therefore, is not to fear conflict, but recognize it as a necessary element in growth and process—necessary to every relationship, every group, and every organization. The healthy attitude recognizes that people can resolve differences and conflicts if they acquire the attitudes, values, and interpersonal-negotiation skills that accompany constructive use of conflict.

Secondly, we identified conflicts as being: (1) nondivisible and nonsharable goal conflicts; (2) partially sharable goal conflicts; and (3) fully sharable goal conflicts. Conflicts were further categorized by their level of intensity—controversies, competitions, and combats.

Third, we considered four possible outcomes of conflict situations. Conflicts can result in victory for one participant and defeat for the other. Or the conflict can become so costly to each participant that both are losing; the participants agree to cessation of the conflict. The third possible outcome is to redefine the conflict so that it becomes a shared-goals situation in which each wins some and loses some. The fourth possible outcome is to realize the goal is fully sharable or redefine the situation so no conflict exists.

The principles of negotiation for conflict resolution were next discussed, and six principles were found and developed at length: open communication lines, accuracy, substantive messages, a rational approach, compromise, and cooperative action. When conflicts cannot be won, ceased, or resolved through negotiation, however, mediation may be used. The last resort may be arbitration, in which a person or agency outside the conflict is given the power legally to resolve the conflict.

SELECTED READINGS

Coser, Lewis. *The Functions of Social Conflict.* Glencoe, Ill.: Free Press, 1956.

Miller, Gerald R., and Simons, Herbert W. *Perspectives on Communication in Social Conflict.* Englewood Cliffs, N.J.: Prentice-Hall, Inc., 1974.

Rapoport, Anatol. *Fights, Games, and Debates.* Ann Arbor: University of Michigan Press, 1961.

Simmel, George. *Conflict.* Translated by Kurt H. Wolff. Glencoe, Ill.: Free Press, 1965.

Interpersonal Communication Contexts

Alan R. Bagg/Tom Stack & Associates

10

Dyadic Communication

Each of us is involved in numerous dyadic communication situations daily. Sometimes we are seeking information; sometimes we are attempting to secure someone's agreement or approval; sometimes we are making a new acquaintance; sometimes we just enjoy visiting with a friend or a social acquaintance; and sometimes we are engaged in intimate talk, disclosing and sharing with another our deepest feelings and concerns. Dyadic situations are virtually endless. We spend more time in dyadic communication than we spend in groups of three or more.

Dyadic communication is two-person communication. We usually think of it in terms of an informal interpersonal situation involving dialogue, or two-way, face-to-face verbal interaction. In dyadic communication two persons initiate messages and responses as they mutually influence each other. Each person simultaneously sends and receives information so as to create shared meanings. This free interchange gives to dyadic communication a high potential for information sharing and an opportunity for effective integration. It is not surprising, then, that some of the most influential and satisfying communication experiences for each of us are dyadic situations.

Dyadic Communication: Foundation of Other Forms of Communication

Dyadic communication represents a basic or "foundation" phenomenon in interpersonal communication. The ability to establish and maintain a relationship with another person on a one-to-one basis is the basic, primary foundation upon which all other forms of interpersonal communication rest. It is important, then, to take a close look at the dynamics of dyadic communication.

It is not possible to provide a complete or accurate understanding of dyadic communication by considering only one person at a time. No matter how intensely and thoroughly we look at one person alone and then at the other person alone, we cannot understand either person accurately in their dyadic situation. To understand this dyadic situation, we have to study the two personalities as they interact.

In dyadic communication, each person creates the other person as the transaction process occurs. (You may want to reread our discussion of the process nature of communication in chapter 2.) Person A is not the same person to the stranger in an elevator as to a class friend, or the boss, or any other person with whom A establishes a relationship. Each person is a unique personality, and each relationship he or she establishes with other persons is a unique relationship.

As Laing has explained, a person's behavior is always in relation to someone or something other than self.[1] He points out that the very simplest schema for understanding a person's behavior has to include at least one other person. The behavior of each toward the other is mediated by the experiencing by each of the other, and the experiencing of each is mediated by the behavior of each. This is the transaction process, the process of each creating, together, the meaning of each other in their relationship. Each dyad as an entity constitutes a social system in which each person is simultaneously influencing and being influenced by the other.

This chapter on dyadic communication has two areas of concern. First, we are going to look at the life of a dyadic relationship: how a relationship is initiated or formed, how it is maintained, and how some relationships are terminated. Second, we will investigate two basic types of relationships: intimate interaction and social communication.

1. R. D. Laing, H. Phillipson, and A. Russell Lee, *Interpersonal Perception: A Theory and a Method of Research* (London: Tavistock Publications, 1966).

The Life of a Relationship

In a way, a relationship has a life. It is born, grows, and ends. Some relationships last a lifetime, while others are short-lived. Some relationships grow strong and deep, while others are occasional and light. Whether they are old or young, long-lived or short-lived, deep or shallow, each dyadic relationship of which you are now a part had a beginning. There was a period of becoming acquainted with that person and of forming a relationship with that person.

Initiating and Forming a Relationship

The formative period of an interpersonal relationship has at least two stages—an initial, exploratory stage and a "getting-acquainted" stage. The first stage might be called the "entry phase," while the second stage might be called the "acquaintance process." The latter stage has been described in

The acquaintance process.

Cornelius Sinclair

detail by Newcomb in *The Acquaintance Process,* by Byrne in *The Attraction Paradigm,* and by Jourard in *Self-Disclosure: An Experimental Analysis of the Transparent Self.*[2] The entry phrase has been described by Zunin, by Altman and Taylor, and by Berger.[3] The entry phase occurs in the first few minutes, while the acquaintance process occurs over a more extended period of time.

The entry phase—the initial contact phase—is an extremely unstable encounter. Each member of the dyad must rely exclusively on the reactions of the other. Either member of the dyad can terminate the continuation of the interaction. Each holds a virtual veto power in this regard. This initial encounter situation is usually characterized by verbal fencing, a process in which each person "sizes up" the other person—each trying to find out who this other person is. Each seeks to discover the other's identity, attitudes, and values. If you discover that the other person has attitudes, values, and beliefs like your own, and if you feel "safe" with the other person, you will tend to

2. Theodore M. Newcomb, *The Acquaintance Process* (New York: Holt, Rinehart & Winston, Inc., 1961); Donn Byrne, *The Attraction Paradigm* (New York: Academic Press, Inc., 1971); and Sidney M. Jourard, *Self-Disclosure: An Experimental Analysis of the Transparent Self* (New York: John Wiley & Sons, Inc., 1971).

3. Leonard Zunin, *Contact: The First Four Minutes* (Los Angeles: Nash Publishing Co., 1972); Irwin Altman and Dalmas A. Taylor, *Social Penetration: The Development of Interpersonal Relationships* (New York: Holt, Rinehart & Winston, Inc., 1973); and Charles R. Berger, "The Acquaintance Process Revisited: Explorations in Initial Interaction" (unpublished manuscript, Northwestern University, 1973).

4. Newcomb, *Acquaintance Process*, p. 261.

reveal yourself more freely. If, however, you feel threatened or insecure with this stranger, you will reveal as little of yourself as is possible. Newcomb calls this process "reciprocal scanning,"[4] and says that it is "a crucial part of the interactional behavior that goes on between persons who are getting acquainted. . . . Following any opportunity for reciprocal scanning—even a brief one on early acquaintance—there is apt to be some delineation on the part of the interacting persons of the area of mutually shared orientations—of at least some small sector about which they agree that they agree or disagree."[5]

5. Ibid.

Those who have studied this initial or entry phase in becoming acquainted believe that the first few minutes of verbal and nonverbal communication between strangers may determine, or at least strongly influence, subsequent communication attempts to become acquainted. These first few minutes (two, three, or four minutes) may determine future interaction patterns and influence the development, or lack thereof, of a subsequent relationship. Though the research of scholars such as Berger and Zunin,[6] we have some idea of what happens during the initial contact phase. Zunin claims that by analyzing the first four minutes of communication of strangers, one can predict with relatively high probability whether or not the persons involved will interact in the future.[7] Jourard reports that persons who are willing to disclose personal information to others in initial contact tend to induce others to engage in self-disclosure. He calls this tendency for disclosure to beget disclosure the "dyadic effect."[8] We have discussed it earlier in this book. The research of Altman and Taylor and of Berger, however, indicates that the disclosure occurring during the first two or three minutes, i.e., during the entry phase, is of a particular type. Namely, it is relatively shallow, safe, conservative, nonevaluative, and demographic. Altman and Taylor describe the talk during this initial contact phase as "light, undertaken at a superficial and noncommittal level, including areas such as whom one knows, where one lives, where one has traveled, what one's profession is, where one works, etc."[9] Although these topics may be and, in fact, are dealt with overtly at a superficial level, Berger's research leads him to believe that these data serve as bases for making inferences about the individual.[10] He says:

6. Berger, "Acquaintance Process Revisited," p. 4; and Zunin, *Contact*, preface.

7. Zunin, *Contact*.

8. Jourard, *Self-Disclosure*.

9. Altman and Taylor, *Social Penetration*, p. 11.

10. Berger, "Acquaintance Process Revisited," p. 4.

> By knowing a person's age, one might be able to accurately infer the person's musical preferences. The kinds of topics covered in initial interaction do help to generate a network of propositions about the persons revealing the information. The propositions or predictions generated from the initial data may be in error; however, the fact that such "theories" are generated on the basis of "superficial" interaction is indeed significant. For if the inferences made on the basis of data obtained in the first few minutes of the encounter suggest that persons may be dissimilar on other, more salient, attributes, the probability that they will continue to interact might well be lowered. By contrast, if the

inference pattern suggests a high level of similarity on attributes not yet sampled, the probability that the interaction will continue will be increased. Thus, inferences based on "superficial" interaction may well determine whether persons will continue their relationship.[11]

11. Ibid.

Berger's research has given us a detailed account of the communication patterns in the initial interaction situations he studied. He wanted to know what kinds of information were exchanged and when patterns shifted in the entry phrase. Zunin postulated a "four-minute barrier," that is, information exchange patterns shifted after four minutes.[12] Berger found that the talk of thirty-six persons (strangers who were interacting) could be classified within seven categories: (1) demographic information: having to do with background characteristics of the person, such as hometown, major family characteristics, and year in school; (2) attitudes and opinions: information concerning the person's attitudes and opinions toward any object or person; (3) future plans: information about future plans of any kind, like summer jobs, career plans, and plans for school; (4) personality: having to do with one's own or the other person's personality; (5) past behavior: concerning the antecedent conditions for the person's present behavior, for example, "Why did you come to this school?"; (6) other persons: any references to persons other than those involved in the interaction, such as "Do you know Jane Smith?" and (7) hobbies and interests.[13]

12. Zunin, Contact, p. 6.

13. Berger, "Acquaintance Process Revisited," p. 7.

Demographic Exchanges

Some of Berger's dyads were given two minutes to talk, some five minutes, and some ten minutes. His results showed that the first four to five minutes were characterized by requests for and the giving of demographic information. In fact, this preoccupation with demographic concerns seemed to suppress the passing of other kinds of information until after the first four or five minutes.[14] Berger's first category dominated the initial interaction. The pattern then shifted to attitudes and opinions (second category) and to other persons (sixth category). The third, fourth, fifth, and seventh categories were "rare conversational topics during initial interaction."[15] Berger points out that one of the prime functions served by exchange of demographic information is to reduce uncertainty about the other or others in the interaction. Specifically, by exchanging demographic information, clues may be gained as to the possible attitudes and opinions a person is likely to hold. Thus, by ascertaining into which "categories" a person falls, we can begin to make inferences about that person's attitudes and opinions without directly asking for them. Reducing uncertainty through demographic scanning may aid in attaining smooth social conduct by enabling persons to predict areas of probable opinion discrepancy so that they can be avoided.

14. Ibid., p. 14.

15. Ibid., p. 7.

Closely related to the uncertainty-reduction function is the search for similarity function that demographic exchange might also serve. For example, if two persons discover that they are from the same hometown, they will probably pursue the matter in an attempt to determine whether they were from the same part of town and/or whether they know the same people. The search for similarity function of demographic exchange is analogous to, if not the same, as Newcomb's notion of reciprocal scanning of "orientations."[16]

16. Ibid., pp. 15, 16.

The Instantaneous General Impression

These studies by Berger, Zunin, and others have added to our understanding of the kinds and patterns of information exchanged in the entry phase of becoming acquainted, but even before the verbal fencing and innocuous exchanges, there is a general and immediate perceived "image" of the stranger that provides an almost instantaneous "definition" of who this stranger is. In research studies, two-second glimpses have been found sufficient for a person to develop an image and general expectation of the person glanced at. Immediately the stranger is perceived as a unit, as a whole. Specific traits fit together to form the almost instantaneous general impression.[17] Moreover, this impression exerts a powerful influence on subsequent communication with the person. Also, a single dominant or striking factor may heavily influence the general impression. A smile, frown, icy glance, bright color, and so on may be especially influential in the assignment of psychological and personality traits. Some traits are especially influential in their effect upon conversation. One of these is the warmth of the person.[18] If the person is perceived as "warm," then he or she is likely to be perceived as also being sincere, honest, generous, wise, and happy.[19] Interactions between physical and psychological traits also determine our impression of people. Psychological traits influence our perception of physical ones, and physical traits influence our impression of psychological ones. The first impressions are extremely important; therefore, those things first noticed—those things determining first impressions—are of special significance. Social psychologists have found that physical appearance, what the person first says, and what he or she first does are important determiners of another's first image. Hence, gestures, posture, and rate of speech are important first indicators. Similarly, some unusual or especially significant physical appearance factor—unusual clothes or inappropriate dress—may be powerful determiners of the immediate image.

17. See S. E. Asch, "Forming Impressions of Personality," *Journal of Abnormal and Social Psychology* 41 (1946): 258–90. Also, you may recall our discussion of person perception in chapter 4, in which the trait theory of impression formation was explained in detail.

18. H. C. Smith, "Sensitivity to People," in *Social Perception*, ed. Hans Toch and H. C. Clay (New York: Van Nostrand Reinhold Co., 1968), p. 14.

19. Ibid.

The first impression is an important determinant of the interaction that follows, and the verbal interactions of the first few minutes influence subsequent interaction leading to the establishment of that specific dyadic relationship. From such initial encounters fledgling relationships are born. During subsequent encounters in the early stage, each person becomes more fully acquainted with the other and the relationship is clarified and becomes established. Once the relationship has been established, the task then is to maintain and sustain it.

The second phase in the life of a relationship is its maintenance and support. The key word, as represented in the writings and the research of many scholars relative to maintaining satisfactory dyadic relationships, seems to be *equilibrium*. One might think that once a relationship is worked out during the ''being-born'' stage, all problems are forever solved. However, if you will recall our discussion early in this book, wherein we view life as a process, you will remember that virtually nothing is static. Rather, change is the one thing we can count on, and that necessitates specific action to maintain equilibrium—to make adjustments and to perform certain behaviors that maintain the relationship as mutually satisfying to both participants. Probably goals and role-relations will be redefined many times as necessitated by change to maintain a balanced relationship.

We have selected four specific factors that seem to open up significant areas in which balance must be maintained. These factors have been identified and discussed by numerous writers under various labels, but the two sources whose explanations we like best are Schutz and Argyle.[20] Schutz identifies three factors especially important to interpersonal behavior—inclusion, control, and affection.[21] Inclusion (the acceptance of the other person by each member of the dyad), control (the dominance of one person by the other), and affection (the liking and love between the two persons) represent needs that must be met if an effective dyadic relationship is to be maintained. Included among the factors identified by Argyle are intimacy, dominance, appropriate response behavior, nonverbal responsiveness, and emotional tone.[22] It is clear from his discussion of each that they are closely related to Schutz's factors. Argyle's ''intimacy'' seems to parallel Schutz's ''affection''; his ''appropriate responsiveness'' is quite similar to Schutz's ''inclusion factor''; and his ''dominance'' factor is clearly parallel to Schutz's ''control.'' If we put these two lists of factors together, we have the following four factors that are especially important to the maintenance of effective dyadic relations: (1) affection or intimacy, (2) dominance or control, (3) appropriate responsiveness or inclusion, and (4) appropriate emotional tone. If a dyadic relationship is to be maintained, the needs and desires of each member of the dyad relative to these four factors will have to be met. In satisfactory dyadic relationships an equilibrium is established between the members of the dyad relative to these factors. Argyle discusses this balance in terms of a reward-cost model. He says, ''A number of investigators have constructed theoretical models of the reward-cost exchanges active in dyads, and have then incorporated them in rather stripped-down experiments, often in terms of games.''[23] Argyle reviews these various experiments and points out that they show cooperative behavior between the dyads in terms of meeting the needs of each relative to the factors of emotional tone,

20. W. C. Schutz, *FIRO: A Three Dimensional Theory of Interpersonal Behavior* (New York: Rinehart and Company, 1958); Michael Argyle, *Social Interaction* (New York: Atherton Press, 1969).

21. Schutz, *FIRO*.

22. Argyle, *Social Interaction*.

23. Ibid., p. 193.

intimacy, dominance, inclusion, and nonverbal responsiveness. Let us look at each of these factors in more detail.

Affection or Intimacy

Whether the dyad consists of husband and wife, mother and daughter, boss and secretary, teacher and student, and so on, one of the areas in which agreement will be worked out and needs fulfilled is intimacy. This factor has been observed in studies of interpersonal behavior in the field and in the laboratory. So important is the fulfillment of needs of affection and intimacy at the dyadic level that virtually every scholar in interpersonal relations discusses it. Argyle states:

> If two people seek different degrees of intimacy there will be incongruity and awkwardness. . . . If A uses social techniques such as standing nearer, looking more and smiling, to a greater extent than B, B will feel that A is intrusive and over-familiar, while A will feel that B is cold and standoffish. Clearly A is seeking an affiliative response from B: it is not enough for him to be able to look B in the eye—B must look back and with the right kind of facial expression. The Argyle and Dean model postulates that each person tries to maintain his own equilibrium level of intimacy.[24]

24. Ibid., p. 201.

If a satisfactory dyadic relationship is to be maintained, then the affection and intimacy needs of each member of the dyad must be met at the level defined by them as appropriate or necessary for that particular dyad.

Dominance or Control

A second area of concern is dominance or control. Again there must be agreement between the members of the dyad. There must be a balance or agreement as to who will control whom, and when. If the two persons have different ideas about who will make a decision, who will talk most, or who will command, agreement or compromise will have to be worked out. And throughout the life of the relationship, it will be necessary to maintain "agreed-on" dominance behaviors. Argyle states that "the commonest source of conflict in dyadic interaction is where each wants to dominate."[25]

25. Ibid.

Appropriate Responsiveness

As Argyle explains his concept of appropriate responsiveness, "each response of A's must be followed by a response of B's which is 'appropriate.' In a conversation, question should lead to answer, jokes to laughter, for example."[26] One can easily see how inappropriate response has the effect of excluding the dyadic partner. The maintenance of satisfying dyadic relationships requires appropriate responsiveness or inclusion. Even in the area of nonverbal responsiveness that Argyle lists as a separate factor, appropriate participation with the other is necessary. Each interactor must from time to

26. Ibid., p. 202.

time signal his or her attentiveness to the other. If you recall the discussion in the chapter on nonverbal communication, it can be easily seen how nonverbal responsiveness is especially effective in expressing feelings and acceptance toward the other person.

Appropriate Emotional Tone

While interaction can proceed between two persons who are in different emotional states, this is not a stable condition. In all probability, what will happen is either that the interaction will cease or there will be a change of emotional state by one member of the dyad. You are probably not unacquainted with this factor in dyadic communication. You may be able to recall times in your life when you made carefully thought-out plans so as to take advantage of the moonlight, the soft music, and the smell of roses for that very special person. You may have been interested in establishing a congruent emotional state in the other person!

A Harmonious Balance

When needs are satisfactorily met in the four areas just identified, effective dyadic relationships exist. Rather than acting independently or in conflict, the two persons interact compatibly as a smoothly-working social system and enjoy a satisfying dyadic relationship. Argyle says, "It may take some time to establish a steady state. . . . When it has been established, it appears to have some of the properties of a system in equilibrium. A system is said to be in equilibrium if it remains in a steady state and if deviations are met with forces to restore conditions to normal."[27] The idea that a stable equilibrium develops in successful dyads seems to be borne out by several studies.[28] In numerous investigations of compatible and incompatible dyads, incompatibles are often found either to differ in strength of affiliative needs or to be made up of pairs in which both members are high in dominance. In experiments in which these two kinds of incompatibles were placed together as dyads, three results emerged: (1) the members of the dyad did not enjoy the interaction and did not like each other, (2) meshing (appropriate response behavior) was poor, and (3) task performance was poor.[29] This inability to develop a harmonious balance that provides a mutually satisfying relationship should be apparent during the formative stage of the dyadic relationship. If, however, relationships and roles are worked out and defined satisfactorily over a period of time—during the formative stage—then the task relative to maintenance of the relationship is to perpetuate the balance and thus satisfy each other's needs through reciprocal behavior, with A responding to needs of B and B responding to needs of A so that the needs of each are met. When harmonious, mutually agreed on, and mutually satisfying interaction occurs relative to affection or intimacy, control, inclusion, and emotional needs, then relationships are maintained.

27. Argyle, *Social Interaction*, p. 203.

28. See, for example, Henry Lennard and Arnold Bernstein, *Patterns in Human Interaction* (San Francisco: Jossey-Bass, Inc., Publishers, 1969); Erving Goffman, *Relations in Public: Micro Studies of the Public Order* (New York: Harper & Row Publishers, Inc., 1972).

29. See, for example, Neil J. Smelser, *A Theory of Collective Behavior* (New York: Free Press of Glencoe, 1962).

Exiting a Relationship

Toffler, like several other writers, has written poignantly about the "speeded-up pace" of life today in technological societies. He calls this ever-increasing pace of living "the accelerative thrust," and points out that the result of accelerative thrust is transiency, or a temporariness and impermanence in all of our experiences, including dyadic relationships. He describes the situation as follows:

> The acceleration of change shortens the duration of many situations. . . . To survive, to avert what we have termed future shock, the individual must become infinitely more adaptable and capable than ever before. . . . He must understand in greater detail how the effects of acceleration penetrate his personal life, creep into his behavior, and alter the quality of existence. He must, in other words, understand transience. . . . Transience is the new temporariness in everyday life. . . . Our relationships with people seem increasingly fragile or impermanent. . . . Relationships that once endured for long spans of time now have shorter life expectancies. . . .[30]

30. Alvin Toffler, *Future Shock* (New York: Random House, Inc., 1970), pp. 33–35, 45, 46.

31. Ibid., pp. 96–98.

If Toffler's observations are true, exiting relationships is an important problem with which we ought to be concerned. In fact, it is the inability of persons to handle this problem that has led, in part, to shallow relationships, even to the avoidance of meaningful relationships and to consequent alienation.[31] This phenomenon, you will recall, we discussed in the chapter on behavior patterns. The point we wish to make at this time, however, is that exiting relationships is as much a part of the real world as is initiating and maintaining interpersonal relationships. Unfortunately, there is almost no research literature on this topic. It is an area in interpersonal communication yet to be studied extensively by communication scholars. There are, however, a few commonsense principles we might suggest.

First, it seems clearly evident that to maintain an ongoing relationship with every person one meets and knows is impossible. Too many persons flow in and out of our lives yearly, weekly, and even daily. We must, so it seems to us, accept the fact that many relationships will terminate. Acknowledgment of that fact would seem to be a necessary and healthful stance. At the same time, it is probably necessary to have some relationships that are long lasting and even permanent through these times of accelerated thrust. If that is true, then a second principle is that we must learn to discriminate clearly and carefully among types of interpersonal relationships. This principle is in accordance with the concepts of change and process. We dare not lock ourselves into a narrow, frozen pattern of behavior as regards our interpersonal relationships. Each relationship is unique. Some will terminate quickly. Others need to be relatively permanent.

Third, we must restrain the temptation to avoid forming relationships because impermanence is so pronounced. Such behavior is contradictory to our basic social nature and to our most important means of survival—integration through communication. The attempted avoidance of all relationships is pathological.

These three observations, of course, simply point once again to the need for great adaptability and sensitivity to our own needs, to the needs of others, and to the environment in general.

Two Dyadic Communication Forms

In this section of the chapter we will look at two specific dyadic communication forms. We believe this will clarify the applications of the dyadic communication factors we have been discussing to specific settings. Further, by thinking in terms of some selected types of dyadic communication, we can focus attention on the interaction of numerous dyadic communication variables and, thus, once again illustrate the complexity and the forceful energy of human communication. The two forms we will consider are intimate communication and social communication.

Intimate Communication

Among the situations included in intimate communication are courtship communication, marital communication, communication with a very close friend, and communication within the family. These communication situations are characterized chiefly by their intimacy and the comparative permanence of relationships. Cooley refers to such groups (marriage, family, friends) as the "springs of life, not only for the individual but for social institutions."[32] With a close friend, the family, or a spouse, we can communicate in a trusting and supportive environment.

The effect of intimate interaction in the marital relationship upon interpersonal perception, interpersonal understanding, and interpersonal acceptance is greater than in other communication situations. In marriage, for example, the effect of this strong interpersonal relationship is illustrated by the *honi phenomenon*. In 1949, a woman observed the faces of her husband and another man through a window of a specially constructed room, which had floors and walls that sloped at odd angles. This room had been constructed for the conducting of experiments, and a person observed walking from one corner of it to another would appear to grow or shrink in size, depending upon the direction in which the person was moving. When this woman observed her husband walking in the room, however, he did not shrink or grow in size, but the other man did change as he walked along with her husband. This unusual observation was named the *honi phenomenon*. Replications of this experiment have substantiated the 1949 finding—the

32. Charles H. Cooley, "Primary Group and Human Nature," in *Symbolic Interaction*, ed. Jerome G. Manis and Bernard N. Meltzer (Boston: Allyn & Bacon, Inc., 1967), p. 156.

33. Warren J. Wittreich, "The Honi Phenomenon: A Case of Selective Perceptual Distortion," in *Social Perception*, ed. Toch and Clay, p. 82.

finding that strong interpersonal relationships operate to influence perception.[33] Married couples with a strong perception of each other are able to overcome the distorting influence of the physical background of the room. The honi phenomenon is illustrative of one of the many strong influences produced by intimate communication. Such influences occur not only in the area of perception but in many other areas discussed in our study of interpersonal communication. The significant point to be made is that in intimate interaction situations such as those with a friend, in the family, and in marriage, communication can be the fullest and most accurate of all interpersonal communication situations. It should be stressed that the opportunity for such communication development is provided in these situations, but there is no absolute guarantee that such development will actually take place. There are communication failures in marriage, there are parents and children who do not communicate with each other successfully, and there are sometimes broken friendships. If a person's intrapersonal communication is extremely inaccurate and ineffective, failure in intimate interaction situations is to be expected.

One of the absolutely essential elements in successful intimate interaction is trust. We cannot be truly intimate without being vulnerable, that is, without opening ourselves, sharing ourselves, and trusting ourselves to another. Trust is necessary for the growth, development, and existence of an intimate relationship. The person who desires to experience intimacy must learn to communicate in such a way as to create a climate of trust that reduces fear of rejection on the part of both parties.

Trust is established through disclosure to a loving, caring, responding person coupled with reciprocal disclosure by that person. Getting to know each other well and building an intimate relationship depends upon both persons being self-disclosing. When each discloses to the other, trust is built as the other responds with acceptance and support. Trust is destroyed when the risk-taking disclosure behavior of one is rejected, ridiculed, or betrayed. Two elements, then, are especially important in intimate communication— risk taking through self-disclosure, and the acceptance and support of the responding person.

We met these elements previously when we discussed self-growth and again in our discussion of initiating and maintaining relationships. They are prominent indeed in the acquaintanceship process and in the control, affection, responsiveness, and appropriate emotional tone necessary to the satisfactory maintenance of relationships. The implications for us of each of these elements ought to be clear. We cannot expect to be able to engage in satisfying intimate communication if we are unwilling or too fearful to take the risk of making disclosures to the other person. We cannot hide behind masks or protect ourselves by being tight-lipped and closed to everyone. Rather, we must learn to open ourselves to others—to take intelligent risks through self-disclosure. And we must become aware of the responsibility placed on

Arnold Kapp/Tom Stack & Associates

us when another discloses himself or herself to us. Can we be supportive and accepting? We find trust as we demonstrate our trustworthiness.

In courtship the emphasis is on the discovery and development of an interpersonal relationship that culminates in the establishment of the most intimate of human relationships. Courtship is then, an extended and deepening acquaintance process. Argyle says of courtship:

> Falling in love means that A is very strongly rewarded by B in the sexual sphere, with the result that A likes B very much, and becomes dependent on B for further rewards. On the other hand A incurs costs—through loss of independence and the difficulties of synchronising; thus he is in an approach-avoidance conflict, and this is confirmed by the common phenomenon of lovers repeatedly breaking off and then coming together again. . . . The process of love is marked by two public rituals—

One of the significant dyadic relationships for most of us is the marital relationship.

Dyadic Communication   275

engagement and marriage. The usual purpose of such rites of passage is to proclaim publicly a change of state, in this case the relationship between two people. A further interesting ritual is the honeymoon . . . there are two main interpersonal tasks to be completed during the honeymooning—to work out mutually satisfactory ways of regulating sexual behaviour, and of living together at closer quarters. A working agreement has to be arrived at over a huge range of interpersonal issues, and towards many outside situations. In other words a new level of equilibrium has to be worked out, with synchronising at a greater level of intimacy, and a higher rate of interaction. . . .[34]

34. Argyle, *Social Interaction*, pp. 214–15.

Let us look specifically at marital communication in terms of two topics—disclosure (openness and closedness, honesty and duplicity) and freedom to grow (to adapt to change and to retain one's individuality while being one with the other).

Disclosure

If we want to be loved, we must disclose ourselves. If we want to love someone, that someone must permit us to know him (or her). That seems so obvious, doesn't it? But, it is, apparently, one of the most common difficulties in marital communication. Jourard and Whitman, psychologists and marital counselors, say:

We discovered that even with those they cared most about, people shared little of their true feelings or their most profound longings and beliefs; revealed little of what they really thought on such touchy subjects as sex, self-image, religion. . . . As a therapist and research psychologist I often meet people who believe that their troubles are caused by things outside themselves—by another person, bad luck or some obscure malaise—when in fact they are in trouble because they are trying to be loved and seeking human response without letting others know them. . . . Even in families—good families—people wear masks a great deal of the time. Children don't know parents; parents don't know their children. Husbands and wives are often strangers to each other.[35]

35. Sidney M. Jourard and Ardis Whitman, "The Fear That Cheats Us of Love," *Redbook*, October 1971, p. 83.

Unfortunately, this concealing and wearing of masks often begins in courtship—right at a time when masks ought to be coming off and deepening acquaintance ought to be occurring. The story is told of one couple on their honeymoon whose refusal to be open with each other resulted in unnecessary misunderstanding and hurt for eight years. What happened was that on their honeymoon, in the restaurant where they took their first meal, she started up a conversation with a strange couple. He refused to participate in this extended conversation with strangers. Both became quite angry, and a big fight between the newlyweds ensued. Eight years passed, with each probably recalling the incident and experiencing renewed anger again and again. It was revealed in counseling sessions some eight years later why he and she had behaved as they did! He thought the honeymoon was a time

Self-disclosure is necessary for the development of an intimate and satisfying dyadic communication.

Ron Seymour

to be alone with his new wife—a time purposefully to close out other people. For her to seek out strangers to engage in conversation was perceived by him to be an insult to his masculinity and to his role on the honeymoon. On the other hand, she saw his refusal to join in the conversation as an insult and rejection of her. She began the conversation with the strange couple because she "had never had a conversation as a wife" and she wanted to try out this new role. The honeymoon seemed to her to be the ideal time to try this aspect of her new role. Isn't it tragic that eight years of pain and misunderstanding resulted from two persons' inability or refusal to communicate openly!

I suspect each of us has been guilty of unnecessary closedness and concealment. We say that we feel things we really do not feel, and that we believe things we really do not believe. We try to present our best selves, sometimes false selves, to be loved. Also, we hide to protect ourselves from change, because change is so frightening. But often these behaviors are counterproductive. They produce an effect exactly the opposite of what we really intend.

Although disclosure of feelings, attitudes, and beliefs is a necessary characteristic of intimate and satisfying dyadic relationships, we want to emphasize that it must be intelligent and benign disclosure. We are not suggesting that you can be or should be brutally open as regards every feeling, attitude, and thought. McCroskey, Larson, and Knapp make this point:

> Disclosure is a particularly important concept in our discussion of interpersonal communication in marriage. Much writing in the popular literature suggests that open communication on all aspects of marital life leads to greater understanding and adjustment. However, there are serious limitations that one should place on that generalization. We have all encountered situations in which individuals in particularly playful or rueful moods give in to momentary impulses to make intense personal disclosures. We sometimes regret these disclosures, even beyond the point where we can derive any comfort from the convenient cop-out, "I'm telling you this for your own good." From the marital situation, the effects of such intense disclosures are long-range and cumulative and may even be destructive. The intensity of the involvement and the commitment which characterizes the marital situation are such that the married couple experimenting with "truth sessions" may discover that their momentary experimentation will have consequences that go far beyond their expectations. The critical questions which should be asked are "Is the disclosure necessary or likely to have productive consequences?" Can the other person handle it?" The second question implies an almost moralistic assertion. The assertion is that when we disclose personal information to another, we are in effect "messing with his mind." If what we say has deep personal implications for the other, then the responsibility for the consequences clearly lies with the person who is doing the disclosing.[36]

36. James C. McCroskey, Carl E. Larson, and Mark L. Knapp, *An Introduction to Interpersonal Communication* (Englewood Cliffs, N.J.: Prentice-Hall, Inc., 1971), pp. 175, 176.

Despite the acknowledgment that one cannot always be totally open, we stress the need for disclosure and honesty when they meet the criteria identified by McCroskey, Larson, and Knapp. Otherwise, courtship communication and marital communication fail in their purposes, and courtship, rather than being a time of mutual exposure of the self and acquaintance with the other, is a period of mutual deception, a period in which the couple constructs false images, one of the other. The result, of course, is that each marries a stranger. It is quite difficult to establish a satisfying relationship if each person's concept of the other is inaccurate. How can a person who selects someone he or she does not know or understand behave in loving ways and reciprocate in fulfilling needs?

Failure to disclose and to be open is especially dangerous to a close and meaningful sexual relationship. Jourard states:

> Given a reasonable lack of prudery, a lusty sex life grows best out of a relationship between two persons who can disclose themselves to each other in all areas of their lives without fear of being hurt. . . . Sex deteriorates when a couple cannot establish a close, mutually revealing, *nonsexual* relationship; the very defenses one uses to keep from being known and possibly hurt by the spouse one cannot understand are the same defenses that impede spontaneity in sex.[37]

37. Jourard and Whitman, "Fear That Cheats Us," p. 157.

Indeed, disclosure, openness, and honesty are important interpersonal communication skills in courtship and marriage.

Freedom to Grow

The second topic we want to consider is freedom to grow, the freedom to adapt to change, and the freedom to retain one's individuality. Jourard, again speaking of marital communication, says, "Once we have formed our image of who and what we are, we proceed to behave as if that were all we ever could be. We 'freeze,' as though we had taken a pledge to ourselves that even if we did change, we'd try not to notice it. And we don't want the other person to change either."[38] In fact, sometimes one person tends to smother the other, to absorb the other person so as to destroy his or her individuality, and to deny the other person the freedom to grow and to change in response to an ever-changing world. Again, Jourard says:

38. Ibid.

> Freedom and the right to grow are a difficult and painful gift for a couple to give each other, but there is no alternative. People outgrow the roles in which they have been cast by their partners, and when they have grown and changed, each must be able to let the fact be known so that the partner he or she loves can take it into account. . . . Husbands and wives need tough and candid talk aimed at dispelling misunderstandings. They need to understand how they differ, what they respect and love in each other, what they hold in common—yes, and what enrages them in each other. If we speak honestly, we must be able to say, "What you are doing right now makes me angry."[39]

39. Ibid., p. 158.

A healthy marital relationship allows both parties the freedom to grow and change as individuals.

40. McCroskey et al., *Introduction to Interpersonal Communication,* p. 170.

Too often the members of intimate dyads become locked in habitual behavior patterns so that change is virtually impossible. As McCroskey, Larson, and Knapp say, "One important implication of this observation must be pointed out, however obvious it may already be to you. We tend to develop habitual ways of responding to others. And these habitual response patterns may be more characteristic of marital communication than of other interpersonal contexts."[40] They go on to point out that when change is responded to by one partner and they vary from the "locked-in patterns," the other member of the dyad often does one of two things—either of which is counterproductive. He or she simply dismisses the other as unreasonable, messed up, unintelligent, or even in need of professional help of some kind. And since we all know how useless it is to talk to someone who is incapable of thinking straight, or following our own clear and concise patterns of reasoning, why bother? Second, if we decide to try to resolve the differences, it is easy for us to invest all our energies and resources into "correcting" the faulty thinking of the other; hence, we enthusiastically embark on a small but holy crusade to convert the other, to save the other from the pitfalls of his or her own thinking, to prove that the other is wrong and we are right. Either of those two courses of action is likely to be unproductive.[41]

41. McCroskey, *Interpersonal Communication*, pp. 170–171.

Not only do we become slaves to habitual behavior, thus denying change and growth, but sometimes the marital relationship acquires an even more counterproductive characteristic—that of "ownership" of the other. It is understandable, of course, how this characteristic might develop, since all of the marriage liturgy, either religious or civil, urges the couple to become one; and indeed, there is a "oneness" in an intergration as deep and close as marriage. There is, however, a seductiveness about this phenomenon, to the effect that one of the dyad may be tempted to cease to exist as an individual. To become "one" in marriage and never be "me" and "you" is directly counter to an important concept in interpersonal communication, the concept of self! When "oneness" is the only perception either or both members of the marriage dyad have, then undue and unhealthy control usually results. One person, the controller, begins to determine all of the outcomes of their interaction. This "ownership" has a stifling effect on the marriage or on any other intimate dyadic relationship in which that phenomenon exists. In such a situation there is no freedom for the "owned" to grow and to respond to an ever-changing world.

In terms of intimate dyadic relationships it appears that disclosure, freedom to grow, and the retaining of one's "selfness" are important variables. Attention to behavior in these areas would seem to be warranted.

Before leaving this section on intimate dyadic communication and going to the section on social communication, we do want to emphasize again that observing the principles of communication so as to communicate smoothly does not of itself guarantee a satisfactory dyadic interpersonal relationship. It may mean only that two persons agree to disagree easily, smoothly, and clearly—that each member of the dyad has his or her own goals, values, needs, and the like. Genuine incompatibility in these areas cannot be compensated for by more "talk." These substantive differences must be resolved as they relate directly to the specific dyadic relationship, or the relationship will have no reason to exist.

Social Communication

Conversation is the most characteristic behavior of sociability. Social conversation as distinguished from other talk is consummatory talk (of primary value at the moment only) and quite different from instrumental talk (used to accomplish a specific goal or to solve a specific problem). In social conversation, talk is its own purpose. This does not mean that any kind of talk satisfies. There is a science and art of conversation with rules of its own, but the identifying characteristic of social conversation is its sociability—its existence for its own sake. Other forms of communication via conversation—the

Social conversation fosters a feeling of harmony.

quarrel, debate, gossip, confessional, interrogation, public speech, interview, and so on—are used to obtain practical ends. The purpose of social conversation is to give pleasure, thus no content, idea, or theme need be dominant. As soon as the talk becomes objective (instrumental), its purpose changes, and it ceases to be social communication. In social conversation we seek to achieve harmony, a consciousness of being together, and enjoyment of one another. We reject conversation that is "too intimate" and "too individual" because it cannot be shared by others. Those topics are appropriate in intimate interaction situations such as talk with a close friend or between husband and wife, but they are not appropriate in social conversation. That is why stories and jokes are common at parties—they provide a content that can be shared by the group.

Stroking

42. Eric Berne, *What Do You Say After You Say Hello?* (New York: Grove Press, Inc., 1972), p. 448.

Because the primary purpose of social communication is the enjoyment of the company of others, something known as *stroking* is a common kind of communication. Berne defines stroking as "a unit of recognition."[42] He elaborates by stating:

Stroking may be used as a general term for intimate physical contact; in practice it may take various forms. Some people literally stroke an infant; others hug or pat it, while some people pinch it playfully or flip it with a fingertip. These all have their analogues in conversations, so that it seems one might predict how an individual would handle a baby by listening to him talk. By an extension of meaning, "stroking" may be employed colloquially to denote any act implying recognition of another's presence. Hence a *stroke* may be used as the fundamental unit of social action. An exchange of strokes constitutes a *transaction,* which is the unit of social intercourse.[43]

Stroking is the "basic unit of social communication."[44] We are social beings. Berne makes the point well that human beings *require* social stimulation. In fact, "stimulus hunger" results ultimately in hallucinations, and if the condition persists, the person regresses more and more and eventually dies. We need social stimulation. It is a requirement of life. There are few real hermits in this world. Most of us need to be stroked. Some persons require more stroking than others, but all persons need it sometimes. Stroking may be verbal or nonverbal, positive or negative. In fact, you can recall the types of feedback we discussed in chapter 7 and apply those types to stroking without much difficulty. Whatever the type, we need it as a confirmation of our existence among others in a social world. We need acceptance. As Borden and Stone say:

> We have shown that stroking may be either positive or negative. It may also be verbal (the words "I love you") or nonverbal (a kiss), vocal (a spoken endearment) or nonvocal (a written note). . . . *Most stroking is done nonverbally.* We trust the nonverbal strokes more than the verbal ones. It's easy to say "I love you" because it is a conscious behavior, but the way you say it (the vocal-nonverbal part) is usually unconscious and thus more to be trusted.
>
> The eyes, rather than the voice, are the most active strokers we have. RECOGNITION is shown there first. (That is why we have the term "poker face.") If you show no emotions in your eyes, people do not know where you are in relation to them. This can be very disconcerting. The reverse is also true. If you are able to control the expressiveness of your eyes so you can stroke without meaning it, then you set up all kinds of false perceptions in others. If you were to smile at us with your eyes, we might think you were recognizing us approvingly when really you were faking it and hate us both (which may be the case if you don't like what you are reading). The only way we can find out is to have a session of strokes to see if our first perceptions were correct. This constitutes communication, or as Berne states it, "social intercourse." . . . If we engage someone in conversation, the very fact that we are talking to him or her is a positive stroke. What we say, as well as the way we say it, may add some more strokes. Sometimes these two types of strokes cancel each other out, but we are always left with the initial stroke, that of contact.[45]

43. Eric Berne, *Games People Play* (New York: Grove Press, Inc., 1964), p. 15.

44. George A. Borden and John D. Stone, *Human Communication: The Process of Relating* (Menlo Park, Calif.: Cummings Publishing Co., 1976), p. 82.

45. Borden and Stone, *Human Communication,* pp. 82–83.

Stability

Social communication, like most other types of communication, evidences a certain amount of orderliness and stability. Transactions in social communication are kept on track by adjustments and corrections so that predictability and stability are maintained. The forms of behavior, even at parties, are more stable than one might realize. The physical environment is generally quite structured and stable, and even the people and groupings tend to be stable as well. This is true for all groups who *are* groups meeting together regularly in social situations. Every sorority, fraternity, family, club, and so on, evidences stability through formalized as well as informalized patterns of interaction.

Social communication takes place in areas where space is controlled, equipped, and decorated in ways that produce stability. In conversational areas, for example, the way chairs are normally arranged takes into consideration specific interpersonal distances.

From the first group, the family, other groups develop. Peer groups of associates, friends, neighborhood networks, and the like are social units that are often interconnected with families. These social groups often gather in each other's homes, where rather stable functions are carried out. Food and drinks are provided, attention and stroking are given to others, and other communicative behaviors are engaged in to maintain bonds, confirm values and beliefs, and in general to reinforce social organization toward stability.

Although each person has many selves—has a multifaceted personality—in any given type of transaction, that person is expected to specialize. From among his or her repertoire of roles, each person is expected to take a particularly appropriate role for this transaction. Therefore, even in social communication, the presence of a given person provides a rather stable source of behavior as that person takes a particular role that is carried out in a customary and predictable way. That person's presence provides a predictable environment for the others who know him or her. The outcome is relative stability of the ways in which we provide stimulation and fulfill social needs.

Pastimes and Games

Pastimes are played by persons (often in dyadic communication situations) at social gatherings. They can be defined as talking about things to "pass the time." Their purpose is to structure time, to provide stroking, and sometimes to select a person with whom we will engage in a more complex dyadic relationship—the game.

Pastiming includes talking about the weather, the gas shortage, the flowers in bloom, cars, hobbies, clothes, travel, sports, and other chitchat topics. Such dyadic communication provides opportunity for stroking and for meeting positive social needs at a relatively shallow and safe level. Sometimes, however, pastiming leads into games.

Interpersonal, social games have several purposes: to avoid intimacy, to avoid reality, to conceal motives, to rationalize activities, to compete, and to combat or fight.[46] Games may be destructive or not destructive, and games can be won or lost; but they do seem to be necessary. At least this is what one writer says:

46. Berne, Games People Play.

> Games are a series of transactions with predictable outcomes and concealed motivations. Although every game is basically dishonest, most are often unconscious; and many are necessary because we cannot be intimate, spontaneous, and game-free with all the many people who move through our lives.[47]

47. Jacquelyn B. Carr, Communicating and Relating (Menlo Park, Calif.: Cummings Publishing Co., 1979), p. 306.

Berne, among others, has observed and described some of these destructive party games.[48] Four of the games that are played most often, according to him, are "Ain't It Awful," "Blemish," "Schlemiel," and "Why Don't You—Yes But."

48. Berne, Games People Play, p. 113.

"Ain't It Awful" has several versions, but all are characterized by people's *seeking* and enjoying suffering and telling about their suffering or hardships to win sympathy. The Ain't-It-Awful player says, "Ain't it awful how you can't trust people today! Ain't it awful about divorce, juvenile delinquency, and crime nowadays!" Or he or she may tell of excruciating pain, operations, and other misfortune. College students play the game, too. For them, it usually takes the form of "Look what the administration is doing to us now!"

"Blemish" is another unwholesome game played in social situations. It is simply the game of discovering a blemish in someone and telling others about it. At parties you will notice that the behavior of the person playing Blemish can be characterized by morbid curiosity, prying, getting in digs, and putting down others. "That's the dress she wore last week. Do you suppose it's the only one she has?" Or "Haven't you read Toffler, John?" These and questions or statements like them are characteristic of the game of Blemish. Blemish, so Berne's studies show, is played most often by the sexually insecure person.

Another social game is "Schlemiel." Berne describes it as follows: the Schlemiel spills his drink on the hostess's evening gown. The hostess or her husband can respond with rage or anger, and thus the Schlemiel wins. Or, the hostess can maintain poise and forgive the Schlemiel, in which case the Schlemiel is free then to inflict more damage—break something, let his cigarette burn the chair, and so on. The payoff for the Schlemiel is to be forgiven publicly. That is what he wants. He can then say he is sorry and feign contrition. The object of the game is to test whether or not he can be destructive and still be forgiven.

"Why Don't You—Yes But" is the oldest subject of game analysis and the most commonly played game at parties and all other kinds of social situations.

The following is an example of the "Why Don't You—Yes But" game.

John:	"Mary always wants to type my papers, but she never does them right!"
Harry:	"Why doesn't she take a course in typing?"
John:	"Oh, she hasn't got time for that."
Roger:	"Well, why don't you type your own?"
John:	"Are you kidding? Have you seen my typing?"
Harry:	"Have you thought of hiring someone else?"
John:	"Listen! I can't even afford the paper for all the typing I need done."
Harry:	"Then why don't you just accept what she does and how she does it?"
John:	"Yes, and flunk my courses because of her lousy typing!"

The idea of the game is to counter every proposed solution with a "Yes, but" until no one has a solution left to propose. Then the instigator of the game, the one who introduced the problem, wins the game! The "Yes, butter" may not make friends, but he or she wins the game. A good player can stand off any number of others until they all give up.

Berne also identifies some sexual games that are played in social communication situations: "Let's You and Him Fight," a game in which a woman maneuvers two men into competition for her favors or company; "Rapo," a game between a man and a woman consisting essentially of mild flirtation to attract the man and get him to "pursue." The woman gets her pleasure from the man's pursuit and response to her signals. She can make the game quite sophisticated as she makes it difficult for him to respond or follow her without being obvious. Of course, as soon as he "catches her," she rejects him and gets her payoff or gratification in watching his discomfort when she repulses him. In some instances, the game has become vicious and has ended tragically in suicide, murder, or in the courtroom. After leading him into the sexual act, she may then cry "Rape!" Male versions of the male game are the "casting couch" and then she doesn't get the part, or "Cuddle-Up" and then she gets fired anyway.

SUMMARY

In this chapter we have observed that the dyadic relationship is the foundation on which other social relationships rest. We have emphasized how the dyadic relationship is best understood as a process in which each participant is created as unique to that relationship through the transactions of the two persons involved. The dyadic relationship has been discussed in terms of initiating, sustaining, and terminating that relationship. The variables or phenomena we chose to study were the maintenance of relationships (including affection and intimacy, dominance or control, responsiveness or inclusion, and emotional tone) and the process of terminating a relationship. In addition, we have looked at two specific dyadic forms—intimate dyadic communication and social communication.

SELECTED READINGS

Byrne, Donn. *The Attraction Paradigm.* New York: Academic Press, Inc., 1971.

Homans, G. C. *Social Behavior: Its Elementary Forms.* New York: Harcourt, Brace and World, 1961.

Jourard, Sidney M. *Self-Disclosure: An Experimental Analysis of the Transparent Self.* New York: John Wiley & Sons, Inc. 1971.

Knapp, Mark L. *Social Intercourse: From Greeting to Goodbye.* Boston: Allyn & Bacon, Inc., 1978.

Newcomb, Theodore M. *The Acquaintance Process.* New York: Holt, Rinehart & Winston, Inc., 1961.

Watzlawick, Paul; Beavin, Janet H.; and Jackson, Don D. *Pragmatics of Human Communication.* New York: W. W. Norton & Co., Inc., 1967.

Zunin, Leonard. *Contact: The First Four Minutes.* Los Angeles: Nash Publishing Co., 1972.

11

Small Group Communication

Americans are very fond of forming committees. We have committees to plan picnics, homecoming decorations, dances, automobiles, and even committees to investigate committees. Just think of how many organizations you know in which every problem to be solved is referred to a committee. We are a very "committee-oriented" people. We like to work on problems in small groups.

With so many small groups about us at work, in government, at church, and at school, it must be apparent that an understanding of communication in small groups is necessary if we are to function effectively at work and at play, and if we are to enhance our comprehension of the events around us. It is for this reason that we now focus our attention upon communication in the small group context.

There are many questions about small groups that should concern us. What are the characteristics of a leader, and how does a person assume leadership in a small group? Are small groups' decisions as good as those made by individuals? Can an individual working alone solve a problem better than a group of people working on it together? Are several heads better than one, or do too many cooks spoil the broth? What is the effect on an individual of being in a small group? Does the small group cause us to be less or more conservative? All of these are legitimate questions about small group communication. We hope to answer some of these questions in this chapter (and if not answer them, at least point out some possible directions of thought regarding them).

Communication in a small group context has probably been studied as completely as almost any other communication phenomenon. As far back as the 1940s there was an intense concern with what was then called "group dynamics."[1] The concern was with making people into better group participants. Attention was focused on determining what made a good leader, and countless studies investigated various personality correlates with leadership. In subsequent years empirical research has focused on small group behavior ranging from leadership to seating arrangements to conformity behavior and to group cohesiveness. Interest in the small group as such has become so

1. Fred L. Strodtbeck, "Communication in Small Groups," in *Handbook of Communication*, ed. Ithiel de Sola Pool et al. (Chicago: Rand McNally & Co., 1973), pp. 658–60.

great that we can easily find dozens of texts on small group behavior today in several different fields—communication, education, political science, psychology, and sociology.

The Nature of Small Group Communication

Before we can adequately discuss small group communication, it is necessary to explain what we mean by *small group*. It is easier to define small groups through concrete examples than by abstract terms. Small groups include three-person committees; families with a mother, father, sister, and brother; a jury in a court trial; and a group of five people planning a party. Just as those examples obviously seem to be small groups, it is equally obvious that the United States Senate, the United Nations General Assembly, the Republican or Democratic national conventions, and all of the people at any given moment in Times Square in New York City are not examples of small groups. Now that we have considered examples of what very clearly is and is not a small group, we will try to suggest some guidelines for differentiating small groups from other groups of people.

What Is Small Group Communication?

2. Michael Burgoon, Judee K. Heston, and James McCroskey, *Small Group Communication: A Functional Approach* (New York: Holt, Rinehart & Winston, Inc., 1974), pp. 2–3; Marvin E. Shaw, *Group Dynamics* (New York: McGraw-Hill Book Co., 1971), p. 4.

3. B. Aubrey Fisher, *Small Group Decision Making: Communication and the Group Process* (New York: McGraw-Hill Book Co., 1974), pp. 16–24; Gerald M. Phillips and Eugene C. Erickson, *Interpersonal Dynamics in the Small Group* (New York: Random House, Inc., 1970), pp. 171–174.

Small groups include groups that range anywhere from two or three in size to twenty as an upper limit.[2]

Having given a numerical range, we should mention that number of people is not the distinguishing characteristic of small groups. Although small groups usually fall within this range, their inclusion as a context of interpersonal communication is more related to other factors[3] that permit equal opportunity for all group members mutually to influence one another. In addition, commonly shared goals among members are a defining characteristic of small groups. Although it is not the identifying characteristic of small groups, size is nevertheless fairly consistently within the range just mentioned because as groups surpass this range in size, the size itself inhibits interaction. This can then prevent group members from mutually influencing one another and sharing goals.

In this chapter we will not discuss groups of two, since dyads were covered separately in chapter 10. For this chapter, then, we will operationally define a small group as including from three to twenty people who can interact with one another on a face-to-face basis, who are not inhibited from interacting because of group size, and who share in common some need or needs that can be satisfied through participation in the group's activities.

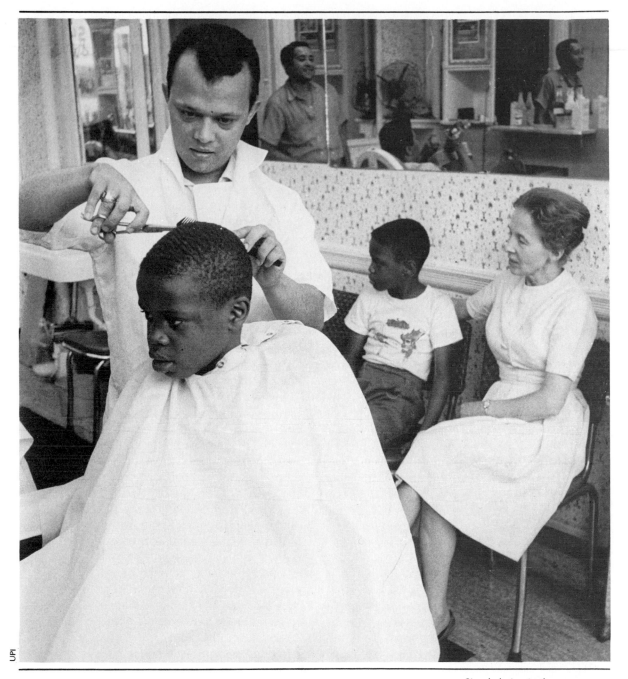

Simply being in the same room does not make several people into a small group.

4. L. Richard Hoffman, "Group Problem Solving," in *Advance in Experimental Social Psychology*, ed. Leonard Berkowitz (New York: Academic Press, Inc., 1965), p. 107.

Using a few of our examples, it must be obvious that a group of people at any given moment in Times Square in New York City are too many in number to interact with one another on a face-to-face basis, with each having an equal interaction opportunity uninhibited by the size of the group. Once there are additional people in a group, size itself begins to inhibit contributions from members of the group.[4] Within a specified amount of time, as the number of people increases within a group, the opportunity for talking decreases, because the amount of time available for discussion must be shared by more persons. In addition, a group of people in Times Square do not share a need or needs that can be satisfied by their interacting as a group.

However, if we consider a group of five people planning a party, we begin to see that the characteristics of a small group are evident. Five people is few enough to permit the opportunity for freedom of interaction in an uninhibited manner. Likewise, more often than not, people who have volunteered to be on a committee to plan a party have social or ego needs that the party as such can satisfy, and thus, being a part of that group can be a step toward satisfying those needs.

Actually, this discussion of small group communication is an outgrowth of our definition of interpersonal communication in chapter 1. There we defined interpersonal communication as a process in which individuals attempt mutually to influence one another through the use of a common symbol system in a situation that permits equal opportunity for all persons involved in the process to influence one another. The only difference now is that we have restricted our view to a specific number of people, because so much research has been conducted examining communication as it occurs in groups within that range. Most of the research has focused upon groups of two to six people; however, enough research has been done with groups larger than that to warrant including them in our definition of a small group.[5]

5. Edwin J. Thomas and Clinton F. Fink, "Effects of Group Size," *Psychological Bulletin* 60 (1963):371–84.

6. Robert Ardrey, *The Social Contract* (New York: Atheneum Publishers, 1970), p. 368.

7. Alex Osborn, *Applied Imagination* (New York: Charles Scribner's Sons, 1957), p. 234.

Robert Ardrey speculated that eleven or twelve may be some sort of a "natural size" for a group.[6] Alex Osborn, in his *Applied Imagination*, suggested that the ideal size for a brainstorming group was about twelve.[7] These suggestions indicate that "ideal group size" is greater than that which has been predominantly studied in experimental situations, so we will include somewhat larger groups within our definition of small group communication. However, it became apparent to us in the course of our teaching experiences that once we get beyond fifteen or twenty people, the character of interaction among teachers and students changes significantly. Somewhere in that fuzzy range of fifteen to twenty members, groups cease being small groups and begin to take on the characteristics of a public communication situation in which one person is predominantly in charge of talking to other people.[8]

8. Burgoon, Heston, and McCroskey, *Small Group Communication*, pp. 2–3; Shaw, *Group Dynamics*, p. 4.

9. Phillips and Erickson, *Interpersonal Dynamics*, p. 40.

Probably more important than size of the group is *a commonality of goals of the members*.[9] In our definition we indicated that members of a small group should have needs in common that can be satisfied through membership and participation in the group. We cannot stress this too much. Many clubs and organizations find themselves in a situation in which members no longer want to attend meetings and participate in activities. In situations like this, the group probably no longer satisfies the needs of its members. When this occurs, the group begins to disintegrate, since it no longer has a reason, or need, for survival. There is no longer a group goal that satisfies the various needs of individuals in the group.

Effectiveness of Small Group Communication

At this point, let us move on to consider a question that has, no doubt, crossed your mind whenever you have seen a committee formed. How effective is the small group? Have you ever had the feeling that you might have been able to solve the problem better by yourself than the small group that attempted to solve it? Have you ever thought that your solution might have been better than the one a committee came up with? That question has been examined in a number of experiments. We will now consider some of the findings.

In determining whether groups or individuals are more effective, we must consider the kind of task to be faced. Generally speaking, tasks that are somewhat repetitive or mechanical in nature are better handled by individuals than by groups.[10] It makes very little sense to have a committee formed within an organization to make regular purchases of paper supplies. That kind of task occurs on a regular basis and can usually be handled as well, if not better, by one competent individual than by several persons working at it together.

The kind of task that seems best suited to group work is one involving some degree of complexity and/or a task requiring creativity for solution of the problem.[11] It is true that sometimes an extremely bright, capable, and creative individual can produce a solution superior to that of a group of average individuals working together; however, since we do not always have an extremely bright, creative person at our disposal, the possibilities for solving complex problems and problems demanding creativity is greater when approached by a group than by an individual, providing certain assumptions are met.

First, the problem must be dividable in some way.[12] It must be possible for us to divide the labor among the various members of the group. It should be possible for one person to gather information about one aspect of the problem, another person to gather information about another aspect of the problem, a third person to gather information about another aspect, and so on. This enables the group to make maximum use of the total resources that are available to it.

10. J. Tuckman and I. Lorge, "Individual Ability as a Determinant of Group Superiority," *Human Relations* 15 (1962):45–51; R. W. Husband, "Cooperative Very Solitary Problem Solution," *Journal of Social Psychology* 11 (1940):405–9; and Fisher, *Small Group Decision Making*, pp. 39–42.

11. Ibid.

12. Barry E. Collins and Harold Cuetzkow, *A Social Psychology of Group Processes for Decision-Making* (New York: John Wiley & Sons, Inc., 1964), pp. 18–27.

13. Osborn, *Applied Imagination,* p. 84.

Second, we should establish an atmosphere of acceptance within the group so as to encourage free and uninhibited contributions by all members of the group.[13] This is especially true when solutions are being suggested. All members should feel free to contribute whatever ideas they have without fear of criticism from other members of the group. If this is possible, the group can elicit more ideas relevant to solving the problem. Therein lies the advantage of several heads being superior to one, for out of several different heads a good solution to the problem is more likely to come. Likewise, assuming that members of the group are aware of effective small group behavior, it may be possible for the members of the group to build on ideas, synthesize different ideas from different persons, and thus produce a group solution superior to any solution that could be offered by any one individual.

14. R. A. Hoppe, "Memorizing By Individuals and Groups: A Test of the Pooling-of-ability Model," *Journal of Abnormal and Social Psychology* 65 (1962):64–71.

Finally, in addition to complex problems being well suited to a group approach, problems that require the remembering and recall of information seem particularly well suited to small groups (rather than to individuals).[14] With more people in a group, there is a greater probability that a given piece of information will be recalled by at least one group member. Putting it all together more information is remembered in total by a group than by any one individual.

Small Group Communication Takes Time

15. J. H. Davis and F. Restle, "The Analysis of Problems and Prediction of Group Problem Solving," *Journal of Abnormal and Social Psychology* 66 (1963):103–16; D. W. Taylor and W. L. Faust, "Twenty Questions: Efficiency in Problem Solving as a Function of Size of Group," *Journal of Experimental Psychology* 44 (1952):360–68.

One aspect of small group ineffectiveness in problem-solving situations is related to the total man-hours expended whenever a group interacts.[15] If a problem takes one hour to be solved by one person and if five persons can solve it in a half hour, on the surface it may appear that the small group is more efficient than the individual, since the small group takes less time (as a group) to solve the problem than an individual would. However, if we are talking about a situation within a large corporation (where time costs money), it becomes apparent that the small group is particularly inefficient in the situation just described because the small group actually consumes two and a half hours, whereas an individual solving the problem has only required one hour (a half hour per person in a five-person group totals two and a half hours). Thus, we are not simply trying to decide what is the "best" way of solving a problem at any given time. Frequently, we are trying to balance the most efficient problem-solving method against the cost of using that method. (Cost is sometimes figured in terms of time spent by the persons involved.) This is a very real consideration we should keep in mind at all times.

If there are some problems that are not amenable to small group solutions, and if the number of total hours consumed by small groups is so great, then why do so many organizations turn to small groups in their quest for solutions to problems? The answer to this question is not readily available by simple consideration of the kinds of tasks suitable to small group solution. Instead, it can be found in an examination of the effects of small groups on the individual (which we will do later in this chapter). To consider fully the effects on the individual of working in a small group, along with other topics, we now move to a consideration of interaction in small groups.

Interaction in Small Groups

Many students are disturbed at attempts made to classify them and to generalize about their behavior. We have often heard students complain in class, "But I am not at all that way," "I do not at all act that way," and "I am different." It is true that individuals deviate from some of the patterns that have been observed in empirical research; however, the consistency of behavior by most individuals is striking. Of these striking consistencies, one that has been observed over time has to do with the phases of interaction that small groups share in common. While different people have labeled these phases differently, there are consistencies among the observations, which become apparent as we consider these observations.

Interaction Phases

Since the phases of small group interaction have been covered by other writers,[16] we will focus on four primary phases that appear to crop up rather consistently within the many different studies that have been conducted. These were confirmed by Fisher[17] and appear to be consistent with those discovered by other researchers.[18] Fisher labeled the four phases *orientation, conflict, emergence,* and *reinforcement.* We will use his terminology.

The first phase, *orientation,* is one you may have noticed when you have taken part in small groups. During this phase, group members try to get to know one another, feel one another out, discover roles and status, and get to know the lay of the land, so to speak. They become oriented toward one another and the problem that faces the group.

During the second phase, *conflict,* there are increasing instances of disagreement among members. There is a greater tendency to maintain positions indicating disagreement. There is a mounting atmosphere of polarization and controversy among members.

Whereas negative comments and behaviors occur in the conflict phase, there is a greater tendency toward positive, favorable comments and interpretation in phase three, *emergence.* Group members use more ambiguous language and make more ambiguous statements to indicate disagreement without appearing quite so disagreeable in phase three. Comments are made that indicate a more favorable attitude toward the position that is emerging from within the group.

16. Lawrence B. Rosenfeld, *Human Interaction in the Small Group Setting* (Columbus, Ohio: Charles E. Merrill Publishing Co., 1973), pp. 39–62.

17. B. Aubrey Fisher, "Decision Emergence: Phase in Group Decision-Making," *Speech Monographs* 37 (1970), 53–66.

18. T. M. Mills, *The Sociology of Small Groups* (Englewood Cliffs, N.J.: Prentice-Hall, Inc., 1967); B. W. Tuckman, "Developmental Sequence in Small Groups," *Psychological Bulletin* 63 (1965):384–99.

The last phase, *reinforcement,* is readily apparent to anyone who has ever participated in a group decision. During reinforcement, everyone makes comments about how well the group worked together and how good a solution was reached. Essentially, people say things that they feel reinforces the decision and the decision-making process. Statements are made that are very positive and that enable people to view the decision and the decision-making process positively.

In essence, the last phase is probably an example of dissonance reduction. If you will recall, in chapter 1 we discussed our need for consistency. Phase four is an excellent example of this need. Typically, if we have been through an arduous decision-making situation that involved conflict and took up our time, it is probably important for us to perceive that experience positively. Otherwise, we are faced with the inconsistency of having wasted our time. Thus, during the reinforcement phase we spend much time telling ourselves and others what a good job we did. Therefore, whatever mental pain or time loss we experienced is at least justified or rationalized in our minds.

Polarization and controversy increase during the conflict phase of a problem-solving group.

These stages of interaction are primarily related to problem-solving groups. However, most groups, whether they be problem-solving groups or not,

© Eric Kroll 1979/Taurus Photos

Chapter 11

very likely go through similar stages. Moreover, these phases are not peculiar to problem-solving groups but could probably be expected in a group of any kind.

According to Tuckman,[19] any kind of group goes through a *forming phase*. This is a testing situation in which members try to find out what the task is, who the leader is, and how the various members relate to one another. This can be true whether the group is task-oriented or not. The primary difference is that in non-task-oriented groups there is no attempt made to find out what the task is.

19. Tuckman, "Developmental Sequence."

The second phase (still following Tuckman) would be a *storming phase* in which there are conflicts between subgroups and may be rebellion against a leader. This kind of thing could occur if the conflict is over proposed solutions in a task-oriented group, or could even involve conflict over the leader's role in something as non-task-oriented as an encounter group.

A third phase that a group probably goes through is a *norming phase*. This is essentially an emergence phase. Nevertheless, it is important for us to note that in addition to the emergence of task solutions and group cohesiveness, the development and emergence of norms occurs.

Every group develops norms of behaviors, dress, attitudes and beliefs, and it is in this norming stage that the future behavior patterns of the group are developed. Not only are these norms developed, but the group enforces adherence to those norms at all times. The reason for the development and enforcement of norms is that without them it is impossible to predict an individual member's behavior. These norms enable us to know what to expect from other people in our groups, so consequently groups develop norms regarding the ways in which ideas are introduced and decisions are made so that all members of the group can know what to expect from other members. This is one reason that so many of our social clubs have attitudinal norms we are expected to meet, so that the members know that they can talk about and what positions they can take without creating future conflict. Thus, the norms actually promote the continuance of cohesiveness within groups.

Finally, we move into a stage of *performing*. In this phase the interpersonal structure of the group is established, roles are flexible and functional, and the group can deal with the task. Of course, in a problem-solving group, this fourth stage is one in which solutions emerge.

One more phase, which is frequently overlooked in discussions of small groups, is called *dissolution*.[20] In this stage the group has ceased to satisfy the needs of its individual members and the members are preparing to bring the group's existence to a close. The behavior at this point consists of discussions of earlier phases of the group. The members talk about the conflicts they have had and of how they have enjoyed getting to know one another and working together. They also reminisce about how they worked out conflicts and reached solutions to problems. They begin to discuss how they will

20. Michael Argyle, *Social Interaction* (Chicago: Aldine-Atherton, 1969), pp. 219–20; R. D. Mann et al., *Interpersonal Styles and Group Development* (New York: John Wiley & Sons, Inc., 1967).

go back out into the outside world or back into the larger organization the group is a part of, and they prepare for this reentry.

It is also not an infrequent thing for members to plan for reunions—talk about getting together sometime in the future for old time's sake. If we may be permitted a cynical observation at this point, it is our feeling that groups typically, after going through the dissolution stage, do not get together for reunions very often, if ever. In fact, we have the distinct impression that after the needs that caused the formation of the group have been met, or once the group can no longer meet those needs, its members, after dissolving the group, actually tend to avoid getting together again. When these reunions do occur, one frequently senses a considerable feeling of embarrassment and awkwardness on the part of former members who are attending the group reunion—a feeling resulting from the realization that no reason for them to be together any longer exists. Their needs of the moment are no longer satisfied by the get-together. It is a futile exercise.

By paying close attention to the kinds of comments being made by people in small group communication, it is possible for us to determine the stage a group is in and use that knowledge to guide our own comments and behavior. If we begin to perceive that a group has gone into a stage of emergence or norming, we should adapt to that and not continue conflict behavior lest we be rejected by the group as deviates. This is, in essence, a suggestion that, when you are a member of a group, you should try to proceed according to whatever stage the group is in. To use an older cliché, slightly modified, "When in conflict phase, conflict, but when in norming phase, norm."

Problem-Solving Phases

The phases of small group communication just discussed are descriptive in nature. Fisher and Tuckman were both attempting to describe what normally happens in small groups. Keep in mind that they were not attempting to describe an ideal or suggest that all groups *should* go through these phases. From their research, they discovered that most groups do go through these phases as described. We are not going to discuss a *prescriptive* approach to stages in small group problem solving. In a prescriptive discussion, our orientation will change from a consideration of what *does* happen in small group problem solving to what *should* happen.

The approach we will consider is widely accepted by people who teach small group communication and was originally developed by Dewey (1910) as an attempt to prescribe an ideal set of steps for individual problem solving.[21] After he developed this approach, based upon "the scientific method," writers in small group communication and discussion texts employed the approach to suggest an ideal set of steps groups should go through to discuss and solve problems adequately. There are six steps in Dewey's model:

21. J. Dewey, *How We Think* (Boston: D.C. Heath, 1910).

Chapter 11

1. *A felt need.* Before a problem can be solved, a difficulty, problem, or need must be expressed. For instance, in a fraternity or a sorority, if pledging has not been successful in past years, a committee may be formed called a membership committee. The "felt need" facing this small group is that of low membership and the need to recruit pledges more effectively. At this stage of problem solving, the group must be able to agree that there is a need. However, at this point the need is somewhat vague and generally stated and serves the function of providing the reason and motivation for group formation and effort.

2. *Problem definition.* It is not enough to have a vague awareness of the problem, although, unfortunately, many groups are content to proceed from a vague awareness. Using Dewey's approach, however, the membership committee just described should proceed from the general statement of low membership to a more specifically defined problem. This could include anything from determining that the fraternity or sorority house looks shabby, to "we don't get out and meet people and ask them to join the group," to "our rush activities during rush week are too unorganized, and thus we have low credibility on the part of potential pledges." In other words, during this stage of problem solving, the group must focus upon the generalized need to determine the *specific* nature of that need so it will then be possible to move to the next step of the problem-solving sequence.

3. *Problem analysis.* Having specifically defined the problem, it is necessary for us to analyze the problem in terms of causes, history, component parts, and the like. The membership committee we have been discussing might analyze the problem of the appearance of the house. This could result in a statement that the sorority or fraternity lacks an approach to maintenance and cleaning, which results in the shabby appearance perceived by prospective pledges. Likewise, an analysis of why people do not get out to meet prospective pledges may result in a conclusion that members are shy. The analysis might also suggest that the type of social gathering provided to meet prospective pledges during rush week is not attractive to prospective pledges. Thus, they do not come to the house, and the members do not have a chance to meet them. Whatever is decided during this step of problem solving, the group should try to explore all the various possible causes of the problem as well as implications of the problem for the future. This kind of analytical approach can frequently be surprising to groups if they go through it conscientiously. It can result in previously unrecognized components of the problem being noticed, as in our example of low membership in a fraternity or sorority.

4. *Solution proposals.* Having defined and analyzed the problem, the group members should propose solutions. There is frequently a tendency to be critical of suggested solutions, but during this stage of problem solving there should be no critical comments. People should be encouraged to suggest answers to the problem, no matter how bizzare or strange they may

seem. In our example, if someone suggests that the fraternity or sorority should have a party at which classical music is played and everyone dresses formally, it is not appropriate *during this step of problem solving* for another committee member to comment that nobody would come or that such a party would be dull. During this stage everyone on the committee should provide encouragement for people to give ideas, no matter how wild they may sound.

5. *Solution testing and comparison*. During this phase of problem solving, the solutions are compared against one another and criticized. The previous suggestion regarding the classical music party might be torn to shreds by members who feel strongly that classical music at a rush party would not work. It is also possible that someone might decide that this is a good idea. Although in step 4 the solutions are proposed and not criticized, in step 5 they are criticized. The practicality of proposed solutions is discussed. Different proposals are compared with one another so that better alternatives can be selected from among all the solutions proposed in step 4. At this point solutions may be criticized on the basis of their cost, the time involved, the number of people it takes, available materials, and the like. It is also quite appropriate during this stage for ideas to be combined. It may well be that one part of idea A and one part of idea B are workable, and therefore the group may decide to combine the workable parts of both ideas A and B and discard what are considered to be the unworkable parts.

6. *Solution/implementation*. In what would seem logically the final step in the problem-solving sequence, the solution/solutions to the problem is selected and put into action. Some people in public speaking have referred to this as an *action step*.

Although this sixth step concludes Dewey's model, it is our feeling that a seventh step should be added—an *evaluation process*. During this last step, the group should meet after the solution to the problem has been implemented to evaluate their success or lack of it. The group should first determine the standards by which they will evaluate the solution. For instance, in the committee just discussed, the standard might be the number of pledges actually recruited into the fraternity or sorority. On the other hand, the group might decide that in addition to the number, the quality of pledges is equally important. Whatever the standards agreed on, the group should next employ these standards in their evaluation of the success or failure of the group's solution. If the solution has been successful according to the group's standards, it should be continued into the future. In our example, the rushing procedures developed by the group should be continued in future years. On the other hand, if the group in our example decides that the rushing procedures did not work, as evaluated against the group's criteria, then it is necessary to go back to step one of the problem-solving process and begin all over again. The group cannot know for sure where they went awry in trying to solve the problem and what caused their problem not to work unless they go back to the beginning in the problem-solving sequence. This is a circular process, in which groups solve problems, put solutions into effect, evaluate them, and then try to solve them all over again. This is a continuing process, one based upon the assumption that people can solve problems rationally.

Dewey's model has a considerable appeal to many scholars. We have used the method in small group discussion courses and have found it to have great utility. It works. Groups that conscientiously and intelligently follow this model solve problems rather efficiently. It is important to follow the steps in this model in the order indicated, and to keep in mind that there are other dynamics in any group process in addition to the problem-solving steps. As will be discussed subsequently, there are group pressures and other factors that also affect the outcome of problem solving in a group. It is not always possible to proceed through a group discussion in as orderly a fashion as this idealistic model would suggest, but we present it with the hope that you will keep it in mind as you are taking part in problem-solving discussions. At the very least, you can strive for this ideal, fully realizing that it never may be completely obtainable.

Group Influence
Conformity

An exeedingly important consideration regarding small groups is the matter of recognizing how much influence a group has over us. Many of us have experienced being with a group in which people were smoking and drinking. While with the group, because everyone else is smoking and drinking, we often find ourselves doing the same thing, even though we may never have smoked or drunk previously. This is the result of pressure to conform. It is common for us to conform to group pressures.[22] For instance, it is not unusual to see a group of teenagers all dressing alike, or wearing their hair the same way. Sometimes a group will go so far as to dictate the kind of socks members may have on their feet (or decree no socks). Group power to cause conformity is observable all around us in untold numbers of situations. It is important for us to understand how and why this happens and what those conditions are that seem to cause greater conformity than others.

It is apparent that some personality characteristics cause a person to be more conforming in behavior than do other characteristics. Rosenfeld suggests drawing the conclusion that personality affects conformity in the following ways:[23] When a person is somewhat submissive, or if a person's self-concept is low, he or she is more likely to conform to the wishes of a group. The higher a person's intelligence, the less likely it is that he or she will conform to the wishes of the group. We cannot totally change our personality, and yet it is important that we be aware of the effect of these personality characteristics on our conforming behavior and, even more importantly, on other people's tendency to conform.

22. R. S. Crutchfield, "Conformity and Character," *American Psychologist* 10 (1955):191–98.

23. Rosenfeld, *Human Interaction*, p. 70.

A. Devaney, Inc., N.Y.

Friendship groups frequently cause us to conform, even in matters of the clothing we wear.

24. J. N. Jackson and H. D. Saltzstein, ''The Effect of Person-Group Relationships on Conformity Processes,'' *Journal of Abnormal and Social Psychology* 57 (1958):17–24; E. J. Thomas, ''Effects of Facilitative Role Interdependence on Group Functioning,'' *Human Relations* 10 (1957):347–66.

These characteristics relate to some of the needs we discussed in chapter 1. For instance, if a person has very high social needs and these needs can be satisfied by the group, that person is more likely to conform to the group's wishes. Likewise, a person with great ego needs is very likely to conform to the group's wishes if the preson perceives that the group can satisfy his or her ego needs. Furthermore, we would suggest this rule of thumb: the more the individual believes his or her needs can be satisfied through membership in a group, the more likely that person is to conform to the group's wishes. As a group becomes more important to you, the group's influence over you increases.[24] Of course, the reverse is true also.

There are other factors that apparently increase the amount of conformity. As the size of a group increases up to about four people, conformity increases.[25] However, as the group increases beyond that size, there is a possibility for deviates to find support, and thus there will not be as much group conformity. Another important factor that appears to increase conformity in groups is the crisis situation.[26] The existence of a crisis, the perception by the group that a task is important, or the existence of competition appear to cause us to conform more. We are willing to conform to expedite matters. This tendency toward conformity for expediency's sake may have been one of the factors that led to the Watergate cover-up during the administration of President Nixon. It may have been that a crisis atmosphere inhibited persons from taking positions deviant from the group. This, in turn, may have caused a great number of people to conform to a position taken by the group—a position with which they were not wholly in agreement.

Another factor that seems to increase our tendency to conform is a perception of common fate.[27] If we perceive that the rewards we are going to receive will depend upon the result of a group decision as opposed to our own individual decision, we develop a greater tendency toward going along with the group—toward conformity. As we perceive that we will all share in the same reward or punishment, we are more likely to accept whatever decisions and behaviors the group decides on. You have, no doubt, experienced this kind of occurrence in a class in which the teacher assigned group projects with the understanding that each group would receive one grade, and everyone in the group would receive that grade. As you perceived that everyone in the group was going to receive the same reward, or share a common fate, you were more likely to conform to the wishes of the group.

Conformity is a word that has negative connotations for many people. We do not like to hear someone say that we are likely to conform. It is important for us to recognize, however, that conformity serves an essential function within groups. Members of groups choose to share behavior patterns because it helps them satisfy their own needs. If people did not develop and conform to norms in groups, it would become almost impossible to predict behavior. This unpredictability would keep the group from functioning effectively as a group because members need to be able to predict what a fellow member is going to do. Try to imagine how groups would function if members could not predict one another's behavior. The more we can predict the behaviors of other members of the group, the more we are able to predict their responses to our messages.

Individual Deviation

While it is true that the group has considerable power over individuals and that most of us tend to conform to group wishes, it is also true that groups do have deviates. There are people in many groups who do not conform to the norms or wishes of the group. This deviation serves at least three functions.[28] First, deviates supply new ideas. Second, their deviation makes norms more explicit. Third, their presence also makes apparent what happens to those who break the norms.

A deviate is someone whose behavior is significantly different from that of most of the members of the group. Consequently, deviates frequently contribute new ideas that others of the group do not have. Also, when a deviate engages in behavior contrary to the norms of the group, that points up those

25. S. E. Asch, "Effects of Group Pressure Upon the Modification and Distortion of Judgements," in *Groups, Leadership and Man,* ed. Harold Guetzkow (Pittsburgh: Carnegie Press, 1951), pp. 177–90.

26. H. Cantril, "The Invasion from Mars," in *Readings in Social Psychology,* ed. E. E. Maccoby and T. M. Newcomb (New York: Holt, Rinehart & Winston, Inc., 1958), pp. 291–99.

27. Jackson and Saltzstein, "The Effect of Person-Group Relations"; E. J. Thomas, "Effects of Facilitative Role Interdependence," in Collins and Guetzkow, eds. *A Social Psychology of Group Processes,* pp. 143–45.

28. Argyle, *Social Interaction,* pp. 226–27.

norms, making them far more graphic. Of course, the net outcome of a deviate's punishment, or of the norms being made more explicit, is probably that other members who are having their needs satisfied through membership in the group are likely to adhere to those norms more than ever.

Why does an individual become a deviate? Once we are members of a group, why should we want to become deviates and run the risk of being outcasts? There are four reasons we may become deviates.[29] First, we may simply be more influenced by norms of another group than we are by the norms of the group we are in. This may occur because another group is more likely to satisfy our needs (or at least we think it will). Second, it is possible that we may have personality characteristics that prevent us from accepting a norm. For example, there are some people whose personalities are extremely argumentative and aggressive and who, if placed in a group where the norm is one of nonconflict and compromise, may find it impossible to accept that norm. Third, a member of the group may think of something nobody else in the group has thought of, and this can turn him or her into a deviate. When this occurs, it is important for the individual first to make himself or herself a valuable member of the group and then try to persuade the group to accept the new idea or point of view. Otherwise, the person will simply remain a deviate in the eyes of the members. Finally, a person will sometimes deviate within a group simply for the purpose of challenging the leader. No doubt you have experienced a situation in which you watched someone challenge the ideas, evidence, or facts a leader was proposing when, seemingly, there was no good reason for the challenge. If you examined this phenomenon very closely, you may have observed that what was being challenged was not really the ideas being expressed but rather the position of leadership occupied by the leader. Sometimes, through taking a deviate position, it is possible to challenge leadership.

Now that we have considered some of the reasons for a person deviating, let us consider what happens to the person who deviates. The first response of a group to a deviate is to increase the amount of communication directed toward that person.[30] There is an attempt made by group members to persuade the individual to adopt the norms of the group and "come back into the fold." If this does not work, a second group response involves the practice of members cutting off communication with the deviate. The person becomes an isolate and is literally isolated from the group's communication. The third and most extreme response is one in which the deviate is so radical in his or her view, and the group is so totally unable to change the person back to the norms, that isolation is not enough. The group will then expel the deviate—[31]physically reject the person and not allow him or her to be in the group at all. This possibility is what has necessitated clauses in fraternity charters explaining how members can be expelled from the brotherhood. Likewise, some churches have procedures for expelling deviates from the fold.

29. Ibid.

30. S. Schachter, "Deviation, Rejection and Communication," *Journal of Abnormal and Social Psychology* 46 (1951):190–207.

31. Collins and Guetzkow, *A Social Psychology of Group Processes*, pp. 180–82.

Sonia Johnson's excommunication by the Church of Jesus Christ of Latter-Day Saints was that church's response to her role as a deviate.

The Risky Shift

32. Kenneth L. Dion, Robert S. Baron and Norman Miller, "Why do Groups Make Riskier Decisions than Individuals?" in *Advances in Experimental Social Psychology*, ed. Leonard Berkowitz (New York: Academic Press, Inc., 1970), pp. 305–11.

Another effect of the group on the individual is the "risky shift phenomenon." This occurs when an individual becomes more radical and less conservative as a result of being in a group.[32] It is not unusual for individuals who would, when working alone, develop a fairly conservative solution to the problem, to become radical with their solutions and become more willing to take risks while part of a group. Groups seem to produce more risky solutions to problems than individuals do. Almost a "mob psychology" begins to occur, even though within a small group. We have often observed faculty, as well as student, groups adopting actions that later preplexed the individual members of the groups because they were so radical or "off the wall." You have probably experienced similar events yourself.

33. M. A. Wallach, N. Kogan, and D. J. Bem, "Diffusion of Responsibility and Level of Risk Taking in Groups," *Journal of Abnormal and Social Psychology* 68 (1964):263–74.

There are several suggestions as to why this may be so. First, there apparently is a *diffusion of responsibility* in a group.[33] If you, working alone, are to solve a problem, you personally take full responsibility for the solution you suggest. However, if you are part of a five-member committee, the solution produced by the committee is only partly your responsibility. As professors, we have frequently observed that students in a class who know they are going to be called on are usually prepared, since they know they are going to have to confront the teacher on a one-to-one basis. However, if the entire class is going to discuss a reading, it is not unusual for some students to skip the reading. We believe this to be a good example of diffusion of responsibility. When the entire group is involved, everyone is more willing to take a risk because the responsibility for having read the material is diffused over more people. On a one-to-one basis, the individual feels full responsibility and is less willing to take risks.

34. Roger Brown, *Social Psychology* (New York: Free Press, 1965), pp. 698–70.

Second, it has also been suggested that *people take greater risks in groups because that is the norm in our society.*[34] This explanation is based on the assumption that in our society a conservative individual is not as valued as a risk-taking individual. Because they are more highly valued, the risk-takers have more influence on the group than do the more conservative members. The reason for this is that a more risky position is usually a more dramatic position, more exciting, and easier to present in a graphic manner. Thus, the risk-inclined individual can exert more influence on the group with less op-position. Third, *risk-oriented members are more extroverted,* which may enable them to interact more effectively.[35] It is apparent that the group can cause both conformity and risk-taking in individuals.

35. Y. Rim, "Machiavellianism and Decisions Involving Risk," *British Journal of Social and Clinical Psychology* 5 (1966):30–36.

36. M. A. Wallach and J. Marli, "Information Versus Conformity in the Effects of Group Discussion on Risk Taking," *Journal of Personality and Social Psychology* 14 (1970), 149–156; E. Burnstein and A. Vinokur, "Testing Two Classes of Theories about Group-Induced Shifts in Individual Choice," *Journal of Experimental Social Psychology* 9 (1973), 123–137.

Finally, during group discussions the more conservative members become aware of their position relative to others in the group. As they discover that others in the group are more risk-taking, they, too, may become more risk-taking. An information function is served by the group, which contributes to the risky shift. Both information regarding the position of others and the arguments supporting those positions influence people to become more risk-taking.[36]

Finally, an effect of interaction with the individual members is the greater acceptance of a decision a group member feels once he or she has taken part in the group discussion leading to it. For example, if a person hears a lecture or receives an order asking him or her to do a particular thing, there is frequently a tendency on the person's part to resist doing what is asked. However, if that same person participates in a group discussion about the same topic and the group reaches the same decision as that advocated in the lecture or in the order, the person is more likely to accept and act on that position, inasmuch as it is based on a group decision he or she has taken part in.[37] This probably is one of the reasons classroom teaching has changed so much in recent years in colleges and universities. The classroom lecture used to be the primary mode of presentation of material for students. Today the classroom discussion, in which the professor sits down and discusses the material with the students, is more and more common. Students generally reach the same conclusions whether the teacher is presenting the material in a lecture or in classroom discussion (sometimes teachers guide these discussions in a rather heavy-handed manner to have the students reach the conclusions they desire). The reason for this change in teaching procedure is an awareness on the part of many college professors that students are more likely to accept the material if they themselves have participated in a discussion of it and if they have arrived at many of the conclusions themselves rather than receiving them through a lecture.

37. J. R. P. French, Jr., I. C. Ross, S. Kirby, J. R. Nelson, and P. Smith, "Employee Participation in a Program of Industrial Change," *Personnel* 35 (1958):16–29.

The use of the small group as a persuasive device was recognized by the late President John F. Kennedy in some of his political campaigns. During his senatorial and House campaigns Kennedy organized, with the aid of his family (and especially the women of his family), a number of "teas." These tea-and-cookie hours took place in the homes of private citizens throughout his state of Massachusetts. Of course, the objective was to get people in the neighborhood to come together and participate in small group discussions about the candidate and to meet the candidate. By doing these things, the people participating became publicly committed to the candidate, and, of course, by taking part in these discussions they were more likely to support the group's conclusion that the candidate was someone they ought to vote for. This was far more effective than a series of speeches or a series of television advertisements in which the candidate was telling them that they should vote for him. Kennedy's use of the small group as part of the political campaign was most effective. Many other candidates have since followed his example.

The effectiveness of small group participation is one of the reasons small groups frequently are used for problem solving, even when they may be less efficient than the individual's making the decision alone and then communicating it to other people. If we can have our fellow employees take part

John F. Kennedy Library

John F. Kennedy was one of the first to make extensive use of small groups as part of a political campaign.

in a decision through a small group discussion, we can, in all likelihood, find them supporting the decision with far greater enthusiasm than if we reached the very same conclusion independently and passed it on to the others through an order. True, small group communication may not be the most efficient means of problem solving in terms of hours expended, yet it may nevertheless prove more effective because it results in greater acceptance of decisions reached.

Communication Patterns

38. Collins and Guetzkow, *A Social Psychology of Group Processes*, pp. 170–177.

Whenever you have been in a small group discussion, you have probably noticed that everyone in the group does not spend the same amount of time talking. Some talk more, some talk less. In addition, you may have noticed that these differences follow fairly predictable patterns. For example, messages flow according to the status, or power, held by individual group members, with high-status and high-power individuals initiating more messages than low-status and low-power persons.[38] Likewise, once power and status is well established within a group, group members direct more of their mes-

sages toward the person or persons with high power and high status.[39] One
of the high-power/high-status persons acts as the "hub" of the small group,
giving and receiving more messages than anyone else in the group.

39. Ibid.

Although high-power/high-status persons give and receive more messages than anyone else in the small group, this is primarily true after the
power structure of the group has already been developed. Before the power
structure has been established, it is more common for people who aspire to
high status/power to direct more of their messages to potentially low-status
persons than to other aspiring high-status persons. Group members who aspire to high status see the potentially low-status members as people on
whom they can build their power base. They therefore direct many of their
messages toward these individuals in a bid to develop support for their desired high status/power.

One of the results of differences in status and power within the small
groups is demonstrated by communication networks—the pattern of message flow among the members—that form within such groups. After a group
has functioned for a while, a specific pattern evolves in which certain members repeatedly talk with one another, thus forming a "network." Of importance in communication networks within small groups is the factor of centrality. This is the degree to which a small group is more or less centralized in
its message flow and decision making. As a small group is more centralized,
the communication pattern is one in which messages are funneled primarily
to one or possibly two people with high status/power and then emanate from
the same one or two people.[40] Also, the decisions tend to be made by the
same one or two people who are central to the communication patterns of
the group.

40. Marvin E. Shaw,
"Communication Network," in
Advances in Experimental Social
Psychology, vol. 1, ed. Leonard
Berkowitz (New York: Academic
Press, Inc., 1964), pp. 111–47.

Studies that have created these communication networks artificially include the classic studies of Leavitt[41] and Bavelas,[42] which established that
the *more decentralized communication networks are faster whenever complex problems are being solved.* However, *for less complex problems the
centralized networks are more efficient.* The relative efficiency of networks
is, thus, dependent on the complexity of the problem to be solved. As problems are more simple, solutions are reached faster and with fewer errors in
centralized communication networks.[43] As problems become more complex, the decentralized networks are more efficient and the problems are
solved faster with fewer errors. Whether the problems are complex or simple, however, centralized networks bring about solutions with the fewest
messages.

41. H. J. Leavitt, "Some Effects of
Certain Communication Patterns on
Group Performance," Journal of
Abnormal and Social Psychology
465 (1951): 38–50.

42. Alex Bavelas, "Communication
Patterns in Task-oriented Groups,"
Journal of the Acoustical Society of
America 22 (1950):725–30.

43. Shaw, "Communication
Networks," pp. 122–24.

It is probably also important to consider, in addition to efficiency, the
degree of member satisfaction present within both the decentralized and the
centralized networks. Members of small groups with decentralized communication networks experience greater satisfaction from their participation
in the small groups.[44] In the centralized network the position of the individual within that network greatly affects satisfaction. As we occupy a more

44. Leavitt, "Effects of Certain
Communication Patterns,"
pp. 38–50.

central role (a position through which more messages are directed and from which more decisions flow), we experience a higher degree of satisfaction. On the other hand, the more peripheral positions within any communication network, whether centralized or decentralized, cause and reflect greater member dissatisfaction.

Leadership

In research and writings covering the area of small group communication, probably the most attention has been paid to the subject of leadership. We suspect this is so because many people are intensely concerned with obtaining leadership positions and being leaders. Whatever the reason, the results of research on leadership have been very mixed. Early attempts to examine the subject through empirical research were directed toward a determination of the personality factors that caused leadership. Just about everything you can think of was correlated with leadership. The one conclusion we can safely draw from this research is that it is impossible to say, with any certainty, which particular personality characteristics lead to leadership positions within small groups.[45] At one time it was suggested that honest, trustworthy persons are good leaders. Research has indicated that this is not necessarily so.

A communication-based factor that results in a person being chosen as leader is the *quantity* of verbal interaction of that person.[46] The more a group member interacts verbally, the greater the likelihood is that he or she will be chosen as leader of the group. In groups that exist for a short duration, the quality of verbal interaction is probably not as important as the quantity, although this may not be true of groups that function over longer time periods. People who interact a lot are perceived as having greater motivation and interest in the group. This perception often leads to their selection as group leaders. The quantity of verbal interaction is not the only factor related to leadership, however.

The factor most closely associated with leadership is the situation itself. The demands of a group's task, along with the needs of the group and its members, dictate the kind of person who will be chosen as a leader for that group.[47] The person who evolves as a leader in a street gang in a large city is not very likely to become the leader of an academic department in a university. The personality characteristics and personal qualities demanded in each of those two situations are poles apart: whereas honesty may be demanded of the person chosen to lead a university academic department, dishonesty may be a highly valued characteristic for a person who is going to lead an urban street gang. Indeed, the leader of a street gang may be the person who can steal the most cars.

The most effective leadership provided by an individual is that which grows out of the situation itself.[48] If the situation calls for aggressiveness, then an aggressive person will be the most effective leader. If a situation calls for

45. Fisher, *Small Group Decision Making*, pp. 74–76.

46. R. M. Sorrentino and R. G. Boutillier, "The Effect of Quantity and Quality of Verbal Interaction on Ratings of Leadership Ability," *Journal of Experimental Social Psychology* 11 (1975), 403–411.

47. Shaw, *Group Dynamics*, p. 278.

48. Fred E. Fiedler, *A Theory of Leadership Effectiveness* (New York: McGraw-Hill Book Co., 1967), pp. 133–80.

patience and calm, a person who is patient and calm will be the most effective leader. This approach to leadership suggests that at any given time, any member within a group may be a potential leader, depending on the demands of the situation. This is not to say that all members of a group will become leaders. Rather, it suggests that no qualities we know of will absolutely guarantee effective leadership for all situations. In fact, short courses and mail-order classes that purport to teach you how to be a leader and focus upon the development of certain qualities in an individual are undoubtedly misleading at best.

The primary prerequisites, if any can be stated, for effective leadership would probably be *intelligence and sensitivity to the needs of the group*. For a person to be able to cope with the many tasks that confront a leader, intelligence (not necessarily super intelligence) is probably a necessity. Sensitivity is necessary for enabling the individual to perceive the needs to the group and know how to respond to them. It would be nice if we could unequivocally name the qualities that will make a person into a leader. Unfortunately, that does not seem to be possible. The situation will determine the qualities necessary, and since there are any number of situations facing groups, it is apparent that we cannot list qualities that will be appropriate to each and every situation.

Intelligence and sensitivity as such are probably related to two kinds of leadership roles that have been discovered through empirical studies. These are the *task and social-emotional leadership roles*.[49] Groups have what can be called task and social-emotional needs. The task needs of a group are those which are related to a problem external to the group. For instance, if a fraternity at a university is preparing a house decoration for homecoming, the task need of the group is related to the external university pressures for the construction of the decoration. Frequently, a small group is formed to handle this task with a person as leader who is qualified regarding the task of house decoration construction—often someone who has had some previous experience designing, planning, and/or building house decorations. Thus, this person, with these special qualifications, is a task leader, fulfilling the task needs of the group.

In addition to the task leader, there is the social-emotional leader. This person is someone who can respond to the internal interpersonal needs of the group. Within every group there are personality conflicts and behaviors of members that interfere with the interaction of the group. It helps to have someone who can be a social-emotional specialist in the group. This person can help "pour oil over troubled waters" and help group members work together despite their differences. This person is what we might call a *people specialist* or a *people leader* as opposed to a task leader, although the terminology most commonly used is *social-emotional leader*. This person coordinates and facilitates the efforts of the other members of the group, despite the fact that he or she may not have much expertise in the area

49. Collins and Guetzkow, *A Social Psychology of Group Processes*, pp. 210–22.

Bruce Quist

Teachers can be thought of as either task leaders or social-emotional leaders in education settings. Sometimes they are both.

relating to the group's task. For instance, in the example we have been using, this person may not know very much at all about the construction of house decorations. However, it may be that the group could never get the house decoration constructed, in spite of considerable expertise on the part of the task leader, were it not for the presence of the social-emotional leader, who can help by stimulating the members of the group and urging them to get along and work together so that they can make use of the task expertise in their midst.

Probably the best example of a person with whom we are all familiar who is more of a social-emotional leader than a task leader is the President of the United States. Most often, people of the United States elect someone as president who is a social-emotional leader. The reason for this is obvious: there are so many different kinds of tasks facing a president at any given time that it is impossible to elect someone to that office who qualifies as an expert in all of the task areas that will confront the White House. Electing someone who is an expert in economic affairs may be fine as long as the president is dealing only with economic affairs. Unfortunately, the president also has to deal with military problems, foreign relations, and ecological problems. All of these demand task expertise of many different sorts, far too many for any one individual to possess. Therefore, we tend to elect as president a person who is able to manipulate and work with people—a person who has the social-emotional expertise that facilitates the finding of task experts for each individual problem facing the country. Then the president can coordinate the efforts of all these people, thus enabling them to work together, just as a social-emotional leader would do in a small group. It seems to us that this is the mark of a good administrative leader: a person who can help other people work together.

It is important to point out that the task leader and the social-emotional leader can be one and the same person in a group. It is possible for one individual to have expertise in both areas. It is not unusual, however, to find that the formally designated leader of a small group is either a task leader or a social-emotional leader, while the other leader in the group is an "informal leader." It is not an unusual thing to have a task leader who is formally designated as being in charge of the house decoration committee, to return to our example. While this person is directing the activities of the group and leading its members in the task at hand, we not infrequently find another person who is handling the social-emotional problems of the group. Thus, in many groups we find two leaders, one of them formally, the other informally fulfilling each of the group needs.

One final comment regarding leadership has to do with the question of whether a leader actually leads or follows. It is our impression that leaders never really lead their groups but instead manage to be a mere half step ahead of them at best. From our earlier discussion of needs, it should be obvious that people do not do something they are aware of as being contrary to their own needs. The person who is chosen as a leader, and the person who is most effective as leader, is someone who responds to the needs of the group. Thus, it is our feeling that more often than not, a would-be "leader" takes positions and says things that are acceptable to the group, as a result of which the group members perceive that that person should lead them where they want to go. There has been a controversy among historians for many years about "whether or not great men make great events happen or whether events make the man great." Implications of our discussion here would be that there really is no such thing as a leader who causes a small group to go off in a direction the group does not wish to go, inasmuch as people cannot accept a position they are not prepared to accept.[50] Rather, the likelihood is that the leadership is simply someone who is sensitive to the group and is willing to go in the direction the group is ready to go, and who simply coordinates and helps its members reach a goal towards which they are already prepared to strive.

50. Carolyn W. Sherif, Muzafer Sherif, and Roger E. Nebergall, *Attitude and Attitude Change* (Philadelphia: W. B. Saunders Company, 1965), pp. 18–59.

Where Small Groups Occur

Up to this point our discussion has been largely theoretical and to a certain extent abstract. We have been discussing principles of communication behavior in all small groups. One of the questions that might be running through your mind at this point is: "That's all well and good, but how often is this going to affect me and be of importance to me? When am I going to be in a small group and have to know about these principles of small group communication?" To which we reply that there are at least three different areas within which you are likely to find yourself engaged in small group communication: the family, working groups, and friendship groups.

The Family

51. Theodore M. Newcomb, "Attitude Development as a Function of Reference Groups: The Bennington Study," in *Readings in Social Psychology*, 3d ed. Eleanor E. Maccoby, Theodore M. Newcomb, and Eugene L. Hartley (New York: Holt, Rinehart & Winston, Inc., 1958), pp. 265–75.

52. T. Parsons and R. F. Bales, *Family Socialization and Interaction Processes* (Glencoe, Ill.: Free Press, 1965).

The family is the first small group one is a part of. Small group characteristics of the family are easily observable. The size of this particular group is usually within the range we suggested as appropriate for a small group. The family influence upon its members is so strong that probably the best criterion for predicting someone's political or religious philosophy is the political or religious philosophy of that person's family.[51] Group influence is significant in the family.

It is also apparent that the family has a division of leadership roles very comparable to those discussed earlier. The task role in American society is filled by the father, who most often earns money for the family and makes the task decisions regarding houses, money, and cars.[52] The social-emotional leadership role is most often filled by the mother. She is concerned about the children—when they are ill, when tempers flare, when feelings are hurt—and looks after the social relationships within the family and even those with other small groups. We should add that these leadership roles have been undergoing considerable change in recent years in America. Fathers are beginning to respond to the social-emotional needs of families to a greater extent, while mothers are also acting in response to the task needs of the family. The family in this country may be evolving into a group in which two leaders share both leadership roles.

In light of the similarities between the family and other small groups, one might expect that communication patterns would have effects on members of the family similar to those they have on other small groups. The highly centralized communication pattern in which the leadership is autocratic would, as in earlier times, very likely be the most efficient, yet would probably produce the least member satisfaction. If the family were to become more centralized in its communication patterns, those not in authority would very likely experience dissatisfaction. On the other hand, a decentralized pattern within the family would very likely produce a great deal of satisfaction for members of the family. Inclusion in discussion of affairs and

Roles in the family are in a state of change, with some husbands taking over what has traditionally been the role of the housewife.

Harry Smedley, Jr.

decision making for the family would probably be satisfying for all members of the family.

One of the most interesting similarities between a family and other small groups concerns dissolution of the family. Families as small groups inevitably experience this phenomenon as children grow up and leave home. As in other small groups, members of a family tend to reflect back upon earlier phases of the family's life as the family is about to break up. As children grow up and leave home to go to school or to be married, it is not an uncommon thing to find children and parents talking about earlier times and various arguments that people engaged in and the ways in which they were resolved. Members of the family focus on happy times and express great satisfaction with their family. At the dissolution phase it appears to be necessary to say positive things about having been in the family to reduce the dissonance experienced by seeing the family broken up. This dissonance is evidently so great that family members, as they are leaving the small group, engage in the ultimate rationalization, by saying in effect, "We are not breaking up. We are going to be apart, but we'll stay in contact and we'll be together often." Unfortunately, in our mobile society this rarely happens, but the rationalization at the time seems to make dissolution more tolerable.

Working Groups

Another kind of small group that most of us find ourselves part of is the working group. We have been discussing, up to this point, the problem-solving group, primarily because it has been the focal point for most of the research in small group communication, but also because it is the kind of working group with which the majority of us have most frequent contact. Whether at work or in a club (or even sometimes in the family), we find ourselves engaged in problem-solving situations with three or four other people. This is a common occurrence, and all of the principles we have discussed up to this point are certainly applicable here.

Therapeutic Groups

53. C. Argyris, "On the Future of Laboratory Education," *Journal of Applied Behavioral Science* 3 (1967):153–83.

Another kind of working group, if it can be called that, is the therapeutic group. Group therapy has become a common approach to handling personal problems by psychologists and counselors. Likewise, for people who are not mentally disturbed, functioning with an encounter group, a T-group, or a sensitivity group has become a common means of working out interpersonal problems.[53] These groups, while not at first glance working groups, do have a specific task set for them: that of improving the members of the group or helping them to improve themselves. These groups typically follow the patterns of other small groups in that they have a task leader (trainer) and generally a social-emotional leader or leaders as well. Frequently, the latter is the same person as the task leader, although it is sometimes true that others assume this role. The groups go through phases very comparable to those already discussed, and people are very enthusiastic about their membership in these groups.[54]

54. Warren G. Bennis, "Patterns and Vicissitudes in T-Group Development," in *T-Group Theory and Laboratory Method,* ed. Leland P. Bradford and Kenneth D. Benne (New York: John Wiley & Sons, Inc., 1964), pp. 248–78.

55. Phillips and Erickson, *Interpersonal Dynamics,* p. 19.

We have frequently been asked in classes how effective encounter groups, sensitivity groups, and T-groups are. We almost always have hesitated to answer that question. We have had experience in sensitivity groups, and that experience has been positive. It has resulted in changes in behavior patterns that seem to have improved interactions with other people. For many people, however, a sensitivity group has little effect in the long run.[55] There is no question that there is an immediate effect, which lasts through the next day or couple of days after the sessions. However, in the long run,

Paul Fusco/Magnum Photos, Inc.

A therapeutic group can be a positive experience for some participants.

over several weeks or months, it appears that the effect of being in a sensitivity group is somewhat negligible. Participation in such a group is an intensely dramatic occurrence; indeed, it is very difficult to have gone through the experience of being told that you are too aggressive or that you are too passive without feeling that the experience has been an intense one. The impact of a session seems to be somewhat short-lived, however, because upon completion of an encounter session people return to their original environments and regress to their original behavior patterns. This is one of the problems that many mental patients experience after treatment. They go back into the original environment that caused the difficulty, and the likelihood is that that environment will cause the difficulty all over again. Likewise, upon leaving an encounter group and returning to the original environment that created the behavior patterns we have, it appears that we tend to resume our old ways.[56]

There has been some question about the harm of encounter groups. However, the rate of breakdowns as a result of these experiences is very small, and the likelihood is that the people who have experienced problems in encounter groups probably would have experienced them anyway.[57] We could go a little further and say that experiencing one's problems in encounter groups is probably a better thing than experiencing them out in the real world, where people would be far less sympathetic.

56. Ibid.

57. Martin Lakin, *Interpersonal Encounter: Theory and Practice in Sensitivity Training* (New York: McGraw-Hill Book Co., 1972), pp. 140–41.

Coacting Groups

Another kind of working group is simply a group of people who work together—for instance, four or five people who work side by side in an office. They are really more coacting than interacting, so one could almost question our reference to these people as a small group. However, they do not have a common goal, and they can interact with one another in an uninhibited manner. There are indications that working together in a group appears to facilitate getting work done.[58] In fact, simply being aware of the presence of other people causes us to work more effectively at some kinds of tasks. Of course, it is also true that if we are in a work group in which the interpersonal attraction is very considerable and the social-emotional structure is very positive, people may interact with one another so well and to such an extent on a personal basis that the work may not get done the way it should.[59]

58. R. B. Zajonc and S. M. Sales, "Social Facilitation of Dominant and Subordinate Responses," *Journal of Experimental Social Psychology* 2 (1966):160–68.

59. R. H. Van Zelst, "Validation of a Sociometric Regrouping Procedure," *Journal of Abnormal and Social Psychology* 47 (1952):299–301.

Friendship Groups

One of the best examples of the principle of group influence is the adolescent friendship group, ranging from the early teens to somewhere in the midtwenties. These groups exert an exceptionally strong influence on the individual member. The norms developed regarding clothing, eating habits, and other behavior patterns are very strong.[60] It is of special interest to note that the norms for all groups, conservative and liberal alike, are strongly enforced. At this stage in our lives we have very high ego and social needs, and our peer group seems to be the group most able to satisfy them. We are trying to break away from our other small group, the family, so as a consequence we seek out another group, our peer group, to which we can relate and which will accept us.[61] Because we desire this acceptance so much and because our needs are so thoroughly satisfied through group recognition, we are very willing to conform to the wishes of the group. These groups have incredible influence over the individual members and can cause the individual members to do things that they would never ordinarily even consider doing as individuals.[62] Lest you begin to feel that this is only true of adolescent groups, you might bear in mind that the same thing is true of any friendship group, so long as the group is satisfying the needs of the individual members. Through friendship the group possesses an enormously powerful hold on the individual.

60. M. Sherif and C. W. Sherif, *Reference Groups* (New York: Harper & Row Publishers, Inc., 1964).

61. Argyle, *Social Interaction*, pp. 246–49.

62. Sherif and Sherif, *Reference Groups.*

Of course we should also indicate that most friendship groups do not have the usual task external to the group that a work group would have, for instance. These groups are primarily socially-emotionally oriented. The leaders in these groups are social-emotional leaders who facilitate interaction among members of the group. Occasionally a friendship group will be faced with a specific task, and in that case a task leader will probably be developed or called on. However, it is more usual for the groups to remain primarily social-emotional.

SUMMARY

Small groups play a very important role in our lives, whether by way of government, industry, family, the church, or the school. We hope that you are now able to think of small groups in terms of the type of interaction that occurs within them, and that a better understanding of small groups can increase your interaction effectiveness within such groups. While size of group alone does not determine interaction, there is probably a range from three to fifteen or twenty people in a small group. We also hope this chapter has focused your attention upon the power of the small group over the individual member. Not only does the small group demand conformity, it even causes the "risky shift" and can determine who is selected as leader because of the group's needs. With these things in mind, we hope your understanding of small group communication will improve your own interpersonal effectiveness within the small group context.

SELECTED READINGS

Brilhart, John K. *Effective Group Discussion.* 3d ed. Dubuque, Iowa: William C. Brown Co., Publishers, 1978.

Burgoon, Michael; Heston, Judee K.; and McCroskey, James. *Small Group Communication: A Functional Approach.* New York: Holt, Rinehart & Winston, Inc., 1974.

Cathcart, Robert S., and Samovar, Larry A. *Small Group Communication: A Reader.* 3d ed. Dubuque, Iowa: William C. Brown Co., Publishers, 1979.

Collins, Barry E., and Guetzkow, Harold. *A Social Psychology of Group Processes for Decision-Making.* New York: John Wiley & Sons, Inc., 1964.

Fisher, B. Aubrey. *Small Group Decision Making: Communication and the Group Process.* New York: McGraw-Hill Book Co., 1974.

Phillips, Gerald M.; Pedersen, Douglas J.; and Wood, Julia T. *Group Discussion: A Practical Guide to Participation and Leadership.* Boston: Houghton Mifflin Co., 1979.

Rosenfeld, Lawrence B. *Human Interaction In a Small Group Setting.* Columbus, Ohio: Charles E. Merrill Publishing Co., 1973.

Shaw, Marvin E. *Group Dynamics.* New York: McGraw-Hill Book Co., 1971.

12

Interpersonal Communication in Organizations

One of the areas in which interpersonal communication is used as much or more than in any other is on the job. Most of us hold a job, and for many of us that job is within an organization. And we probably do our work using interpersonal communication. We talk with colleagues, receive instructions and requests, give instructions and requests, have formal and informal conferences with another person, and attend group meetings. Besides that, there is a lot of informal chitchat and conversation that is simply social communication. This is important in every organization because it is directly related to the climate of the organization, to job satisfaction, and to the creation of personal networks in the organization. In addition to those uses of interpersonal communication in organizations, there is the grapevine and rumor mill.

Interpersonal communication is one of the primary, critical factors in the successful operation of any form of organized activity. All of the essential functions of the management of most organizations—planning, organizing, staffing, directing, and controlling—are accomplished primarily through communication. So important is communication to businesses and other organizations that organizational communication has become a major area of study in colleges and universities and receives considerable attention from business and organizational leaders in workshops and in-service training programs in communication. Communication specialists are hired to diagnose and overcome communication problems in organizations.

What does one study in organizational communication? In instructional communication? In intercultural communication? In all these types of communication we are concerned with essentially the same factors—the major elements of interpersonal communication—the topics of this book. What is different is the setting. Each setting, by its nature, uses some forms of communication (interviewing, order-giving, formal, informal, etc.) more than other forms, and finds some interpersonal communication variables more important to the successful operation of the organization than are other variables. A prison, a church, a hospital, a classroom, and a production line are different in terms of their communication needs. Therefore, any selection of special topics for this chapter is arbitrary. We have selected five topics that seem to be generally important to organizations. These are: (1) the employment interview, (2) the persuasive conference or the persuasive interview, (3) organized or formal communication, (4) social communication, and (5) grapevine and rumor.

The Interview

Probably the first interpersonal communication experience in connection with our work and organizations is the job interview. Unless we are successful in that interpersonal communication situation, we have no job in an organization. Of course, there are interviews other than job interviews that are important in organizations. In fact, the conference situation is parallel to the interview in terms of purposes, skills, and procedures.

The *interview* is defined as a form of communication involving two parties, at least one of whom has a preconceived and serious purpose, and both of whom speak and listen from time to time.[1] This definition of interviewing clearly identifies the interview as dyadic communication while at the same time differentiating it from other forms of dyadic communication, such as intimate and social communication. It is different in that at least one person, and perhaps both, has a preconceived and serious purpose. Two persons getting together and talking, with neither having thought in advance about the purpose or objective to be accomplished, does not constitute an interview. It might be social conversation, but it is not an interview. The words *serious purpose* differentiate the interview from social conversation for enjoyment. The interview is a form of instrumental communication, and we are interested in those variables that are especially prominent in this dyadic communication situation.

The three most common objectives of interviews are to obtain information, to provide information, and to persuade. Informational interviews aim either to obtain beliefs, attitudes, feelings, or objective data from the interviewee, or to explain to, instruct, or appraise the interviewee. Public opinion polls and research surveys are typical, well-known examples of the "information-getting" interview, while explaining the procedures and policies of an organization to a new employee is an example of the "information-giving" interview. Also considered in the informational category are: counseling, reprimand, and appraisal interviews, problem-solving conferences, police and insurance investigations, the receiving of complaints, and informative interviews of celebrities or experts for newspapers, radio, or television.

Often, however, a person wishes to modify the beliefs or attitudes of another person and attempts to do so through a conference—a persuasive

1. Robert S. Goyer, W. Charles Redding, and John T. Rickey, *Interviewing: Principles and Techniques* (Dubuque, Iowa: Kendall/Hunt Publishing Co., 1968), p. 6.

interview. The sales interview is an example, with the interviewer (the sales-person) attempting to sway the interviewee (the customer) toward adopting his or her point of view. Another example of the persuasive conference is the attempt of a subordinate to persuade a superior to accept a proposal; or when you go to the bank to secure a loan, you are a persuader engaged in a persuasive interview. Throughout life each of us engages in interviews in which we try to persuade another person to agree with us. This topic will be discussed later in this chapter.

A persuasive interview.

In considering the employment interview, we must learn some essential skills and principles that apply to any interview situation. These common areas of concern are the question-answer process and the structure and planning of any conference or interview. Let us now consider the question-answer process.

The Question-Answer Process

Here the questioning skill of the interviewer is called into play. Obviously, one of the first steps in the development of that skill consists of becoming acquainted with the various types of questions and their applications. Following are the major types of questions to be used:

Open *questions* call for a response of more than a few words. One type of open question, the *open-ended question,* is extremely vague in that it may do nothing more than specify a topic and ask the respondent to talk. Examples: "What do you think about life?" and "Tell me a little about yourself." A second kind of open question is more direct in that it identifies a more restricted topic area and asks for a reply on that restricted topic. In some classification systems this question is classified separately from open questions and is known as the *direct question.* An example: "What did you do on your weekends last winter?"

Closed *questions,* a second category, call for a specific response of a few words. One type of closed question is the yes-no, or bipolar, question. It calls for a "yes" or a "no" answer—or, perhaps, an "I don't know" reply. "Did you attend the last home basketball game last winter?" is a closed question. Similarly, "What two courses did you like most, and what two courses did you like least in high school?" is a closed question, though not a yes-no question.

One important principle derivable from the use of open or closed questions is that both types tend to influence the length of the interviewee's responses. Open questions encourage the respondent to talk at greater length, while closed questions inhibit participation by the respondent.[2] Since one of the problems in most interviews is getting the interviewee to become freely involved and to participate in the interview, it is unwise for the interviewer to use only closed questions. Open questions are more likely to be used in the early part of the interview or at the introduction of each new topic; closed questions are used as follow-ups for the responses to open questions.

Mirror questions are nondirective. The reason for using a mirror question is to encourage the interviewee to expand on a response that the interviewer believes was incomplete. Mirror questions are usually restatements of what the interviewee has just said. If the interviewee has said: "I don't approve of legal abortion," a mirror question might be: "You say that abortion should not be legal?"

Probing questions are asked to probe more deeply into the reasons for an attitude or belief, or to elicit more specific information. Not all probes are questions of why or how, although these are the most common probing questions. There are a variety of other vocalizations that act effectively as probes and encouragements. Brief sounds or phrases such as "Uh-huh," "I see," "That's interesting," "Oh?" "Good," "I understand," and "Go on," have the effect of requesting further comment from the respondent. Probes and encouragements are introduced at any time—during pauses, or while the interviewee is speaking. They indicate careful attention and interest and are intended to encourage the respondent to "tell more" without the interviewer's specifying or disclosing in a closed way the further response. It is important, however, that an interviewer avoid the habit of relying on only one reinforcing or probing word.

Silence is fully as important as direct probing questions and sounds. As indicated in chapter 6 (in the discussion on nonverbal communication), si-

2. Stephen A. Richardson, Barbara S. Dohrenwend, and David Klein, *Interviewing: Its Forms and Functions* (New York: Basic Books, Inc., 1965), p. 147.

lence communicates. The inexperienced interviewer is often afraid of pauses and silences. He or she tends to fill every silence, and by so doing rushes through the interview. Sometimes, if the respondent is slow in answering a question, the inexperienced interviewer may rush in to rephrase the question or to ask a new question. With experience, interviewers can learn when to use silence as a means of communication—as a probe. Research findings indicate that silences of three to six seconds are most effective in getting the respondent to provide more information.[3] Hence, when we use silence as a probe, we should be prepared to terminate the silence within six seconds or at such interval as silence seems destined to fail as a probing technique.

Leading questions strongly imply or encourage a specific answer. They "lead" the respondent to an answer the interviewer expects. The leading question can be quite detrimental when used for the wrong reasons. An interviewer who wants straightforward, valid, and reliable information from the respondent will carefully avoid using leading question. Cannell and Kahn state: "Questions should be phrased so that they contain no suggestion as to the most appropriate response,"[4] and Bingham, Moore, and Gustad state: "Avoid implying the answer to your own question."[5] If, however, the interviewer wishes to test the respondent to see if the respondent really understands or is genuinely committed, then the leading question may be useful. For example, when the speech therapist asks the parent of a stuttering boy, "You are slapping his hands every time he starts to stutter, aren't you?" the therapist is leading the parent to an incorrect answer unless the parent clearly understands before responding that slapping the child for stuttering is inappropriate behavior.

One type of leading question is the *yes-response* or the *no-response question*. "Naturally, you agree with the decision, didn't you?" is an example of a yes-response question. One of the components of leading questions is expectation. If the interviewer asks, "Are you twenty-one years old?" the question is a direct, closed question, but it is not leading. If, however, the interviewer asks, "Of course, you are twenty-one years old, aren't you?" this indicates an expectation. Expectations can be identified by the syntax and logic of the question, but, as noted in chapter 6 (on nonverbal communication), intonation can also communicate expectation. Through intonation and emphasis one might make the question, "Did you agree with that decision?" a leading question—by implying surprise and incredulity at anything other than the expected answer.

Another form of the leading question is the *loaded question,* which uses loaded words and has highly emotional connotations. It reaches touchy spots and strikes strong feelings. It may present a dilemma from which it is difficult for the respondent to escape. Questions that are not stated objectively are considered loaded. Various techniques are used to indicate the bias or expectation. Prestige may be used. "The President of the United States believes that the problem is serious. Don't you agree?" is an example

3. See R. L. Gordon, "An Interaction Analysis of the Depth-Interview" (Ph.D. dissertation, University of Chicago, 1954); G. Saslow et. al., "Test-Retest Stability of Interaction Patterns During Interviews Conducted One Week Apart," *Journal of Abnormal and Social Psychology* 54 (1957):295–302.

4. C. F. Cannell and R. L. Kahn, "The Collection of Data by Interviewing," in *Research Methods in the Behavioral Sciences*, ed. L. Festinger and D. Katz (New York: Dryden Press, 1953), p. 346.

5. W. V. D. Bingham, B. V. Moore, and J. W. Gustad, *How to Interview* (New York: Harper & Brothers, 1959), p. 74.

of using prestige to indicate the bias. The interviewer may also associate positive stereotypes with responses that are desired or negative stereotypes with responses that are not desired.

To gain an understanding of the question-answer process, you need to become familiar with and be able to recognize the various types of questions that may be used. Through guided practice, you can develop skill in using questions.

Interview Structure

This is the second topic we wish to discuss in connection with the interview. *Structure* can be thought of in two ways: (1) as the composition of the interview in terms of opening, body (or substantive part), and closing; and (2) as the composition or organizational plan of the body of the interview.

First let us consider the structure of the interview in terms of its parts—opening, body, and closing. The initial stage, opening the interview, is quite important, for during this time the relationship between the interviewer and the respondent is established. The objectives of the opening are to establish confidence, trust, clarification of purpose of the interview, and the identification of mutual goals. Rapport, an important element throughout the interview, is largely established in the opening stage. Some preinterview acts also relate to the establishment of rapport. The request for an interview should not be made in terms that alarm or threaten the interviewee; and the place selected for the interview should be private, comfortable, and conducive to a smooth and satisfactory interviewing operation.

The second phase of the interview is the substantive part, which relies heavily upon the question-answer process previously discussed. Structure, as it relates to this part of the interview, will be discussed shortly.

The final stage of the interview is the closing. Some interviews come to natural closings as a result of the nature of the progress of the discussion or as a result of the inclination of the participants. Other interviews really need to be continued, but circumstances dictate that they must be closed. Still other interviews could be continued profitably because things are going so well, but time dictates that they must be ended. Regardless of the reasons or conditions, the interview closing ought to contain a short summary by the interviewer, an opportunity for the interviewee to make additions and corrections, and an indication of the next steps, or "where we go from here."

Now, let us consider the second way structure is used in interviewing—as the organizational plan or strategy used to guide the question-answer process within the body of the interview. The interview can be structured in terms of questions used and in terms of general pattern so as to be directive or nondirective. With the directive structure the interviewer decides what questions will be asked, what topics will be covered, the sequence of the topics and questions, and the overall procedure that will be followed in the interview. Using the nondirective approach, the interviewer allows the interviewee to make almost all of these decisions. The interviewee is reinforced and encouraged to talk about whatever he or she wishes. When interviews are used for research purposes, it may, of course, be necessary to standardize the procedure so that there can be a basis for response comparisons; but if the purpose is to get information from one interviewee in a non-research situation, then a flexible, alert approach may be profitably used. If the interviewer is using a nondirective structure, then open questions, mirror questions, and indirect probes will be used; but if he or she is using a direct approach, then closed questions and direct probes may be used.

The direct structured interview may be described further in terms of degree of directness. The most highly structured interview pattern would be the standardized interview. In this type of structure each question in the interview is precisely worded; each question is carefully ordered in terms of where it fits in the entire sequence of questions. In other words, every question is asked in exactly the same words and at the same place in the interview for every person interviewed. All verbal content of the interviewer, as well as the sequence of the content, is rigidly controlled. Such an interview structure is most frequently used in research interviewing, in which one of the requirements is to compare interviewee responses to common or standardized stimuli.

Some direct interviews, on the other hand, are not so rigidly standardized. They may use a directive structure and cover a specified number of areas, but the interviewer is free to move into one area or another as the situation seems to warrant. The interviewer is also free to add questions, to probe on a given topic, or to shorten his or her investigation on a given topic. The structure is basically directive rather than nondirective, but it utilizes a great amount of flexibility so as to adjust to the interviewee.

These different structures vary in value and efficiency according to the purpose of the interview. Counseling and therapy interviews are often non-directive in structure, since it is desirable to reduce threat to the interviewee, to give the interviewee control over his or her own information sharing, and to make the interviewee responsible for information acquisition and growth. On the other hand, the employment interview often utilizes a direct approach, but with considerable flexibility built into it. Research interviewers are normally structured so as to be standardized.

Now, let us specifically consider the employment interview.

The Employment Interview

Before you get a job interview, it is necessary to make application for the job. And before you walk in to fill out the organization's application sheet or before you mail your letter of application, you should have prepared a data sheet, sometimes called a résumé or vita. You may want to include this data sheet with your letter of application. It is also easier to fill out the on-the-spot information sheet when you apply for a position at the site of the organization if you have given thought and careful attention to assembling data about yourself. This preparing a careful inventory of yourself is helpful, also, in terms of getting yourself ready for the interview.

A résumé has three general categories: personal history, educational history, and work experience. In addition, you will want a list of possible references—people who are able and willing to furnish recommendations for you. Following is an outline you might use to prepare a data sheet or résumé.

I. General information
   A. Your name
   B. Address
   C. Telephone number
   D. Date of birth
   E. Marital status
II. Education
   A. Schools attended
   B. Honors earned
   C. Grade point average
   D. Major
   E. Minors
   F. Activities
III. Experience
   A. Prior work
   B. Experience-related activities
IV. References
   In addition to listing an individual's name, address, and phone number, you can give a brief sentence that summarizes the particular qualities or abilities he or she might be able to comment on.

The employment interview combines several purposes—to inform, to get information, and to persuade. Moreover, the employment interview is unique in that both the applicant and the employer share the power of decision. Generally, the applicant should consider the employment interview as a situation in which he or she is in the position of persuading the prospective employer that he or she (the applicant) represents a good investment for the employer, but sometimes situations arise in which the procedure is reversed and the primary burden is upon the employer to sell the job to the applicant.

The employment interview represents a communication situation in which almost every person in college will participate sooner or later—an extraordinarily important communication situation. An understanding of and skill in interpersonal communication can enhance your performance in employment interviews. Consider, therefore, three topics that can be of particular value: personal conduct, what the typical interviewer wants to know about the applicant, and what the applicant needs to learn about the position.

Personal Conduct in the Employment Interview

The following six elements are important as far as personal conduct in the interview is concerned. From these behaviors, appearances, and physical traits, the interviewee is judged and his or her image constructed. They are set forth here as a convenient checklist rather than as a discussion of each item.

I. Dress, appearance, and physical bearing
II. Bodily behavior during the interview
   A. Walking (entering and exiting)
   B. Shaking hands
   C. Posture
   D. Facial expression and eye contact
   E. General animation
   F. Mannerisms indicating tension; aimless movements
III. Use of the voice
   A. Quality of voice
   B. Pitch level
   C. Audibility
   D. Intelligibility (rate, phrasing, and articulation)
   E. Expressiveness
IV. Use of language
   A. Vocabulary
   B. Grammar
   C. Slang and triteness
V. Attitudes (minimum essentials for the average interview)
   A. Directness—not withdrawal (revealed in eye contact, body tone, and posture)
   B. Responsiveness—active participation
   C. Mental alertness
   D. Sincerity
   E. Emotional control (poised, controlled, open; but no cockiness)
   F. Honesty
VI. Ability to listen

Using this checklist and applying the principles and concepts discussed in the chapters on interpersonal communication and nonverbal communication, we can describe, evaluate, and establish self-improvement objectives for participation in employment interviews.

The results of several studies of employment interviews indicate that the major areas of concern to the interviewer are the applicant's ability, desire to work, social-emotional maturity, and character. An applicant, knowing that these areas are important to the interviewer, would be wise to give some thought to these questions so that full and accurate information can be provided in an effective manner.

In terms of *ability,* interviewers are especially interested in the applicant's vocational and avocational experiences. It is wise for the applicant to know in substance how these experiences contribute toward making him or her capable for the position. It is to the advantage of the applicant to be able to point out such relationships or applications rather than leaving them to the "assumed knowledge" of the interviewer.

Education and training, both formal and informal, are part of one's ability and should be fully explored in the employment interview. Similarly, intelligence—as revealed through grades in school, activities, honors, recognitions, and conduct during the interview—is related to ability. The questions asked by the interviewee, as well as the responses the interviewee makes to questions asked by the interviewer, are used to evaluate intelligence and general ability.

A second area of major concern is *desire to work.* Studies of interviewing show that questions and information relating to three areas—past record of changes in jobs, applicant's reasons for wanting the job for which he or she is applying, and knowledge of this company or organization—are used to evaluate the applicant's desire to work.

The third major area of concern for the employer is the *social-emotional level of maturity* of the applicant. The typical interviewer may attempt to discover the applicant's personal goals, independence, self-reliance, creativity, imagination, and ability to exercise authority, to take orders, or be corrected.

Finally, the *character* of the applicant is of importance to the interviewer. Character may be judged on the basis of personal behavior, honesty, history of financial responsibility or irresponsibility, and the accuracy and objectivity of self-reports (the things the interviewee divulges about himself or herself during the interview). Dishonesty, sham, and boastfulness are extremely detrimental and even disastrous in the employment interview.

Not only should the applicant be concerned and prepared to satisfy the employer in terms of what the employer wants to know, but it is also necessary that the applicant systematically and thoroughly discover some things that he or she needs to know.

Verbal and nonverbal communication are important for both the interviewer and the interviewee.

Jean-Claude Lejeune

One of the most important areas of concern is that of *job expectation* or *requirements*. There are many sad stories about jobs that were not at all what the applicants assumed or understood them to be when they accepted the positions. Careful thought and effort should be given to understanding and fully satisfying yourself as to what the job entails.

A second area is that of discovering who your co-workers are. A common background in education, values, philosophy, and training will enhance the relationships with co-workers and increase potential job satisfaction.

The applicant should also be concerned with the opportunities and policies for advancement, benefits, hours, pay, job security, and working conditions. It is helpful for the applicant to have these areas clearly in mind so that he or she can secure the information necessary for a good decision.

6. pp. 23–25.

The following list of suggestions should be considered as general guidelines for interviewers and interviewees in the employment interview.[6]

Suggestions for the applicant
1. Clarify the job requirements.
2. State why you are applying for this job with this company.
3. Present your qualifications in terms of having something of value to offer the company. Deal as much as possible in specific details and examples—job experiences, avocations, travel, activities, offices held, organizations, and schoolwork.
4. Do not hesitate to admit potential weaknesses. Under no circumstances should you attempt to bluff or fake on these, but wherever possible, make a transition from a weakness to a strength; or at least, when the facts justify it, show some good extenuating circumstance for the "weakness." (This does *not* mean supplying alibis or excuses!)
5. Do not depend merely on a "smooth front" (appearance and smile) to "sell yourself." Provide full information to the prospective employer.
6. Get as much information as possible on such sensitive matters as salary (usually in terms of a range, or of the "going average").
7. Let the employer set the "tone" or atmosphere of the interview. Be a little more formal than usual—but don't be too rigid! Be cautious about jokes, wisecracks, sarcastic asides, and so forth!
8. Watch the opening moments of the interview. Avoid making remarks that create a "negative set" for the rest of the interview. Avoid starting the interview with a remark such as "I'm really not sure that my background will be appropriate for your company or for this job," or "I'm sorry to say I haven't had any experience along these lines."
9. Be informed on the company: its history, geographical locations, general methods of doing business, reputation, and so forth.
10. Try never to have an interview concluded without some sort of understanding about where you stand, what is to happen next, who is to contact whom. This does *not* mean you are to push the employer against the wall and force a definite commitment!

Suggestions for the employer:
1. Take the initiative in getting the interview under way; don't sit back and stare at the applicant. Offer your hand first. Ask the applicant to be seated. Establish rapport *before* probing for information.
2. Make an easy, casual, smooth transition from opening greetings to the first serious topic of the interview.
3. Start off with "easy" materials and aspects on the applicant's background that are not sensitive areas. Encourage the applicant to talk

freely about something which, from information that appeared on the application blank, should be easy for the applicant to discuss with specific details and examples.

4. Don't give a "sales pitch."
5. Do more listening than talking. Encourage the applicant to "open up." Listen carefully—including "between the lines." Insert brief prompters to encourage more talk; use "mirror" techniques.
6. Don't exaggerate the benefits of the company or the job! Create confidence and trust by being honest about potential or actual drawbacks.
7. Avoid evaluative comments on the applicant's answers such as "that's too bad," or "I'm certainly glad you said that!"
8. Without being mechanical about it, try to cover topics in a systematic order. Your objective is not only to avoid hit-and-miss jumping around but also to avoid giving the impression of engaging in an oral examination!
9. Be alert to cues in the applicant's answers and behavior. Adapt immediately to what is said so that you can follow up a promising lead. Probe suspected weaknesses.
10. Ask questions that will reveal the applicant's attitudes and personality in terms of the job's total requirements.

The employment interview is a give-and-take process, highly dynamic and rich in its informational and persuasive potential. The communication skills involved are varied and include those examined in this text in intrapersonal and interpersonal communication. The person who desires to improve his or her behavior as an interviewer or interviewee must learn to be extremely perceptive and accurate in observation and understanding of other persons.

The Persuasive Conference or Persuasive Interview

Persuasive interviews are seldom called persuasive interviews. They are called conferences, sales presentations, or other things; but whatever they are called, they are situations in which one person attempts to persuade or influence another person. In fact, in some conference situations, each person has a proposal or persuasive goal in mind to present. Most organizations make extensive use of conferences to initiate action and to solve problems.

The possibility of success in these persuasive conference situations is increased when the following criteria are met:

1. The proposal satisfies a need of the person to be persuaded.
2. The persuader and persuadee have similar beliefs, attitudes, values, cultural background, and moral standards.
3. The proposal is shown to be workable and practical.

One or both participants in a conference may have proposals or persuasive goals to present.

4. Objections to the proposal can be shown to be outweighed by benefits and advantages.
5. No better alternative is available.

Of these five criteria, the creation of a need or desire is perhaps the most important. In any event, the smart persuader in the conference situation is concerned with all of these factors and organizes his or her efforts in the conference around these objectives.

There are good reasons why the persuasive conference is used extensively. It is far superior to using memos, brochures, meetings of several persons, newspapers, the publication of the organization, or direct orders given orally. The advantages of the conference or interview situation are:

1. The persuasive message can be adapted to the specific person.
2. One can get immediate feedback, verbal and nonverbal.
3. The persuadee can participate in the process.
4. Strategies can be changed as the process is open, alive, and defined at the time.

There is no form of communication so open and so adaptable as the face-to-face conference or interview situation.

To prepare well for a persuasive interview or conference, you need to consider several factors in a systematic way. Kahn and Cannell's illustration of those factors is seen in figure 12.1.

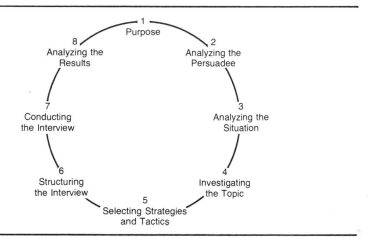

Figure 12.1 This figure is based on one in Robert L. Kahn and Charles F. Cannell, *The Dynamics of Interviewing,* (New York: John Wiley & Sons, Inc., 1964), p. 103.

The first step is to determine the *purpose* of the interview, the goal the persuader has in mind—the action, attitude, or belief the persuader wants the persuadee to accept. It is essential for the persuader to know clearly and precisely what he or she wants the outcome of the conference to be.

The second step in the process is to *analyze the persuadee* carefully. The conference needs to be adapted to that particular person. Age, sex, race, intelligence, group memberships, hobbies, superior and subordinate relationships, work experience, attitudes relative to the goal or proposed action, temperament, personality, interaction history with others—these and other factors that seem to be relevant to the persuasive encounter ought to be considered. The persuadee's values, beliefs, and motives as they relate to the proposal are essential factors to consider. The effective persuader does not plunge blindly into interactions. Rather, he or she attempts to discover as much as possible about the persuadee so that messages and interactions can be adapted to that specific person.

The third step is to *analyze the situation.* Where will this conference take place? Can you obtain privacy and be free of interruptions? Is it a formal or informal setting? Will it be on your ground, the persuadee's ground, or neutral ground? What will be the likely atmosphere? Trust? Suspicion? Apathy?

The fourth step is to *do your homework,* i.e., to do the investigating and research necessary to having thorough knowledge and understanding of the problem under consideration.

The fifth step is to *select the strategies and tactics* you will use in the interview or conference. You will want to use a different strategy for a hostile person from that you would use for a cooperative person, for example. Some strategies are: (1) the common-ground approach, (2) the yes-yes approach, (3) the implicative approach, (4) the climax-order approach, (5) the anticlimax-order approach, (6) the one-sided approach, and (7) the both-sides approach.

The *common-ground approach* is one in which beliefs, attitudes, feelings, and goals that are held in common by the persuader and the persuadee are identified and used to achieve the acceptance of the proposal. The *yes-yes approach* leads logically via an inductive process from small agreements through progressing agreements to acceptance of the major proposition or action. The *implicative approach* is an indirect approach in which the goal is argued for, *not directly,* but by implication. It is not explicitly stated. This approach is often used when the proposal will be met with hostility or negative response, or when the persuadee is so insecure or defensive that he or she has to "have the idea first." Reasons, arguments, and data congruent with the desired proposition are given, but the solution or conclusion is not stated. The persuadee is left to discover that on his or her own. Only by implication is the proposition made known.

The *climax-order strategy* simply means that the strongest argument is given last. *Anticlimax order* means that the strongest argument is given first. *One side* of the argument is given when the persuadee is apt to be in partial agreement already, is not resistant or hostile, and is not accustomed to verbal interpersonal interaction in decision-making situations. On the other hand, when the persuadee is opposed to the proposition, even hostile to it, and is accustomed to verbal argument and decision making, it may be better to present both sides of the issue.

The sixth step in preparing for the conference or persuasive interview is *structuring the interview.* The strategies and tactics just discussed are fitted into an overall structure or pattern of organization for the interview or conference. The standard pattern of organization has been identified as follows:[7]

7. Adapted from Charles J. Stewart and William B. Cash, Jr., *Interviewing: Principles and Practices* (Dubuque, Iowa: William C. Brown, Co., Publishers, 1978), p. 230.

I. Opening
   A. Establish rapport
   B. Give a clear, concise statement of purpose, need, or problem
II. Body
   A. Problem or need
      1. Point-by-point development of the reasons, causes, or aspects of the need or problem
         a) Always point out how the reason, cause, or aspect concerns the persuadee
         b) Employ a variety of evidence and appeals to motives, beliefs, values, and frames of reference

        c) Summarize and get agreement (at least tentative) before moving to a new reason, cause, or aspect of the need or problem

    2. Summarize the need or problem and get overt agreement from the persuadee before proceeding further

  B. Criteria: standards, requirements, norms the solution should meet

    1. Present the criteria

    2. Discuss briefly why each criterion is important in evaluating solutions to this need or problem

    3. Encourage the persuadee to add criteria to the list

    4. Summarize and get agreement on all criteria to be used

  C. Evaluation of solutions

    1. Deal with one solution at a time

    2. Explain the solution in detail

    3. Evaluate the solution criterion by criterion

    4. Handle objections before they arise, if possible

    5. Get agreement on how well the solution meets the criteria

    6. Move to the next solution, if more than one is to be considered

III. Closing

  A. Summarize what has been discussed in the interview and the agreements reached

  B. Obtain a commitment from the persuadee if at all possible

  C. Arrange for the next interview or for the first step in implementing the solution

The seventh step is to *conduct the interview,* as we have described the process earlier in this chapter. And the final step is to *analyze the conference or interview.* While the interaction is fresh in the persuader's mind, he or she should take stock. Is the persuasion completed? Will it require more research? Will it require another meeting or two? Is a new strategy called for? What is the next action?

Organized or Formal Communication in Organizations

Organizations are systems of people, and people are organized, and carry on the functions required to keep themselves organized, through communication of two types—formal and informal. This section of this chapter deals with formal communication in organizations; the following sections focus on informal communication in organizations.

This "organizing" of people to accomplish some objective usually involves creating a structure that provides a hierarchy of functions, status, control, and division of labor, among other things. These patterns of structure can be partially indicated via organizational charts that show titles, tasks, roles, and spans of control. For example, a small kite manufacturing business might indicate its "organization" by a chart, as shown in figure 12.2.

Figure 12.2

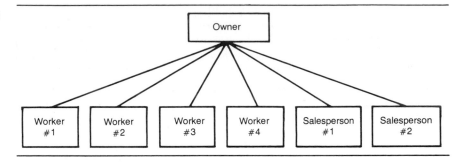

A small realty company might indicate its organization as in figure 12.3.

Figure 12.3

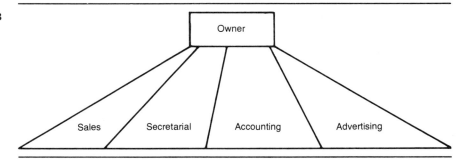

One thing that becomes immediately apparent is that organizations prescribe "roles" for people as they are "systematized" according to the functions the organization needs to have performed. This means that those principles of interpersonal communication involving roles (role relationships, congruity of role and personality, and so on) are of concern and quite applicable in organizational communication.

Secondly, there are various degrees of status and power assigned to the hierarchial positions of persons in an organization. Therefore, variables such as power, status, and superior-subordinate interactions and relationships, among others, are concerns in organizational communication.

Third, we notice that the organizational chart indicates the "height" and the "width" of the organization. Some organizations are flat. The kite business in figure 12.2 is flat; it has only six persons and only two vertical levels. Organizations might have several layers from top to bottom, however. Governmental organizations often seem to have many layers. Figure 12.4 illustrates a complex organization that is tall. It has several layers vertically.

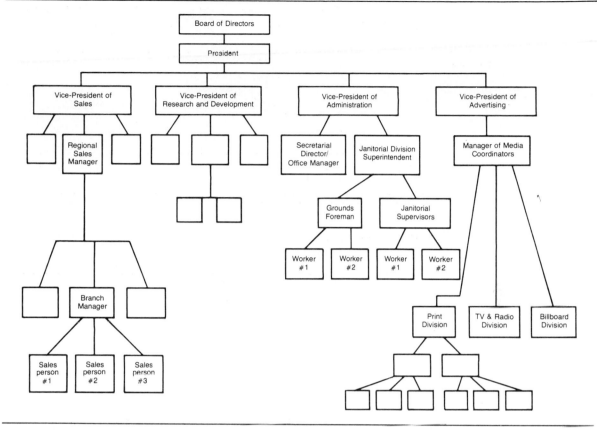

Figure 12.4

Communication Patterns in Organizations

As can be seen from these organizational charts, there is upward-downward communication in organizations, as well as lateral communication. For some time, researchers have studied organizational communication in terms of the characteristics of communication flow, amount of communication, accuracy of communication, and types of messages as they relate to upward, downward, and lateral communication. Role and location in the organization often determines salary, amount of responsibility, rate of promotion, and who talks to whom. Important policy determination communication does not occur between the president and the janitor—at least not in the formal communication prescribed for the organization. It may occur in the informal communication network. Mere location in the organization tends to determine with whom one communicates, inasmuch as people tend to communicate with those near them in the organizational structure.

Policy decisions are usually made by people on the same organizational level.

Organizations tend to produce three kinds of communication patterns—downward, upward, and lateral. Researchers have discovered that the dominant type of formal communication is downward. Everyone except the bottom-level employee has someone below to whom messages can be sent in the formal network. One of the problems in some organizations is getting feedback to downward communication, since feedback to messages sent down involves upward communication, and persons may be cautious when sending messages to superiors and to persons with power over them. Sometimes only "good" messages are sent upward. The bias that can sometimes be found in upward communication may be so strong that the validity of the communication is suspect. It may be difficult to get honest and full communication from subordinates. People may refuse to read information upward or delay it as a strategy of noncompliance with persons who are above them.

Lateral communication occurs mostly between persons on the same organizational level. The direction of the communication (upward, downward, or lateral) has significant influence on the nature of the content of messages sent, the amount of communication, and the motives or purposes of the communication.

Power is an important variable relative to upward, downward, and lateral communication in the formal organization. Salary, promotion, disciplinary action, and evaluations are power-related functions, and they influence communication in the organization.

Another variable related to the organization's height or flatness as well as to its size is *span of control*. Span of control refers to the number of persons who report directly to a superior. In figure 12.4, four vice-presidents report to the president, and four regional sales managers report to the vice-president of sales. These spans of control are four. In centralized organizations, spans of control may be wide so that the top officials have direct power over many persons. In decentralized organizations, the top officials have few people reporting to them directly. Span of control is yet another variable that influences an organization's communication in many ways.

The formal communication of any organization is affected by the informal communication of the persons in that organization. The next two sections of this chapter deal with the informal communication of organization. Suffice at this point to say that when an organization's climate is positive, formal and informal communication are improved. When the climate is negative, informal and formal communication suffer. When lack of trust and disliking develop, then there may be problems in formal communication. In the formal network, diagonal lines may develop. Rather than communicating upward or downward, persons communicate diagonally. A superior has more faith in someone else's subordinate than in his or her own subordinate, and so he or she communicates across and down. Or a subordinate may have more trust in someone else's supervisor and send messages up and across.

Another result of problems in the formal channels is "going-around" or "skip-level communication." A person may choose to violate the rules of the channel hierarchy and skip his or her superior or go directly to an upper-level person. Such practices may be detrimental to the organization as well as to the persons involved. In any event, they are the result of problems in the formal system or of exceptionally strong and positive characteristics of informal networks.

Let us now consider informal communication in organizations.

Informal Social Communication in Organizations

The importance of the social aspects of work roles has been documented in many studies.[8] Most persons enjoy acceptance and desire group inclusion. This is a personal need identified and discussed earlier in this book. Seiler asserts that even the work performance of isolates is influenced by social factors.[9] Social communication contributes to the work in organizations in at least two ways: it is directly related to climate, and it is the vehicle by which interpersonal relationships and climate are established, and these relationships are important to task performance. Secondly, social communication has a strong influence on the establishment of personal networks.

8. John A. Seiler, *Systems Analysis in Organizational Behavior* (Homewood, Ill.: Richard D. Irwin, Inc., 1967), p. 70.

9. Ibid.

Climate

10. Jack Gibb, *Factors Producing Defensive Behavior within Groups* (IV, Annual Technical Report, Office of Naval Research, Contract Nons-2285(01), November 15, 1957).

When a new person enters the organization for the first time, he or she is able to detect almost immediately the climate or atmosphere prevailing in that organization. It may be happy, forward-moving, friendly, and optimistic, or it may be drab, stationary, cold, and withdrawn. In fact, Gibb talks about climates being either supportive or defensive.[10] Of course, there are various degrees of each. Climate is important in an organization and is developed and maintained to a great extent through social communication.

Personal Networks

The concept of personal networks refers to those persons who are trusted, personal friends. Each of us has his or her personal network. There are formal, organizational networks in every organization, as we have seen, but personal networks are different. They can cut across hierarchies of status. They can skip over some people near by and take in other persons in some other part of the organization. They can include newcomers and old-timers. In short, each person's *personal network* is a thing of his or her own creation for whatever reasons, whatever criteria, and whatever procedures he or she chooses. The persons in your personal network are those you call on for information, for advice, and for help or decisions. That network is usually acquired and maintained through social communication. Such networks are essential to "getting the work done" in every organization, and since they come into being through social communication, such communication takes on added importance in the organization.

Grapevine and Rumor: Communication Phenomena in Organizations

We will conclude this chapter on interpersonal communication in organizations with a discussion of two interesting interpersonal communication phenomena—the grapevine and rumor.

The Grapevine

The grapevine uses informal channels to carry information—sometimes true and sometimes false. Mixed in with accurate news is pure gossip; but true or false, grapevine information often affects the affairs of management and the climate of the organization. Keith Davis says, referring to managers:

> Some regard the grapevine as an evil—a thorn in the side which regularly spreads rumor, destroys morale and reputations, leads to irresponsible actions, and challenges authority. Some regard it as a good thing because it acts as a safety value and carries news fast. Others regard it as a very mixed blessing. Whether the grapevine is considered

an asset or a liability, it is important for executives to try to understand it. For one thing is sure: although no executive can absolutely control the grapevine, he can *influence* it. And since it is here to stay he should learn to live with it.[11]

11. Keith Davis, "Management Communication and the Grapevine," *Harvard Business Review* 31 (Jan.-Feb. or: Davis, "Management Communication." 1953):43

The grapevine is known for the following characteristics:

1. It is fast. Traditionally, before news gets into the paper or on television or radio, it is on the grapevine.
2. The grapevine is unpredictable. At times it will carry anything any place. At other times it is highly selective and discriminating. Its capriciousness makes it difficult to predict.
3. The grapevine operates mostly at the place of work in the work milieu.
4. The grapevine does not seem to operate as a means to fill the void of formal communication in an organization. Some organizations with elaborate and efficient formal communication procedures have a powerful grapevine, and some without good formal communication also have grapevines. Actually, the grapevine (informal communication) and formal communication may be used to supplement each other. The grapevine can provide additional information (true or false as it may be) to formal communications; and formal communication may be used to conform or expand what has been in the grapevine.
5. The grapevine is flexible. Formal communication largely follows a chain of command by formal procedures, but the grapevine is more flexible. Davis has identified and described four "chains" in various grapevines.[12] They are the single-strand chain (A to B to C to D, etc.), the gossip chain, the probability chain, and the cluster chain.[13] The single-strand chain is often responsible for distortion and filtering of information in the grapevine. The gossip chain is defined as Person A seeking to tell everyone else. The probability chain is one in which A communicates randomly to one or two persons who, in turn, communicate randomly. The cluster chain is *not* random. Person A tells three or four others, and each of these tell his or her selected others. These "others" told are not selected at random, but are specially and purposefully selected. They constitute a "grapevine" network for the person passing the information along. Davis has stated, "This was virtually the only kind of chain found in the Jason Company, and may well be the normal one in industry generally."[14] These few individuals who had clusters to which they passed information seemed to be the only ones doing so. Most received the information and did not transmit it. This same characteristic has been described by Jacobson and Seashore.[15]

12. Ibid.

13. Ibid., pp. 43–49.

14. Ibid., p. 46.

15. Eugene Jacobson and Stanley E. Seashore, "Communication Practices in Complex Organizations," *The Journal of Social Issues* VII, no. 3 (1951):37.

Three principles seem to be followed in grapevine communication in organizations: (1) the messages have to do with what will affect the persons there, especially job-related items; (2) the grapevine tells people what they want to know about, rather than what any "would-be controller" of the grapevine might want the people to know; and (3) its information is new.

The grapevine is an informal communication system that may supplement an organization's formal communication system.

Robert Eckert

Rumor

Rumor is not unlike the grapevine except that it is not "organization bound." The grapevine remains within a single organization. Rumor knows no bounds. Two basic conditions for rumor seem to be that the rumor must have some importance to the listener, and that the facts of the rumor must be ambiguous. Of course, the more important the subject of the rumor, the greater is the spread, growth, and speed of the rumor. The relationship between importance and ambiguity is multiplicative, for if either aspect is zero, there is no rumor.[16] Rumor thrives by responding to human need. Any human need can provide the motive power. Sex is the topic of much gossip and rumor, but there are pipedream rumors based on hope and desire, rumors of threats based on fears and anxiety, and slanderous rumors based on jealousy and hate. In a way, rumor is a form of rationalization by which strong emotional urges and feelings, as they are associated with confused or murky situations, motivate rumors to provide explanations that restore order and provide understanding and an appropriate answer. In fact, rumors are a group's or society's way of providing closure, of finding a plausible answer to a confusing situation. We each seem to be so prone to "wanting closure," to needing answers, that when we hear an interpretation of some situation that is confusing to us, if that interpretation conforms to our emotional needs and secret lives, we will clasp the rumor to our breasts, believe it, and transmit it to others. Perhaps the fun of rumor is that its perpetrators tend to project themselves, their desires, and their emotional needs into the rumor.

16. Brent D. Peterson, Gerald M. Goldhaber, and Wayne R. Pall. *Communication Probes* (Chicago: Science Research Associates, Inc., 1974), p. 138.

The characteristics of rumor are: (1) it is specific as to topic; (2) it has to do with either specific events or personalities; (3) it implies truth even when the person passing it along says, "Now this is just a rumor, but . . ."; and (4) it grows in acceptance and in transmission in the absence of evidence. As with the grapevine, ambiguity increases the power of rumor.

The best advice for coping with rumor is to nail it down with evidence. Nothing short of valid evidence can halt rumor quickly.

SUMMARY

In this chapter we have considered interpersonal communication in the organization setting. Each of us spends much of our waking time—2,000 hours per year or more—at work. Our interpersonal communication there is an important aspect of our lives. We have discussed the employment interview and the informational and persuasive interview (the conference) as important forms of *instrumental interpersonal communication*. Then we have discussed formal and informal interpersonal communication in the organization. We have noted that informal social communication is important to the establishment of organizational climate and of personal networks. Finally, we looked briefly at the *grapevine and rumor*.

SELECTED READINGS

Amsden, Forrest M., and White, Abel D. *How to Be Successful in the Employment Interview: A Step-by-Step Approach for the Candidate.* Cheney, Wash.: Interviewing Dynamics, 1975.

Berko, Roy; Wolvin, Andrew; and Curtis, Ray. *This Business of Communicating* (Dubuque, Iowa: William C. Brown Co., Publishers, 1980).

Bradley, Patricia, and Baird, John. *Communication for Business and the Professions* (Dubuque, Iowa: William C. Brown Co., Publishers, 1980).

Goldhaber, Gerald M. *Organizational Communication.* 2d ed. (Dubuque, Iowa: William C. Brown Co., Publishers, 1979).

Kahn, Robert C., and Cannell, Charles F. *The Dynamics of Interviewing* (New York: John Wiley & Sons, Inc., 1964).

Redding, Charles, and Sanborn, Georgia A. *Business and Industrial Communication: A Source Book* (New York: Harper & Row, Publishers, Inc., 1964).

Stewart, Charles J., and Cash, William B. *Interviewing: Principles and Practices.* 2d ed. (Dubuque, Iowa: William C. Brown Co., Publishers, 1978).

Tacey, William S. *Business and Professional Speaking.* 3d ed. (Dubuque, Iowa: William C. Brown Co., Publishers, 1980).

Glossary

A

Abstraction process
Verbal process of placing objects, persons, and concepts into categories based on the similarities among members of the categories, while overlooking the differences among category members.

Acquaintance process
When persons come to know each other.

Alienation
Being estranged, separated from, or being alone and withdrawn from others.

Arbitration
Process of resolving a conflict by using a third party, an unbiased outsider, who is given the power to dictate a resolution.

Attitudes
Inferred mental state in which a person evaluates a person, object, or concept as either positive or negative. Attitudes are usually inferred from behaviors that can be observed.

Attributive cues
Physical characteristics unrelated to specific message content that can still affect message reception in interpersonal communication.

Auding
Translating the flow of words into meaning.

Auditory acuity
Sensitivity of ability to receive sounds.

B

Balance theory
Theoretical explanation of the need for consistency developed by Fritz Heider.

Body image
Physical self; size, attractiveness, and socially admired physical characteristics.

C

Categorization
Process of grouping the phenomena in our environment into categories according to their similarities.

Closed-mindedness
Opposite of open-mindedness; evaluates on the basis of inner drives and needs; thinks in black and white, either-or categories; focuses on the source; seeks information to reinforce beliefs; and rejects, ignores, or distorts information inconsistent with own belief system.

Closed questions
Have an expected and predictable answer, i.e., yes or no, or some specific and short answer.

Common ground approach
Persuasive technique in which establishment of "common ground" (beliefs, attitudes, desires, theoretic base, assumptions, or premise are agreed to by the persuader and persuadee) is used as foundation for the persuasive strategy.

Communication apprehension
Fear of speaking situations, either formal or informal.

Communication network
Pattern of message flow among the members of a small group or organization.

Communication context
Combination of the number of people, their relationships, their goals, and the communication phases they evolve through that are used to distinguish among dyadic, small group, and organizational communication.

Communicative cues/behaviors
Nonverbal behaviors used as intended messages to influence others.

Compromise
Process of each party to the conflict giving up some goals or values to resolve the conflict and to win some goals and values.

Congruity theory
Theoretical explanation of the need for consistency developed by Charles E. Osgood and Percy H. Tannenbaum.

Connotative meaning
Emotional associations that affect responses to words.

Consummatory interpersonal communication
that directed toward immediate satisfaction of needs by the communication process itself.

Controversy
Disagreement that is perceived as being controllable and resolvable.

Culture
Combined effects of knowledge, experience, meanings, beliefs, bias, attitudes, religion, concepts of the self, the universe and self-universe relationships, hierarchies of status, role expectations, spatial relations, and time concepts shared by large groups of people across generations.

D

Dating
Process of mentally placing a date beside the words for persons, objects, and concepts to remind us that they change over time.

Defensiveness
Opposite of trusting another; fear of another and protecting oneself from another.

Demographic exchanges
Reciprocal giving of "demographic data," i.e., age, education, where one lives, occupation, etc.

Denotative meaning
Meaning of words that includes properties of concepts, but no emotional responses.

Deviation (in small groups)
Practice of an individual not conforming to the norms or wishes of the group.

Dissonance theory
Theoretical explanation of the need for consistency suggested by Leon Festinger.

Distance
Intimate distance
Distance from 0-18″ used by intimate friends when communicating about intimate topics.

Personal distance
Distance from 18″ to 4′ used for interactions with our friends and families about personal topics.

Social distance
Distance from 4′ to 12′ used for social interactions and business discussions.

Public distance
Distance of 12′ and more used in public presentations to groups.

Double-bind
Having received contradictory messages.

Dyadic communication
Two-person or two-party communication.

E

Encounter groups
Small groups formed for the purpose of self-improvement of the participants.

Environment
Environment of any communication system includes all the factors outside the system which influence the system.

F

Facial communication
All the nonverbal messages produced by the use of facial muscles and organs.

Feedback
Receiving information relative to a message you sent for the purpose of correcting or adjusting that message if needed.

Friendship groups
Small groups formed for the purpose of satisfying the social needs of group members.

G

Generation gap
Misunderstanding between older and younger people that results from different communication behaviors based on differences in experiences.

Gestalt approach to perception
This approach to perception suggests that we perceive *perceptual wholes.*

H

Hidden antagonizers
Words perceived negatively by the recipient

of a message when the originator of the message is unaware of any negative connotations.

I

Identity crisis
Unintegrated self; one who is in a state of being unsure of who he or she is; one who is doubtful of his or her acceptability.

Implicit personality theory
Set of inferences privately developed by one person about another person at an initial meeting.

Indexing
General semantic practice to help people mentally remind themselves that all objects, persons, or concepts referred to by a word are not the same.

In listening indexing refers to the ranking of information according to importance and relationship to other information.

Implicative approach
Arguing by inductive reasoning.

Informative behaviors/cues
Nonverbal behaviors that provide information to an observer even though the observed one does not intend them to do so.

Instrumental interpersonal communication
That directed toward the accomplishment of a task.

Interactive behavior
Nonverbal behavior that can affect interactions between people whether or not the communicators intend it to do so.

Interpersonal attraction
Liking of each other.

Interpersonal communication
Process of from two to twenty persons mutually attempting to influence one another through use of a common symbol system, in a situation permitting equal opportunity for all persons involved in the process to influence each other.

Interpersonal conflict
Situation of competition in which incompatible activities occur.

Interpersonal negotiation
Process of participants in a conflict situation attempting to resolve the situation through communication.

Interpersonal trust
Reliance on the behavior of a person to achieve a desired objective.

L

Language
Processing system composed of two subsystems, the vocabulary and the grammar, both interacting to produce meaning.

Leadership
Situationally based communication behaviors that permit a leader to influence group members relative to social-emotional and task needs of the group.

Leading question
Question that is designed to "lead" the respondent to an expected response.

Listening
Process of hearing, identifying and analyzing, and assigning meaning to incoming aural stimuli.

Loaded question
Leading question that is designed to trap the respondent.

M

Macromeaning
Process of categorizing individual stimuli.

Meaning
Responses people have to words, resulting from a complex process of association.

Dimensions of meaning
Three components of meaning discovered by Osgood, Suci, and Tannenbaum; the evaluative, potency, and activity dimensions.

Mediation
Using a third party in conflict resolution with the third party having no power to dictate a resolution.

Micromeaning
Process of categorizing the relationships among various stimuli and structures.

Mirror question
Nondirective interviewing technique in which a statement of the interviewee is repeated as a statement or question by the interviewer.

N

Needs
Motivational states people respond to in survival-oriented behavior.

Consistency need
Need to have our ideas, values, perceptions, behaviors, and attitudes all be consistent among themselves.

Ego need
Need to think positively of oneself, to have high self-esteem.

Physical need
Need to maintain oneself physically over both a long term and short term basis.

Social need
Need to have positive relationships with other people.

Negative feedback
Evidence that the intended message has not been received correctly.

Nonsharable goals
Winner-take-all situations in which one participant in the conflict situation wins all and the other participant loses all.

Nonverbal communication
Behaviors produced to influence others in ways other than words, such as gestures, eye behavior, facial expressions, and posture.

O

Open-mindedness
Processing information in ways characterized by objective evaluation, use of data, easy differentiation, focus on content, acceptance of and even seeking of information, toleration of ambiguity and dissonant information, and willing to modify beliefs.

Open question
No specific answer is expected; any answer is appropriate.

P

Paralanguage
Nonverbal characteristics associated with the production of words through speech, pitch, voice quality, and rate and rhythm of speech.

Perception
Mental process of selecting, organizing, and intepreting the many stimuli that impinge upon us at any given moment.

Person perception
Mental process of selecting, organizing, and interpreting the available stimuli related to a person we have met.

Personal network
Each person's network of personal, trusted friends.

Positive feedback
Evidence that the intended message has been received correctly.

Power
Dominance, authority, or control.

Probing question
Question that is designed to elicit more information on that topic.

Propinquity
Distance between persons.

R

Reciprocal scanning
Process of "sizing each other up" in the acquaintance time, especially during the initial or entry phase.

Reciprocity phenomenon
Tendency for one behavior to elicit the same behavior in another; in the acquaintance process, it is the tendency to give information about oneself to cause the other person to give information about himself or herself.

Reference process
Mental process by which we connect things symbolized with the symbols themselves.

Risky shift
Phenomenon of an individual becoming more radical and less conservative as a result of taking part in small group communication.

Ritual response
Communication response that is automatic and predictable rather than spontaneous and dynamic.

Roles
Functions one fulfills in relation to others.

S

Self-acceptance
Having a positive and constructive attitude toward oneself.

Self-actualization
Bringing one's ideal self into existence as the real or actual self; fulfilling one's highest need, i.e., to become what one wants to be.

Self-awareness
Being knowledgeable as to "who one is."

Self-concept
Physical, social, and psychological perceptions of oneself.

Self-consciousness
Extent to which a person is shy, embarrassed, anxious, and overly concerned with himself or herself when in the presence of or watched by others; the opposite of social confidence and poise.

Self-disclosure
Making known information about oneself to another.

Self-esteem
Liking, valuing, and regarding oneself highly for high self-esteem and assigning unfavorable and negative attitudes toward oneself for low self-esteem.

Self-fulfilling prophecy
Bringing into fruition a predicted behavior; the living up to or down to a label. Process by which our expectations regarding ourselves or others causes us to engage in behaviors that result in ourselves and/or others behaving according to our expectations.

Small group communication
Communication that occurs in a group of three or more people who can interact with each other on a face-to-face basis, who are not inhibited from interacting because of group size, and who share common needs that can be satisfied through participation in the group's activities.

Social-emotional needs and leadership
Leadership based upon a response to the interpersonal needs of the group.

Span of control
Number of persons who report directly to a superior.

Stereotype
Abstraction process by which we include all persons from a group in a category and expect them all to be identical.

Stroking communication
Unit of recognition; communication to another so as to meet his or her social, affective, or psychological needs.

Structuralist approach to perception
Position that perception is the process of combining all sensations additively into a single perception.

T

Tactile communication
Form of nonverbal communication based on touching behavior.

Task needs and leadership
Leadership based on a response to a problem external to the group.

Trait theory
Approach to person perception in which we develop perception of personality traits and either add them together or combine them wholistically into a perception of those we meet.

W

Warmth
Love, affection, sociability, and liking of.

White noise
Extraneous sounds comprised of all or many frequencies.

Words
Minimal units of meaning; symbolic behaviors that are arbitrary in nature, acquired through a complex process of association.

Working groups
Small groups that respond primarily to task needs.

Y

Yes-yes approach
Technique of eliciting agreement from the persuadee from minor points to the critical decision point.

Index

A

Abner, Edward, 125
Abrahamson, Mark, 231
Abstraction process, 127–31
Acceptance, 22, 72–73
Accidental happenings, 228–29
Acquaintance process, 264, 275
Addington, D. W., 154
Adolescence, 60
  friendship groups, 318
  identity crisis, 61–66
Affection, 211, 227–28, 234
  and self-disclosure, 235–36
Aggression, 240
Agreement, reaching, 134–37
Alienation, 211, 235–39
Allport, G. W., 212
Altman, Irwin, 265, 266
Ambiguity, 207–08, 256
Amsden, Forrest M., 345
Anomia-alienation, 236–37
Anticlimax order, 336
Anxiety, 219, 230
Applbaum, Ronald L., 89
Apprehension, communication, 69–70
Arbitration, 258
Ard, Ben N., 5
Ardrey, Robert, 8, 16, 17, 20, 49, 157, 292
Argyle, Michael, 57, 98, 100, 199, 269, 270,
  271, 275–76, 297, 303–04, 318
Argyris, C., 316
Aronson, E., 165, 229
Asch, S. E., 99, 100, 268, 303
Ashby, W. Ross, 189
Attitudes, similarity of, 232–34
Attraction, 211, 227–34
Attractiveness, 101–04, 165–66
Auding, 172, 175
Auditory analysis, 174
Authoritarianism, 213

B

Bach, George R., 246
Baird, John, 345
Balance theory, 21

Bales, Robert F., 200–01, 255, 314
Barbara, Dominick A., 209
Barker, Larry L., 139, 209
Barnlund, Dean C., 42, 188
Baron, Robert S., 306
Barry, William A., 5
Bartley, S. Howard, 89
Bateson, G., 36
Bavelas, Alex, 309
Beavin, Janet H., 208, 287
Behavior(s), 100, 143, 145–64
Beier, E. G., 231
Bennis, Warren G., 316
Berelson, Bernard, 14
Berger, Charles R., 265–68
Berko, Roy, 345
Berkowitz, Leonard, 98
Berlo, David K., 3, 49, 68, 94, 191, 192
Bern, D. J., 306
Berne, Eric, 56, 282–83, 285–86
Bernstein, Arnold, 271
Berscheid, Ellen, 165
Bickman, Leonard, 148
Bingham, W. V. D., 325
Blacks
  language system, 125
  nonverbal behavior, 163
Blake, Robert R., 60
Blanton, Smiley, 204
Body image, 56, 60
Borden, George A., 283
Boren, Robert R., 106
Bork, K., 231
Boulding, Kenneth E., 243–44
Boutillier, R. G., 310
Bowers, John Waite, 244
Bradley, Patricia, 345
Brewer, M. B., 229
Brewer, R. E., 229
Brilhart, John K., 319
Brock, T. C., 229
Brockopp, G. W., 197
Brooks, William D., 40–42, 118, 215
Brooks-Emmert model, 40–42
Brown, Roger, 130, 306
Broxton, J. A., 231
Bruner, J. S., 92, 93

Hastorf, Albert H., 88, 91–94, 98
Hayakawa, S. I., 113, 131, 132
Hegstrom, T. G., 140
Heider, Fritz, 21, 87, 96, 232
Hertel, Richard K., 5
Heston, Judee K., 237, 290, 292, 319
Heterophily, 104
Hidden antagonizers, 131–34
Hochberg, 89
Hoff, L., 197
Hoffman, L. Richard, 292
Homans, G. C., 229, 287
Homophily, 104
Honi phenomenon, 273–74
Hoppe, R. A., 294
Hostility, 211
    and alienation, 238–39
    techniques for reducing, 239–40
Howe, Richard L., 237–38
Hudson, W., 105
Husband, R. W., 293

I

Ideas, listening for, 184–85
Identity
    crisis, 61–66
    sense of, development, 12–14
Immediate vs. delayed feedback, 194, 198
Implicative approach, 336
Implicit personality theory, 99, 100, 150
Impressions
    of people, 99–100, 147–50, 268
    sensory, forming, 175
Inclusion, 269
Indirect feedback, 192, 194
Indexing, 175
Industry
    communication. See Organizational
        communication
    need satisfaction in, 18–20
Inference, 96–97, 145–47
Informal communication in organizations,
    341–42
Information
    accuracy, 255
    impersonal, 79
    listening for, 177, 185
    overload, 256
    personal, 79–80
Informative behavior, 143, 164
Ingham, Harry, 78
Initiating communicator, 42
Input subsystems, 42
Instantaneous general impression, 268
Instrumental interpersonal communication,
    28–29
Intentional approach to nonverbal
    communication, 143

Intentional behavior vs. inference, 145–47
Intentions of others, 96–97, 215
Inter- and intrafacing, 42, 44
Interference, 41, 47–48
Interfering messages, 42
Internal feedback, 189–90
Interpersonal communication, 3–5
    contexts, 14–15, 36–37, 48
    dyadic, 263–87
    effect of words on, 124–27
    and environment, 168
    function of, 28–29
    and marriage, 5, 6, 273–81
    between men and women, 4–5, 140–41
    models, 38–48
    and need satisfaction, 10–14, 33–34, 37
    negotiation, 252–57
    organizational, 231–45
    origins, 7–8
    patterns and orientations, 211–41
    perception in. See Perception
    as process, 31–33
    and self-concept, 66–70
    social, 281–87
    and survival, 6–14
    systems, characteristics of, 33–37
    trust in, 106–07, 218
    value component in, 27–28
Interview
    defined, 322, 326
    direct vs. indirect, 327
    employment, 327–33
    persuasive, 333–37
    structure, 326–27, 336–37
Intimacy, 270
Intimate communication, 273–81
Intimate distance, 157, 159

J

Jackson, Don D., 208, 287
Jackson, J. N., 302, 303
Jacobson, Eugene, 343
James, Willem, 19–20
Job interview, 322–23, 327–33
Johari window, 78–79
Johnson, David W., 200, 202, 224, 241, 246,
    253, 255, 257
Johnson, Kenneth R., 163
Johnson, Wendell, 189–90, 209
Jones, E. E., 229
Jourard, Sidney M., 60, 161, 234–36, 265,
    276, 279, 287

K

Kahn, R. L., 325, 335
Kahn, Robert C., 345
Katz, D., 60

Ruben, Brent D., 14
Ruesch, Jurgen, 36, 139, 148, 152, 169
Rumor, 344–45

S

Sachs, J., 154
Sales, S. M., 318
Sales interview, 323
Saltzstein, H. D., 302, 303
Samovar, Larry A., 319
Sanborn, Georgia A., 345
Santi, A., 253, 255
Sapir, Edward, 122
Sapir-Whorf hypothesis, 122–25
Saslow, G., 325
Satir, V. M., 253
Schachter, S., 230, 231, 304
Scheflen, Albert E., 150, 152
Schizophrenia, 64
Schneider, David J., 88, 91–94
Schramm, Wilbur, 39, 117
Schutz, William C., 16, 18, 49, 60, 234, 269
Search for order, 91–92, 93, 95
Seashore, Stanley E., 343
Secord, P. F., 60
Seibold, David R., 252
Self
  healthy, characteristics, 70
  multiplicity of selves, 56
  perception, 55, 61
Self-acceptance, 72–73
Self-actualization, 17–19, 73–75
Self-awareness, 70–72
Self-concept, 62
  and communication, 66–70
  definition, 53–55
  development, 12–14, 56–58
  and feedback, 195–96, 200–01
  improving, 70–83
  and self-esteem, 60
  and values, 26–27
Self-consciousness, 58–59
Self-disclosure, 75–83, 274
  in entry phase, 266–67
  and liking, 235–36
  in marriage, 276, 278–79
  and trust, 222
Self-esteem, 17, 56, 58–59
  and self-concept, 60
  and trust, 213
Self-fulfilling prophecy, 66, 68, 105–06
Self-identity, 61, 62
Self-image, 56–58, 63
"Selfishness," 9–10
Sensitivity groups, 36, 316–17
Sensory impressions, forming, 175
Sexual behavior, 23, 205, 207

Shaw, Marvin E., 290, 309, 319
Sherif, Carolyn W., 313, 318
Sherif, Muzafar, 313, 318
Shure, G. H., 253–55
Silence, 77–78, 324–25
Simmel, George, 244, 246, 259
Simons, Herbert W., 259
Simplistic thinking, 226
Skip-level communication, 341
Skolnick, P., 253–54
Slobin, Dan I., 110, 114, 122, 123
Small group communication, 15, 48, 289–319
  and conformity, 301–03
  effectiveness, 293–97
  as persuasive device, 307
  problem solving by, 298–301, 307–08
  size of group, 290–93, 302
Smelser, Neil J., 271
Smith, H. C., 268
Smith, P. A., 60
Smith, Ralph R., Jr., 151
"Snarl words," 131–34
Social distance, 157, 159, 160
Social-emotional leader, 311–14
Social isolation, 230
Social liking, 102, 235–36
Social needs, 16–18, 22
Social survival, 10–11
Solutions, finding, 299–300
Sorrentino, R. M., 310
Sound(s)
  loudness of, measuring, 173
  recognizing, 174–75
Space, used to communicate, 157, 159–60
Span of control, 341
Speech, 5–6, 7
  accents, 162–63
  nonfluencies, 155–56
  origins, 8
  paralanguage, 152, 154–56
  speed, and thought speed, 181–82, 185
Spiker, Charles C., 92
Spitz, R. A., 17
Staats, Arthur W., 116, 121
Staats, Carolyn K., 116, 121
Stability, 284
  in perception, 104–06
Starling, Marion E., 149
Stass, J. W., 150
Status, 338
Steady-state theory, 32
Steiner, Gary A., 14
Steinfatt, Thomas M., 252
Stereotypes, 128
  behaviors, theories of, 100
Stevens, Leonard A., 209
Stewart, Charles J., 345
Stewart, John, 49